THE Twelve
A *THRILLING* NOVEL OF TOMORROW

WRITER: **J. MICHAEL STRACZYNSKI**

PENCILER: **CHRIS WESTON**

INKERS: **GARRY LEACH** WITH **CHRIS WESTON** (ISSUES #4 & #6)

COLORIST: **CHRIS CHUCKRY**

LETTERER: **COMICRAFT'S JIMMY BETANCOURT**

COVER ARTISTS: **KAARE ANDREWS** (ISSUES #1-4)

& **PAOLO RIVERA** (ISSUES #5-6)

ASSOCIATE EDITOR: **MOLLY LAZER**

EDITOR: **TOM BREVOORT**

★

COLLECTION EDITOR: **JENNIFER GRÜNWALD**

ASSISTANT EDITORS: **ALEX STARBUCK** & **NELSON RIBEIRO**

EDITOR, SPECIAL PROJECTS: **MARK D. BEAZLEY**

SENIOR EDITOR, SPECIAL PROJECTS: **JEFF YOUNGQUIST**

SENIOR VICE PRESIDENT OF SALES: **DAVID GABRIEL**

SVP OF BRAND PLANNING & COMMUNICATIONS: **MICHAEL PASCIULLO**

BOOK DESIGNER: **RODOLFO MURAGUCHI**

★

EDITOR IN CHIEF: **AXEL ALONSO** • PUBLISHER: **DAN BUCKLEY**

CHIEF CREATIVE OFFICER: **JOE QUESADA** • EXECUTIVE PRODUCER: **ALAN FINE**

THE TWELVE VOL. 1. Contains material originally published in magazine form as THE TWELVE #1-6. First printing 2012. ISBN# 978-0-7851-2324-8. Published by MARVEL WORLDWIDE, INC., a subsidiary of MARVEL ENTERTAINMENT, LLC. OFFICE OF PUBLICATION: 135 West 50th Street, New York, NY 10020. Copyright © 2008 and 2012 Marvel Characters, Inc. All rights reserved. $16.99 per copy in the U.S. and $18.99 in Canada (GST #R127032852); Canadian Agreement #40668537. All characters featured in this issue and the distinctive names and likenesses thereof, and all related indicia are trademarks of Marvel Characters, Inc. No similarity between any of the names, characters, persons, and/or institutions in this magazine with those of any living or dead person or institution is intended, and any such similarity which may exist is purely coincidental. **Printed in the U.S.A.** ALAN FINE, EVP - Office of the President, Marvel Worldwide, Inc. and EVP & CMO Marvel Characters B.V.; DAN BUCKLEY, Publisher & President - Print, Animation & Digital Divisions; JOE QUESADA, Chief Creative Officer; DAVID BOGART, SVP of Business Affairs & Talent Management; TOM BREVOORT, SVP of Publishing; C.B. CEBULSKI, SVP of Creator & Content Development; DAVID GABRIEL, SVP of Publishing Sales & Circulation; MICHAEL PASCIULLO, SVP of Brand Planning & Communications; JIM O'KEEFE, VP of Operations & Logistics; DAN CARR, Executive Director of Publishing Technology; SUSAN CRESPI, Editorial Operations Manager; ALEX MORALES, Publishing Operations Manager; STAN LEE, Chairman Emeritus. For information regarding advertising in Marvel Comics or on Marvel.com, please contact John Dokes, SVP Integrated Sales and Marketing, at jdokes@marvel.com. For Marvel subscription inquiries, please call 800-217-9158. **Manufactured between 12/15/2011 and 1/3/2012 by QUAD/GRAPHICS, DUBUQUE, IA, USA.**

10 9 8 7 6 5 4 3 2 1

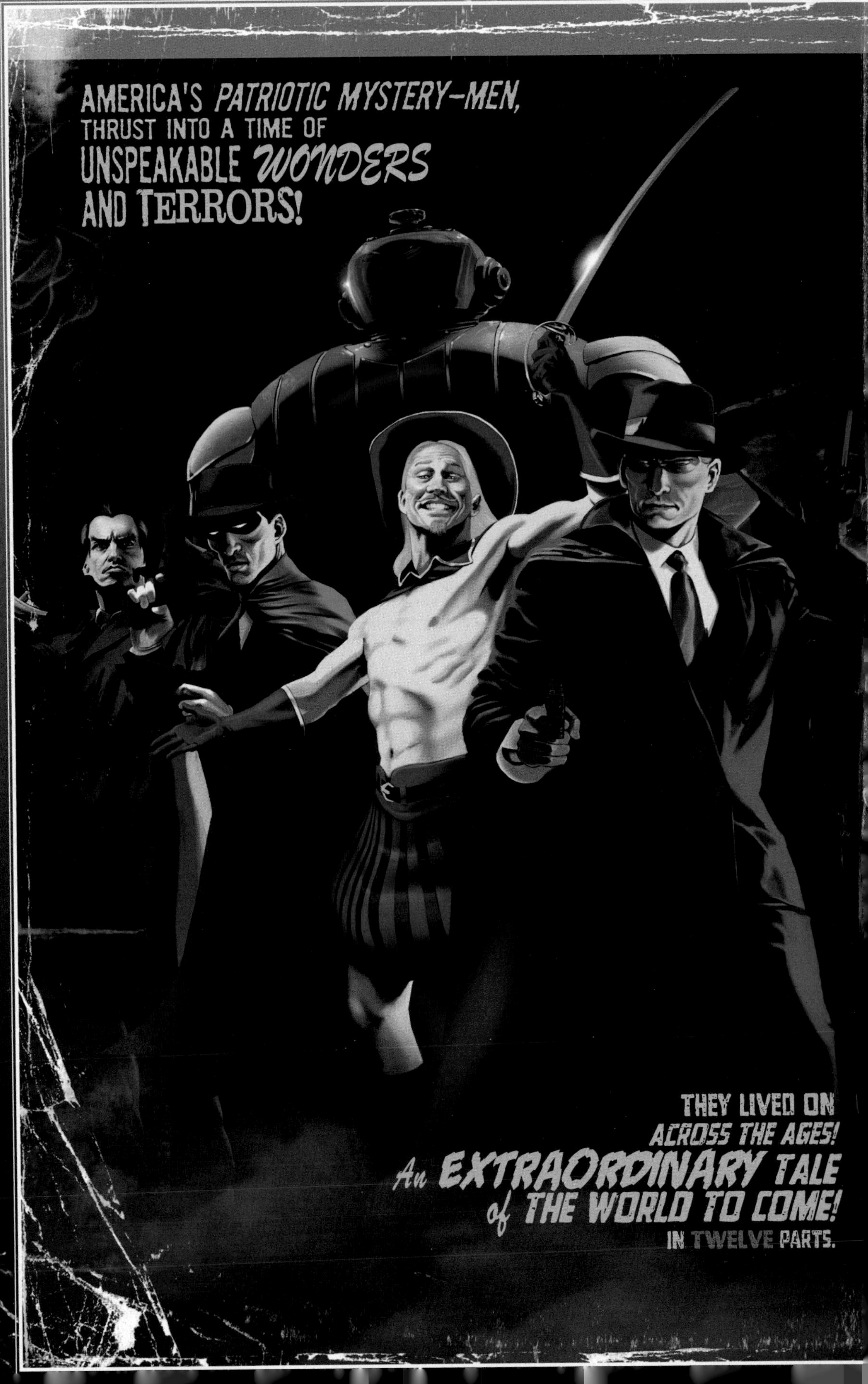
AMERICA'S PATRIOTIC MYSTERY-MEN,
THRUST INTO A TIME OF
UNSPEAKABLE WONDERS
AND TERRORS!
THEY LIVED ON
ACROSS THE AGES!
An EXTRAORDINARY TALE
of THE WORLD TO COME!
IN TWELVE PARTS.

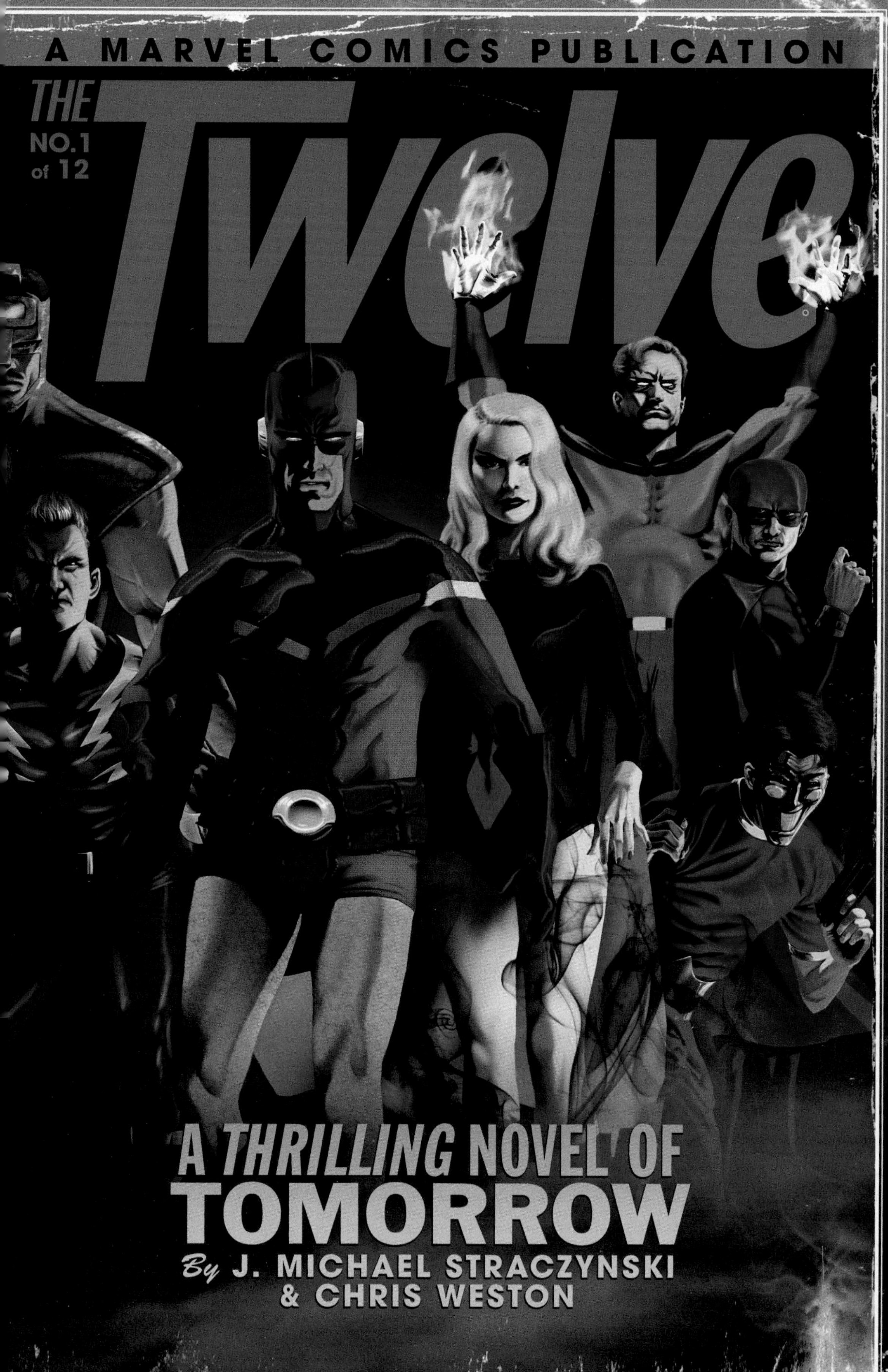
A MARVEL COMICS PUBLICATION
THE
NO.1
of 12
Twelve
A THRILLING NOVEL OF
TOMORROW
By J. MICHAEL STRACZYNSKI
& CHRIS WESTON

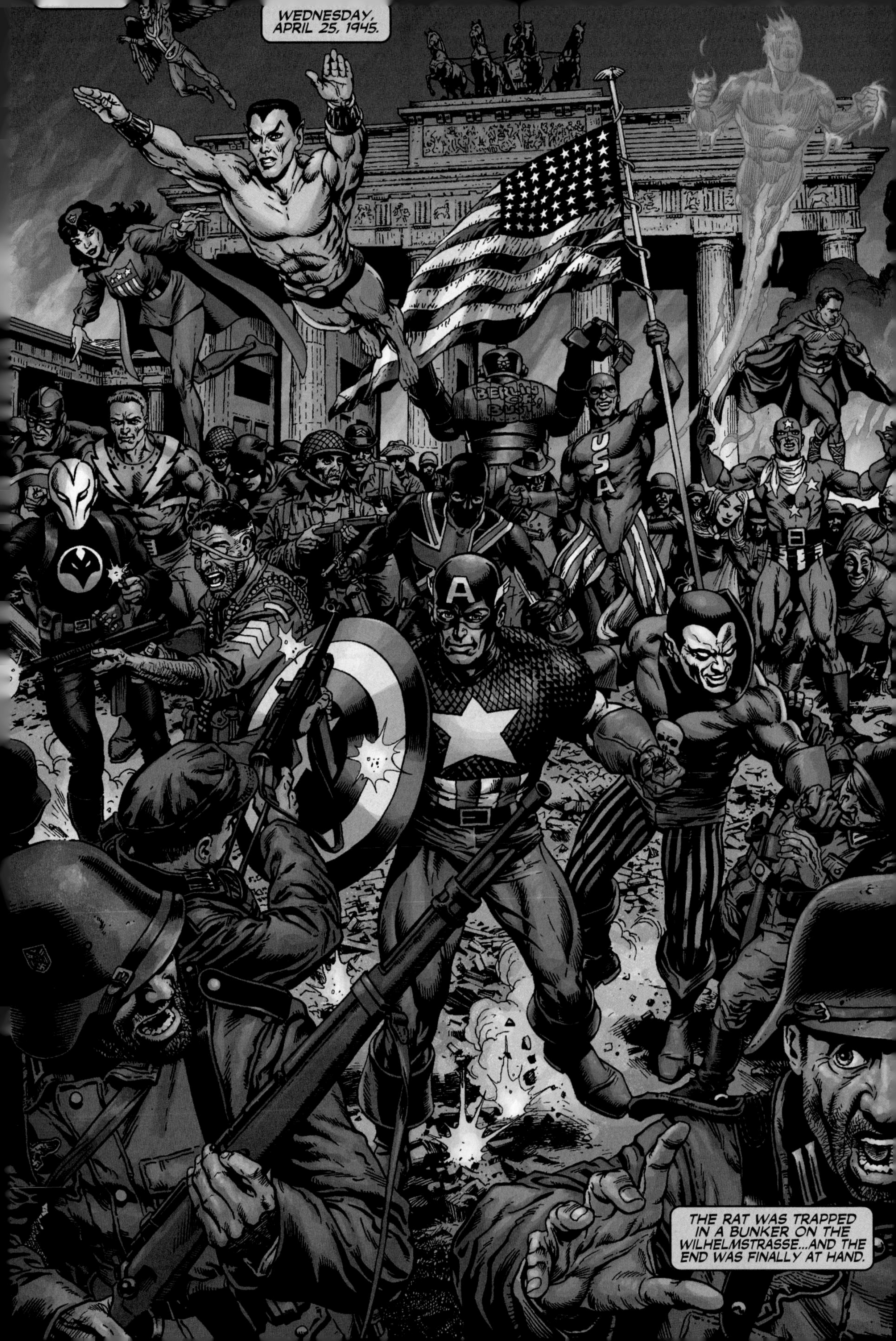
WEDNESDAY, APRIL 25, 1945.
BERLIN OR BUST
USA
THE RAT WAS TRAPPED IN A BUNKER ON THE WILHELMSTRASSE...AND THE END WAS FINALLY AT HAND.

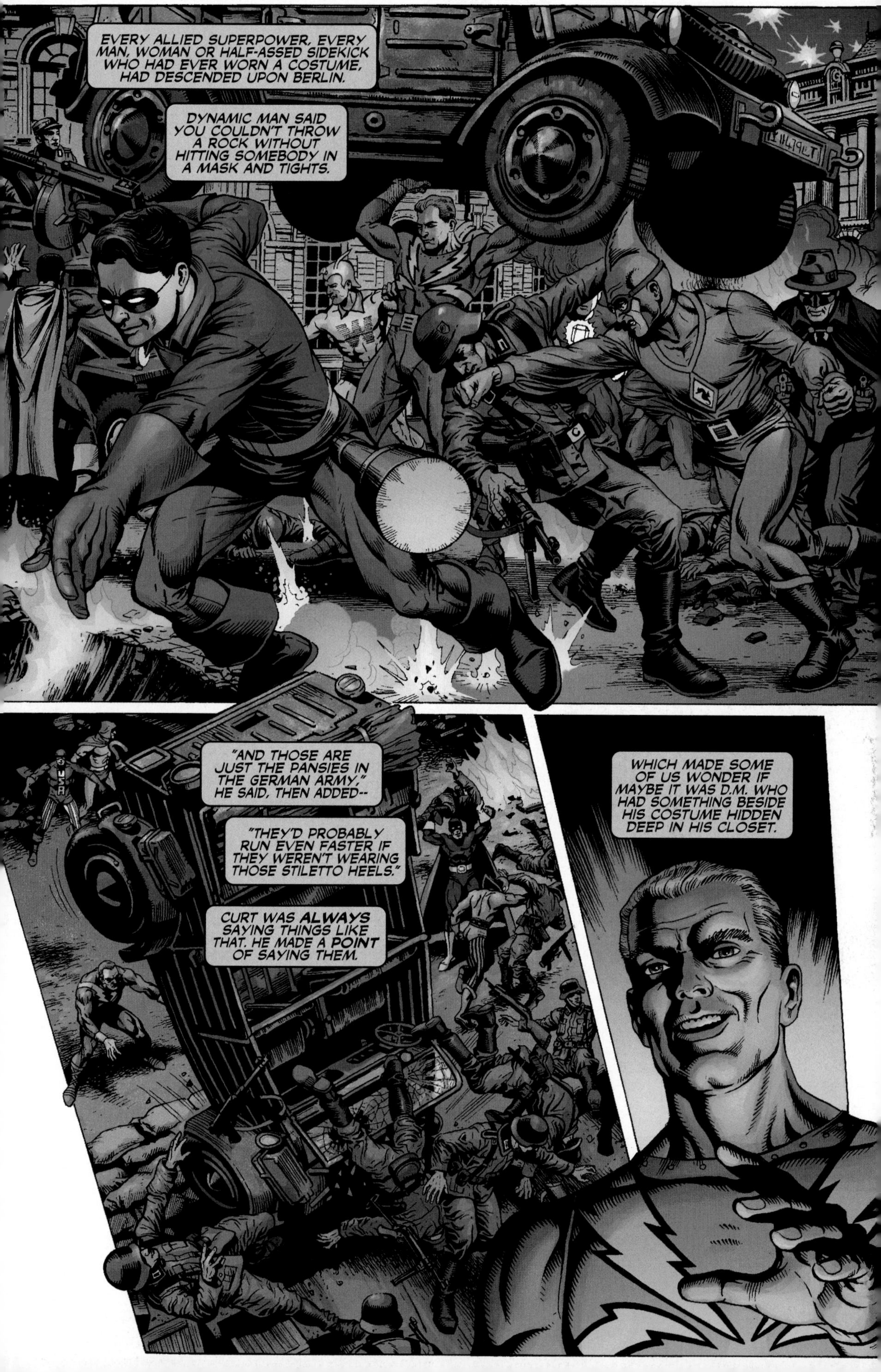

EVERY ALLIED SUPERPOWER, EVERY MAN, WOMAN OR HALF-ASSED SIDEKICK WHO HAD EVER WORN A COSTUME, HAD DESCENDED UPON BERLIN.
DYNAMIC MAN SAID YOU COULDN'T THROW A ROCK WITHOUT HITTING SOMEBODY IN A MASK AND TIGHTS.
"AND THOSE ARE JUST THE PANSIES IN THE GERMAN ARMY," HE SAID, THEN ADDED--
"THEY'D PROBABLY RUN EVEN FASTER IF THEY WEREN'T WEARING THOSE STILETTO HEELS."
CURT WAS **ALWAYS** SAYING THINGS LIKE THAT. HE MADE A **POINT** OF SAYING THEM.
WHICH MADE SOME OF US WONDER IF MAYBE IT WAS D.M. WHO HAD SOMETHING BESIDE HIS COSTUME HIDDEN DEEP IN HIS CLOSET.

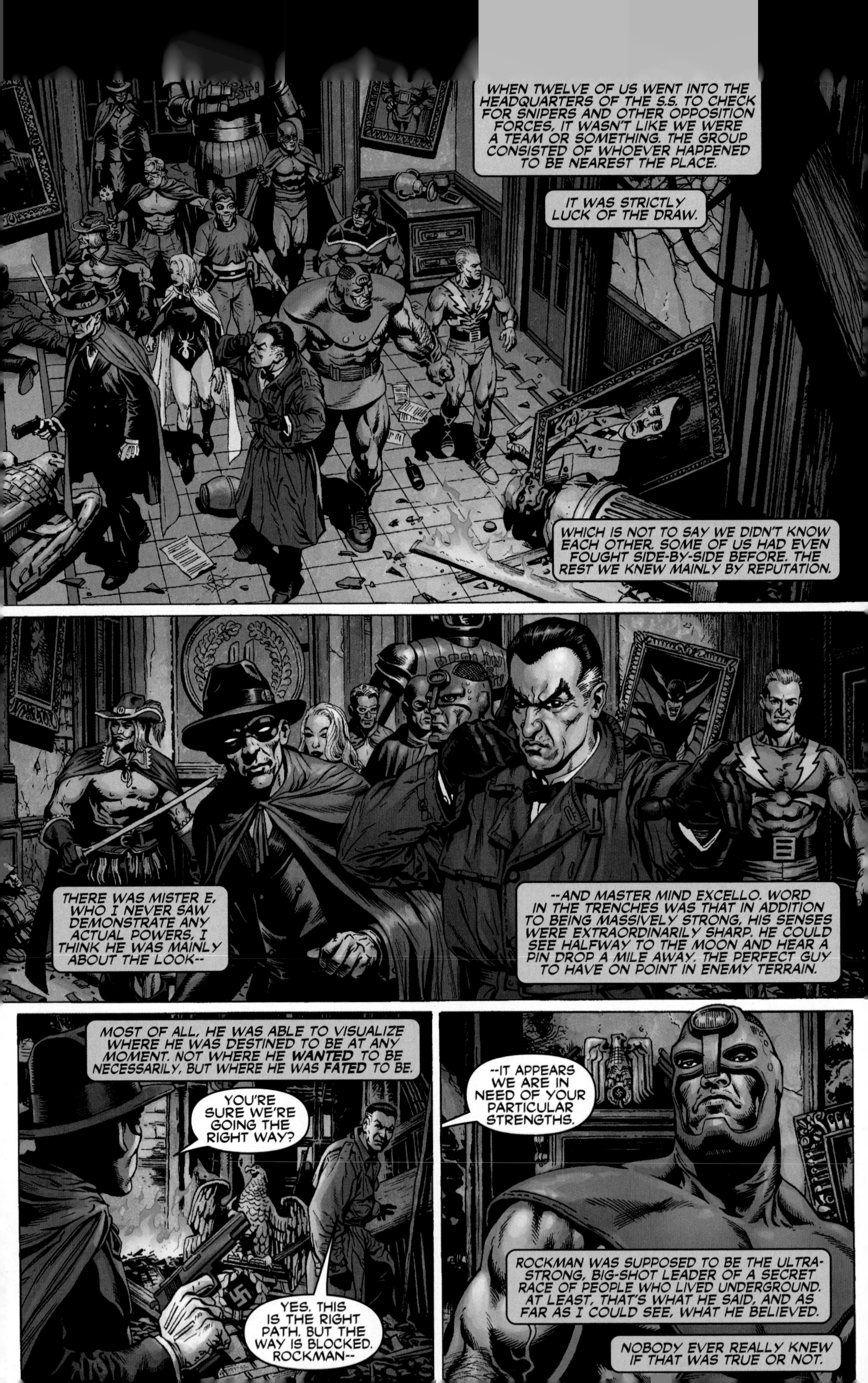
WHEN TWELVE OF US WENT INTO THE HEADQUARTERS OF THE S.S. TO CHECK FOR SNIPERS AND OTHER OPPOSITION FORCES, IT WASN'T LIKE WE WERE A TEAM OR SOMETHING. THE GROUP CONSISTED OF WHOEVER HAPPENED TO BE NEAREST THE PLACE.
IT WAS STRICTLY LUCK OF THE DRAW.
WHICH IS NOT TO SAY WE DIDN'T KNOW EACH OTHER. SOME OF US HAD EVEN FOUGHT SIDE-BY-SIDE BEFORE. THE REST WE KNEW MAINLY BY REPUTATION.
THERE WAS MISTER E, WHO I NEVER SAW DEMONSTRATE ANY ACTUAL POWERS. I THINK HE WAS MAINLY ABOUT THE LOOK--
--AND MASTER MIND EXCELLO. WORD IN THE TRENCHES WAS THAT IN ADDITION TO BEING MASSIVELY STRONG, HIS SENSES WERE EXTRAORDINARILY SHARP. HE COULD SEE HALFWAY TO THE MOON AND HEAR A PIN DROP A MILE AWAY. THE PERFECT GUY TO HAVE ON POINT IN ENEMY TERRAIN.
MOST OF ALL, HE WAS ABLE TO VISUALIZE WHERE HE WAS DESTINED TO BE AT ANY MOMENT. NOT WHERE HE **WANTED** TO BE NECESSARILY, BUT WHERE HE WAS **FATED** TO BE.
YOU'RE SURE WE'RE GOING THE RIGHT WAY?
YES. THIS IS THE RIGHT PATH, BUT THE WAY IS BLOCKED. ROCKMAN--
--IT APPEARS WE ARE IN NEED OF YOUR PARTICULAR STRENGTHS.
ROCKMAN WAS SUPPOSED TO BE THE ULTRA-STRONG, BIG-SHOT LEADER OF A SECRET RACE OF PEOPLE WHO LIVED UNDERGROUND. AT LEAST, THAT'S WHAT HE SAID, AND AS FAR AS I COULD SEE, WHAT HE BELIEVED.
NOBODY EVER REALLY KNEW IF THAT WAS TRUE OR NOT.

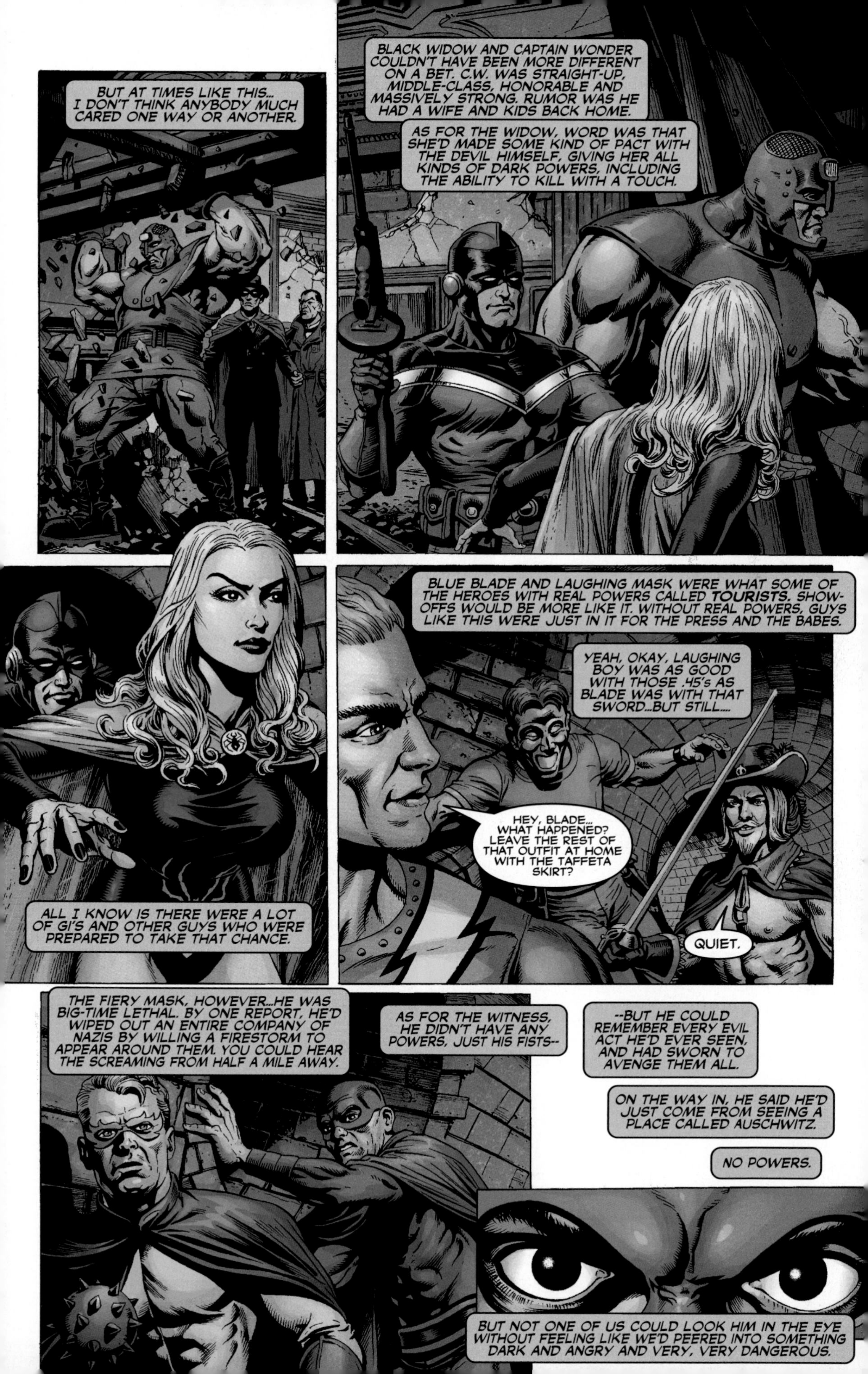
BUT AT TIMES LIKE THIS... I DON'T THINK ANYBODY MUCH CARED ONE WAY OR ANOTHER.
BLACK WIDOW AND CAPTAIN WONDER COULDN'T HAVE BEEN MORE DIFFERENT ON A BET. C.W. WAS STRAIGHT-UP, MIDDLE-CLASS, HONORABLE AND MASSIVELY STRONG. RUMOR WAS HE HAD A WIFE AND KIDS BACK HOME.
AS FOR THE WIDOW, WORD WAS THAT SHE'D MADE SOME KIND OF PACT WITH THE DEVIL HIMSELF, GIVING HER ALL KINDS OF DARK POWERS, INCLUDING THE ABILITY TO KILL WITH A TOUCH.
ALL I KNOW IS THERE WERE A LOT OF GI'S AND OTHER GUYS WHO WERE PREPARED TO TAKE THAT CHANCE.
BLUE BLADE AND LAUGHING MASK WERE WHAT SOME OF THE HEROES WITH REAL POWERS CALLED **TOURISTS.** SHOW-OFFS WOULD BE MORE LIKE IT. WITHOUT REAL POWERS, GUYS LIKE THIS WERE JUST IN IT FOR THE PRESS AND THE BABES.
YEAH, OKAY, LAUGHING BOY WAS AS GOOD WITH THOSE .45'S AS BLADE WAS WITH THAT SWORD...BUT STILL....
HEY, BLADE... WHAT HAPPENED? LEAVE THE REST OF THAT OUTFIT AT HOME WITH THE TAFFETA SKIRT?
QUIET.
THE FIERY MASK, HOWEVER...HE WAS BIG-TIME LETHAL. BY ONE REPORT, HE'D WIPED OUT AN ENTIRE COMPANY OF NAZIS BY WILLING A FIRESTORM TO APPEAR AROUND THEM. YOU COULD HEAR THE SCREAMING FROM HALF A MILE AWAY.
AS FOR THE WITNESS, HE DIDN'T HAVE ANY POWERS, JUST HIS FISTS--
--BUT HE COULD REMEMBER EVERY EVIL ACT HE'D EVER SEEN, AND HAD SWORN TO AVENGE THEM ALL.
ON THE WAY IN, HE SAID HE'D JUST COME FROM SEEING A PLACE CALLED AUSCHWITZ.
NO POWERS.
BUT NOT ONE OF US COULD LOOK HIM IN THE EYE WITHOUT FEELING LIKE WE'D PEERED INTO SOMETHING DARK AND ANGRY AND VERY, VERY DANGEROUS.

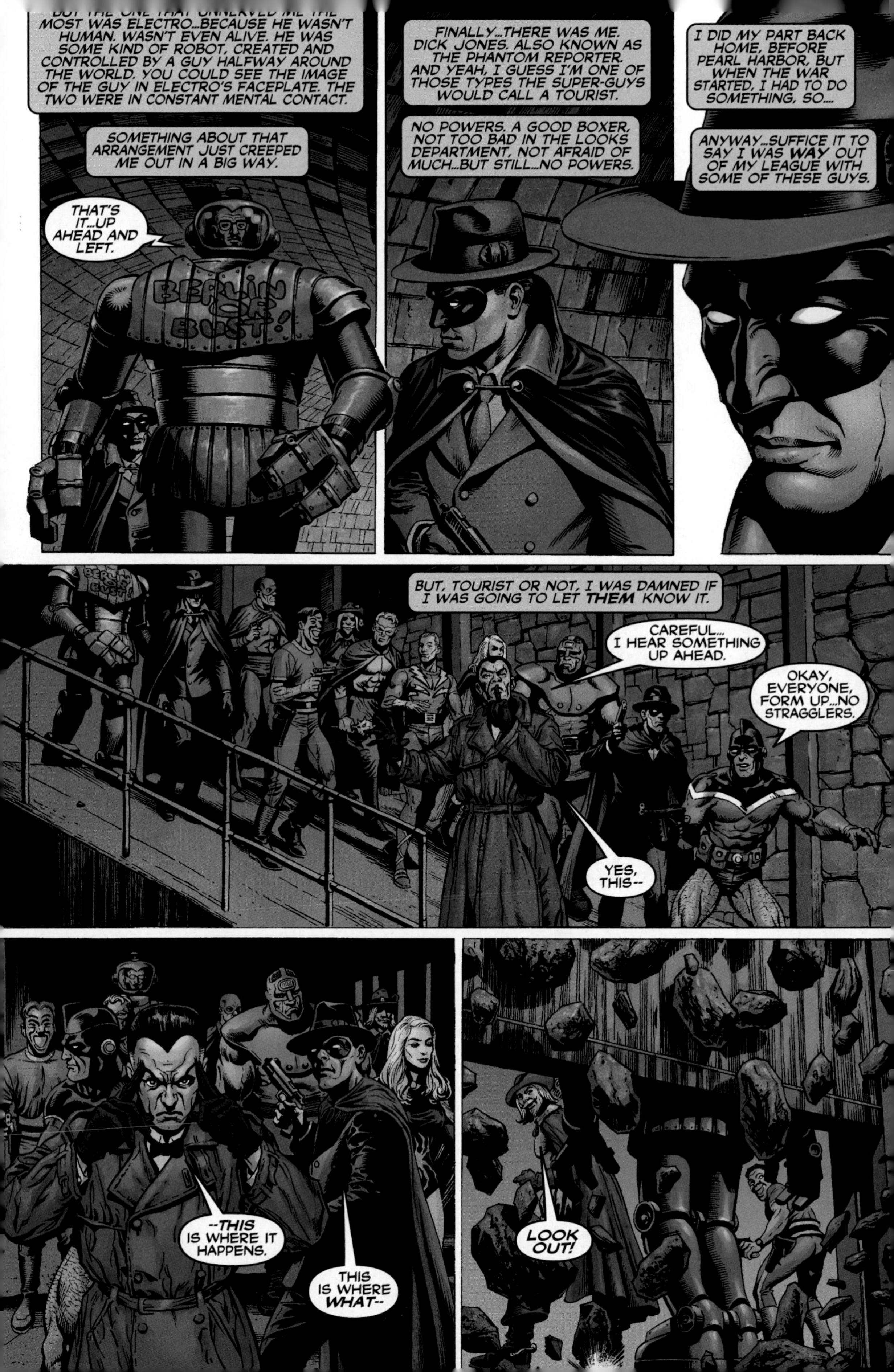
BUT THE ONE THAT UNNERVED ME THE MOST WAS ELECTRO...BECAUSE HE WASN'T HUMAN. WASN'T EVEN ALIVE. HE WAS SOME KIND OF ROBOT, CREATED AND CONTROLLED BY A GUY HALFWAY AROUND THE WORLD. YOU COULD SEE THE IMAGE OF THE GUY IN ELECTRO'S FACEPLATE. THE TWO WERE IN CONSTANT MENTAL CONTACT.
SOMETHING ABOUT THAT ARRANGEMENT JUST CREEPED ME OUT IN A BIG WAY.
THAT'S IT...UP AHEAD AND LEFT.
BERLIN OR BUST!
FINALLY...THERE WAS ME. DICK JONES. ALSO KNOWN AS THE PHANTOM REPORTER. AND YEAH, I GUESS I'M ONE OF THOSE TYPES THE SUPER-GUYS WOULD CALL A TOURIST.
NO POWERS. A GOOD BOXER, NOT TOO BAD IN THE LOOKS DEPARTMENT, NOT AFRAID OF MUCH...BUT STILL...NO POWERS.
I DID MY PART BACK HOME, BEFORE PEARL HARBOR, BUT WHEN THE WAR STARTED, I HAD TO DO SOMETHING, SO....
ANYWAY...SUFFICE IT TO SAY I WAS **WAY** OUT OF MY LEAGUE WITH SOME OF THESE GUYS.
BUT, TOURIST OR NOT, I WAS DAMNED IF I WAS GOING TO LET **THEM** KNOW IT.
CAREFUL... I HEAR SOMETHING UP AHEAD.
OKAY, EVERYONE, FORM UP...NO STRAGGLERS.
YES, THIS--
--***THIS*** IS WHERE IT HAPPENS.
THIS IS WHERE ***WHAT***--
LOOK OUT!

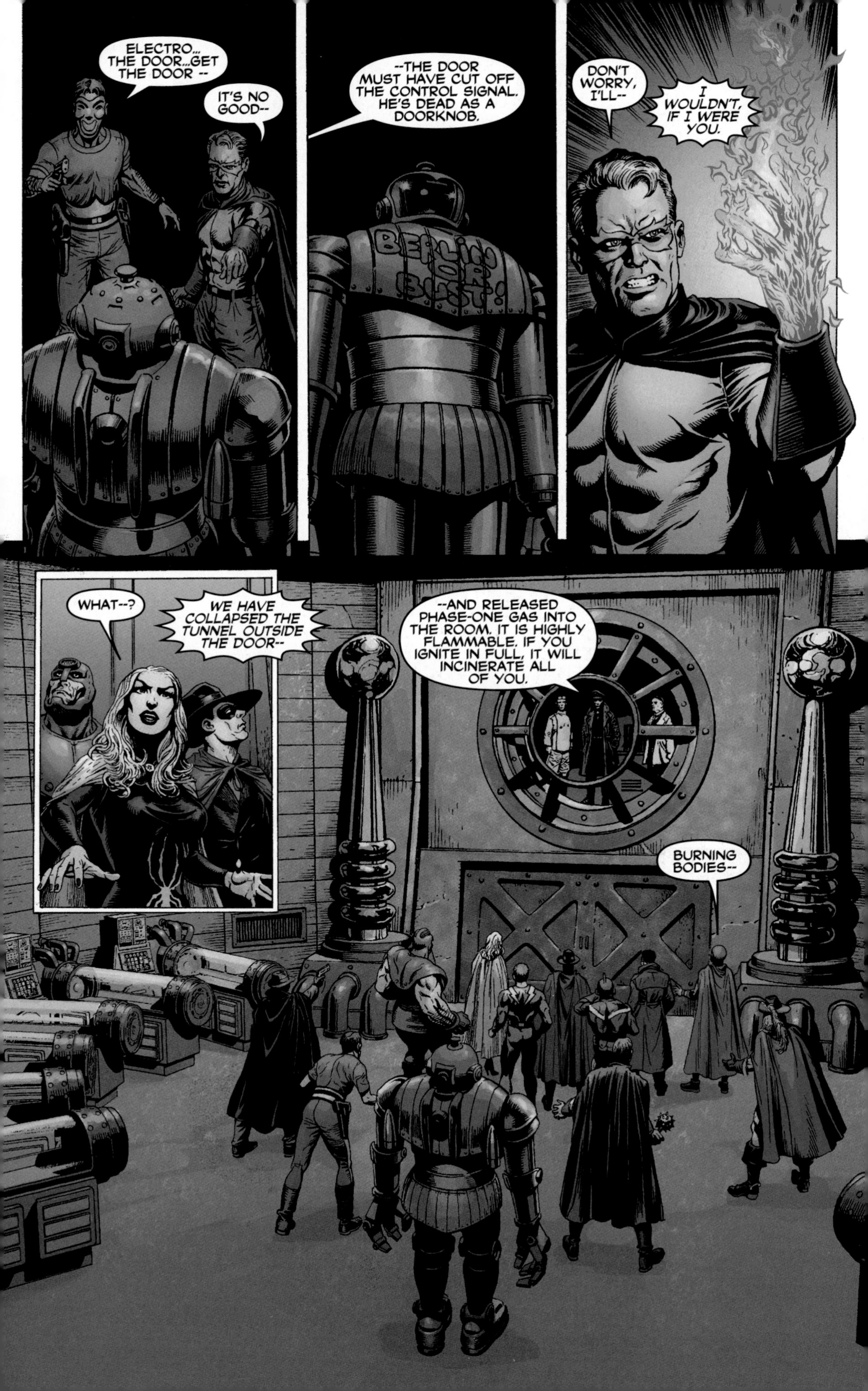
ELECTRO... THE DOOR...GET THE DOOR --
IT'S NO GOOD--
--THE DOOR MUST HAVE CUT OFF THE CONTROL SIGNAL. HE'S DEAD AS A DOORKNOB.
BERLIN OR BUST!
DON'T WORRY, I'LL--
I WOULDN'T, IF I WERE YOU.
WHAT--?
WE HAVE COLLAPSED THE TUNNEL OUTSIDE THE DOOR--
--AND RELEASED PHASE-ONE GAS INTO THE ROOM. IT IS HIGHLY FLAMMABLE. IF YOU IGNITE IN FULL, IT WILL INCINERATE ALL OF YOU.
BURNING BODIES--

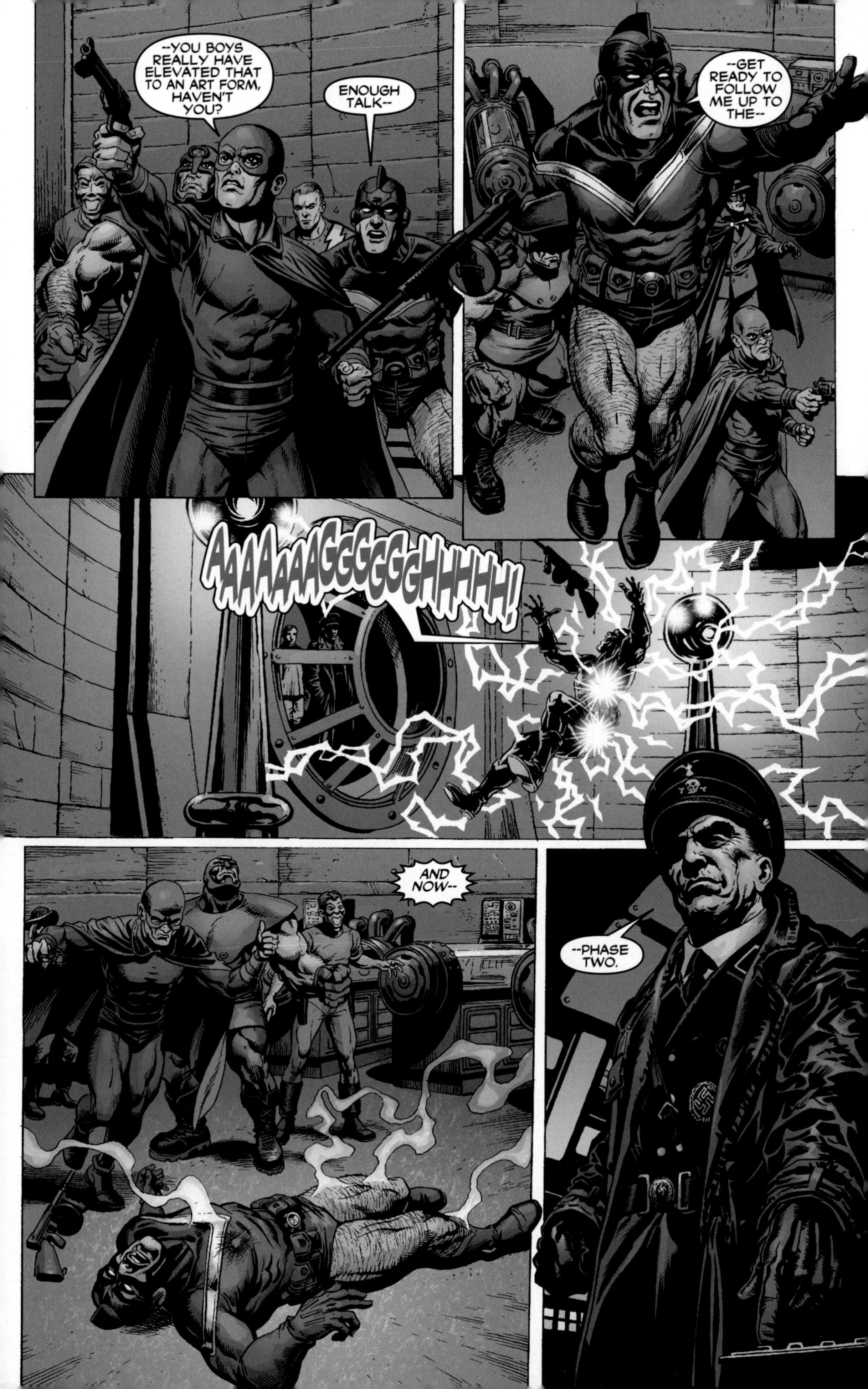
--YOU BOYS REALLY HAVE ELEVATED THAT TO AN ART FORM, HAVEN'T YOU?
ENOUGH TALK--
--GET READY TO FOLLOW ME UP TO THE--
AAAAAAGGGGGHHHHH!
AND NOW--
--PHASE TWO.

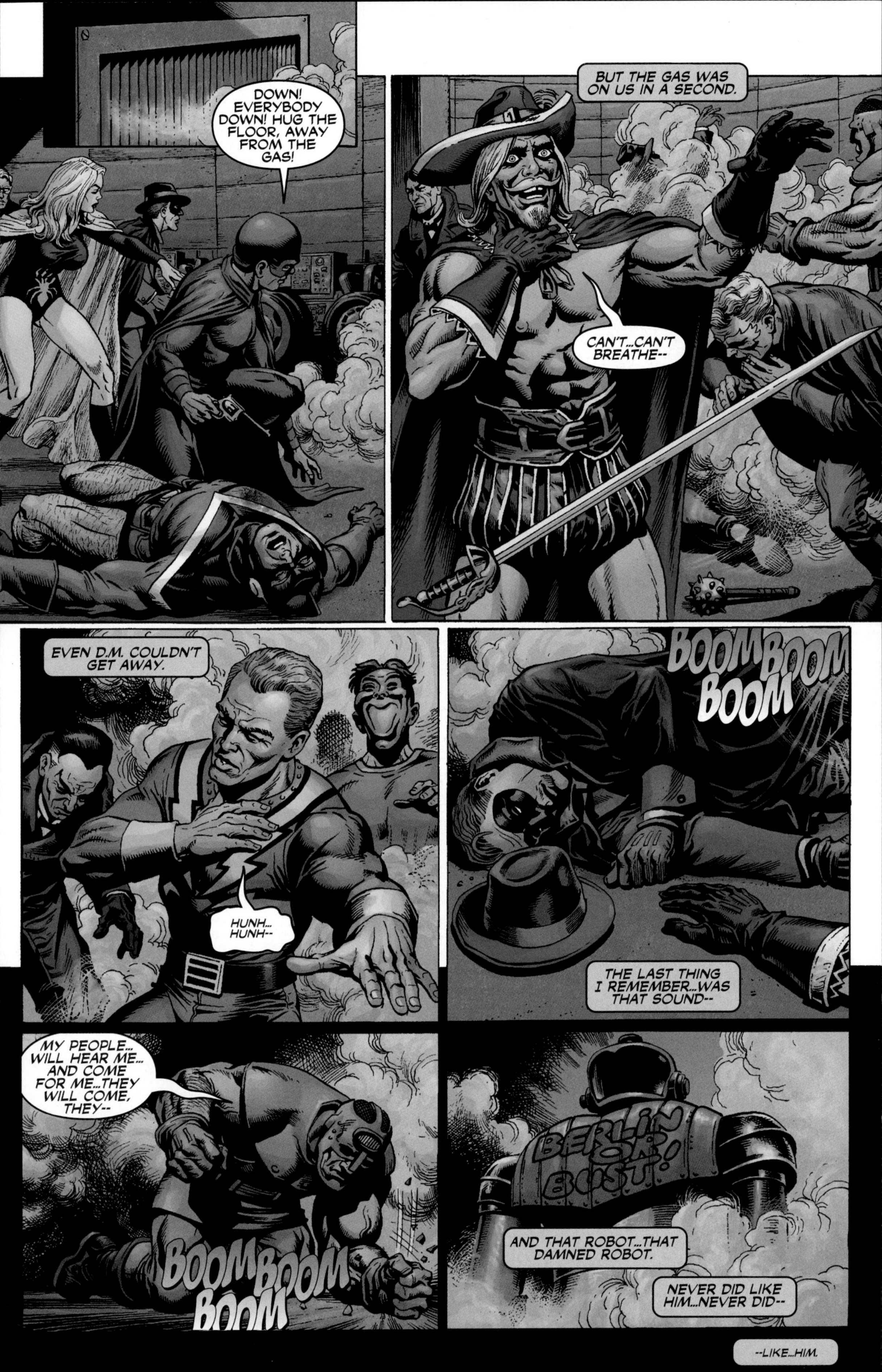
DOWN! EVERYBODY DOWN! HUG THE FLOOR, AWAY FROM THE GAS!
BUT THE GAS WAS ON US IN A SECOND.
CAN'T...CAN'T BREATHE--
EVEN D.M. COULDN'T GET AWAY.
HUNH... HUNH--
BOOM BOOM BOOM
THE LAST THING I REMEMBER...WAS THAT SOUND--
MY PEOPLE... WILL HEAR ME... AND COME FOR ME...THEY WILL COME, THEY--
BOOM BOOM BOOM
BERLIN OR BUST!
AND THAT ROBOT...THAT DAMNED ROBOT.
NEVER DID LIKE HIM...NEVER DID--
--LIKE...HIM.

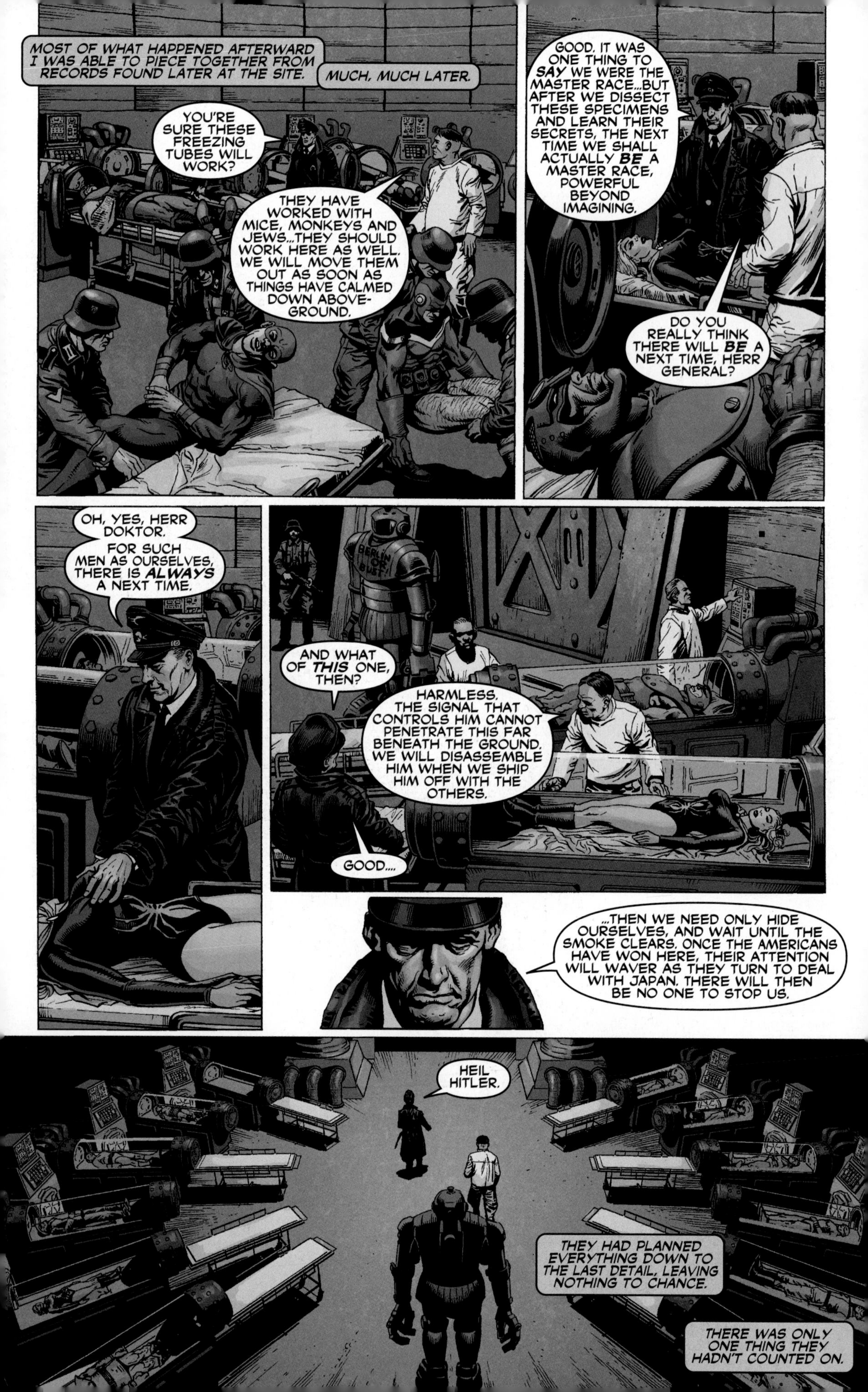
MOST OF WHAT HAPPENED AFTERWARD I WAS ABLE TO PIECE TOGETHER FROM RECORDS FOUND LATER AT THE SITE.
MUCH, MUCH LATER.
YOU'RE SURE THESE FREEZING TUBES WILL WORK?
THEY HAVE WORKED WITH MICE, MONKEYS AND JEWS...THEY SHOULD WORK HERE AS WELL. WE WILL MOVE THEM OUT AS SOON AS THINGS HAVE CALMED DOWN ABOVE-GROUND.
GOOD. IT WAS ONE THING TO SAY WE WERE THE MASTER RACE...BUT AFTER WE DISSECT THESE SPECIMENS AND LEARN THEIR SECRETS, THE NEXT TIME WE SHALL ACTUALLY BE A MASTER RACE, POWERFUL BEYOND IMAGINING.
DO YOU REALLY THINK THERE WILL BE A NEXT TIME, HERR GENERAL?
OH, YES, HERR DOKTOR.
FOR SUCH MEN AS OURSELVES, THERE IS ALWAYS A NEXT TIME.
BERLIN OR BUST
AND WHAT OF THIS ONE, THEN?
HARMLESS. THE SIGNAL THAT CONTROLS HIM CANNOT PENETRATE THIS FAR BENEATH THE GROUND. WE WILL DISASSEMBLE HIM WHEN WE SHIP HIM OFF WITH THE OTHERS.
GOOD....
...THEN WE NEED ONLY HIDE OURSELVES, AND WAIT UNTIL THE SMOKE CLEARS. ONCE THE AMERICANS HAVE WON HERE, THEIR ATTENTION WILL WAVER AS THEY TURN TO DEAL WITH JAPAN. THERE WILL THEN BE NO ONE TO STOP US.
HEIL HITLER.
THEY HAD PLANNED EVERYTHING DOWN TO THE LAST DETAIL, LEAVING NOTHING TO CHANCE.
THERE WAS ONLY ONE THING THEY HADN'T COUNTED ON.

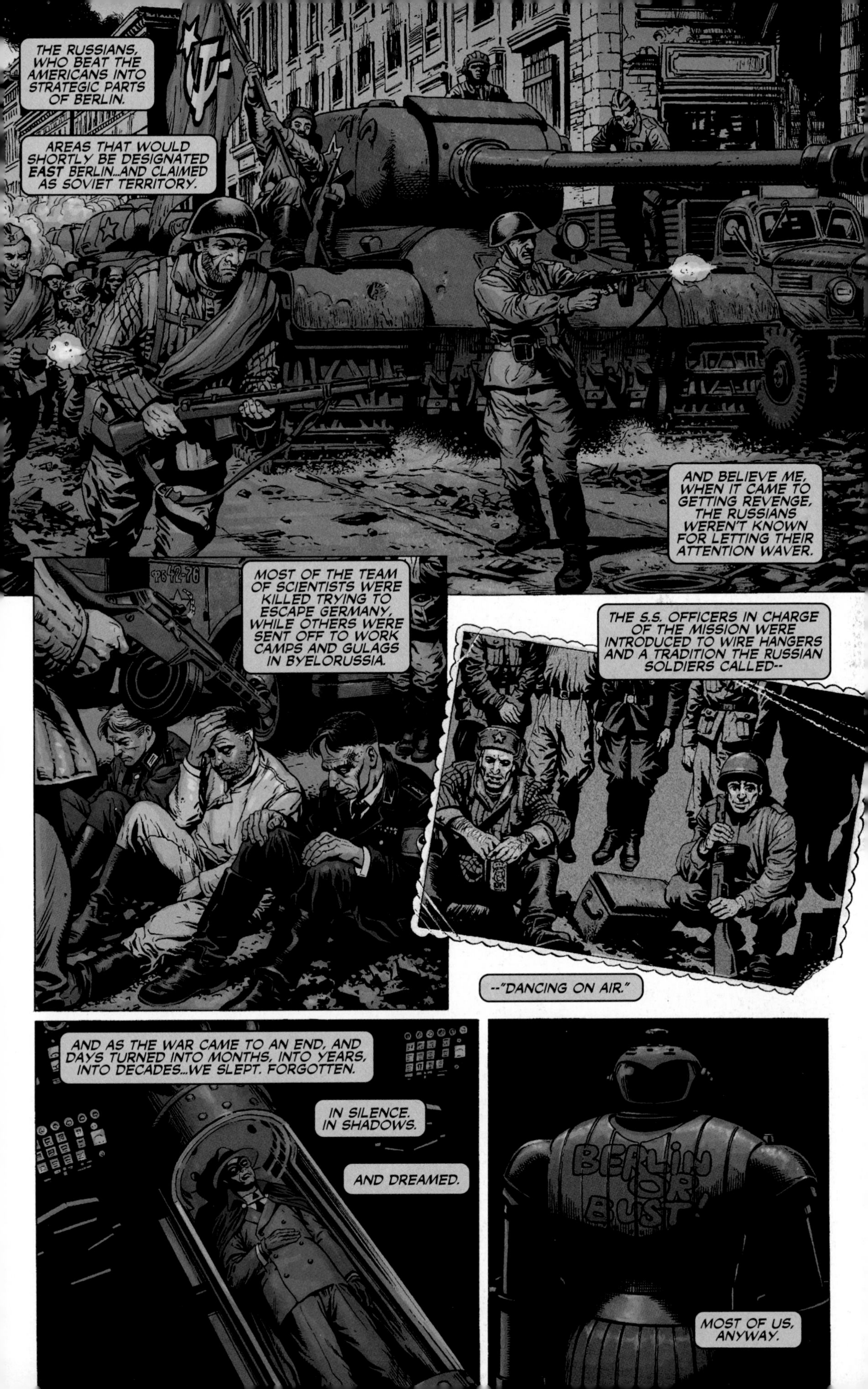
THE RUSSIANS, WHO BEAT THE AMERICANS INTO STRATEGIC PARTS OF BERLIN.
AREAS THAT WOULD SHORTLY BE DESIGNATED EAST BERLIN...AND CLAIMED AS SOVIET TERRITORY.
AND BELIEVE ME, WHEN IT CAME TO GETTING REVENGE, THE RUSSIANS WEREN'T KNOWN FOR LETTING THEIR ATTENTION WAVER.
MOST OF THE TEAM OF SCIENTISTS WERE KILLED TRYING TO ESCAPE GERMANY, WHILE OTHERS WERE SENT OFF TO WORK CAMPS AND GULAGS IN BYELORUSSIA.
THE S.S. OFFICERS IN CHARGE OF THE MISSION WERE INTRODUCED TO WIRE HANGERS AND A TRADITION THE RUSSIAN SOLDIERS CALLED--
--"DANCING ON AIR."
AND AS THE WAR CAME TO AN END, AND DAYS TURNED INTO MONTHS, INTO YEARS, INTO DECADES...WE SLEPT. FORGOTTEN.
IN SILENCE. IN SHADOWS.
AND DREAMED.
BERLIN OR BUST!
MOST OF US, ANYWAY.

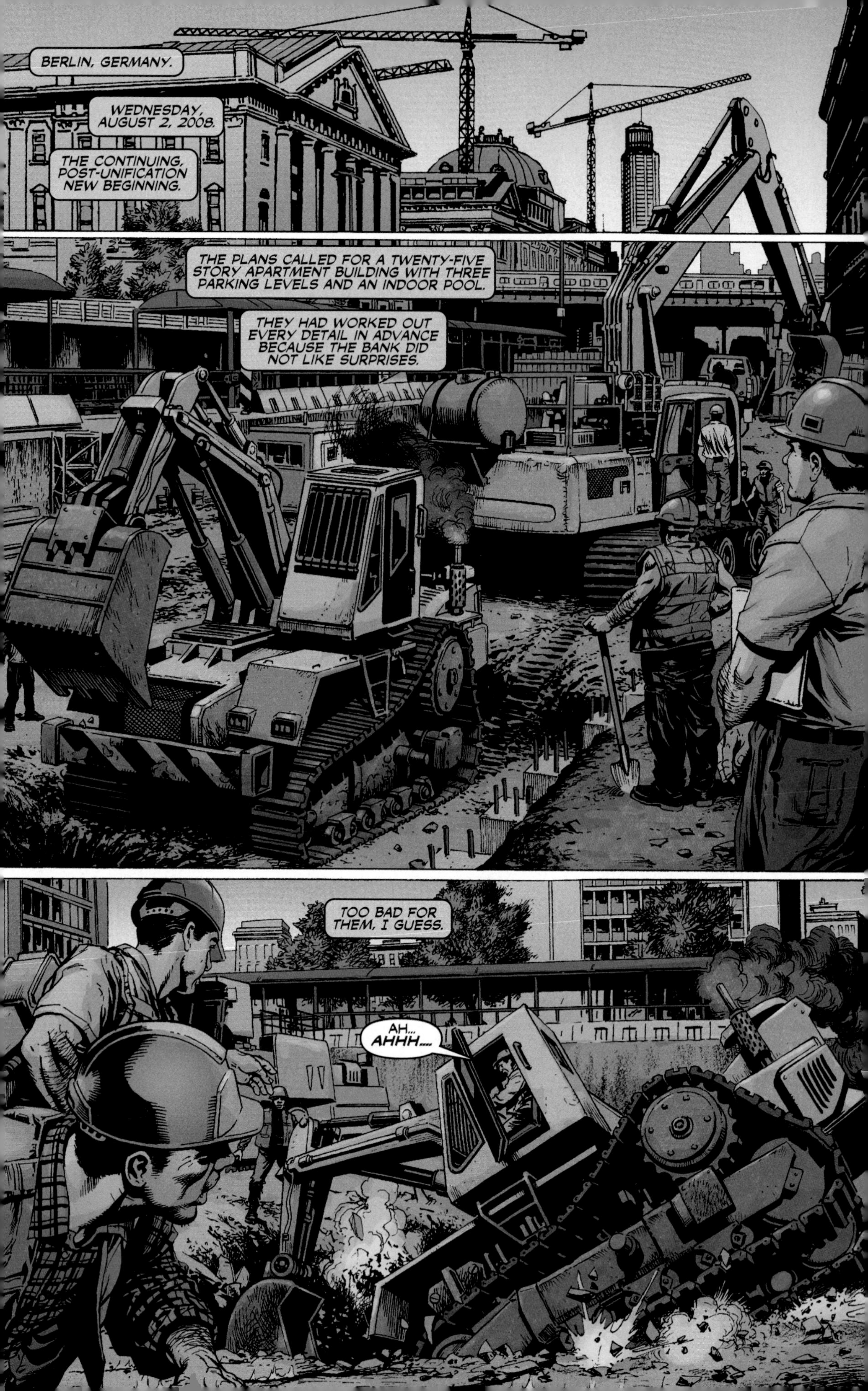
BERLIN, GERMANY.
WEDNESDAY, AUGUST 2, 2008.
THE CONTINUING, POST-UNIFICATION NEW BEGINNING.
THE PLANS CALLED FOR A TWENTY-FIVE STORY APARTMENT BUILDING WITH THREE PARKING LEVELS AND AN INDOOR POOL.
THEY HAD WORKED OUT EVERY DETAIL IN ADVANCE BECAUSE THE BANK DID NOT LIKE SURPRISES.
TOO BAD FOR THEM, I GUESS.
AH... AHHH....

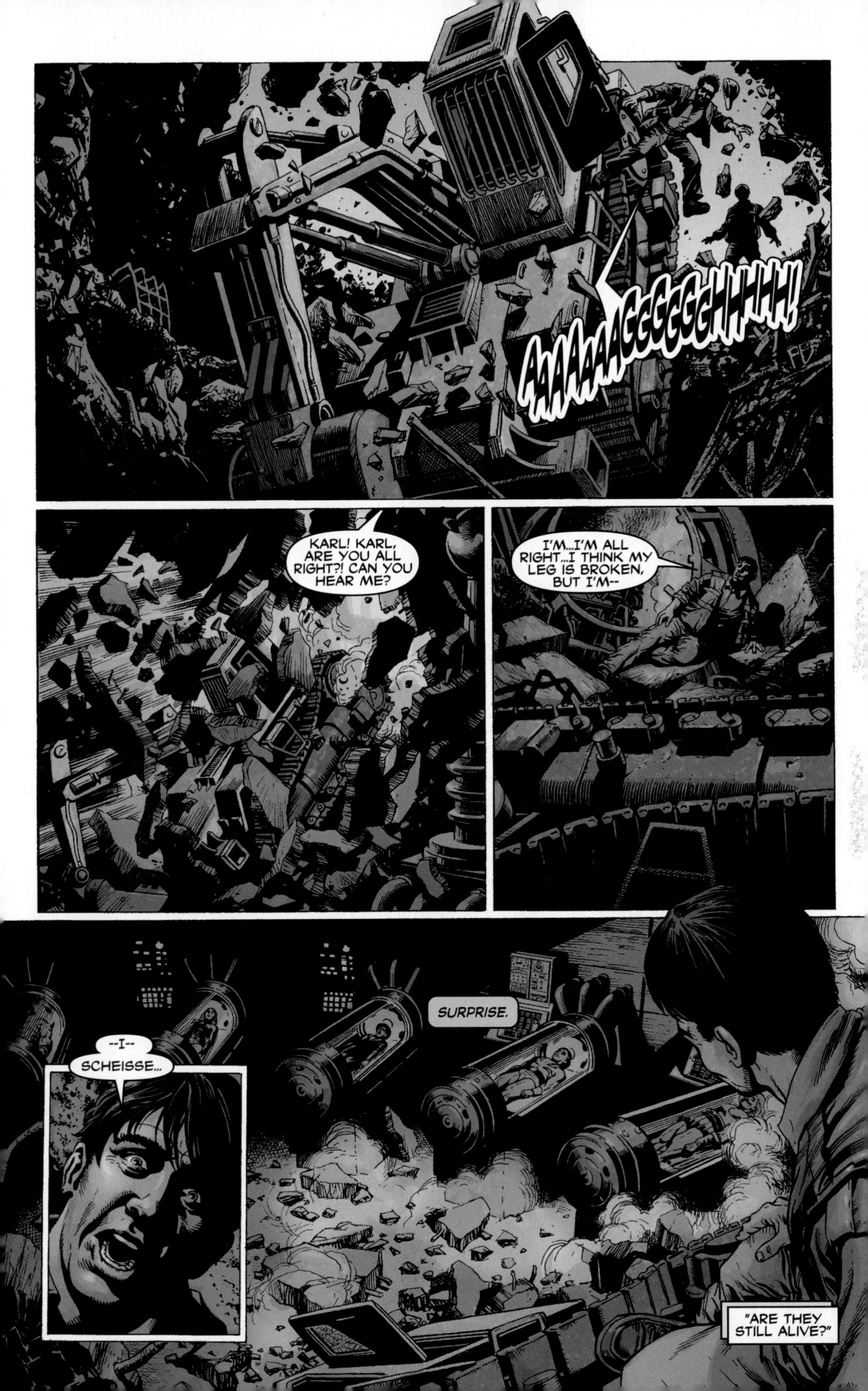
AAAAAAGGGGGHHHHH!
KARL! KARL, ARE YOU ALL RIGHT?! CAN YOU HEAR ME?
I'M...I'M ALL RIGHT...I THINK MY LEG IS BROKEN, BUT I'M--
SURPRISE.
--I--
SCHEISSE...
"ARE THEY STILL ALIVE?"

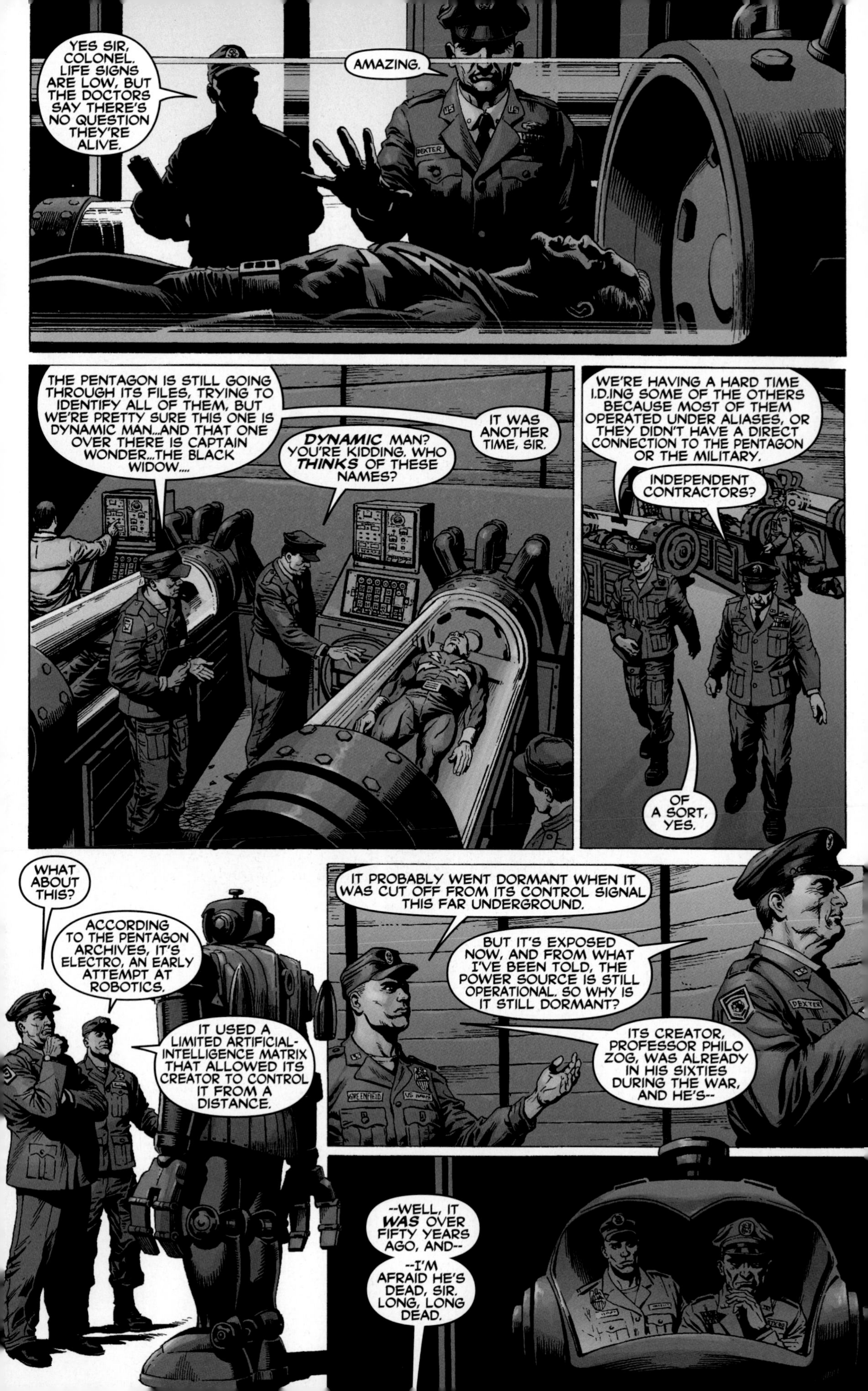
YES SIR, COLONEL. LIFE SIGNS ARE LOW, BUT THE DOCTORS SAY THERE'S NO QUESTION THEY'RE ALIVE.
AMAZING.
DEXTER
THE PENTAGON IS STILL GOING THROUGH ITS FILES, TRYING TO IDENTIFY ALL OF THEM, BUT WE'RE PRETTY SURE THIS ONE IS DYNAMIC MAN...AND THAT ONE OVER THERE IS CAPTAIN WONDER...THE BLACK WIDOW....
DYNAMIC MAN? YOU'RE KIDDING. WHO THINKS OF THESE NAMES?
IT WAS ANOTHER TIME, SIR.
WE'RE HAVING A HARD TIME I.D.ING SOME OF THE OTHERS BECAUSE MOST OF THEM OPERATED UNDER ALIASES, OR THEY DIDN'T HAVE A DIRECT CONNECTION TO THE PENTAGON OR THE MILITARY.
INDEPENDENT CONTRACTORS?
OF A SORT, YES.
WHAT ABOUT THIS?
ACCORDING TO THE PENTAGON ARCHIVES, IT'S ELECTRO, AN EARLY ATTEMPT AT ROBOTICS.
IT USED A LIMITED ARTIFICIAL-INTELLIGENCE MATRIX THAT ALLOWED ITS CREATOR TO CONTROL IT FROM A DISTANCE.
IT PROBABLY WENT DORMANT WHEN IT WAS CUT OFF FROM ITS CONTROL SIGNAL THIS FAR UNDERGROUND.
BUT IT'S EXPOSED NOW, AND FROM WHAT I'VE BEEN TOLD, THE POWER SOURCE IS STILL OPERATIONAL. SO WHY IS IT STILL DORMANT?
ITS CREATOR, PROFESSOR PHILO ZOG, WAS ALREADY IN HIS SIXTIES DURING THE WAR, AND HE'S--
GREENFIELD
US NAVY
DEXTER
--WELL, IT WAS OVER FIFTY YEARS AGO, AND--
--I'M AFRAID HE'S DEAD, SIR. LONG, LONG DEAD.

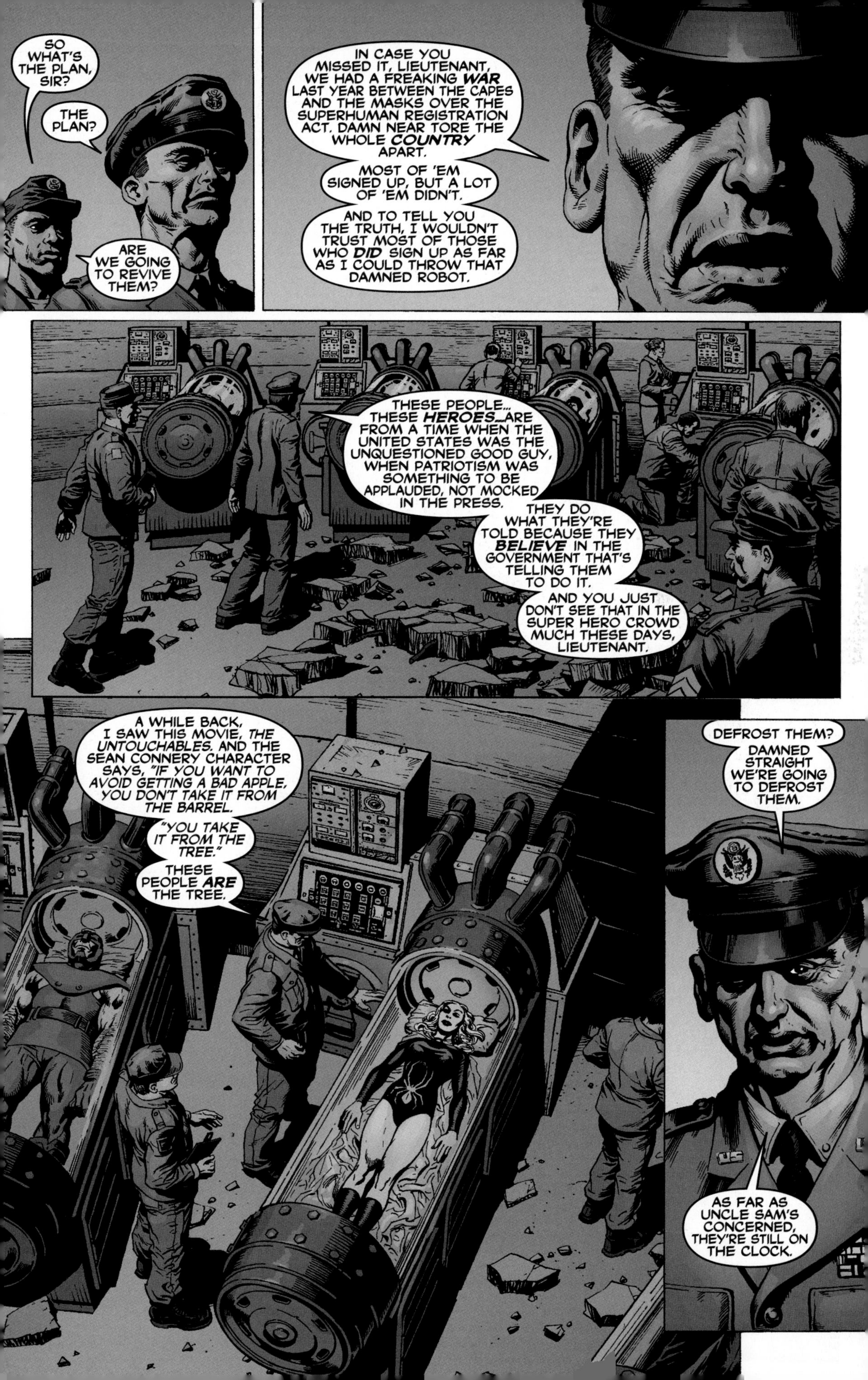
SO WHAT'S THE PLAN, SIR?
THE PLAN?
ARE WE GOING TO REVIVE THEM?
IN CASE YOU MISSED IT, LIEUTENANT, WE HAD A FREAKING WAR LAST YEAR BETWEEN THE CAPES AND THE MASKS OVER THE SUPERHUMAN REGISTRATION ACT. DAMN NEAR TORE THE WHOLE COUNTRY APART.
MOST OF 'EM SIGNED UP, BUT A LOT OF 'EM DIDN'T.
AND TO TELL YOU THE TRUTH, I WOULDN'T TRUST MOST OF THOSE WHO DID SIGN UP AS FAR AS I COULD THROW THAT DAMNED ROBOT.
THESE PEOPLE... THESE HEROES...ARE FROM A TIME WHEN THE UNITED STATES WAS THE UNQUESTIONED GOOD GUY, WHEN PATRIOTISM WAS SOMETHING TO BE APPLAUDED, NOT MOCKED IN THE PRESS.
THEY DO WHAT THEY'RE TOLD BECAUSE THEY BELIEVE IN THE GOVERNMENT THAT'S TELLING THEM TO DO IT.
AND YOU JUST DON'T SEE THAT IN THE SUPER HERO CROWD MUCH THESE DAYS, LIEUTENANT.
A WHILE BACK, I SAW THIS MOVIE, THE UNTOUCHABLES. AND THE SEAN CONNERY CHARACTER SAYS, "IF YOU WANT TO AVOID GETTING A BAD APPLE, YOU DON'T TAKE IT FROM THE BARREL.
"YOU TAKE IT FROM THE TREE."
THESE PEOPLE ARE THE TREE.
DEFROST THEM? DAMNED STRAIGHT WE'RE GOING TO DEFROST THEM.
AS FAR AS UNCLE SAM'S CONCERNED, THEY'RE STILL ON THE CLOCK.

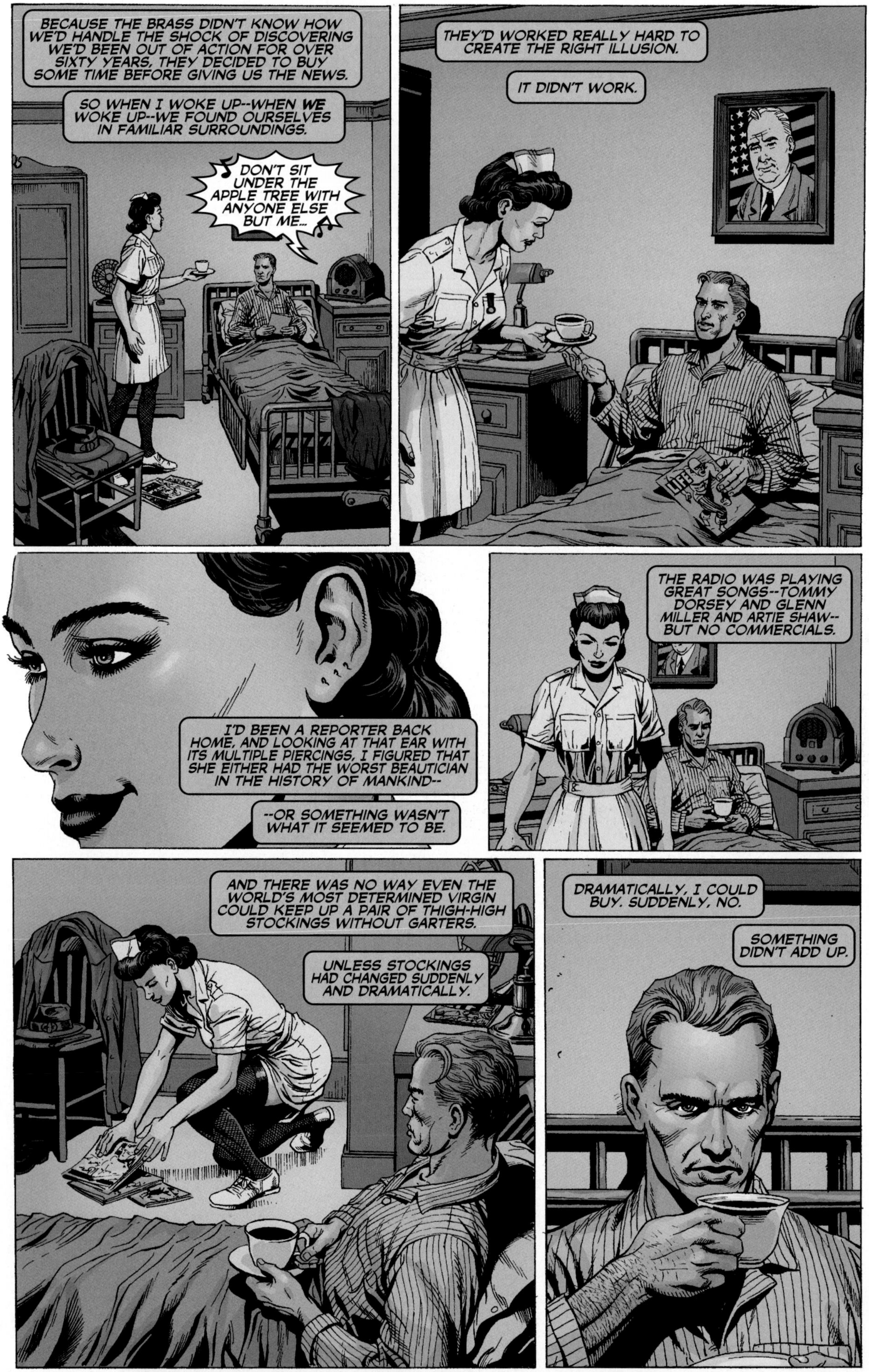
BECAUSE THE BRASS DIDN'T KNOW HOW WE'D HANDLE THE SHOCK OF DISCOVERING WE'D BEEN OUT OF ACTION FOR OVER SIXTY YEARS, THEY DECIDED TO BUY SOME TIME BEFORE GIVING US THE NEWS.
SO WHEN I WOKE UP--WHEN WE WOKE UP--WE FOUND OURSELVES IN FAMILIAR SURROUNDINGS.
DON'T SIT UNDER THE APPLE TREE WITH ANYONE ELSE BUT ME...
THEY'D WORKED REALLY HARD TO CREATE THE RIGHT ILLUSION.
IT DIDN'T WORK.
I'D BEEN A REPORTER BACK HOME, AND LOOKING AT THAT EAR WITH ITS MULTIPLE PIERCINGS, I FIGURED THAT SHE EITHER HAD THE WORST BEAUTICIAN IN THE HISTORY OF MANKIND--
--OR SOMETHING WASN'T WHAT IT SEEMED TO BE.
THE RADIO WAS PLAYING GREAT SONGS--TOMMY DORSEY AND GLENN MILLER AND ARTIE SHAW--BUT NO COMMERCIALS.
AND THERE WAS NO WAY EVEN THE WORLD'S MOST DETERMINED VIRGIN COULD KEEP UP A PAIR OF THIGH-HIGH STOCKINGS WITHOUT GARTERS.
UNLESS STOCKINGS HAD CHANGED SUDDENLY AND DRAMATICALLY.
DRAMATICALLY, I COULD BUY. SUDDENLY, NO.
SOMETHING DIDN'T ADD UP.

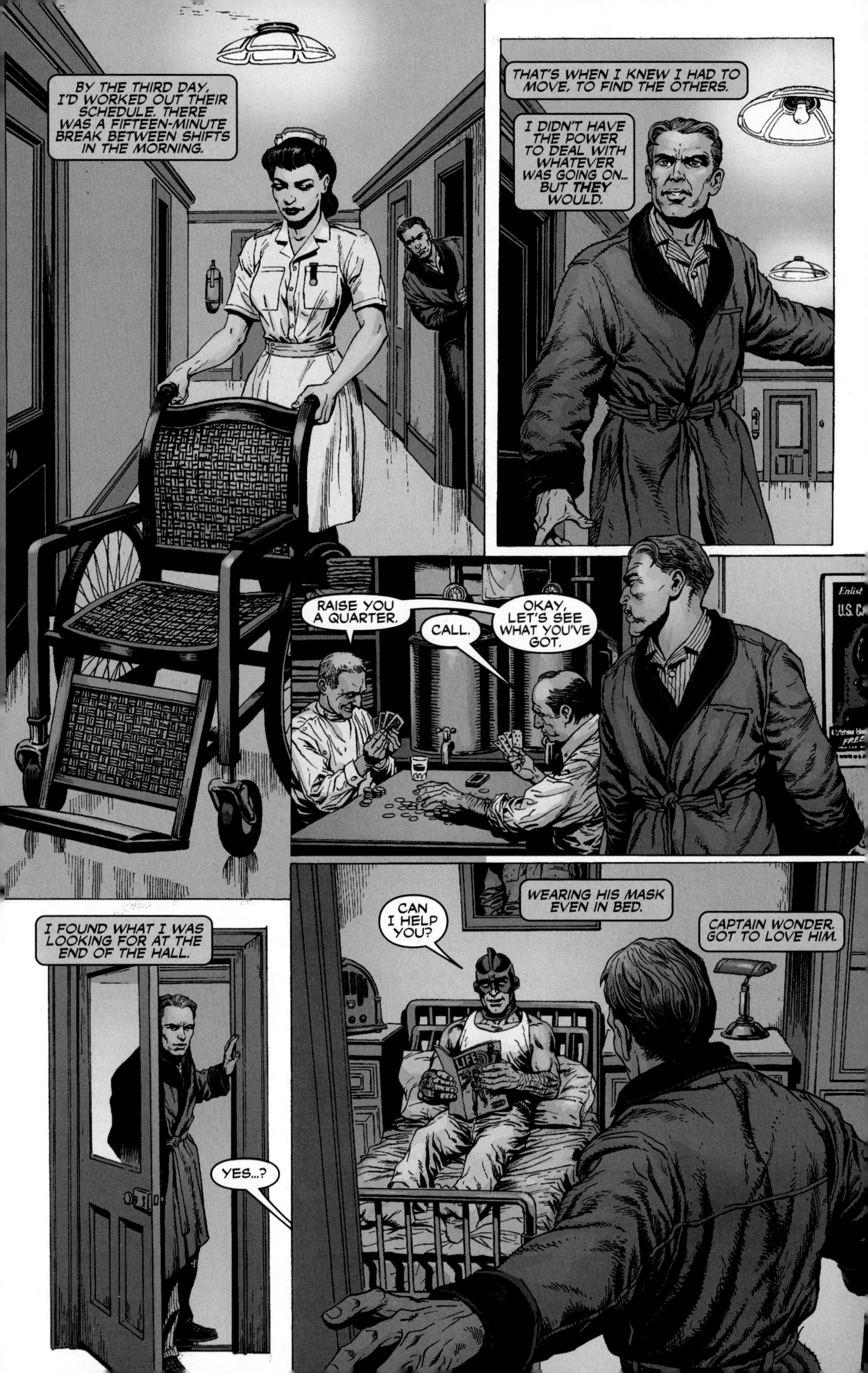
BY THE THIRD DAY, I'D WORKED OUT THEIR SCHEDULE. THERE WAS A FIFTEEN-MINUTE BREAK BETWEEN SHIFTS IN THE MORNING.
THAT'S WHEN I KNEW I HAD TO MOVE, TO FIND THE OTHERS.
I DIDN'T HAVE THE POWER TO DEAL WITH WHATEVER WAS GOING ON... BUT THEY WOULD.
RAISE YOU A QUARTER.
CALL.
OKAY, LET'S SEE WHAT YOU'VE GOT.
I FOUND WHAT I WAS LOOKING FOR AT THE END OF THE HALL.
YES...?
CAN I HELP YOU?
WEARING HIS MASK EVEN IN BED.
CAPTAIN WONDER. GOT TO LOVE HIM.

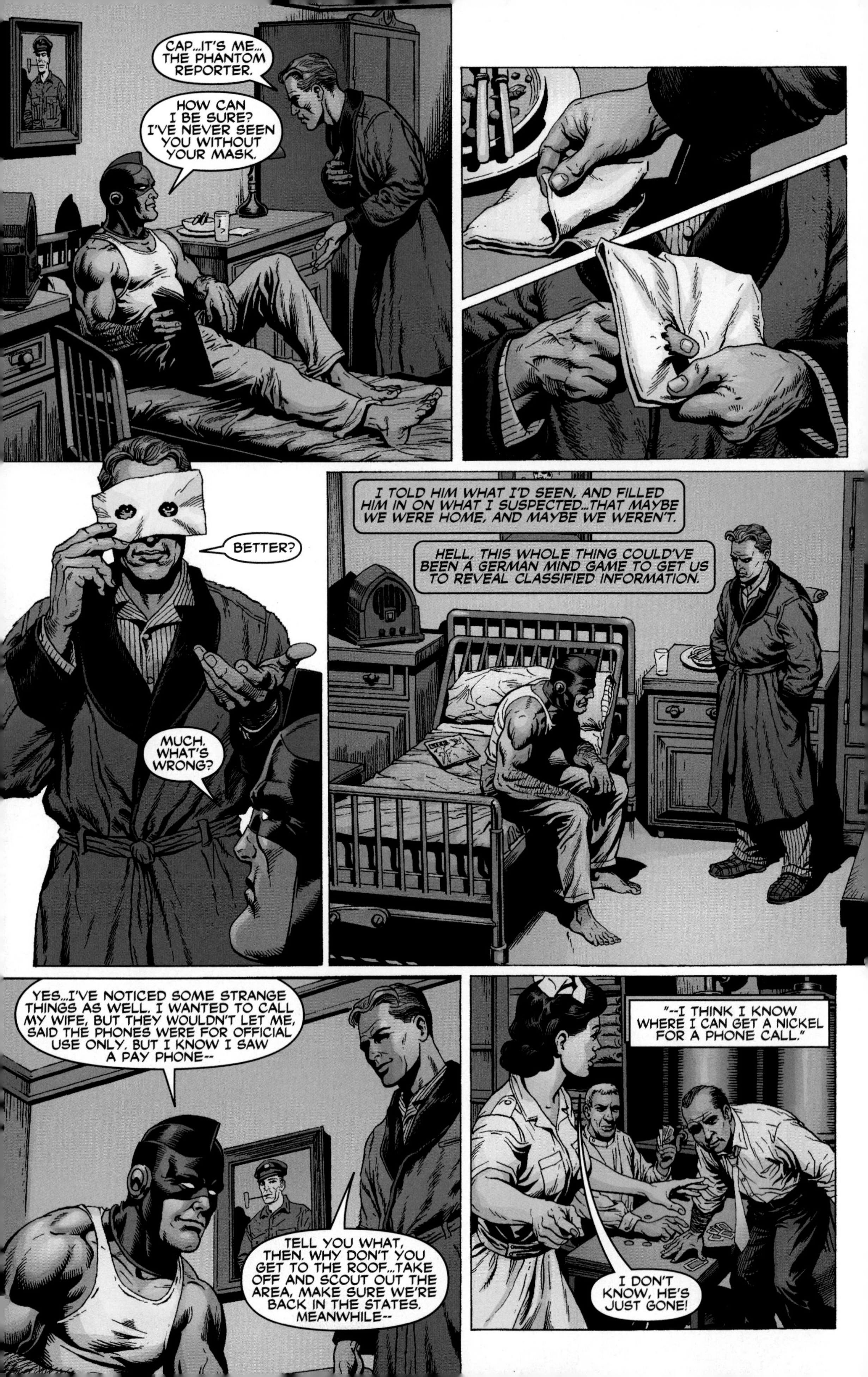
CAP...IT'S ME... THE PHANTOM REPORTER.
HOW CAN I BE SURE? I'VE NEVER SEEN YOU WITHOUT YOUR MASK.
BETTER?
MUCH. WHAT'S WRONG?
I TOLD HIM WHAT I'D SEEN, AND FILLED HIM IN ON WHAT I SUSPECTED...THAT MAYBE WE WERE HOME, AND MAYBE WE WEREN'T.
HELL, THIS WHOLE THING COULD'VE BEEN A GERMAN MIND GAME TO GET US TO REVEAL CLASSIFIED INFORMATION.
YES...I'VE NOTICED SOME STRANGE THINGS AS WELL. I WANTED TO CALL MY WIFE, BUT THEY WOULDN'T LET ME, SAID THE PHONES WERE FOR OFFICIAL USE ONLY. BUT I KNOW I SAW A PAY PHONE--
TELL YOU WHAT, THEN. WHY DON'T YOU GET TO THE ROOF...TAKE OFF AND SCOUT OUT THE AREA, MAKE SURE WE'RE BACK IN THE STATES. MEANWHILE--
"--I THINK I KNOW WHERE I CAN GET A NICKEL FOR A PHONE CALL."
I DON'T KNOW, HE'S JUST GONE!

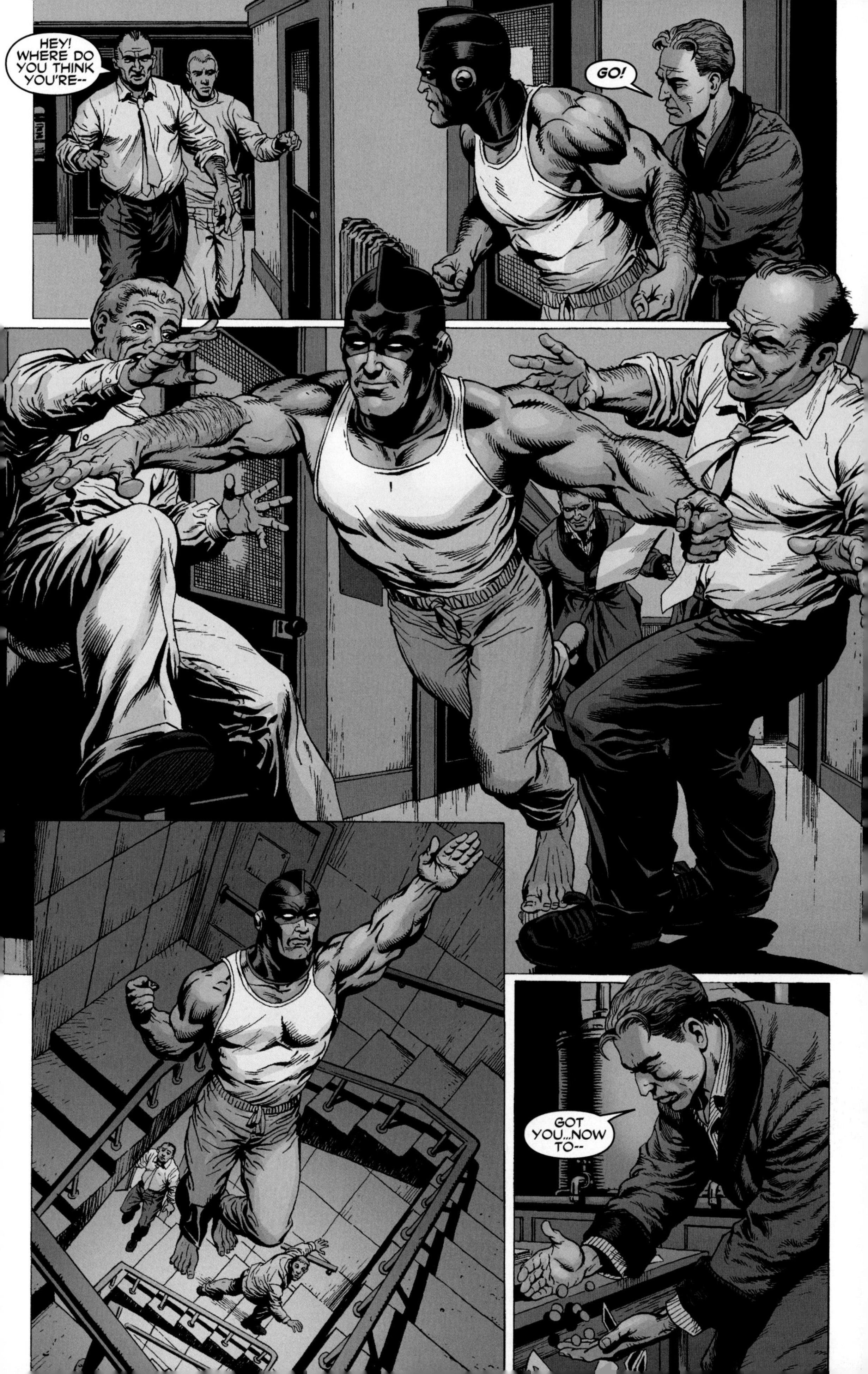
HEY! WHERE DO YOU THINK YOU'RE--
GO!
GOT YOU...NOW TO--

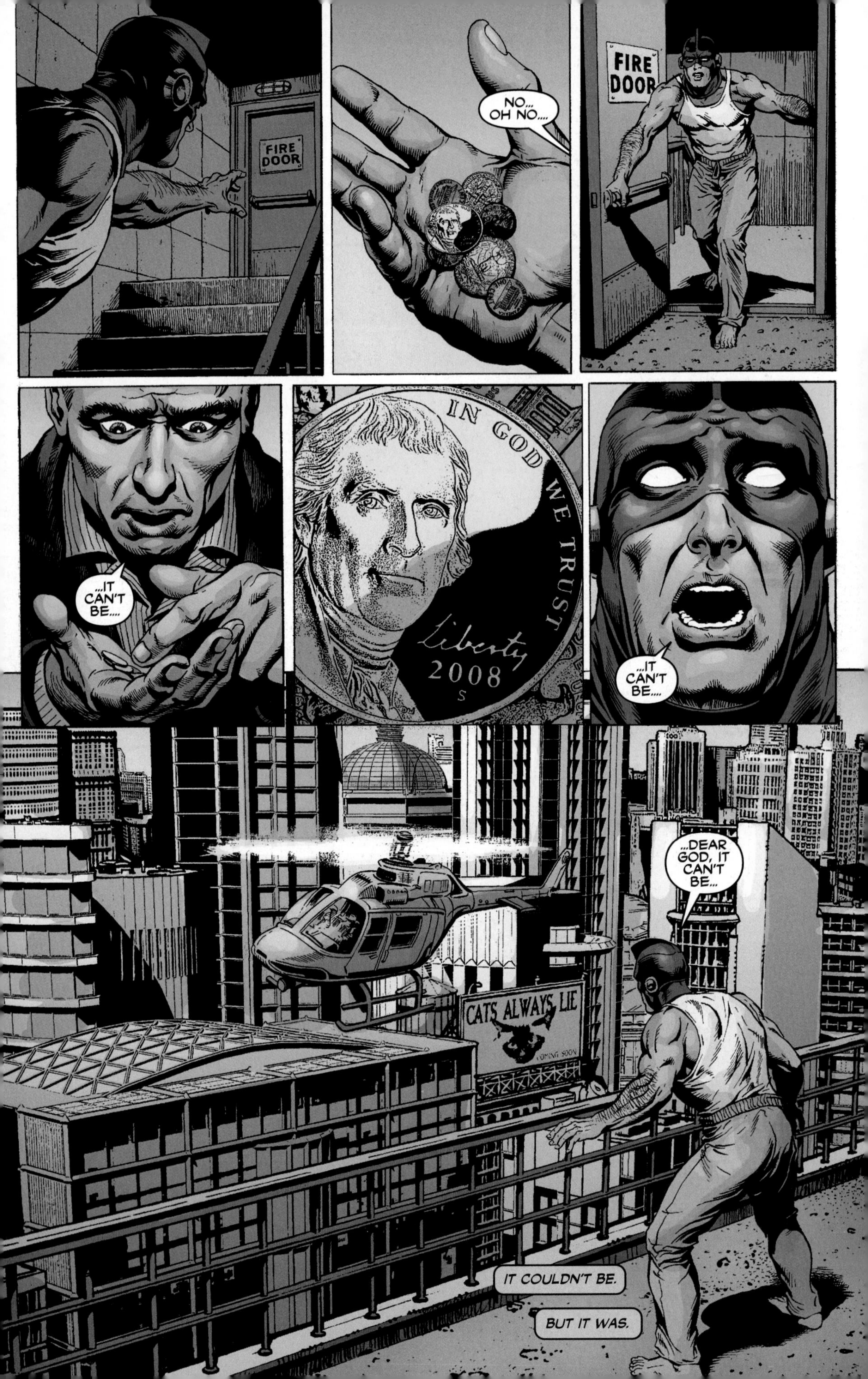
FIRE DOOR
NO... OH NO....
FIRE DOOR
...IT CAN'T BE....
IN GOD WE TRUST
Liberty
2008
S
...IT CAN'T BE....
...DEAR GOD, IT CAN'T BE...
CATS ALWAYS LIE
COMING SOON
IT COULDN'T BE.
BUT IT WAS.

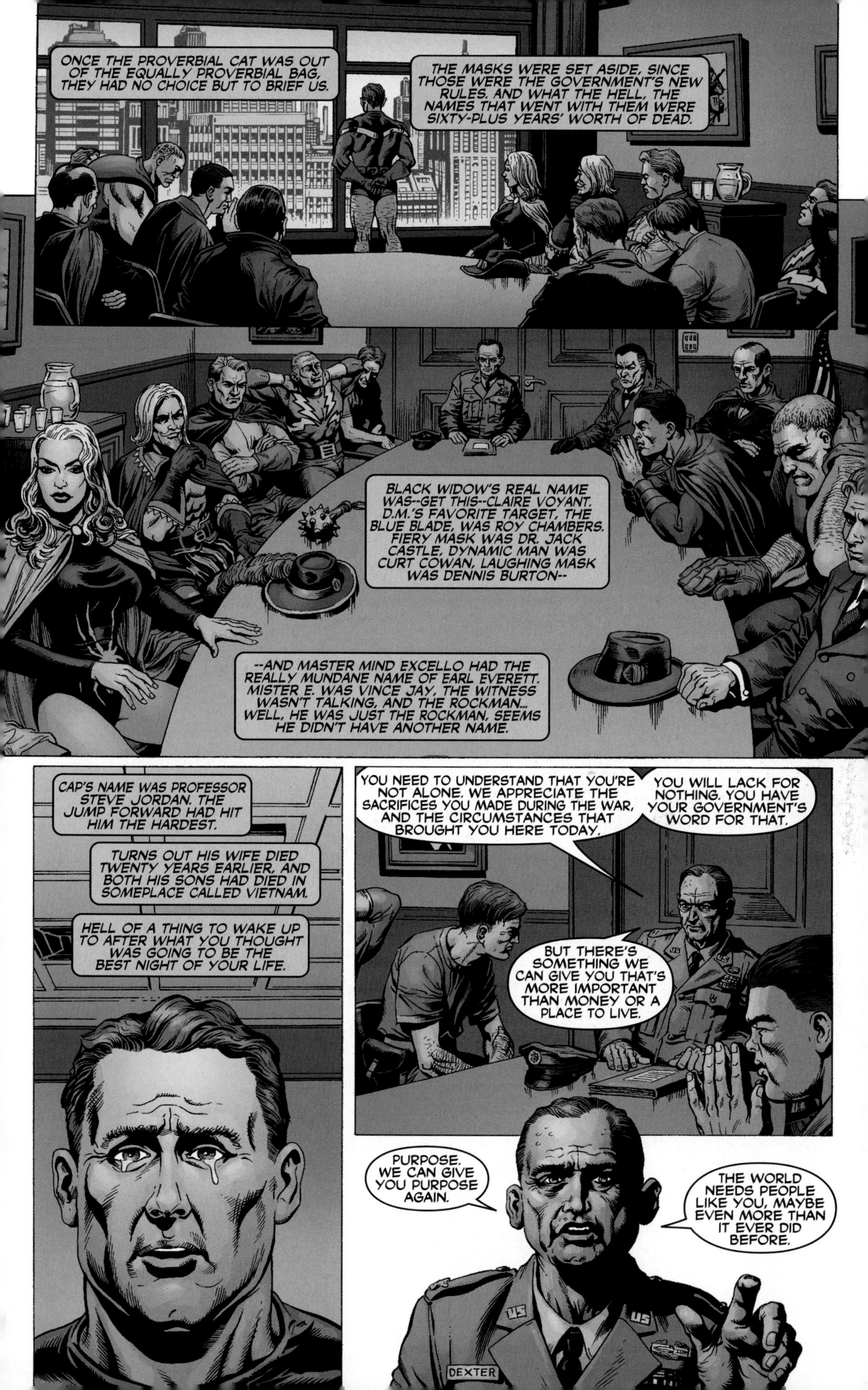
ONCE THE PROVERBIAL CAT WAS OUT OF THE EQUALLY PROVERBIAL BAG, THEY HAD NO CHOICE BUT TO BRIEF US.
THE MASKS WERE SET ASIDE, SINCE THOSE WERE THE GOVERNMENT'S NEW RULES. AND WHAT THE HELL, THE NAMES THAT WENT WITH THEM WERE SIXTY-PLUS YEARS' WORTH OF DEAD.
BLACK WIDOW'S REAL NAME WAS--GET THIS--CLAIRE VOYANT. D.M.'S FAVORITE TARGET, THE BLUE BLADE, WAS ROY CHAMBERS. FIERY MASK WAS DR. JACK CASTLE. DYNAMIC MAN WAS CURT COWAN, LAUGHING MASK WAS DENNIS BURTON--
--AND MASTER MIND EXCELLO HAD THE REALLY MUNDANE NAME OF EARL EVERETT. MISTER E. WAS VINCE JAY, THE WITNESS WASN'T TALKING, AND THE ROCKMAN... WELL, HE WAS JUST THE ROCKMAN, SEEMS HE DIDN'T HAVE ANOTHER NAME.
CAP'S NAME WAS PROFESSOR STEVE JORDAN. THE JUMP FORWARD HAD HIT HIM THE HARDEST.
TURNS OUT HIS WIFE DIED TWENTY YEARS EARLIER, AND BOTH HIS SONS HAD DIED IN SOMEPLACE CALLED VIETNAM.
HELL OF A THING TO WAKE UP TO AFTER WHAT YOU THOUGHT WAS GOING TO BE THE BEST NIGHT OF YOUR LIFE.
YOU NEED TO UNDERSTAND THAT YOU'RE NOT ALONE. WE APPRECIATE THE SACRIFICES YOU MADE DURING THE WAR, AND THE CIRCUMSTANCES THAT BROUGHT YOU HERE TODAY.
YOU WILL LACK FOR NOTHING. YOU HAVE YOUR GOVERNMENT'S WORD FOR THAT.
BUT THERE'S SOMETHING WE CAN GIVE YOU THAT'S MORE IMPORTANT THAN MONEY OR A PLACE TO LIVE.
PURPOSE. WE CAN GIVE YOU PURPOSE AGAIN.
THE WORLD NEEDS PEOPLE LIKE YOU, MAYBE EVEN MORE THAN IT EVER DID BEFORE.
DEXTER

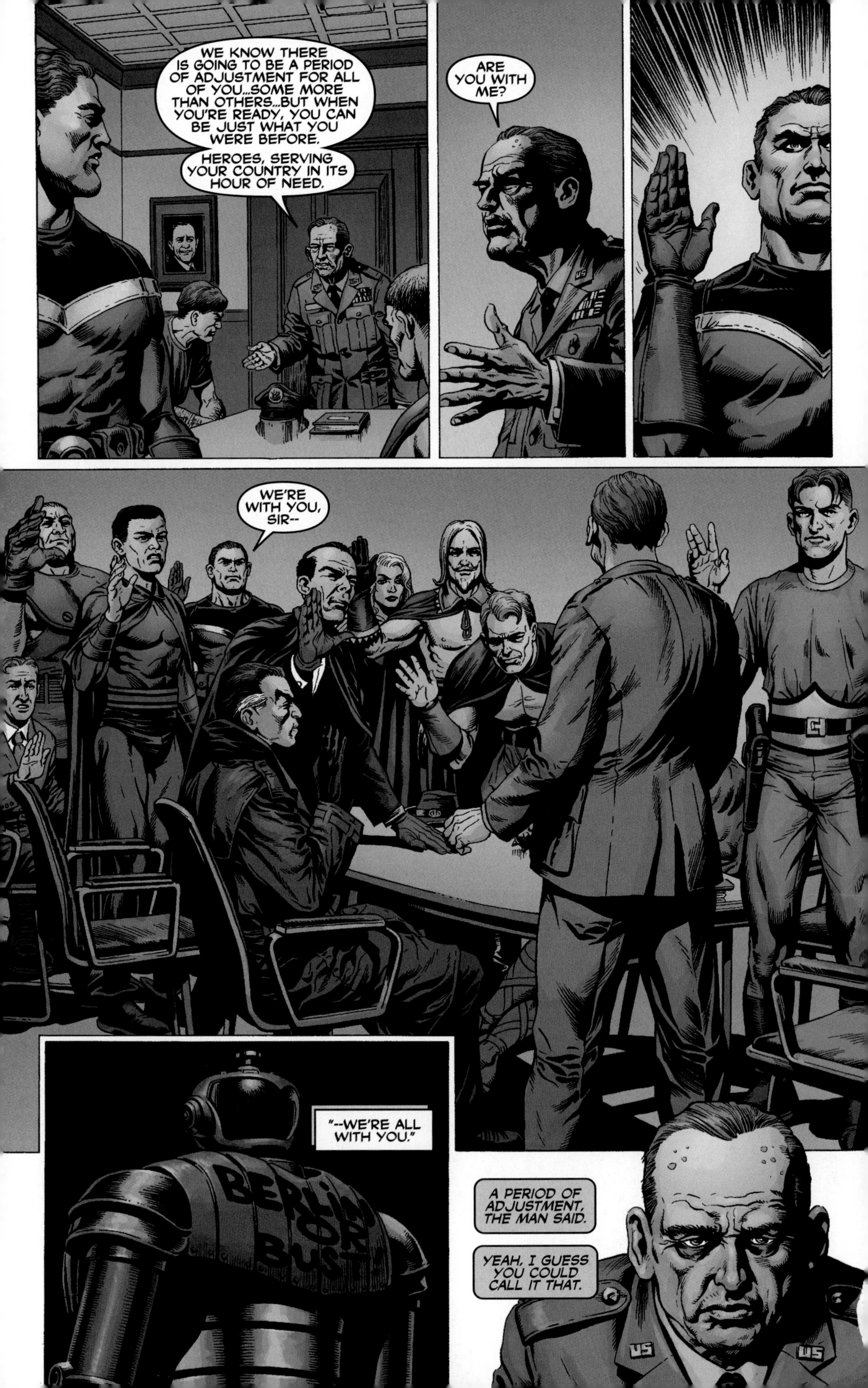
WE KNOW THERE IS GOING TO BE A PERIOD OF ADJUSTMENT FOR ALL OF YOU...SOME MORE THAN OTHERS...BUT WHEN YOU'RE READY, YOU CAN BE JUST WHAT YOU WERE BEFORE.
HEROES, SERVING YOUR COUNTRY IN ITS HOUR OF NEED.
ARE YOU WITH ME?
WE'RE WITH YOU, SIR--
"--WE'RE ALL WITH YOU."
BERLIN OR BUST
A PERIOD OF ADJUSTMENT, THE MAN SAID.
YEAH, I GUESS YOU COULD CALL IT THAT.

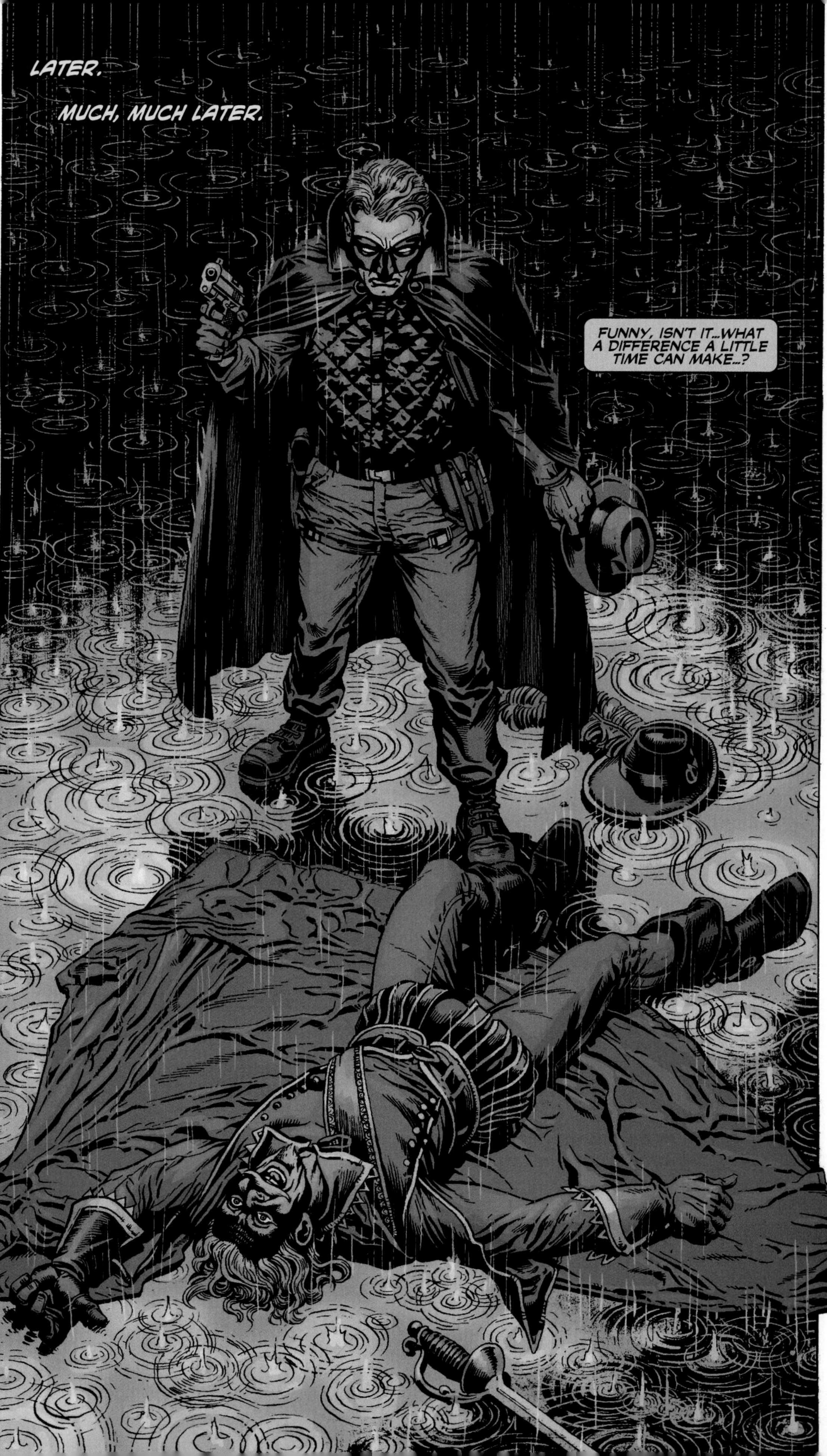
LATER.
MUCH, MUCH LATER.
FUNNY, ISN'T IT...WHAT A DIFFERENCE A LITTLE TIME CAN MAKE...?

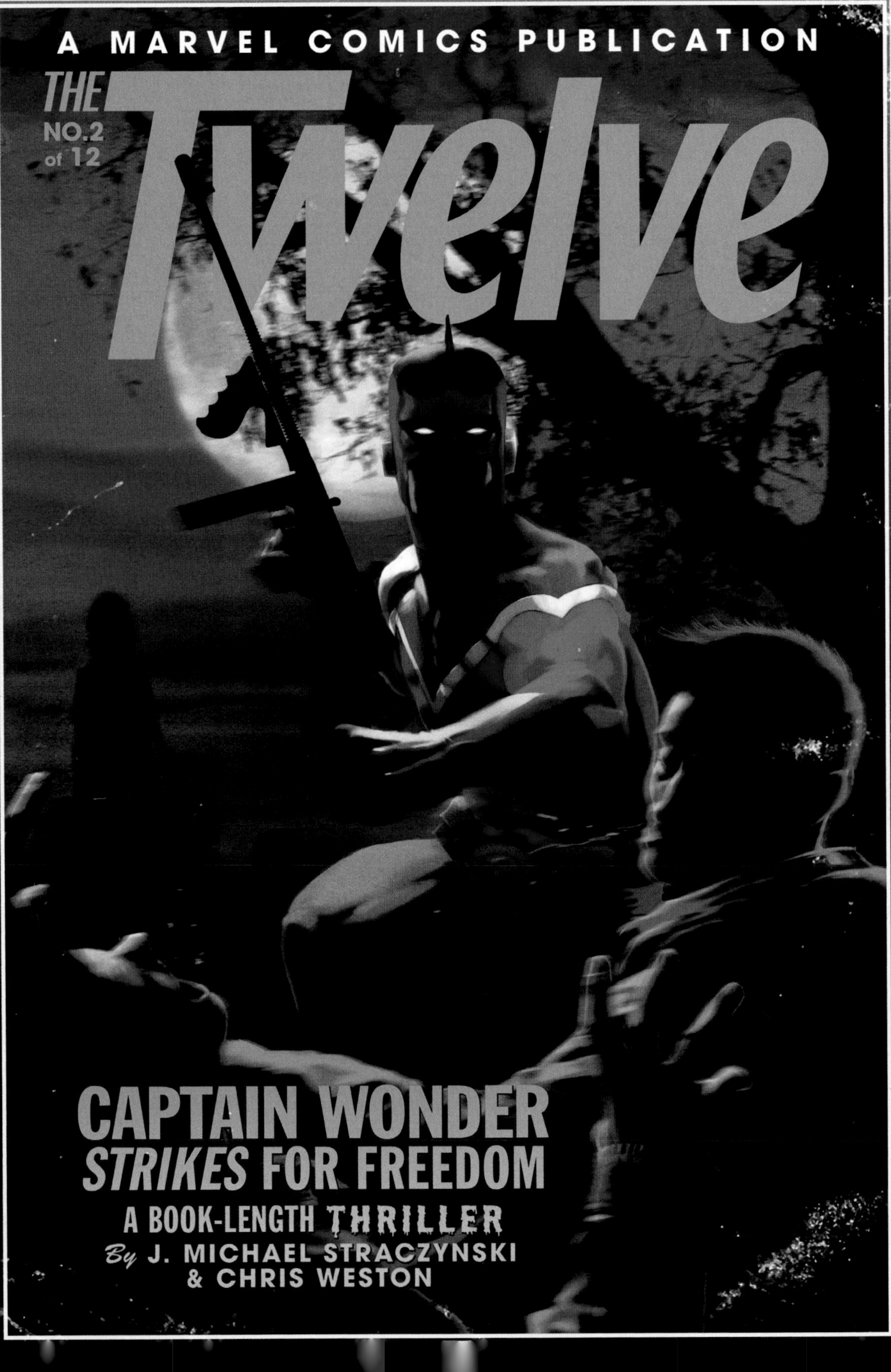
A MARVEL COMICS PUBLICATION
THE
NO.2
of 12
Twelve
CAPTAIN WONDER
STRIKES FOR FREEDOM
A BOOK-LENGTH THRILLER
By J. MICHAEL STRACZYNSKI
& CHRIS WESTON

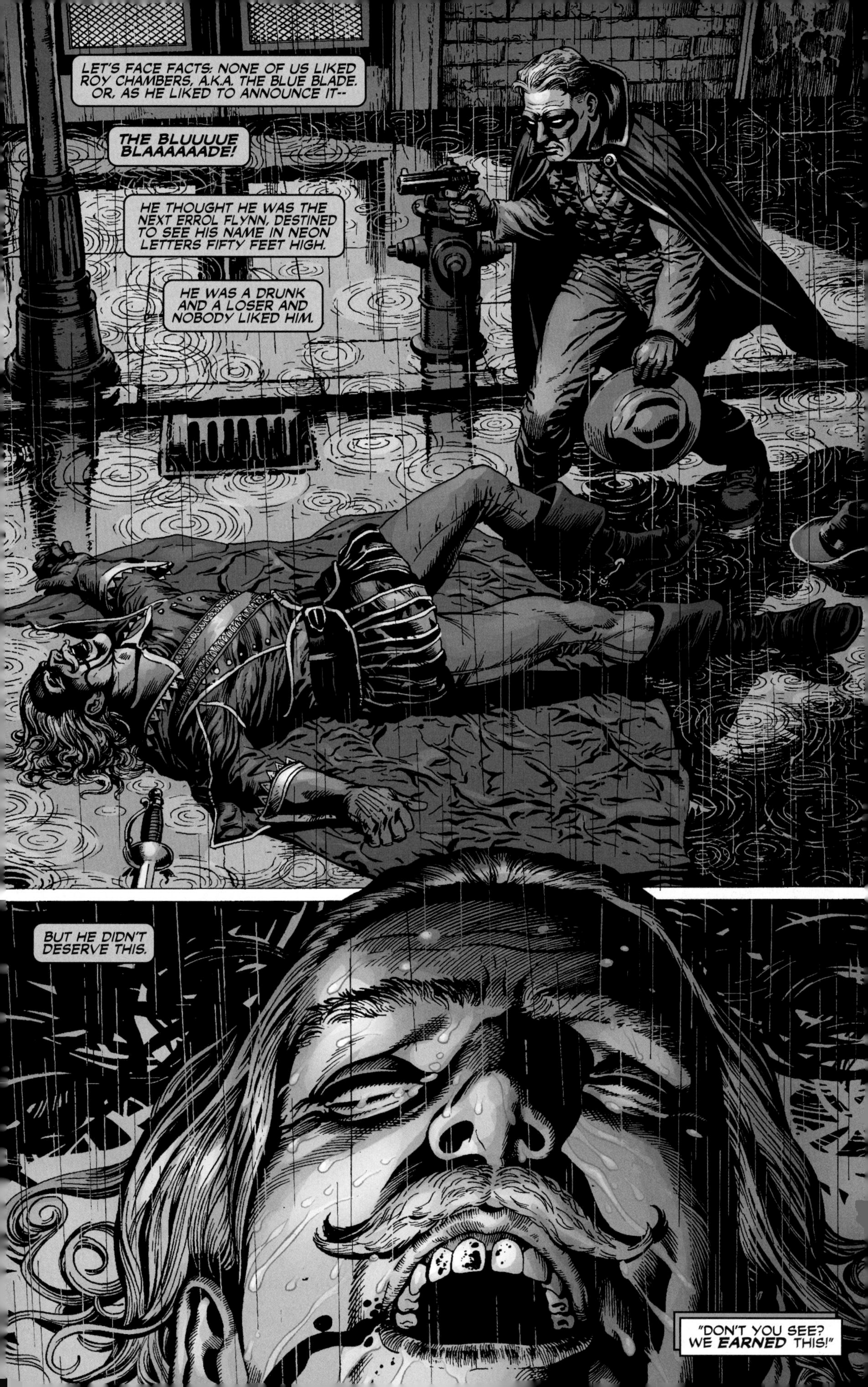
LET'S FACE FACTS: NONE OF US LIKED ROY CHAMBERS, A.K.A. THE BLUE BLADE. OR, AS HE LIKED TO ANNOUNCE IT--
THE BLUUUUE BLAAAAAAADE!
HE THOUGHT HE WAS THE NEXT ERROL FLYNN, DESTINED TO SEE HIS NAME IN NEON LETTERS FIFTY FEET HIGH.
HE WAS A DRUNK AND A LOSER AND NOBODY LIKED HIM.
BUT HE DIDN'T DESERVE THIS.
"DON'T YOU SEE? WE EARNED THIS!"

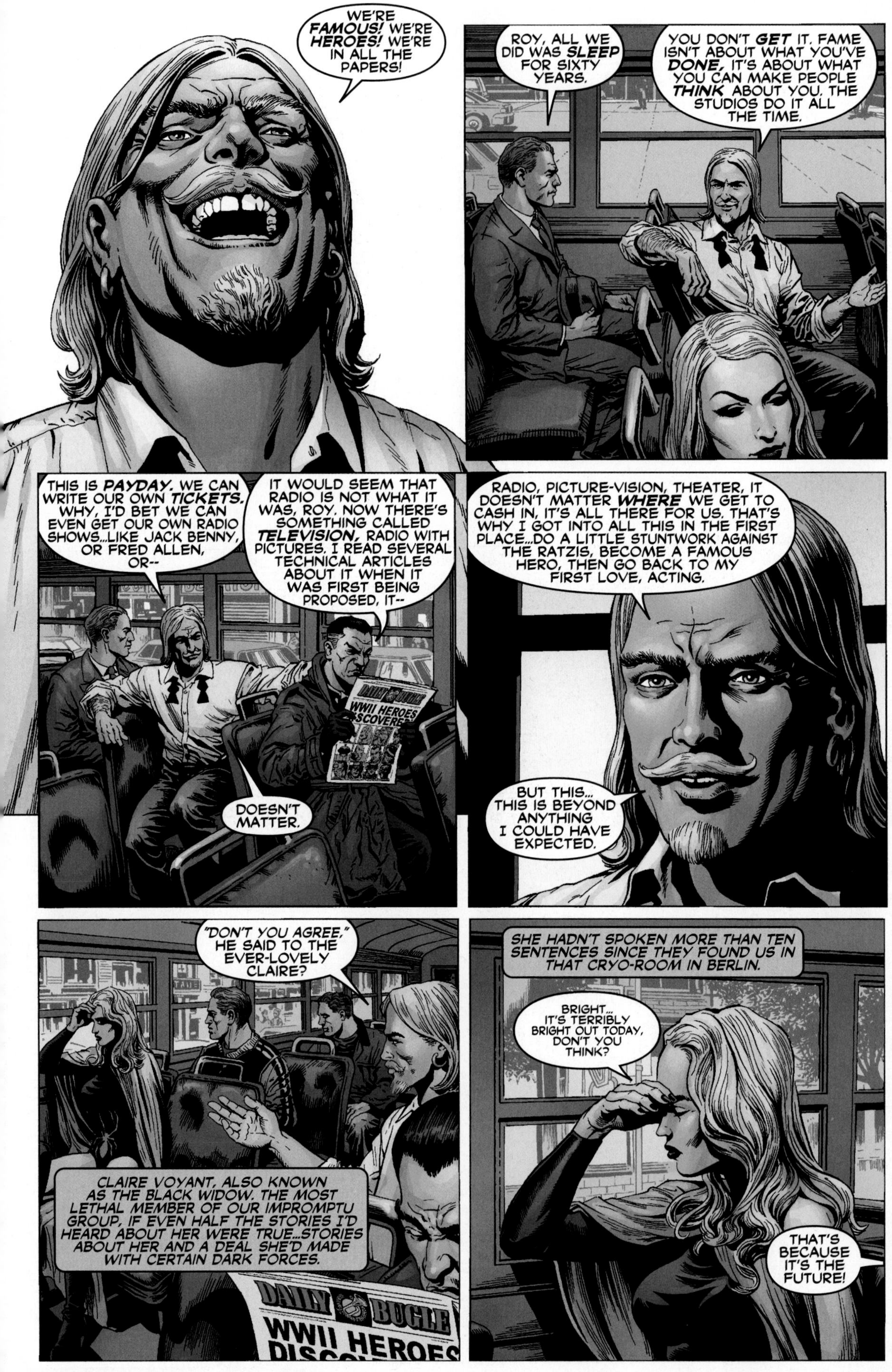
WE'RE FAMOUS! WE'RE HEROES! WE'RE IN ALL THE PAPERS!
ROY, ALL WE DID WAS SLEEP FOR SIXTY YEARS.
YOU DON'T GET IT. FAME ISN'T ABOUT WHAT YOU'VE DONE, IT'S ABOUT WHAT YOU CAN MAKE PEOPLE THINK ABOUT YOU. THE STUDIOS DO IT ALL THE TIME.
THIS IS PAYDAY. WE CAN WRITE OUR OWN TICKETS. WHY, I'D BET WE CAN EVEN GET OUR OWN RADIO SHOWS...LIKE JACK BENNY, OR FRED ALLEN, OR--
IT WOULD SEEM THAT RADIO IS NOT WHAT IT WAS, ROY. NOW THERE'S SOMETHING CALLED TELEVISION, RADIO WITH PICTURES. I READ SEVERAL TECHNICAL ARTICLES ABOUT IT WHEN IT WAS FIRST BEING PROPOSED, IT--
DOESN'T MATTER.
RADIO, PICTURE-VISION, THEATER, IT DOESN'T MATTER WHERE WE GET TO CASH IN, IT'S ALL THERE FOR US. THAT'S WHY I GOT INTO ALL THIS IN THE FIRST PLACE...DO A LITTLE STUNTWORK AGAINST THE RATZIS, BECOME A FAMOUS HERO, THEN GO BACK TO MY FIRST LOVE, ACTING.
BUT THIS... THIS IS BEYOND ANYTHING I COULD HAVE EXPECTED.
"DON'T YOU AGREE," HE SAID TO THE EVER-LOVELY CLAIRE?
CLAIRE VOYANT, ALSO KNOWN AS THE BLACK WIDOW. THE MOST LETHAL MEMBER OF OUR IMPROMPTU GROUP, IF EVEN HALF THE STORIES I'D HEARD ABOUT HER WERE TRUE...STORIES ABOUT HER AND A DEAL SHE'D MADE WITH CERTAIN DARK FORCES.
DAILY BUGLE
WWII HEROES
SHE HADN'T SPOKEN MORE THAN TEN SENTENCES SINCE THEY FOUND US IN THAT CRYO-ROOM IN BERLIN.
BRIGHT... IT'S TERRIBLY BRIGHT OUT TODAY, DON'T YOU THINK?
THAT'S BECAUSE IT'S THE FUTURE!

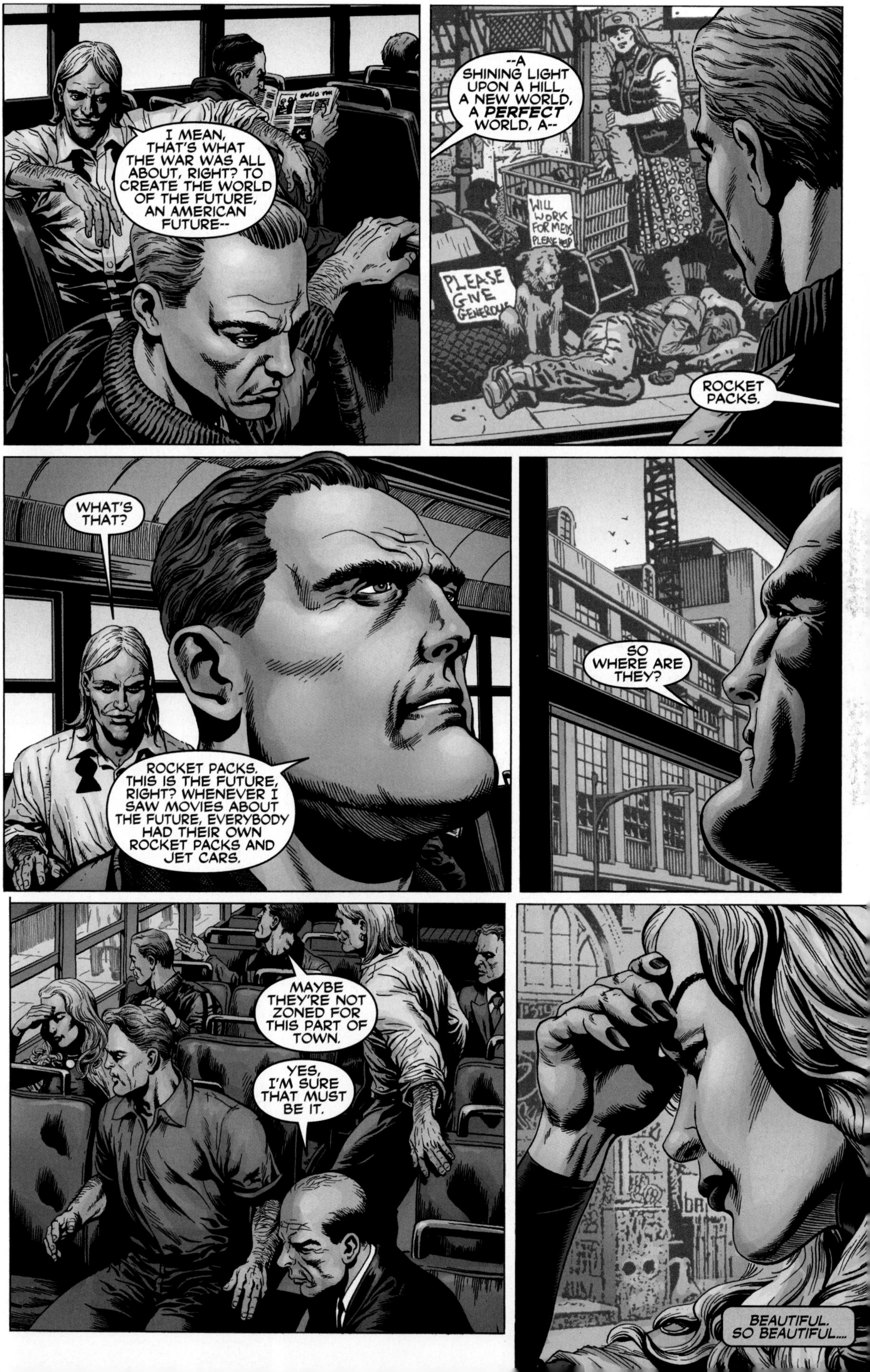
I MEAN, THAT'S WHAT THE WAR WAS ALL ABOUT, RIGHT? TO CREATE THE WORLD OF THE FUTURE, AN AMERICAN FUTURE--
--A SHINING LIGHT UPON A HILL, A NEW WORLD, A PERFECT WORLD, A--
WILL WORK FOR MEDS PLEASE HELP
PLEASE GIVE GENEROUS
ROCKET PACKS.
WHAT'S THAT?
ROCKET PACKS. THIS IS THE FUTURE, RIGHT? WHENEVER I SAW MOVIES ABOUT THE FUTURE, EVERYBODY HAD THEIR OWN ROCKET PACKS AND JET CARS.
SO WHERE ARE THEY?
MAYBE THEY'RE NOT ZONED FOR THIS PART OF TOWN.
YES, I'M SURE THAT MUST BE IT.
BEAUTIFUL. SO BEAUTIFUL....

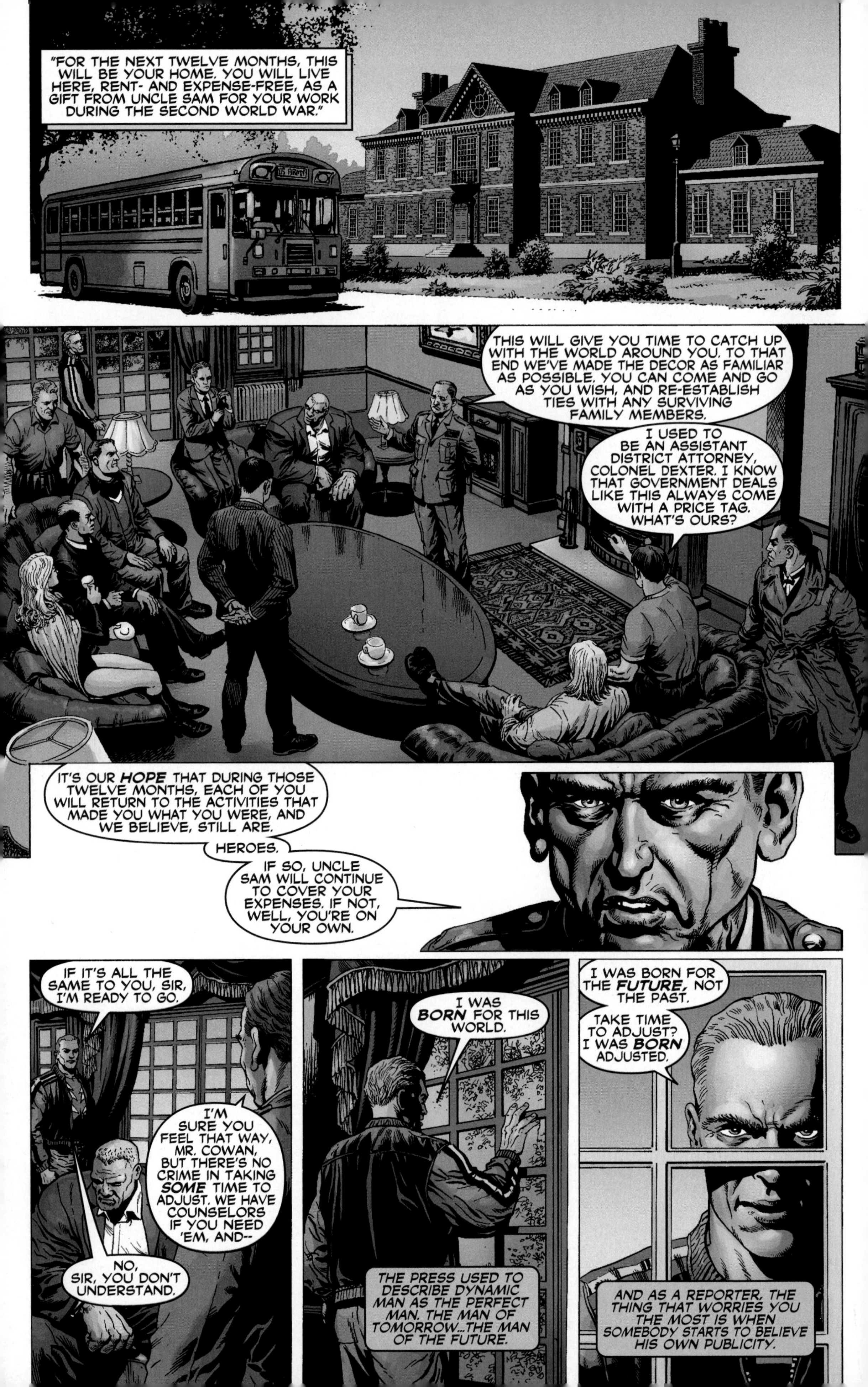
"FOR THE NEXT TWELVE MONTHS, THIS WILL BE YOUR HOME. YOU WILL LIVE HERE, RENT- AND EXPENSE-FREE, AS A GIFT FROM UNCLE SAM FOR YOUR WORK DURING THE SECOND WORLD WAR."
US ARMY
THIS WILL GIVE YOU TIME TO CATCH UP WITH THE WORLD AROUND YOU. TO THAT END WE'VE MADE THE DECOR AS FAMILIAR AS POSSIBLE. YOU CAN COME AND GO AS YOU WISH, AND RE-ESTABLISH TIES WITH ANY SURVIVING FAMILY MEMBERS.
I USED TO BE AN ASSISTANT DISTRICT ATTORNEY, COLONEL DEXTER. I KNOW THAT GOVERNMENT DEALS LIKE THIS ALWAYS COME WITH A PRICE TAG. WHAT'S OURS?
IT'S OUR *HOPE* THAT DURING THOSE TWELVE MONTHS, EACH OF YOU WILL RETURN TO THE ACTIVITIES THAT MADE YOU WHAT YOU WERE, AND WE BELIEVE, STILL ARE.
HEROES.
IF SO, UNCLE SAM WILL CONTINUE TO COVER YOUR EXPENSES. IF NOT, WELL, YOU'RE ON YOUR OWN.
IF IT'S ALL THE SAME TO YOU, SIR, I'M READY TO GO.
I'M SURE YOU FEEL THAT WAY, MR. COWAN, BUT THERE'S NO CRIME IN TAKING *SOME* TIME TO ADJUST. WE HAVE COUNSELORS IF YOU NEED 'EM, AND--
NO, SIR, YOU DON'T UNDERSTAND.
I WAS *BORN* FOR THIS WORLD.
THE PRESS USED TO DESCRIBE DYNAMIC MAN AS THE PERFECT MAN. THE MAN OF TOMORROW...THE MAN OF THE FUTURE.
I WAS BORN FOR THE *FUTURE,* NOT THE PAST.
TAKE TIME TO ADJUST? I WAS *BORN* ADJUSTED.
AND AS A REPORTER, THE THING THAT WORRIES YOU THE MOST IS WHEN SOMEBODY STARTS TO BELIEVE HIS OWN PUBLICITY.

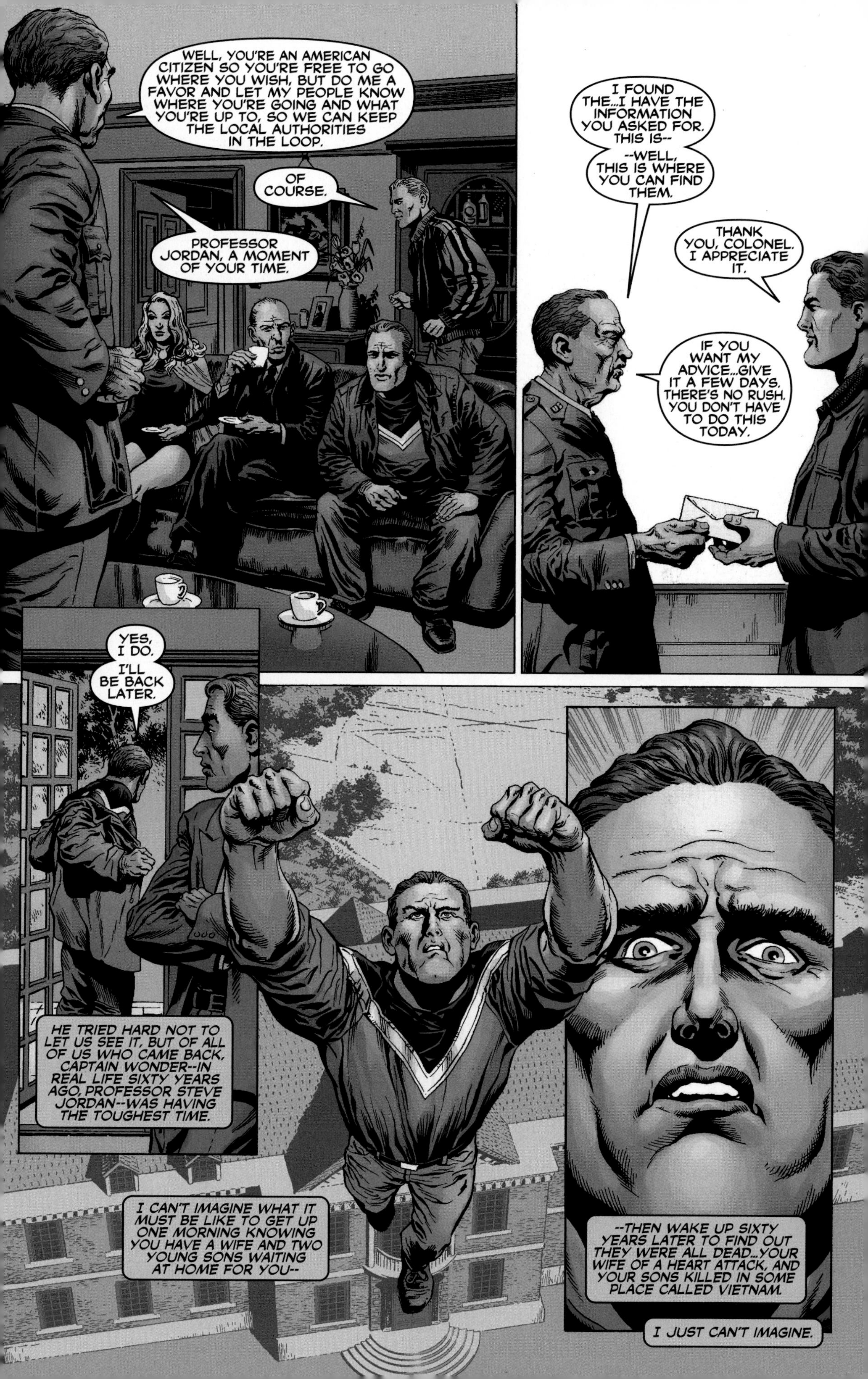
WELL, YOU'RE AN AMERICAN CITIZEN SO YOU'RE FREE TO GO WHERE YOU WISH, BUT DO ME A FAVOR AND LET MY PEOPLE KNOW WHERE YOU'RE GOING AND WHAT YOU'RE UP TO, SO WE CAN KEEP THE LOCAL AUTHORITIES IN THE LOOP.
OF COURSE.
PROFESSOR JORDAN, A MOMENT OF YOUR TIME.
I FOUND THE...I HAVE THE INFORMATION YOU ASKED FOR. THIS IS--
--WELL, THIS IS WHERE YOU CAN FIND THEM.
THANK YOU, COLONEL. I APPRECIATE IT.
IF YOU WANT MY ADVICE...GIVE IT A FEW DAYS. THERE'S NO RUSH. YOU DON'T HAVE TO DO THIS TODAY.
YES, I DO.
I'LL BE BACK LATER.
HE TRIED HARD NOT TO LET US SEE IT, BUT OF ALL OF US WHO CAME BACK, CAPTAIN WONDER--IN REAL LIFE SIXTY YEARS AGO, PROFESSOR STEVE JORDAN--WAS HAVING THE TOUGHEST TIME.
I CAN'T IMAGINE WHAT IT MUST BE LIKE TO GET UP ONE MORNING KNOWING YOU HAVE A WIFE AND TWO YOUNG SONS WAITING AT HOME FOR YOU--
--THEN WAKE UP SIXTY YEARS LATER TO FIND OUT THEY WERE ALL DEAD...YOUR WIFE OF A HEART ATTACK, AND YOUR SONS KILLED IN SOME PLACE CALLED VIETNAM.
I JUST CAN'T IMAGINE.

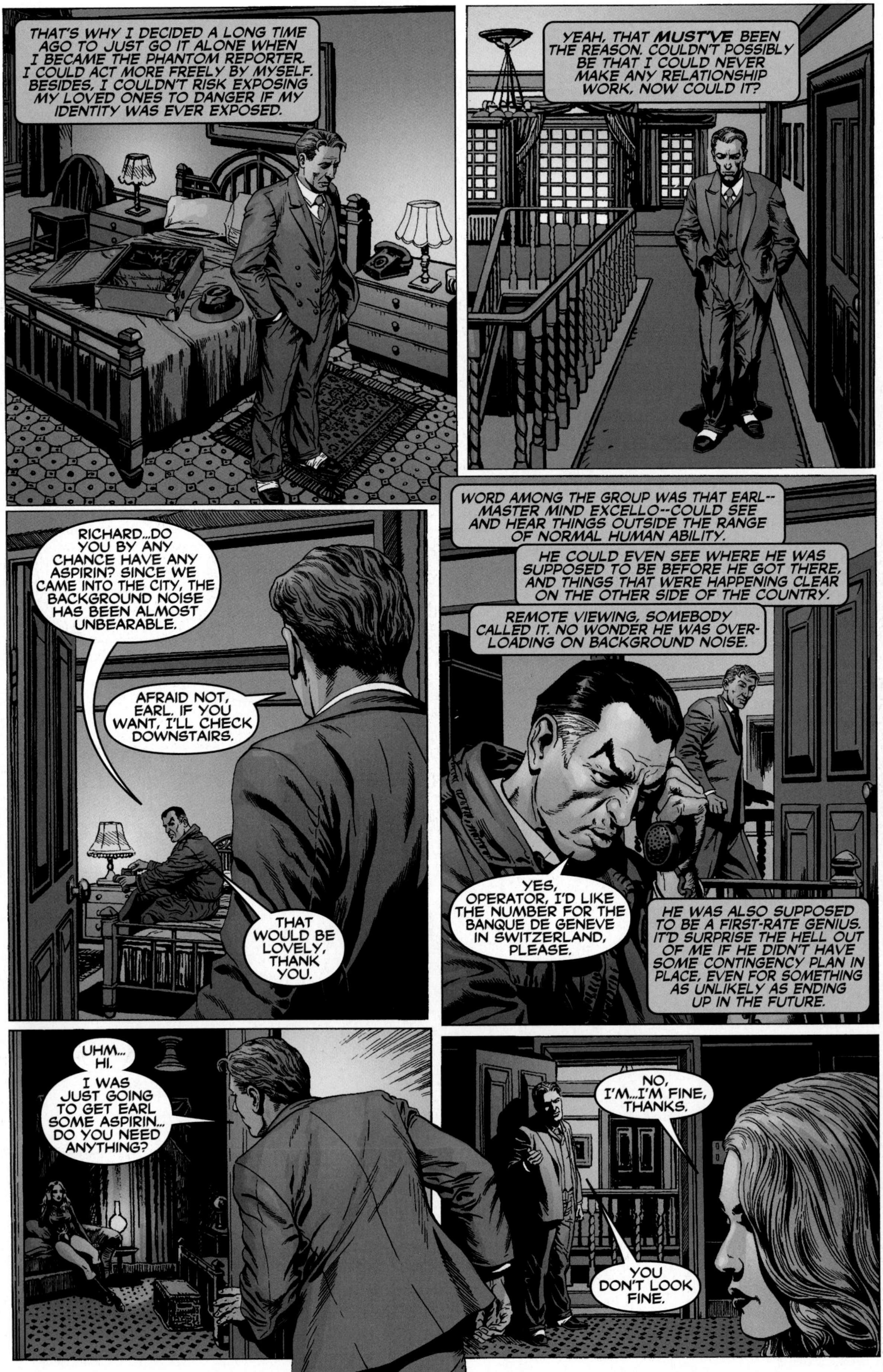
THAT'S WHY I DECIDED A LONG TIME AGO TO JUST GO IT ALONE WHEN I BECAME THE PHANTOM REPORTER. I COULD ACT MORE FREELY BY MYSELF. BESIDES, I COULDN'T RISK EXPOSING MY LOVED ONES TO DANGER IF MY IDENTITY WAS EVER EXPOSED.
YEAH, THAT **MUST'VE** BEEN THE REASON. COULDN'T POSSIBLY BE THAT I COULD NEVER MAKE ANY RELATIONSHIP WORK, NOW COULD IT?
RICHARD...DO YOU BY ANY CHANCE HAVE ANY ASPIRIN? SINCE WE CAME INTO THE CITY, THE BACKGROUND NOISE HAS BEEN ALMOST UNBEARABLE.
AFRAID NOT, EARL. IF YOU WANT, I'LL CHECK DOWNSTAIRS.
THAT WOULD BE LOVELY, THANK YOU.
WORD AMONG THE GROUP WAS THAT EARL--MASTER MIND EXCELLO--COULD SEE AND HEAR THINGS OUTSIDE THE RANGE OF NORMAL HUMAN ABILITY.
HE COULD EVEN SEE WHERE HE WAS SUPPOSED TO BE BEFORE HE GOT THERE, AND THINGS THAT WERE HAPPENING CLEAR ON THE OTHER SIDE OF THE COUNTRY.
REMOTE VIEWING, SOMEBODY CALLED IT. NO WONDER HE WAS OVER-LOADING ON BACKGROUND NOISE.
YES, OPERATOR, I'D LIKE THE NUMBER FOR THE BANQUE DE GENEVE IN SWITZERLAND, PLEASE.
HE WAS ALSO SUPPOSED TO BE A FIRST-RATE GENIUS. IT'D SURPRISE THE HELL OUT OF ME IF HE DIDN'T HAVE SOME CONTINGENCY PLAN IN PLACE, EVEN FOR SOMETHING AS UNLIKELY AS ENDING UP IN THE FUTURE.
UHM... HI.
I WAS JUST GOING TO GET EARL SOME ASPIRIN... DO YOU NEED ANYTHING?
NO, I'M...I'M FINE, THANKS.
YOU DON'T LOOK FINE.

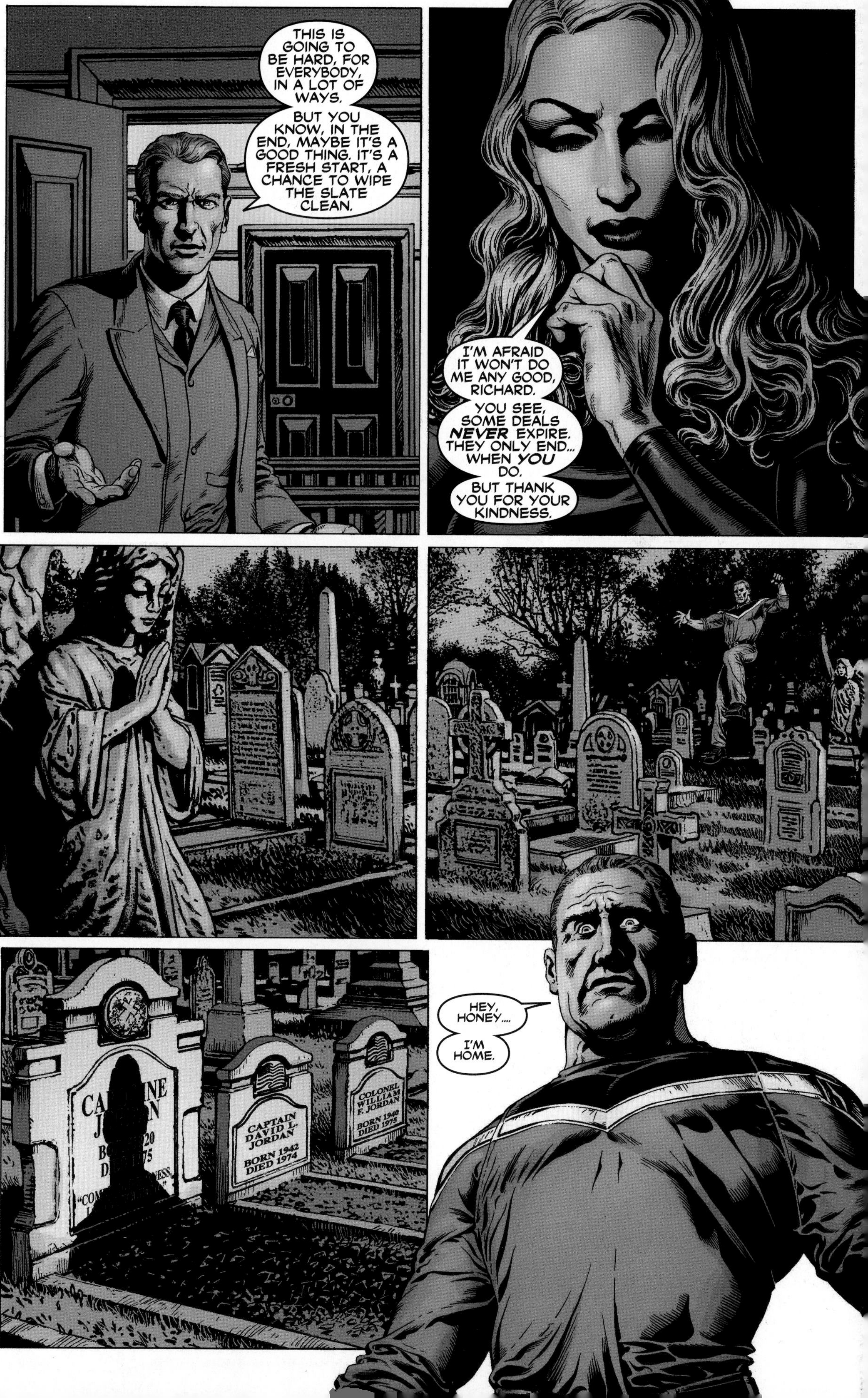
THIS IS GOING TO BE HARD, FOR EVERYBODY, IN A LOT OF WAYS.
BUT YOU KNOW, IN THE END, MAYBE IT'S A GOOD THING. IT'S A FRESH START, A CHANCE TO WIPE THE SLATE CLEAN.
I'M AFRAID IT WON'T DO ME ANY GOOD, RICHARD.
YOU SEE, SOME DEALS ***NEVER*** EXPIRE. THEY ONLY END... WHEN ***YOU*** DO.
BUT THANK YOU FOR YOUR KINDNESS.
CAPTAIN DAVID L. JORDAN BORN 1942 DIED 1974
COLONEL WILLIAM F. JORDAN BORN 1940 DIED 1975
HEY, HONEY....
I'M HOME.

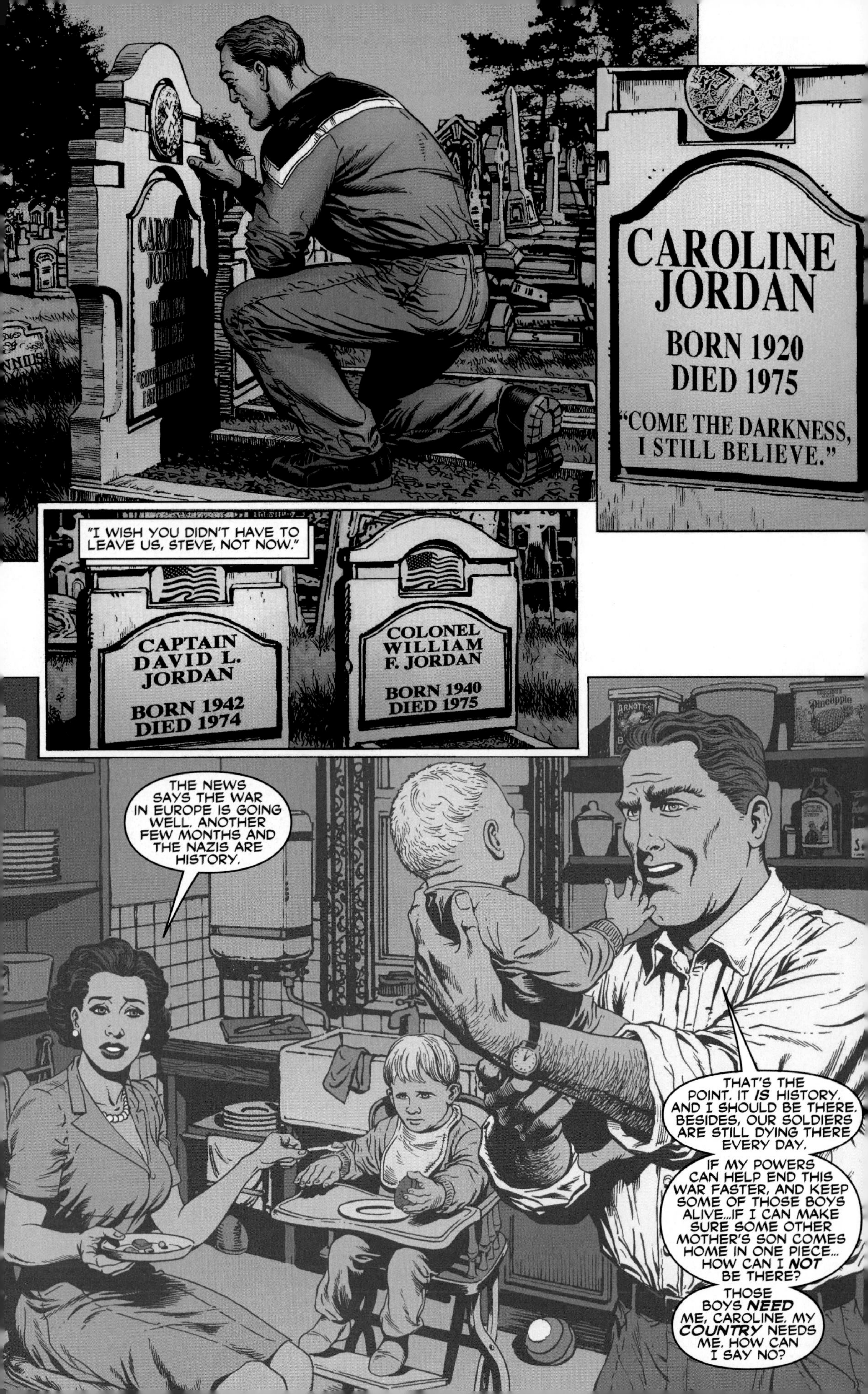
CAROLINE JORDAN
BORN 1920
DIED 1975
"COME THE DARKNESS, I STILL BELIEVE."
"I WISH YOU DIDN'T HAVE TO LEAVE US, STEVE, NOT NOW."
CAPTAIN DAVID L. JORDAN
BORN 1942
DIED 1974
COLONEL WILLIAM F. JORDAN
BORN 1940
DIED 1975
THE NEWS SAYS THE WAR IN EUROPE IS GOING WELL. ANOTHER FEW MONTHS AND THE NAZIS ARE HISTORY.
THAT'S THE POINT. IT *IS* HISTORY. AND I SHOULD BE THERE. BESIDES, OUR SOLDIERS ARE STILL DYING THERE EVERY DAY.
IF MY POWERS CAN HELP END THIS WAR FASTER, AND KEEP SOME OF THOSE BOYS ALIVE...IF I CAN MAKE SURE SOME OTHER MOTHER'S SON COMES HOME IN ONE PIECE... HOW CAN I *NOT* BE THERE?
THOSE BOYS ***NEED*** ME, CAROLINE. MY ***COUNTRY*** NEEDS ME. HOW CAN I SAY NO?

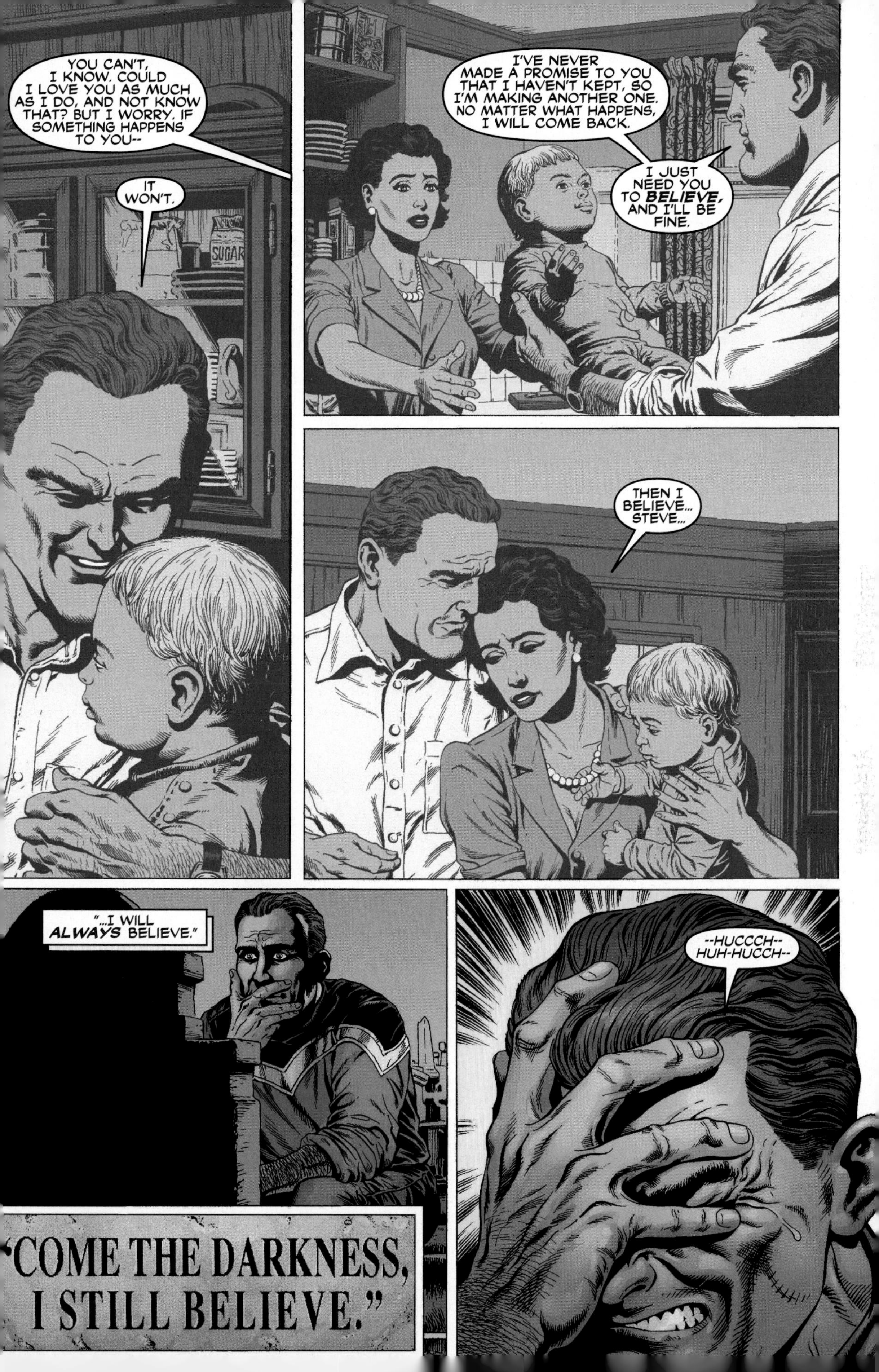
YOU CAN'T, I KNOW. COULD I LOVE YOU AS MUCH AS I DO, AND NOT KNOW THAT? BUT I WORRY. IF SOMETHING HAPPENS TO YOU--
IT WON'T.
SUGAR
I'VE NEVER MADE A PROMISE TO YOU THAT I HAVEN'T KEPT, SO I'M MAKING ANOTHER ONE. NO MATTER WHAT HAPPENS, I WILL COME BACK.
I JUST NEED YOU TO BELIEVE, AND I'LL BE FINE.
THEN I BELIEVE... STEVE...
"...I WILL ALWAYS BELIEVE."
"COME THE DARKNESS, I STILL BELIEVE."
--HUCCCH-- HUH-HUCCH--

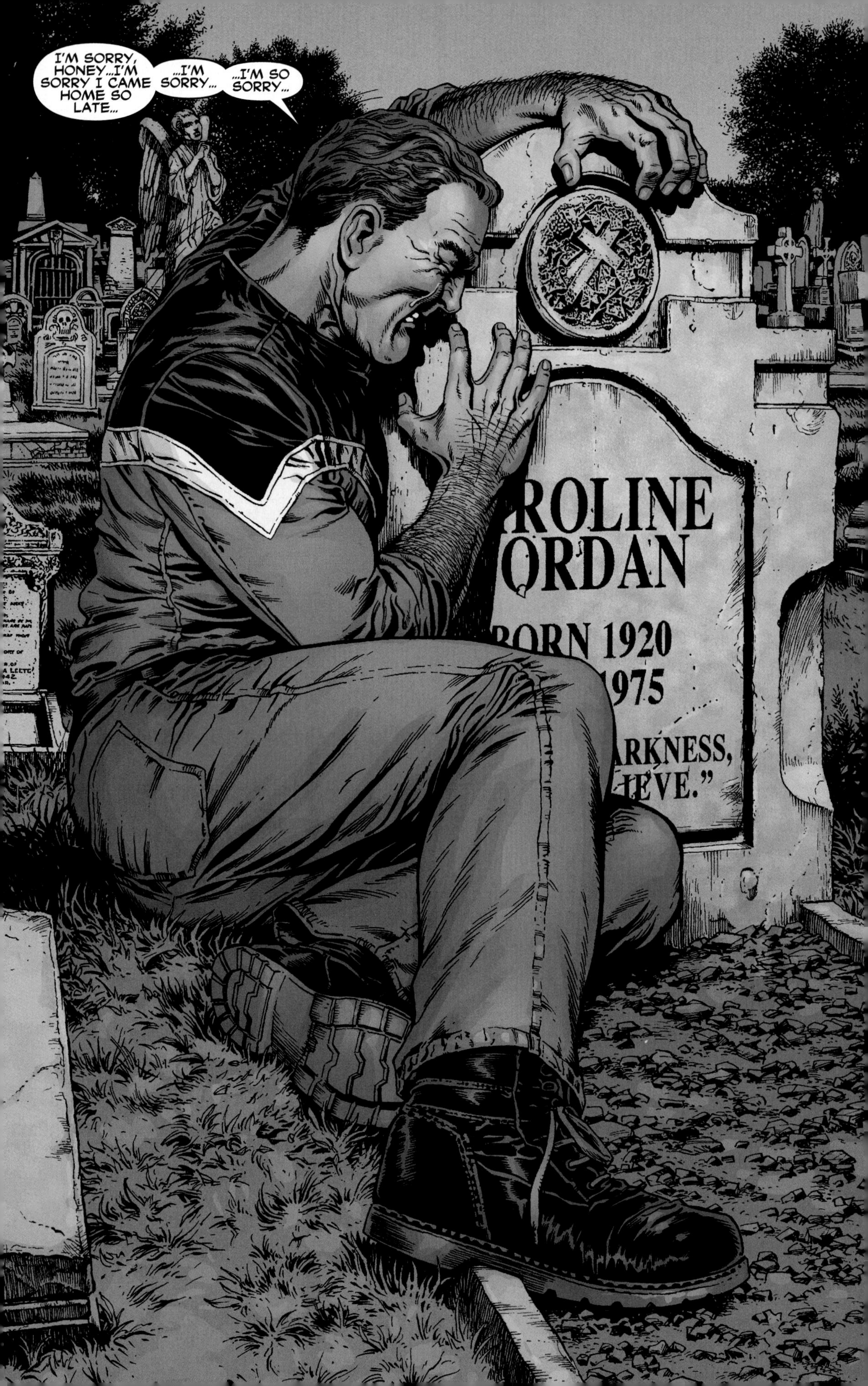
I'M SORRY, HONEY...I'M SORRY I CAME HOME SO LATE...
...I'M SORRY...
...I'M SO SORRY...
ROLINE
ORDAN
ORN 1920
1975
ARKNESS,
IEVE."

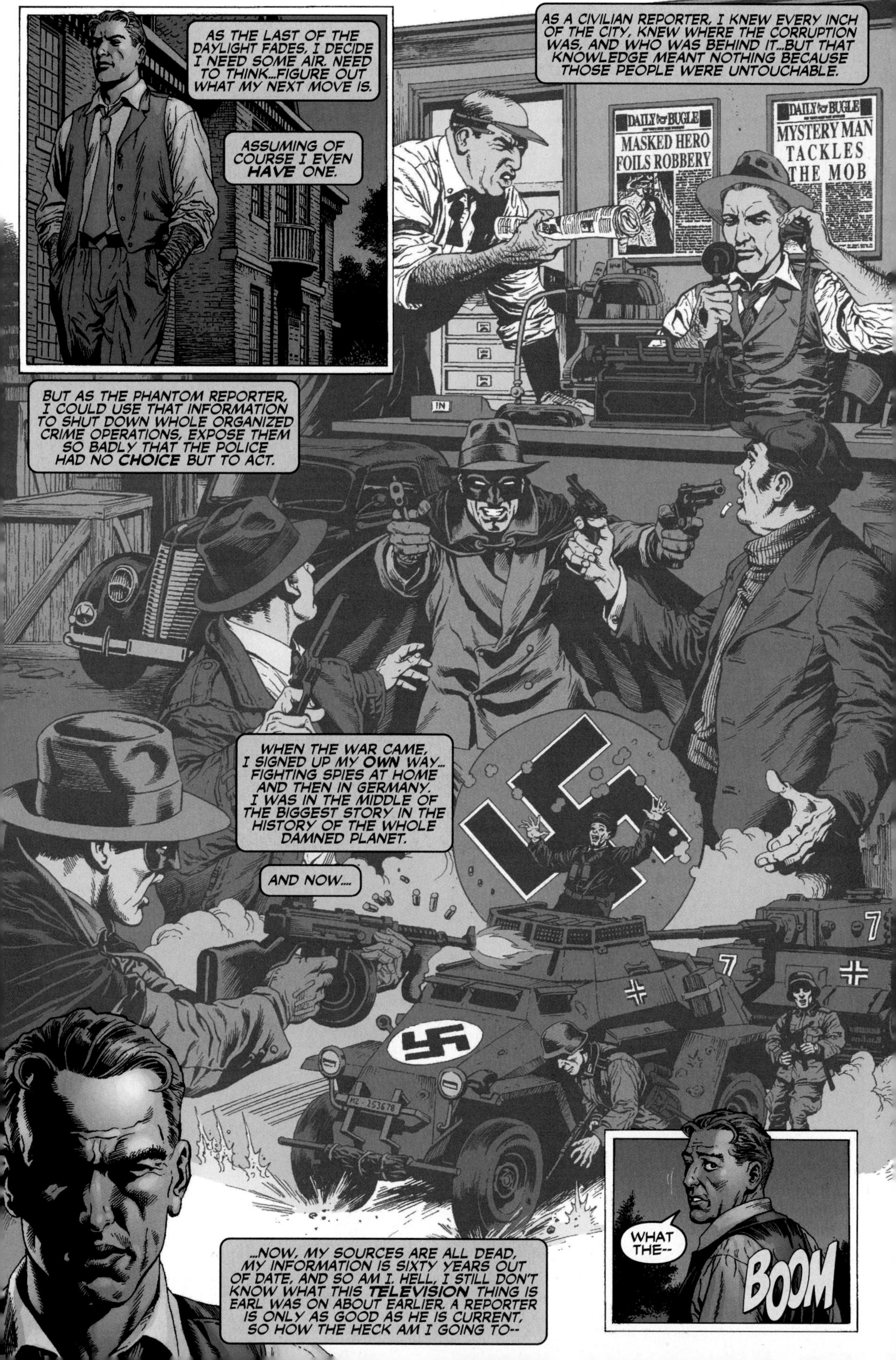
AS THE LAST OF THE DAYLIGHT FADES, I DECIDE I NEED SOME AIR. NEED TO THINK...FIGURE OUT WHAT MY NEXT MOVE IS.
ASSUMING OF COURSE I EVEN HAVE ONE.
AS A CIVILIAN REPORTER, I KNEW EVERY INCH OF THE CITY, KNEW WHERE THE CORRUPTION WAS, AND WHO WAS BEHIND IT...BUT THAT KNOWLEDGE MEANT NOTHING BECAUSE THOSE PEOPLE WERE UNTOUCHABLE.
DAILY BUGLE
MASKED HERO FOILS ROBBERY
DAILY BUGLE
MYSTERY MAN TACKLES THE MOB
IN
BUT AS THE PHANTOM REPORTER, I COULD USE THAT INFORMATION TO SHUT DOWN WHOLE ORGANIZED CRIME OPERATIONS, EXPOSE THEM SO BADLY THAT THE POLICE HAD NO CHOICE BUT TO ACT.
WHEN THE WAR CAME, I SIGNED UP MY OWN WAY... FIGHTING SPIES AT HOME AND THEN IN GERMANY. I WAS IN THE MIDDLE OF THE BIGGEST STORY IN THE HISTORY OF THE WHOLE DAMNED PLANET.
AND NOW...
7
7
...NOW, MY SOURCES ARE ALL DEAD, MY INFORMATION IS SIXTY YEARS OUT OF DATE, AND SO AM I. HELL, I STILL DON'T KNOW WHAT THIS TELEVISION THING IS EARL WAS ON ABOUT EARLIER. A REPORTER IS ONLY AS GOOD AS HE IS CURRENT, SO HOW THE HECK AM I GOING TO--
WHAT THE--
BOOM

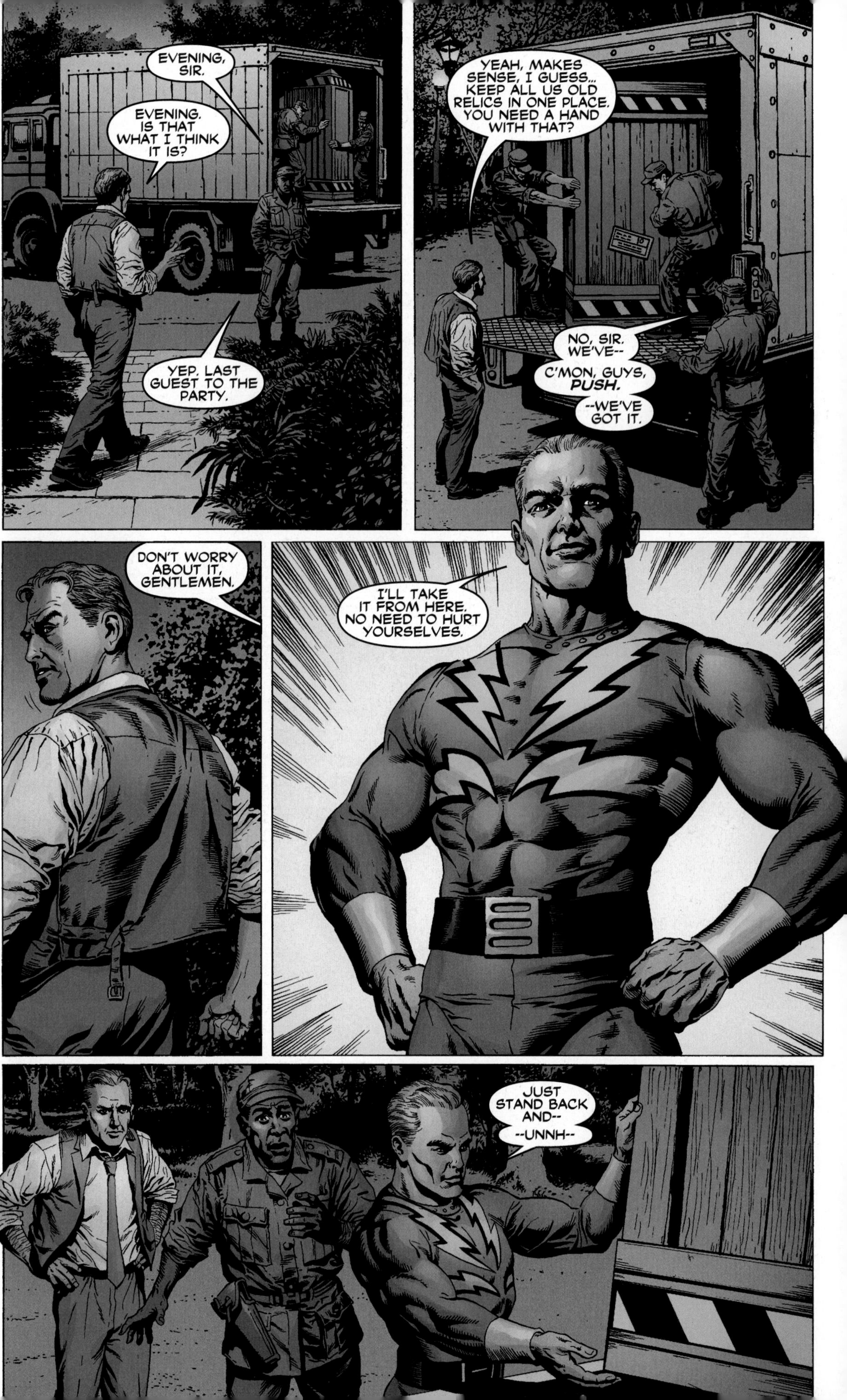
EVENING, SIR.
EVENING. IS THAT WHAT I THINK IT IS?
YEP. LAST GUEST TO THE PARTY.
YEAH, MAKES SENSE, I GUESS... KEEP ALL US OLD RELICS IN ONE PLACE. YOU NEED A HAND WITH THAT?
NO, SIR. WE'VE--
C'MON, GUYS, PUSH.
--WE'VE GOT IT.
DON'T WORRY ABOUT IT, GENTLEMEN.
I'LL TAKE IT FROM HERE. NO NEED TO HURT YOURSELVES.
JUST STAND BACK AND--
--UNNH--

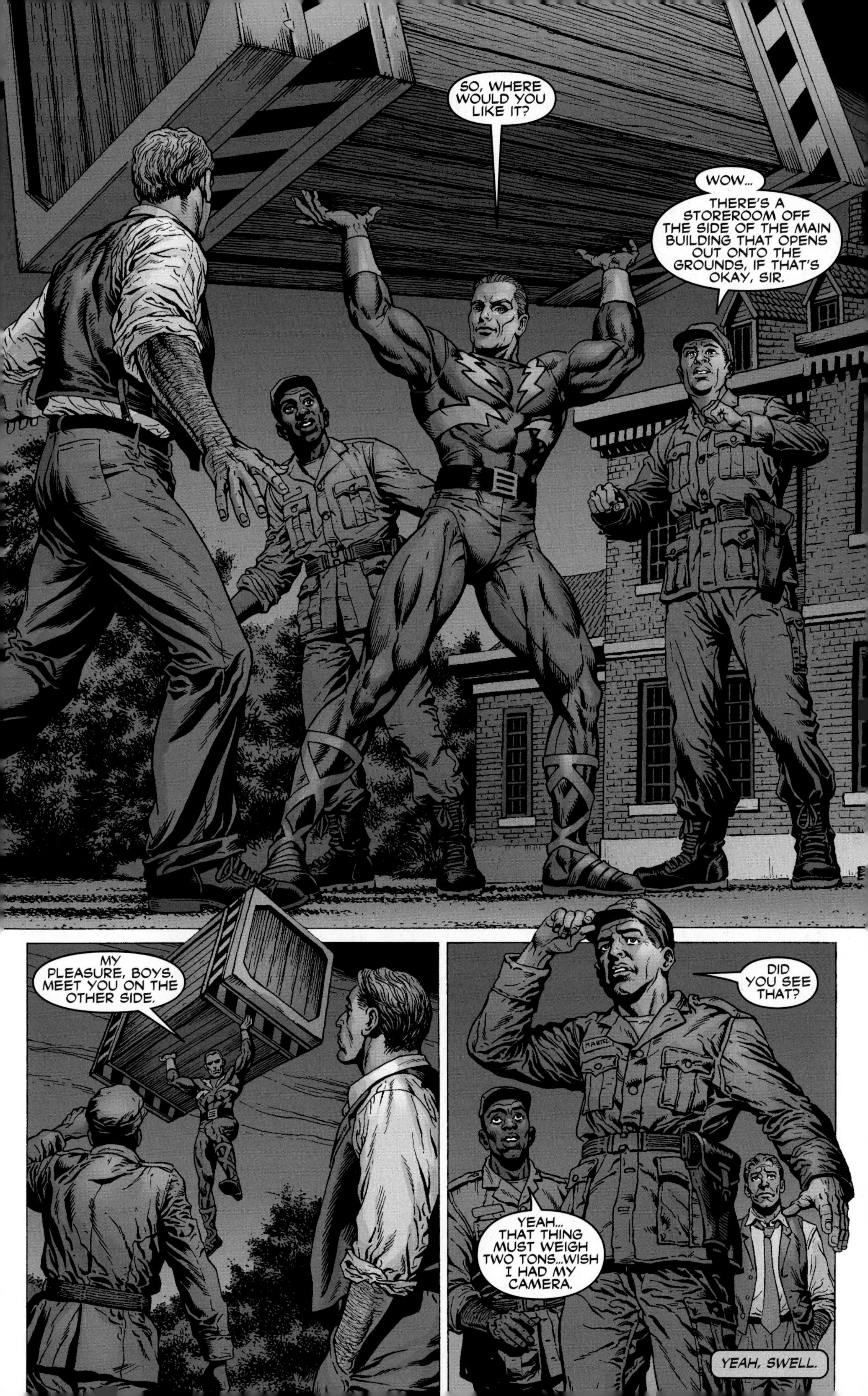
SO, WHERE WOULD YOU LIKE IT?
WOW...
THERE'S A STOREROOM OFF THE SIDE OF THE MAIN BUILDING THAT OPENS OUT ONTO THE GROUNDS, IF THAT'S OKAY, SIR.
MY PLEASURE, BOYS. MEET YOU ON THE OTHER SIDE.
DID YOU SEE THAT?
YEAH... THAT THING MUST WEIGH TWO TONS...WISH I HAD MY CAMERA.
YEAH, SWELL.

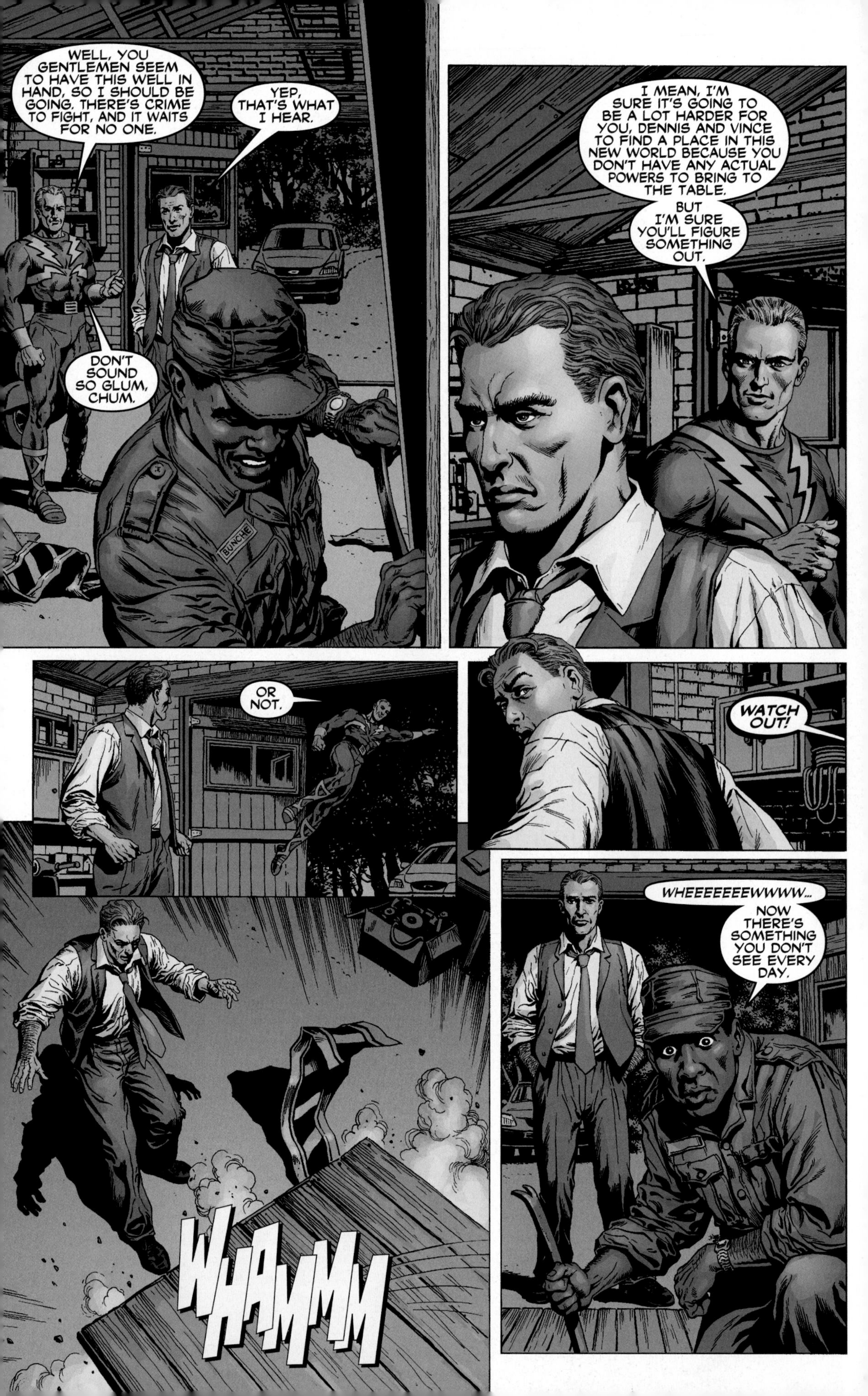
WELL, YOU GENTLEMEN SEEM TO HAVE THIS WELL IN HAND, SO I SHOULD BE GOING. THERE'S CRIME TO FIGHT, AND IT WAITS FOR NO ONE.
YEP, THAT'S WHAT I HEAR.
DON'T SOUND SO GLUM, CHUM.
BUNCHE
I MEAN, I'M SURE IT'S GOING TO BE A LOT HARDER FOR YOU, DENNIS AND VINCE TO FIND A PLACE IN THIS NEW WORLD BECAUSE YOU DON'T HAVE ANY ACTUAL POWERS TO BRING TO THE TABLE.
BUT I'M SURE YOU'LL FIGURE SOMETHING OUT.
OR NOT.
WATCH OUT!
WHAMMM
WHEEEEEEEWWWW...
NOW THERE'S SOMETHING YOU DON'T SEE EVERY DAY.

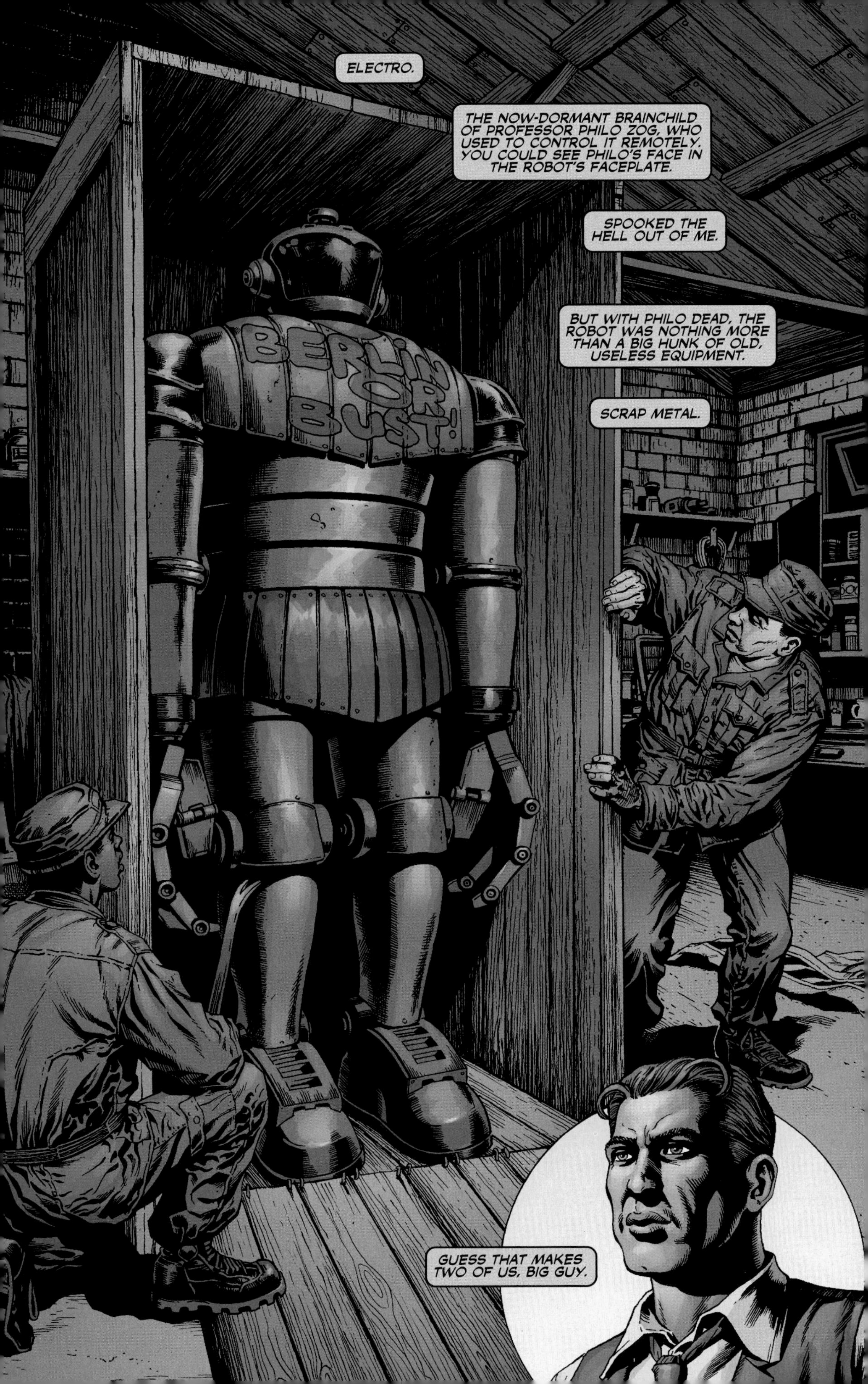
ELECTRO.
THE NOW-DORMANT BRAINCHILD OF PROFESSOR PHILO ZOG, WHO USED TO CONTROL IT REMOTELY. YOU COULD SEE PHILO'S FACE IN THE ROBOT'S FACEPLATE.
SPOOKED THE HELL OUT OF ME.
BUT WITH PHILO DEAD, THE ROBOT WAS NOTHING MORE THAN A BIG HUNK OF OLD, USELESS EQUIPMENT.
SCRAP METAL.
BERLIN OR BUST!
GUESS THAT MAKES TWO OF US, BIG GUY.

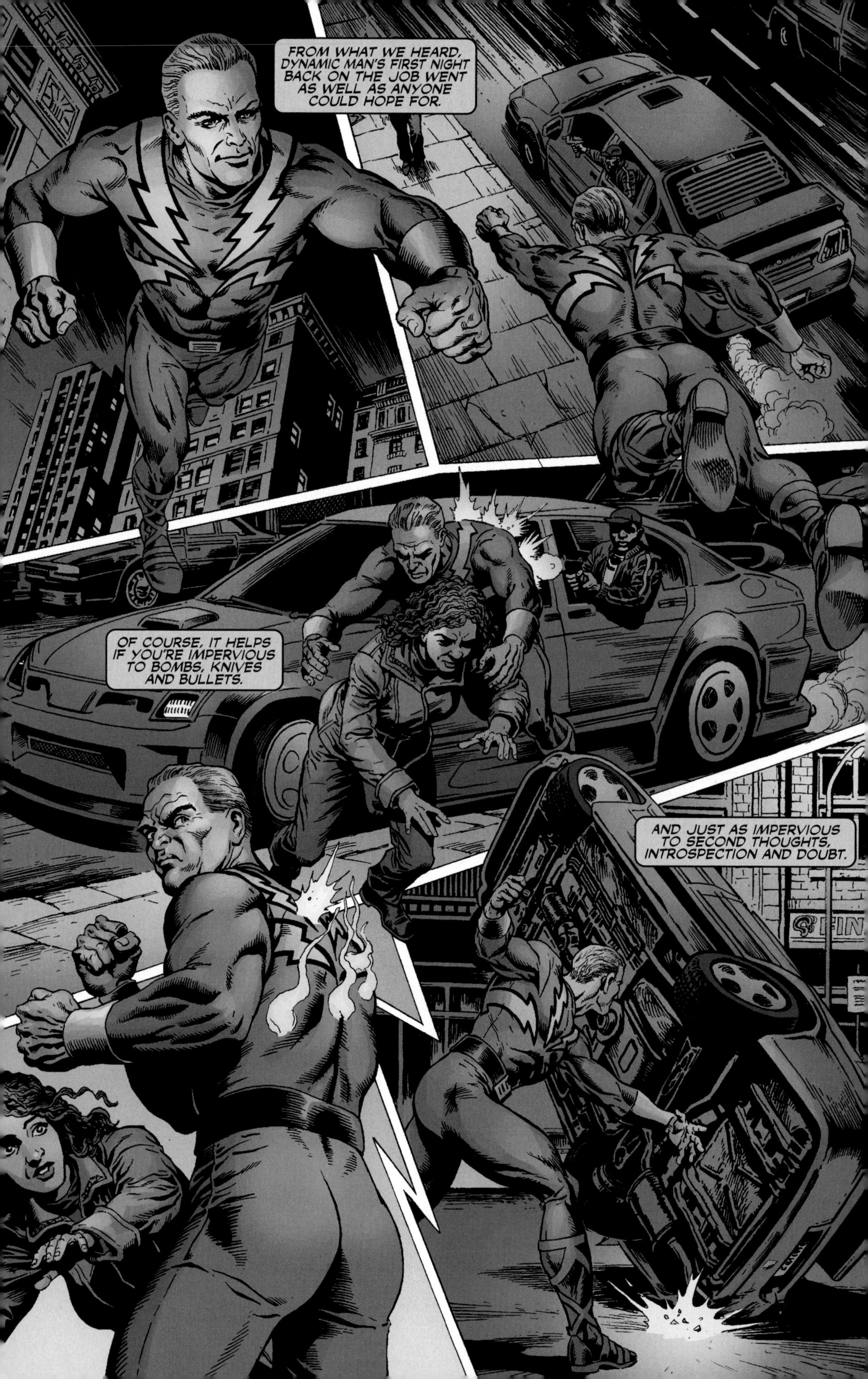
FROM WHAT WE HEARD, DYNAMIC MAN'S FIRST NIGHT BACK ON THE JOB WENT AS WELL AS ANYONE COULD HOPE FOR.
OF COURSE, IT HELPS IF YOU'RE IMPERVIOUS TO BOMBS, KNIVES AND BULLETS.
AND JUST AS IMPERVIOUS TO SECOND THOUGHTS, INTROSPECTION AND DOUBT.

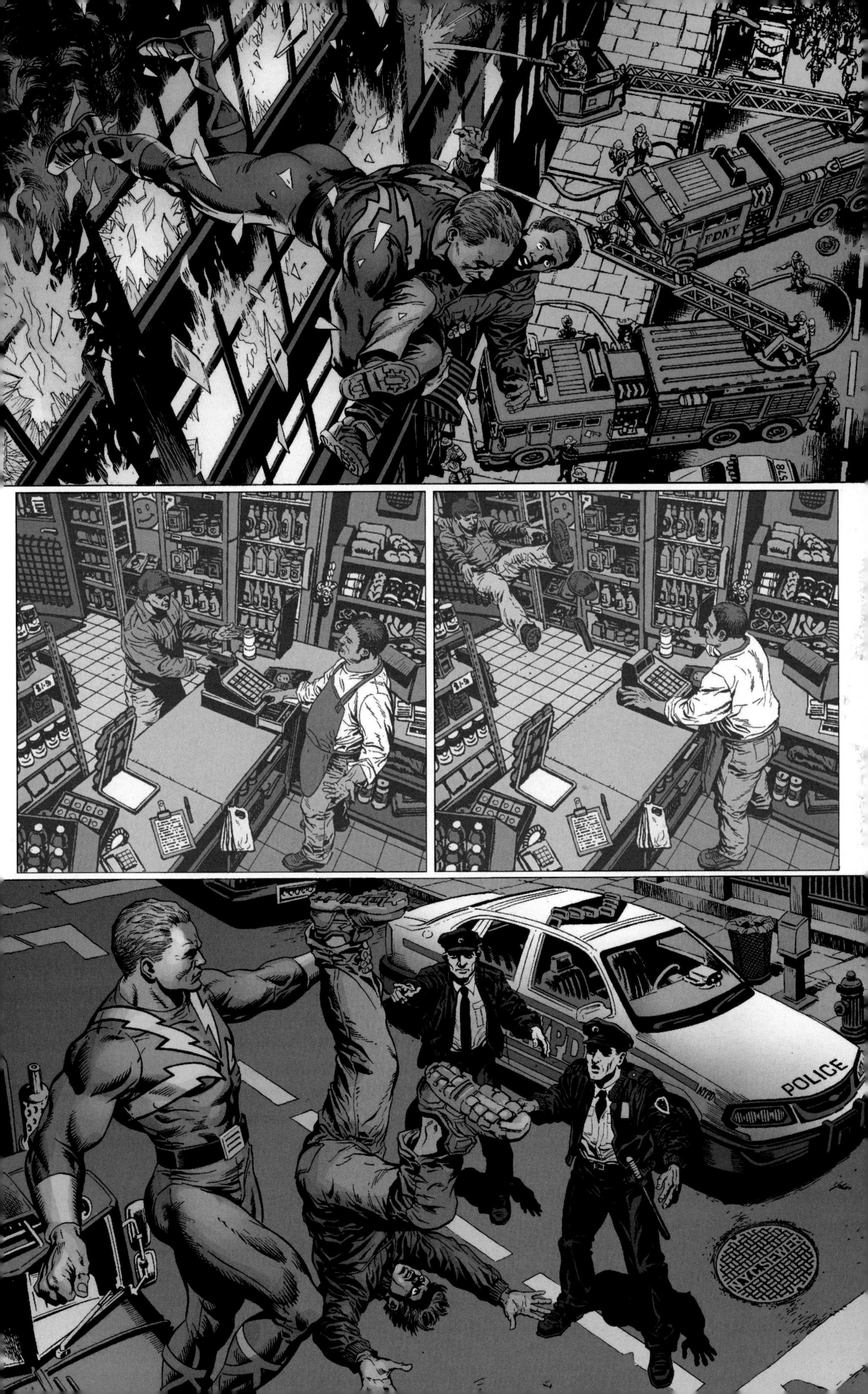
FDNY
NYPD
POLICE

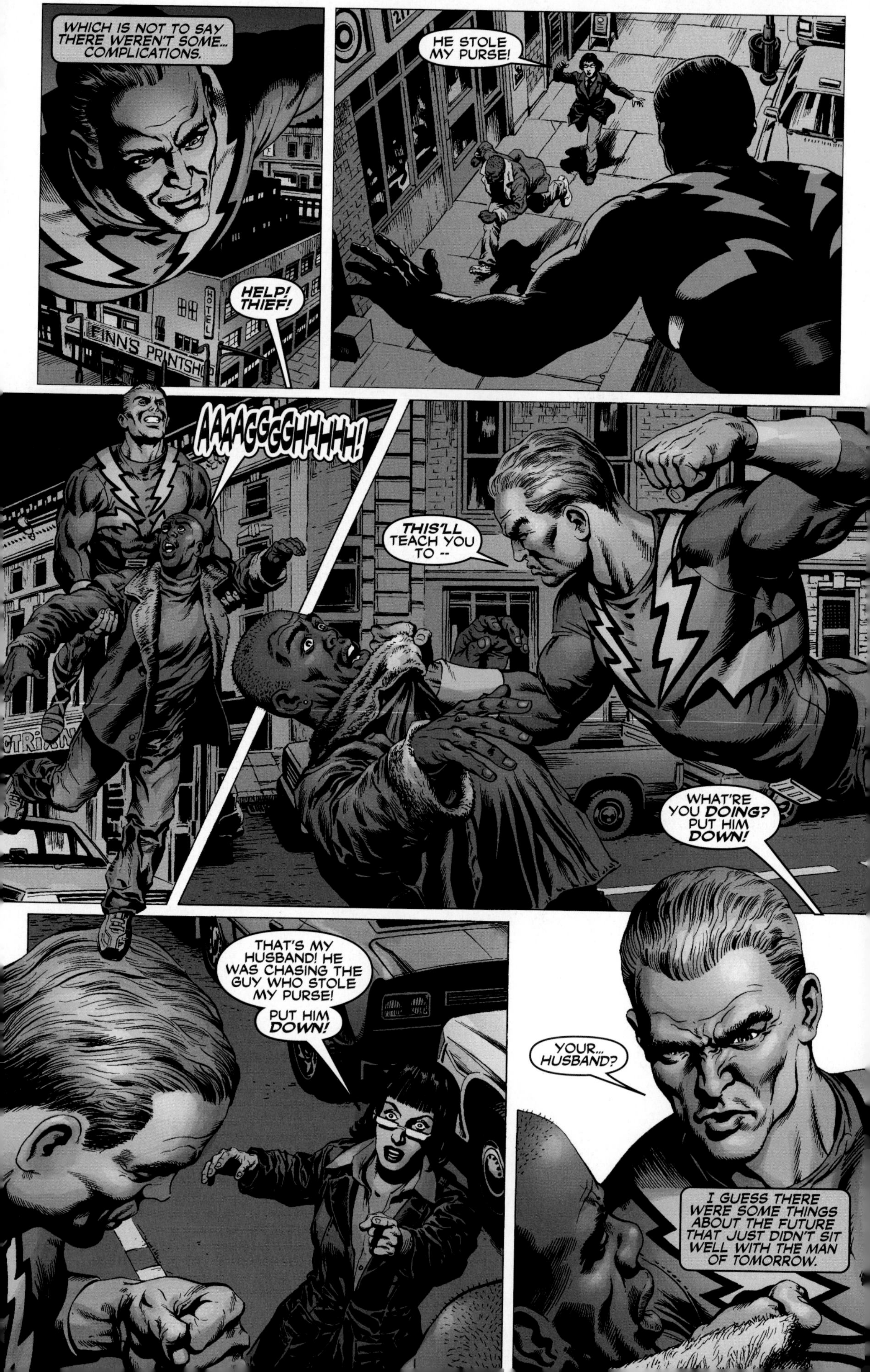

WHICH IS NOT TO SAY THERE WEREN'T SOME... COMPLICATIONS.
FINN'S PRINTSHOP
HOTEL
HELP! THIEF!
HE STOLE MY PURSE!
AAAAGGGGHHHHH!
THIS'LL TEACH YOU TO --
WHAT'RE YOU DOING? PUT HIM DOWN!
THAT'S MY HUSBAND! HE WAS CHASING THE GUY WHO STOLE MY PURSE!
PUT HIM DOWN!
YOUR... HUSBAND?
I GUESS THERE WERE SOME THINGS ABOUT THE FUTURE THAT JUST DIDN'T SIT WELL WITH THE MAN OF TOMORROW.

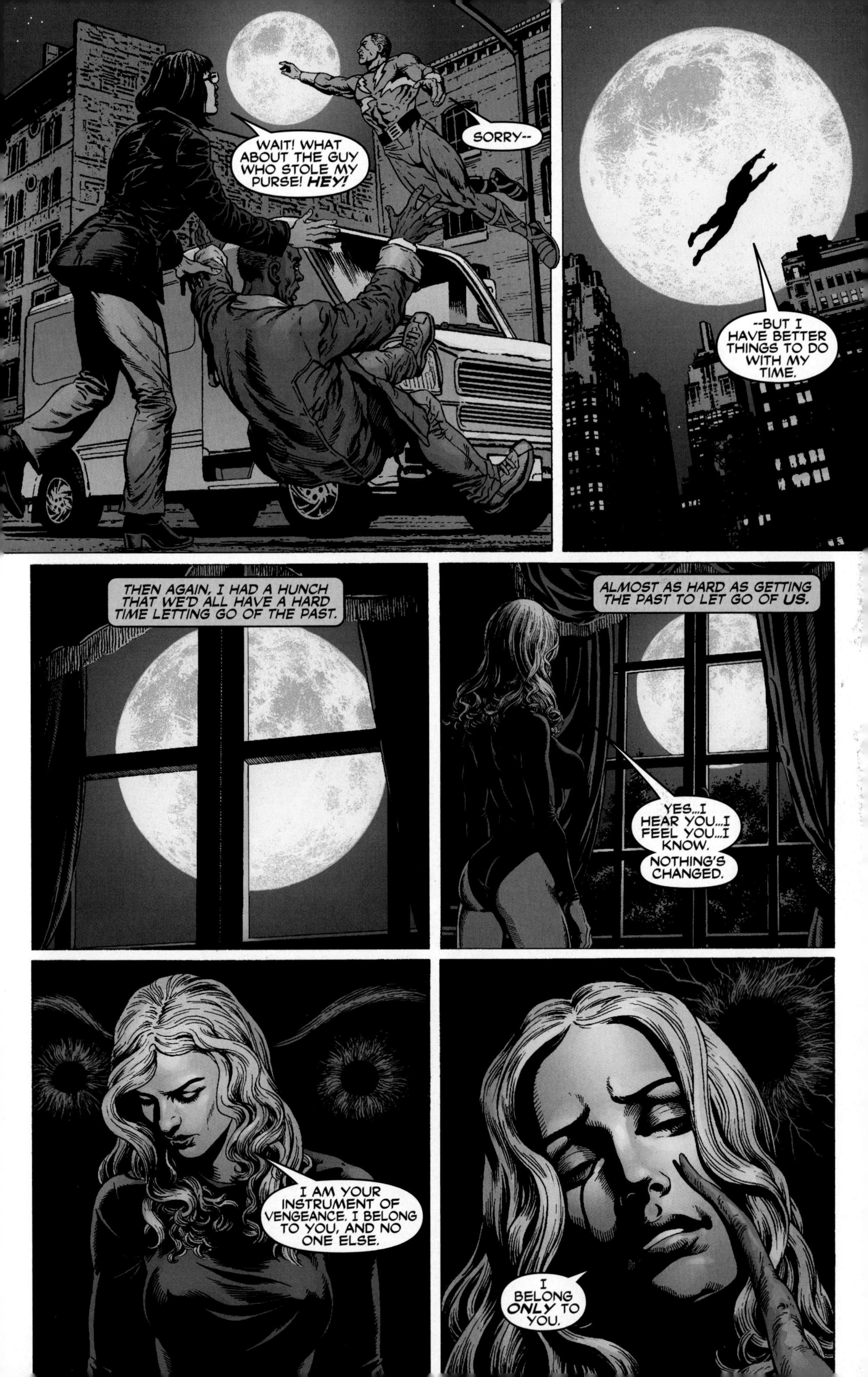
WAIT! WHAT ABOUT THE GUY WHO STOLE MY PURSE! *HEY!*
SORRY--
--BUT I HAVE BETTER THINGS TO DO WITH MY TIME.
THEN AGAIN, I HAD A HUNCH THAT WE'D ALL HAVE A HARD TIME LETTING GO OF THE PAST.
ALMOST AS HARD AS GETTING THE PAST TO LET GO OF **US.**
YES...I HEAR YOU...I FEEL YOU...I KNOW. NOTHING'S CHANGED.
I AM YOUR INSTRUMENT OF VENGEANCE. I BELONG TO YOU, AND NO ONE ELSE.
I BELONG ***ONLY*** TO YOU.

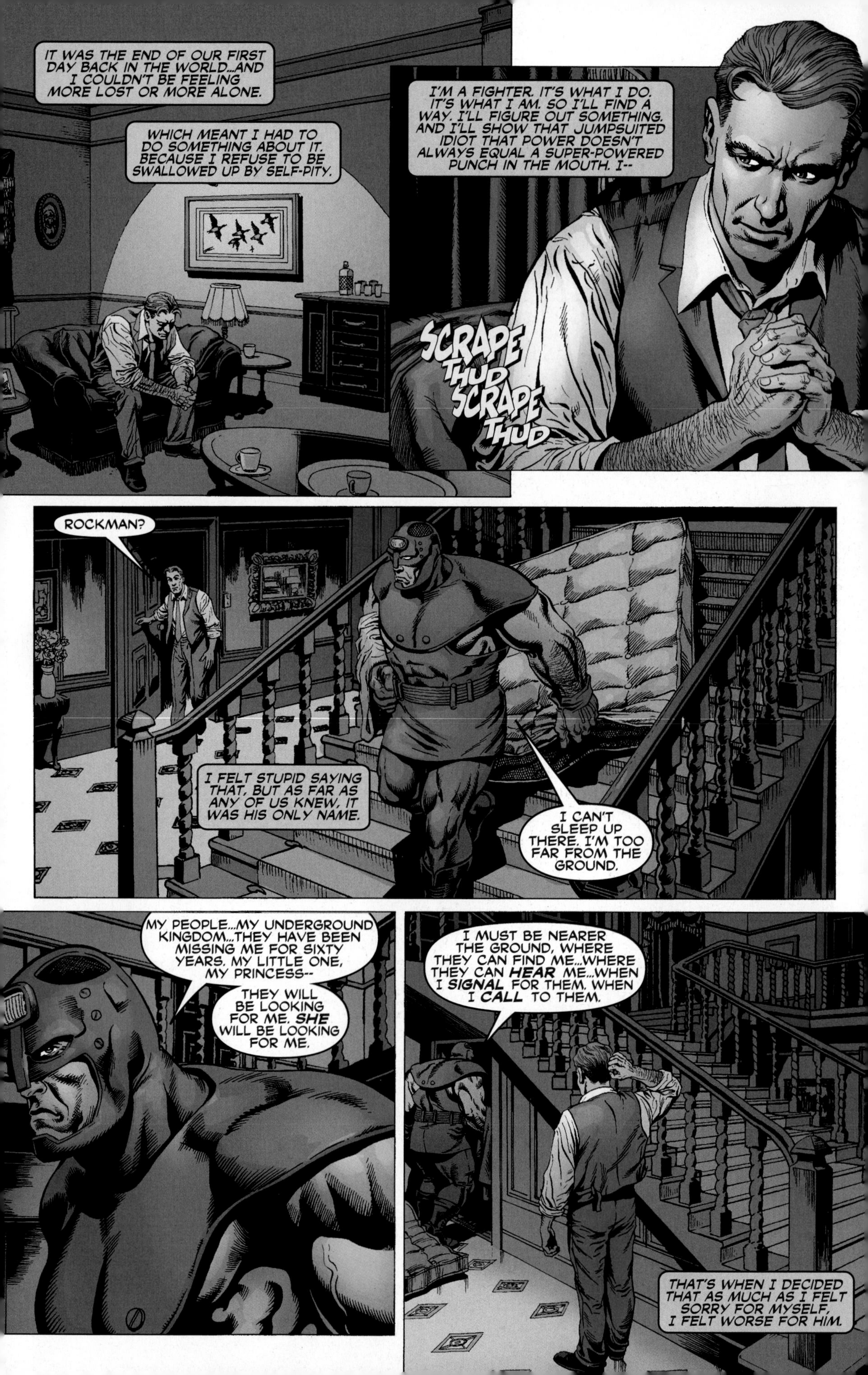

IT WAS THE END OF OUR FIRST DAY BACK IN THE WORLD...AND I COULDN'T BE FEELING MORE LOST OR MORE ALONE.
WHICH MEANT I HAD TO DO SOMETHING ABOUT IT. BECAUSE I REFUSE TO BE SWALLOWED UP BY SELF-PITY.
I'M A FIGHTER. IT'S WHAT I DO. IT'S WHAT I AM. SO I'LL FIND A WAY. I'LL FIGURE OUT SOMETHING. AND I'LL SHOW THAT JUMPSUITED IDIOT THAT POWER DOESN'T ALWAYS EQUAL A SUPER-POWERED PUNCH IN THE MOUTH. I--
SCRAPE THUD SCRAPE THUD
ROCKMAN?
I FELT STUPID SAYING THAT, BUT AS FAR AS ANY OF US KNEW, IT WAS HIS ONLY NAME.
I CAN'T SLEEP UP THERE. I'M TOO FAR FROM THE GROUND.
MY PEOPLE...MY UNDERGROUND KINGDOM...THEY HAVE BEEN MISSING ME FOR SIXTY YEARS. MY LITTLE ONE, MY PRINCESS--
THEY WILL BE LOOKING FOR ME. SHE WILL BE LOOKING FOR ME.
I MUST BE NEARER THE GROUND, WHERE THEY CAN FIND ME...WHERE THEY CAN HEAR ME...WHEN I SIGNAL FOR THEM. WHEN I CALL TO THEM.
THAT'S WHEN I DECIDED THAT AS MUCH AS I FELT SORRY FOR MYSELF, I FELT WORSE FOR HIM.

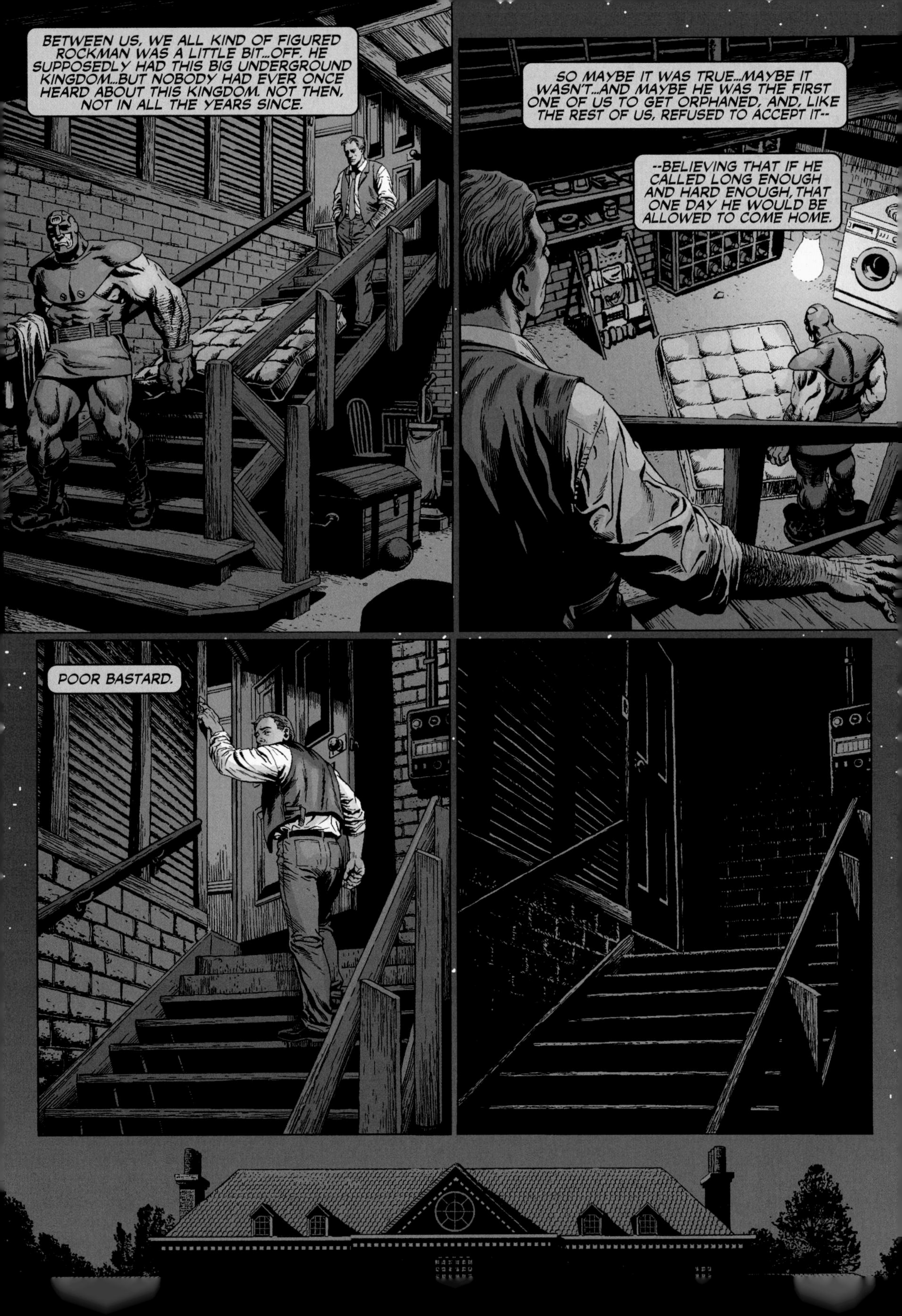
BETWEEN US, WE ALL KIND OF FIGURED ROCKMAN WAS A LITTLE BIT...OFF. HE SUPPOSEDLY HAD THIS BIG UNDERGROUND KINGDOM...BUT NOBODY HAD EVER ONCE HEARD ABOUT THIS KINGDOM. NOT THEN, NOT IN ALL THE YEARS SINCE.
SO MAYBE IT WAS TRUE...MAYBE IT WASN'T...AND MAYBE HE WAS THE FIRST ONE OF US TO GET ORPHANED, AND, LIKE THE REST OF US, REFUSED TO ACCEPT IT--
--BELIEVING THAT IF HE CALLED LONG ENOUGH AND HARD ENOUGH, THAT ONE DAY HE WOULD BE ALLOWED TO COME HOME.
POOR BASTARD.

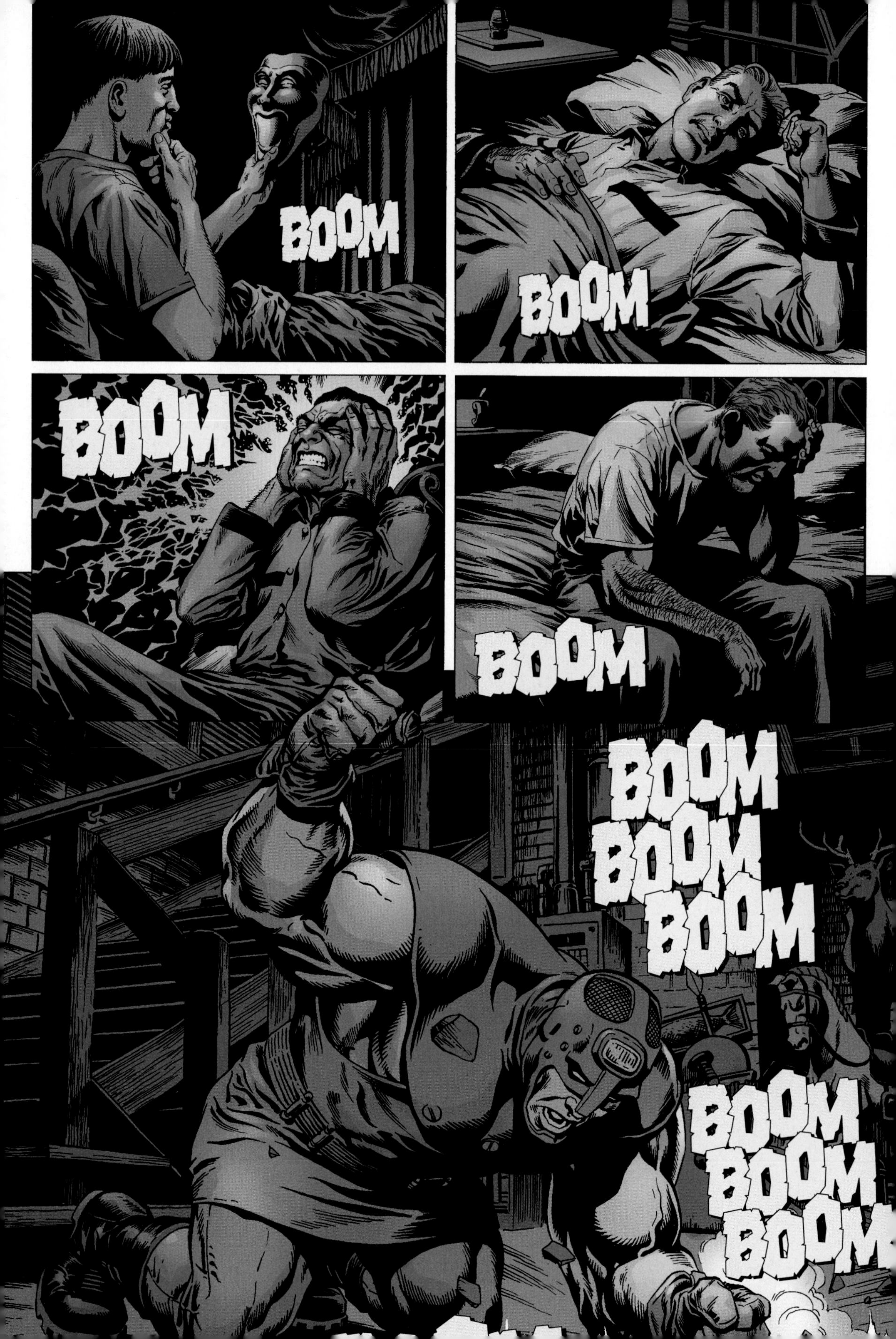
BOOM
BOOM
BOOM
BOOM
BOOM
BOOM
BOOM
BOOM
BOOM
BOOM

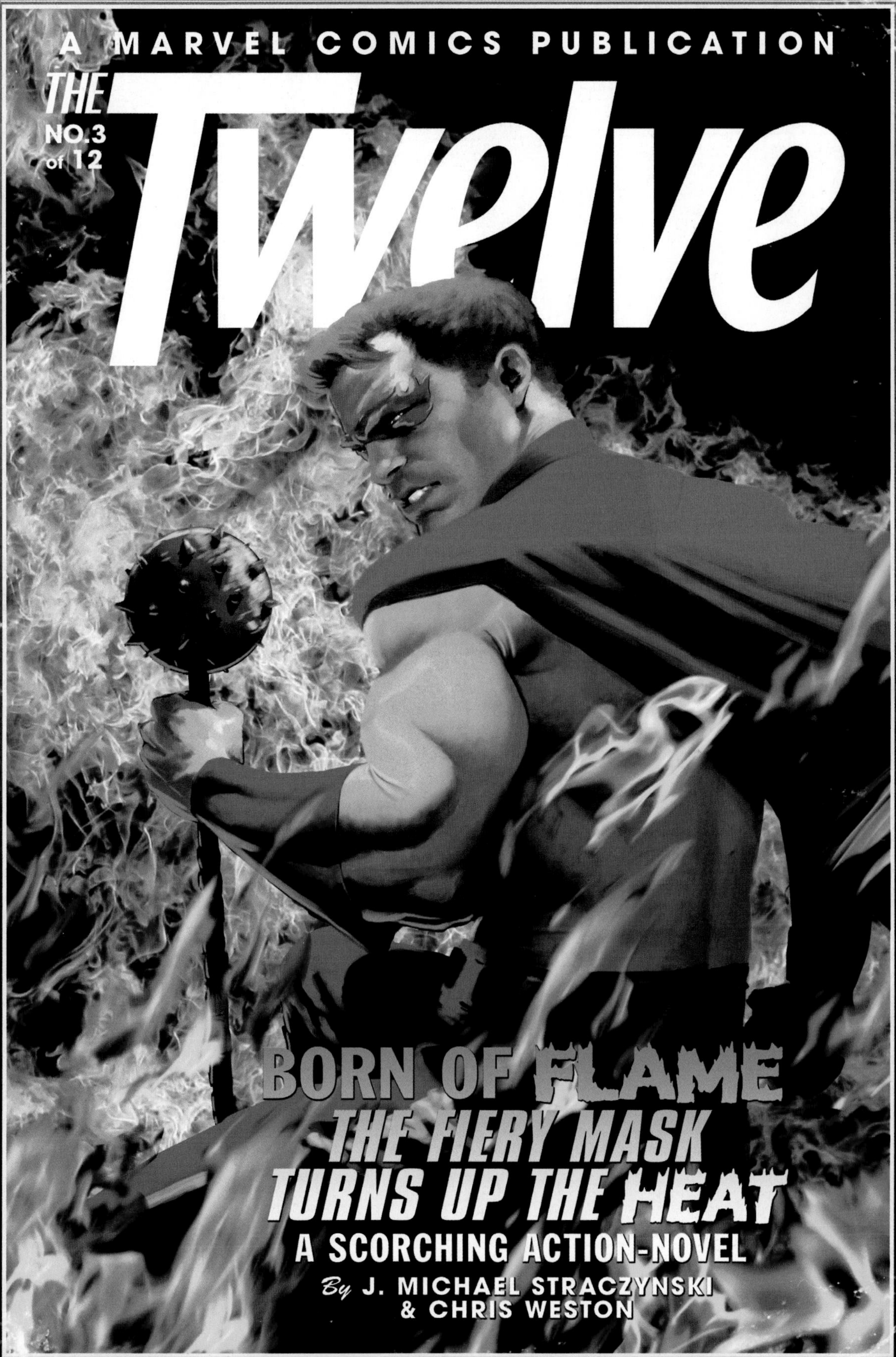
A MARVEL COMICS PUBLICATION
THE
NO.3
of 12
Twelve
BORN OF FLAME
THE FIERY MASK
TURNS UP THE HEAT
A SCORCHING ACTION-NOVEL
By J. MICHAEL STRACZYNSKI
& CHRIS WESTON

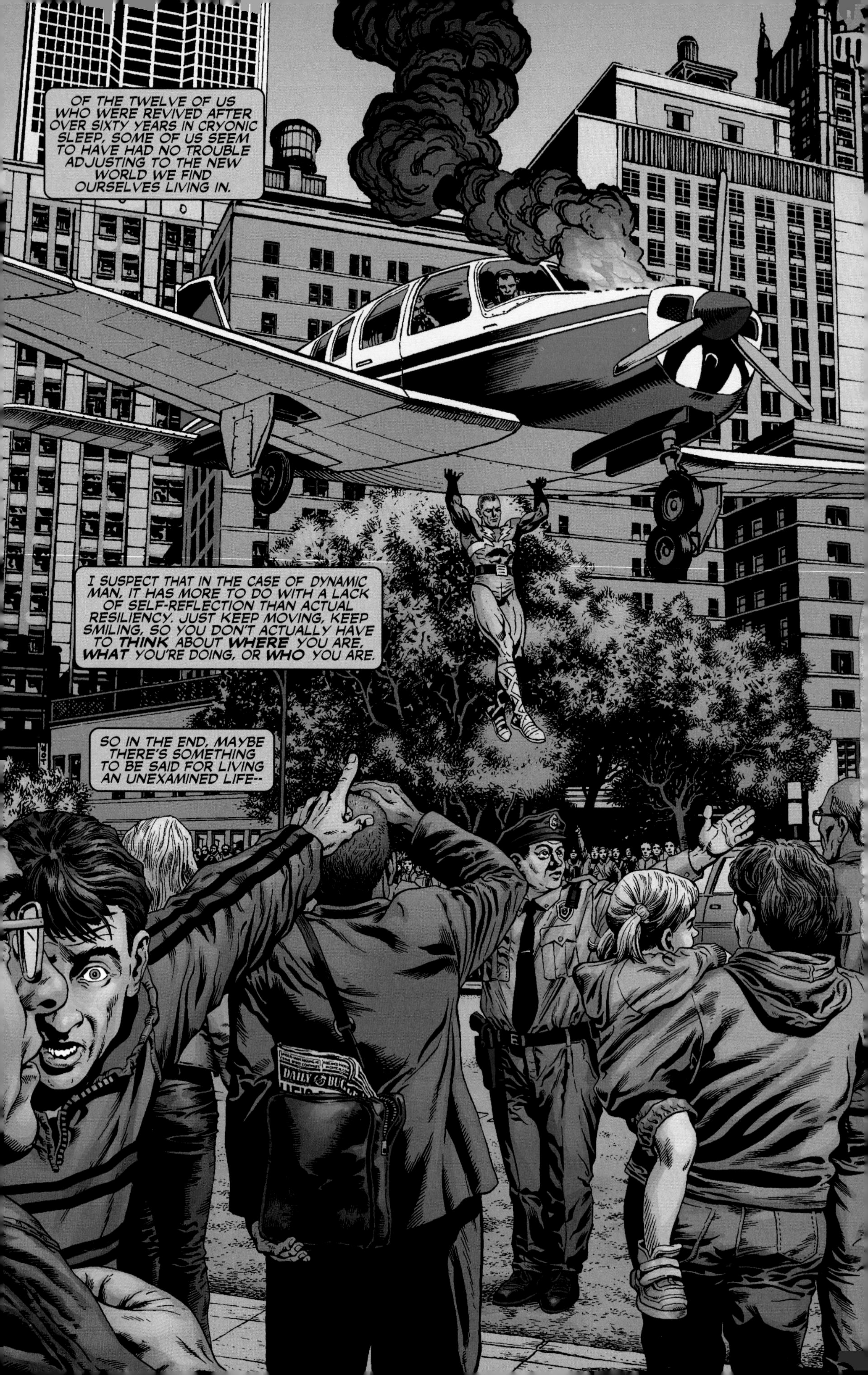
OF THE TWELVE OF US WHO WERE REVIVED AFTER OVER SIXTY YEARS IN CRYONIC SLEEP, SOME OF US SEEM TO HAVE HAD NO TROUBLE ADJUSTING TO THE NEW WORLD WE FIND OURSELVES LIVING IN.
I SUSPECT THAT IN THE CASE OF DYNAMIC MAN, IT HAS MORE TO DO WITH A LACK OF SELF-REFLECTION THAN ACTUAL RESILIENCY. JUST KEEP MOVING, KEEP SMILING, SO YOU DON'T ACTUALLY HAVE TO **THINK** ABOUT **WHERE** YOU ARE, **WHAT** YOU'RE DOING, OR **WHO** YOU ARE.
SO IN THE END, MAYBE THERE'S SOMETHING TO BE SAID FOR LIVING AN UNEXAMINED LIFE--

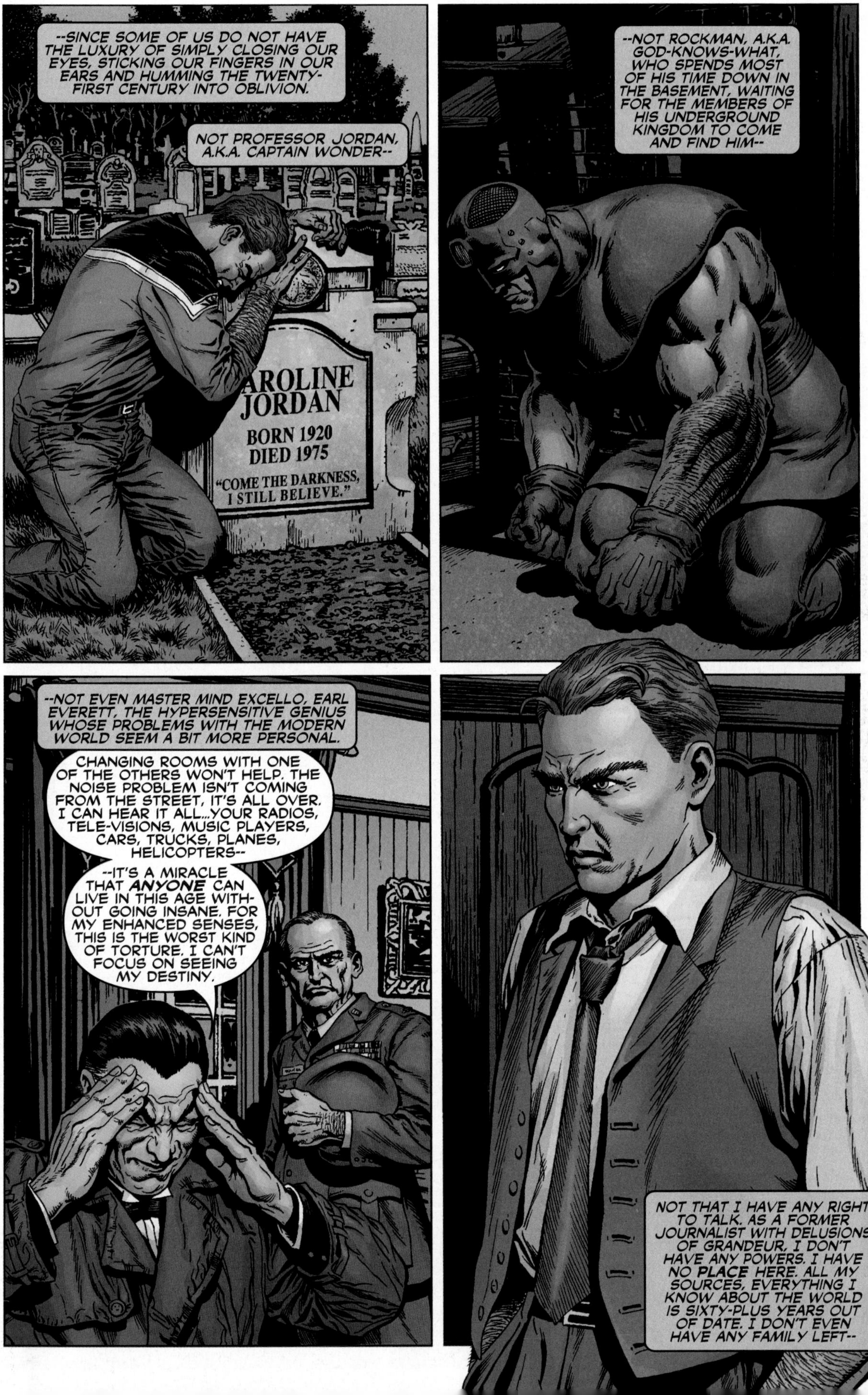
--SINCE SOME OF US DO NOT HAVE THE LUXURY OF SIMPLY CLOSING OUR EYES, STICKING OUR FINGERS IN OUR EARS AND HUMMING THE TWENTY-FIRST CENTURY INTO OBLIVION.
NOT PROFESSOR JORDAN, A.K.A. CAPTAIN WONDER--
AROLINE JORDAN
BORN 1920
DIED 1975
"COME THE DARKNESS, I STILL BELIEVE."
--NOT ROCKMAN, A.K.A. GOD-KNOWS-WHAT, WHO SPENDS MOST OF HIS TIME DOWN IN THE BASEMENT, WAITING FOR THE MEMBERS OF HIS UNDERGROUND KINGDOM TO COME AND FIND HIM--
--NOT EVEN MASTER MIND EXCELLO, EARL EVERETT, THE HYPERSENSITIVE GENIUS WHOSE PROBLEMS WITH THE MODERN WORLD SEEM A BIT MORE PERSONAL.
CHANGING ROOMS WITH ONE OF THE OTHERS WON'T HELP. THE NOISE PROBLEM ISN'T COMING FROM THE STREET, IT'S ALL OVER. I CAN HEAR IT ALL...YOUR RADIOS, TELE-VISIONS, MUSIC PLAYERS, CARS, TRUCKS, PLANES, HELICOPTERS--
--IT'S A MIRACLE THAT ANYONE CAN LIVE IN THIS AGE WITH-OUT GOING INSANE. FOR MY ENHANCED SENSES, THIS IS THE WORST KIND OF TORTURE. I CAN'T FOCUS ON SEEING MY DESTINY.
NOT THAT I HAVE ANY RIGHT TO TALK. AS A FORMER JOURNALIST WITH DELUSIONS OF GRANDEUR, I DON'T HAVE ANY POWERS. I HAVE NO PLACE HERE. ALL MY SOURCES, EVERYTHING I KNOW ABOUT THE WORLD IS SIXTY-PLUS YEARS OUT OF DATE. I DON'T EVEN HAVE ANY FAMILY LEFT--

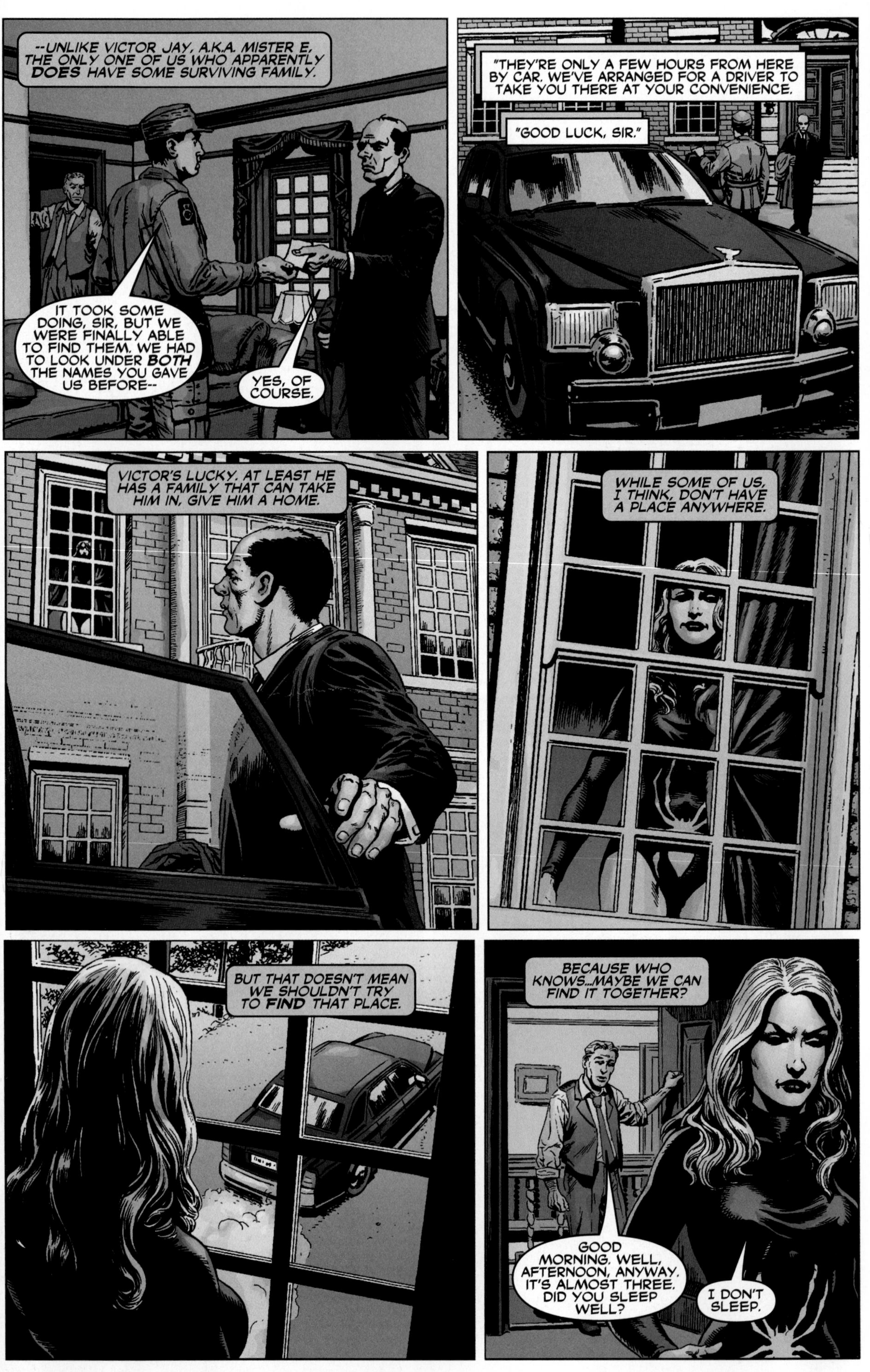
--UNLIKE VICTOR JAY, A.K.A. MISTER E, THE ONLY ONE OF US WHO APPARENTLY DOES HAVE SOME SURVIVING FAMILY.
IT TOOK SOME DOING, SIR, BUT WE WERE FINALLY ABLE TO FIND THEM. WE HAD TO LOOK UNDER BOTH THE NAMES YOU GAVE US BEFORE--
YES, OF COURSE.
"THEY'RE ONLY A FEW HOURS FROM HERE BY CAR. WE'VE ARRANGED FOR A DRIVER TO TAKE YOU THERE AT YOUR CONVENIENCE.
"GOOD LUCK, SIR."
VICTOR'S LUCKY. AT LEAST HE HAS A FAMILY THAT CAN TAKE HIM IN, GIVE HIM A HOME.
WHILE SOME OF US, I THINK, DON'T HAVE A PLACE ANYWHERE.
BUT THAT DOESN'T MEAN WE SHOULDN'T TRY TO FIND THAT PLACE.
BECAUSE WHO KNOWS...MAYBE WE CAN FIND IT TOGETHER?
GOOD MORNING. WELL, AFTERNOON, ANYWAY. IT'S ALMOST THREE. DID YOU SLEEP WELL?
I DON'T SLEEP.

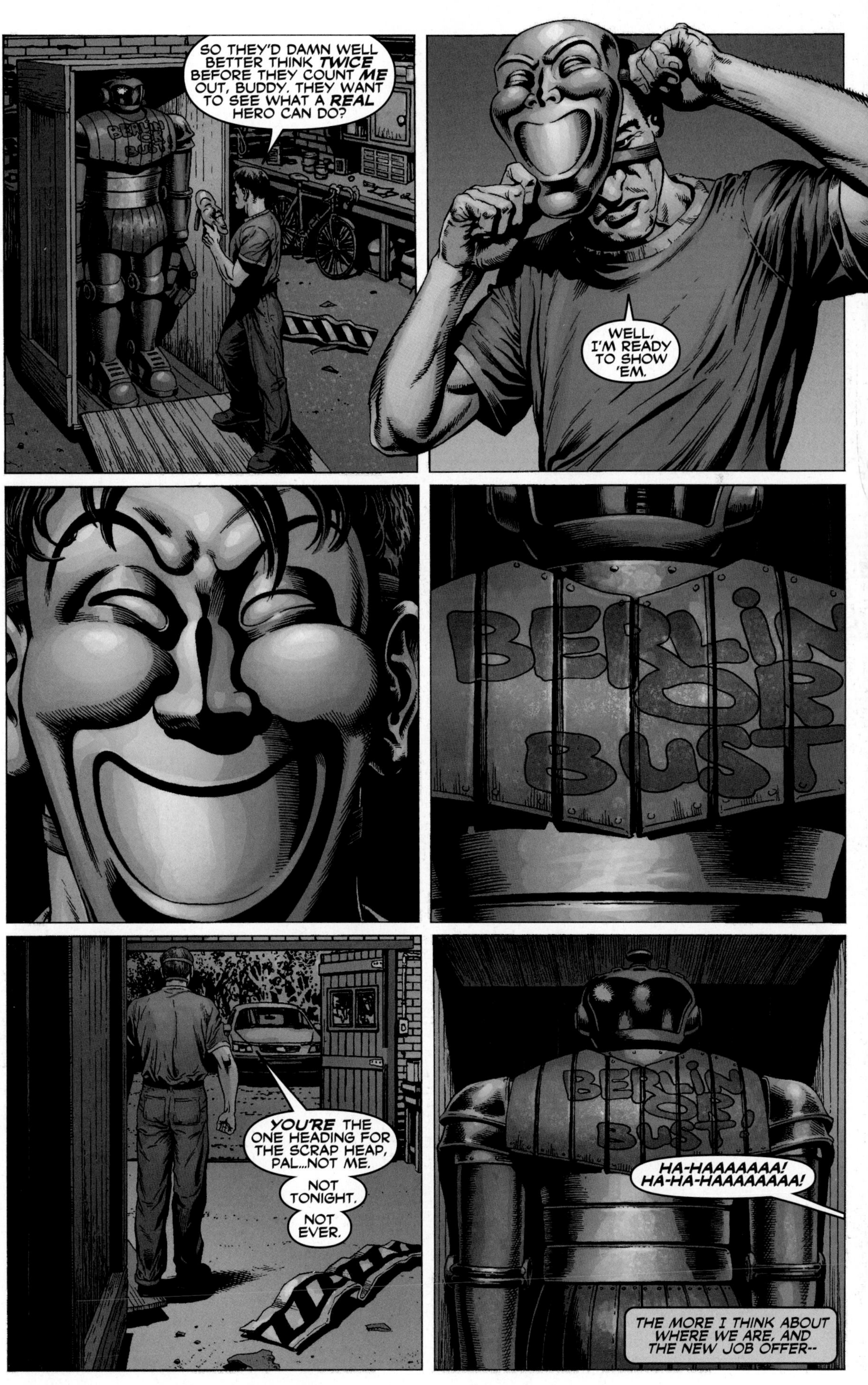
SO THEY'D DAMN WELL BETTER THINK TWICE BEFORE THEY COUNT ME OUT, BUDDY. THEY WANT TO SEE WHAT A REAL HERO CAN DO?
BERLIN OR BUST
WELL, I'M READY TO SHOW 'EM.
BERLIN OR BUST
YOU'RE THE ONE HEADING FOR THE SCRAP HEAP, PAL...NOT ME.
NOT TONIGHT.
NOT EVER.
BERLIN OR BUST
HA-HAAAAAAA! HA-HA-HAAAAAAAA!
THE MORE I THINK ABOUT WHERE WE ARE, AND THE NEW JOB OFFER--

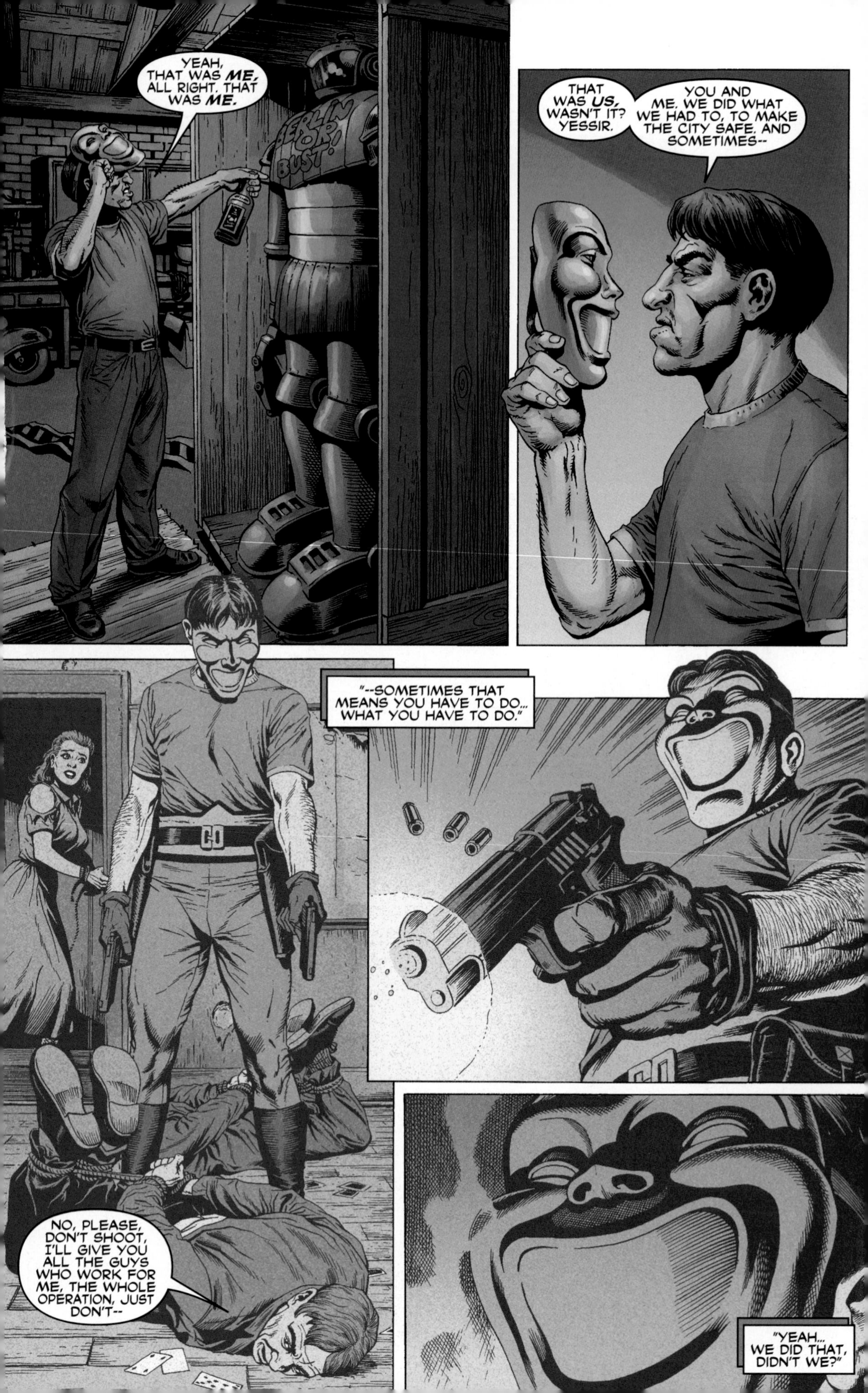
YEAH, THAT WAS ME, ALL RIGHT. THAT WAS ME.
BERLIN OR BUST!
THAT WAS US, WASN'T IT? YESSIR.
YOU AND ME. WE DID WHAT WE HAD TO, TO MAKE THE CITY SAFE. AND SOMETIMES--
"--SOMETIMES THAT MEANS YOU HAVE TO DO... WHAT YOU HAVE TO DO."
NO, PLEASE, DON'T SHOOT, I'LL GIVE YOU ALL THE GUYS WHO WORK FOR ME, THE WHOLE OPERATION, JUST DON'T--
"YEAH... WE DID THAT, DIDN'T WE?"

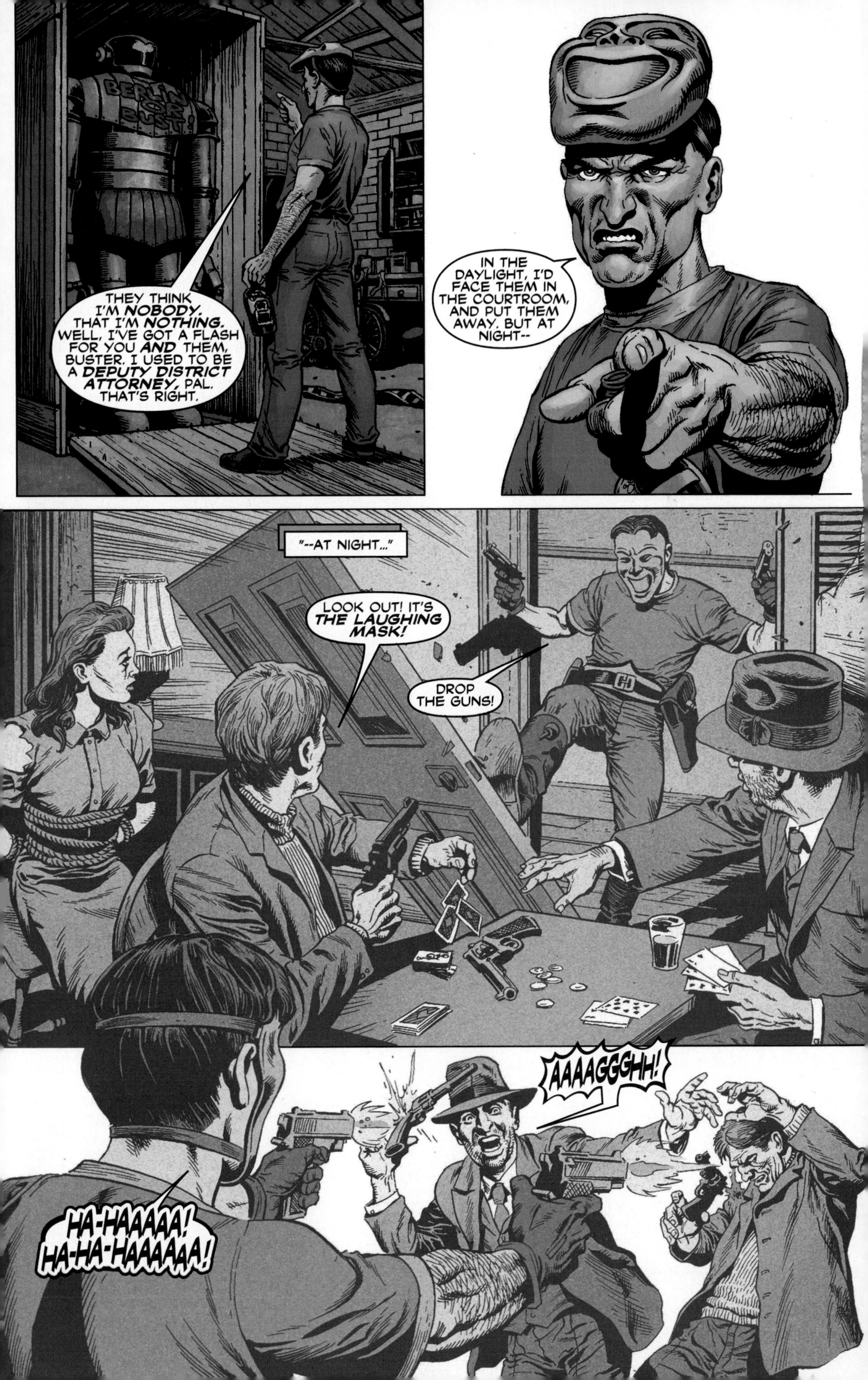
BERLIN OR BUST!
THEY THINK I'M NOBODY, THAT I'M NOTHING. WELL, I'VE GOT A FLASH FOR YOU AND THEM, BUSTER. I USED TO BE A DEPUTY DISTRICT ATTORNEY, PAL. THAT'S RIGHT.
IN THE DAYLIGHT, I'D FACE THEM IN THE COURTROOM, AND PUT THEM AWAY. BUT AT NIGHT--
"--AT NIGHT..."
LOOK OUT! IT'S THE LAUGHING MASK!
DROP THE GUNS!
AAAAGGGHH!
HA-HAAAAA! HA-HA-HAAAAAA!

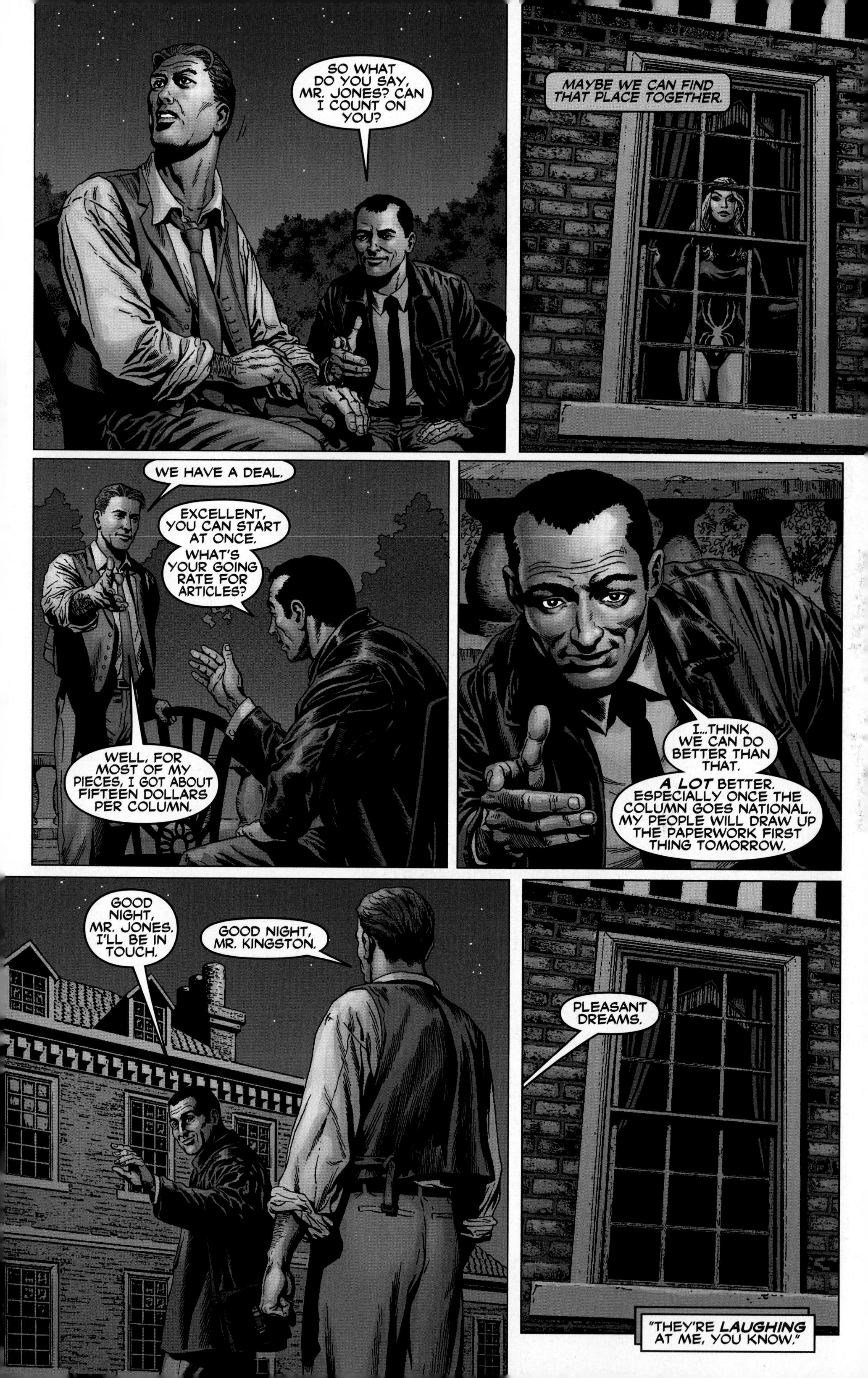
SO WHAT DO YOU SAY, MR. JONES? CAN I COUNT ON YOU?
MAYBE WE CAN FIND THAT PLACE TOGETHER.
WE HAVE A DEAL.
EXCELLENT, YOU CAN START AT ONCE. WHAT'S YOUR GOING RATE FOR ARTICLES?
WELL, FOR MOST OF MY PIECES, I GOT ABOUT FIFTEEN DOLLARS PER COLUMN.
I...THINK WE CAN DO BETTER THAN THAT. A LOT BETTER. ESPECIALLY ONCE THE COLUMN GOES NATIONAL. MY PEOPLE WILL DRAW UP THE PAPERWORK FIRST THING TOMORROW.
GOOD NIGHT, MR. JONES. I'LL BE IN TOUCH.
GOOD NIGHT, MR. KINGSTON.
PLEASANT DREAMS.
"THEY'RE LAUGHING AT ME, YOU KNOW."

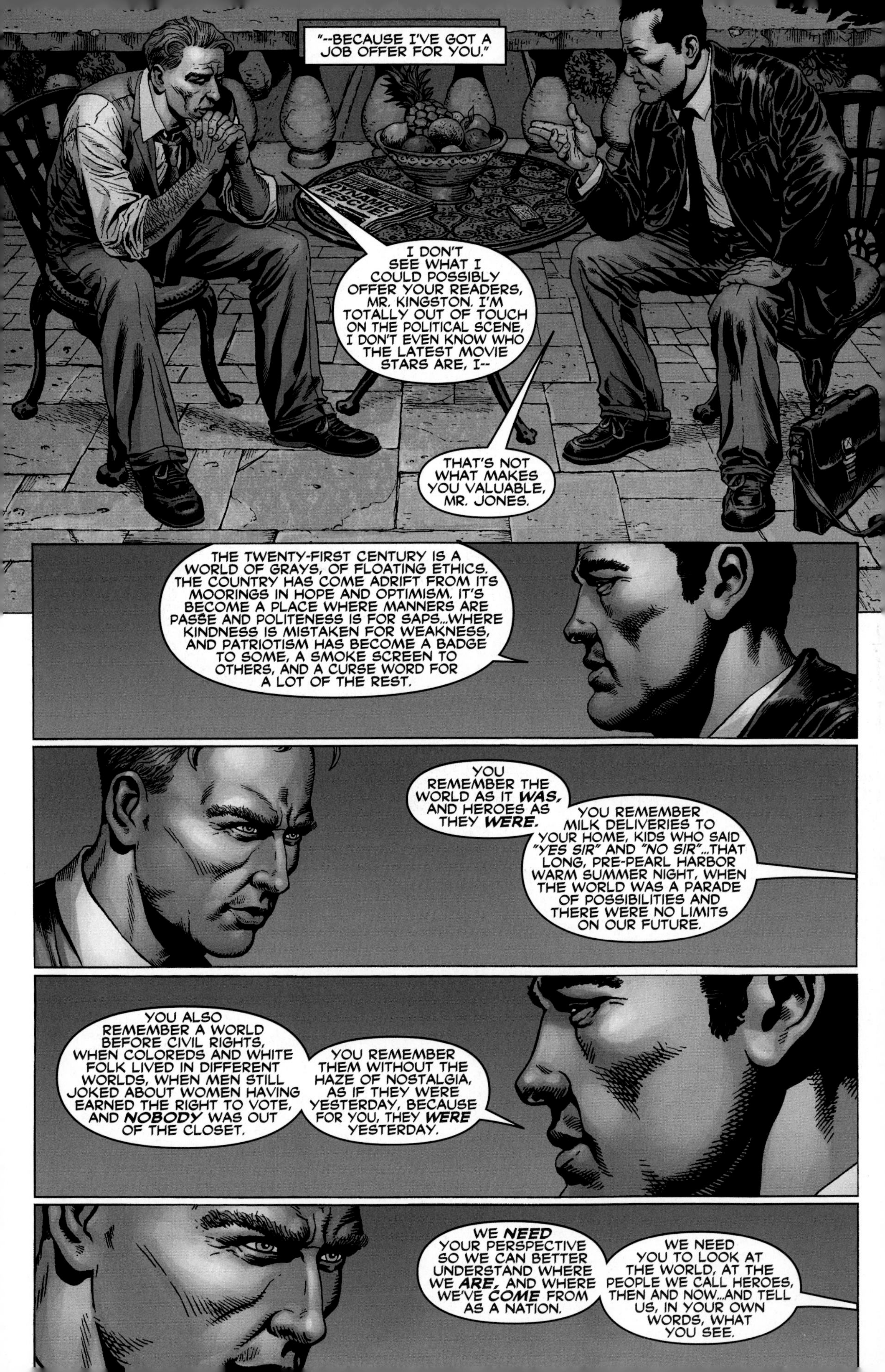
"--BECAUSE I'VE GOT A JOB OFFER FOR YOU."
DYNAMIC RESCUE
I DON'T SEE WHAT I COULD POSSIBLY OFFER YOUR READERS, MR. KINGSTON. I'M TOTALLY OUT OF TOUCH ON THE POLITICAL SCENE, I DON'T EVEN KNOW WHO THE LATEST MOVIE STARS ARE, I--
THAT'S NOT WHAT MAKES YOU VALUABLE, MR. JONES.
THE TWENTY-FIRST CENTURY IS A WORLD OF GRAYS, OF FLOATING ETHICS. THE COUNTRY HAS COME ADRIFT FROM ITS MOORINGS IN HOPE AND OPTIMISM. IT'S BECOME A PLACE WHERE MANNERS ARE PASSE AND POLITENESS IS FOR SAPS...WHERE KINDNESS IS MISTAKEN FOR WEAKNESS, AND PATRIOTISM HAS BECOME A BADGE TO SOME, A SMOKE SCREEN TO OTHERS, AND A CURSE WORD FOR A LOT OF THE REST.
YOU REMEMBER THE WORLD AS IT *WAS,* AND HEROES AS THEY *WERE.*
YOU REMEMBER MILK DELIVERIES TO YOUR HOME, KIDS WHO SAID *"YES SIR"* AND *"NO SIR"*...THAT LONG, PRE-PEARL HARBOR WARM SUMMER NIGHT, WHEN THE WORLD WAS A PARADE OF POSSIBILITIES AND THERE WERE NO LIMITS ON OUR FUTURE.
YOU ALSO REMEMBER A WORLD BEFORE CIVIL RIGHTS, WHEN COLOREDS AND WHITE FOLK LIVED IN DIFFERENT WORLDS, WHEN MEN STILL JOKED ABOUT WOMEN HAVING EARNED THE RIGHT TO VOTE, AND *NOBODY* WAS OUT OF THE CLOSET.
YOU REMEMBER THEM WITHOUT THE HAZE OF NOSTALGIA, AS IF THEY WERE YESTERDAY, BECAUSE FOR YOU, THEY *WERE* YESTERDAY.
WE *NEED* YOUR PERSPECTIVE SO WE CAN BETTER UNDERSTAND WHERE WE *ARE,* AND WHERE WE'VE *COME* FROM AS A NATION.
WE NEED YOU TO LOOK AT THE WORLD, AT THE PEOPLE WE CALL HEROES, THEN AND NOW...AND TELL US, IN YOUR OWN WORDS, WHAT YOU SEE.

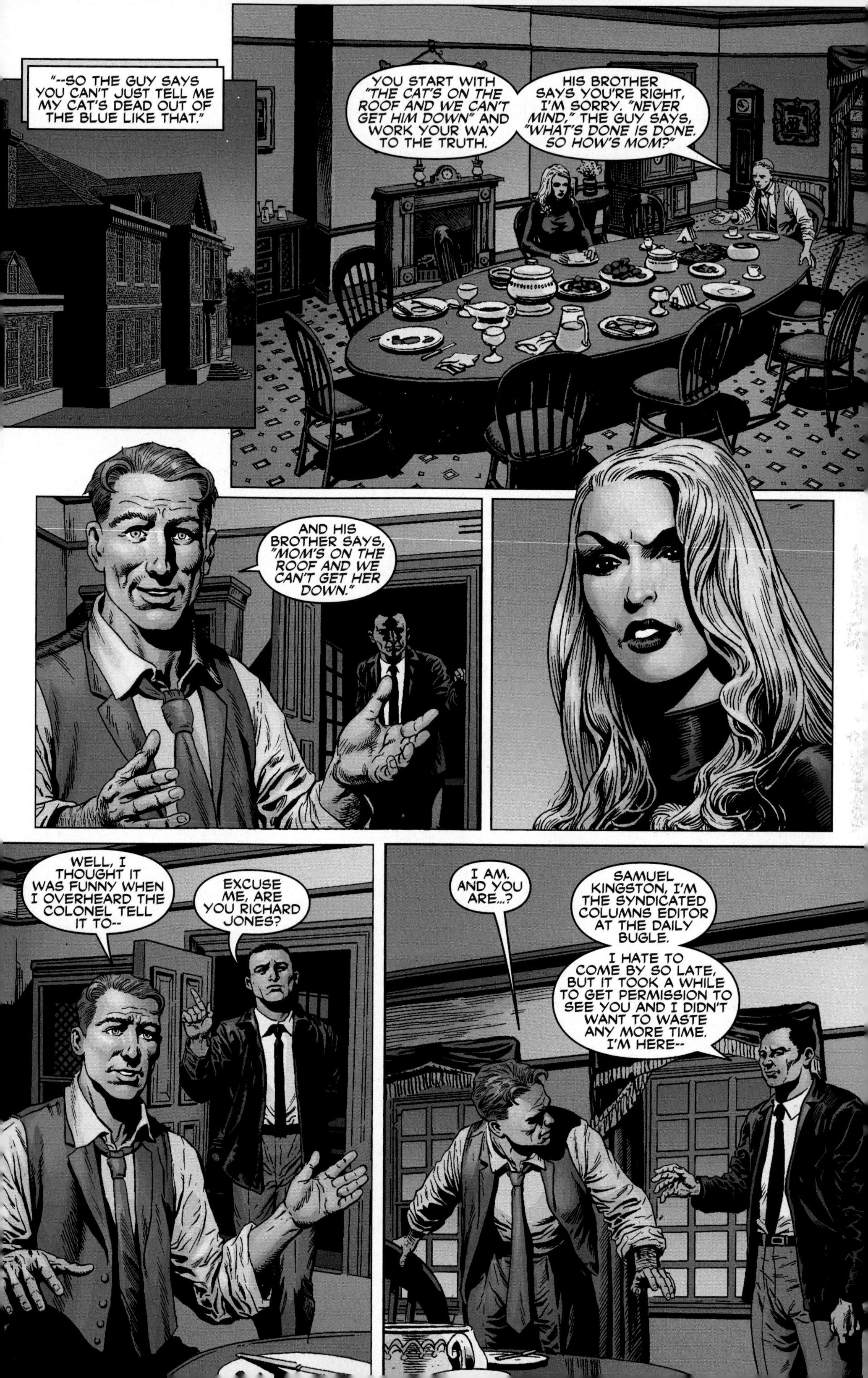
"--SO THE GUY SAYS YOU CAN'T JUST TELL ME MY CAT'S DEAD OUT OF THE BLUE LIKE THAT."
YOU START WITH "THE CAT'S ON THE ROOF AND WE CAN'T GET HIM DOWN" AND WORK YOUR WAY TO THE TRUTH.
HIS BROTHER SAYS YOU'RE RIGHT, I'M SORRY. "NEVER MIND," THE GUY SAYS, "WHAT'S DONE IS DONE. SO HOW'S MOM?"
AND HIS BROTHER SAYS, "MOM'S ON THE ROOF AND WE CAN'T GET HER DOWN."
WELL, I THOUGHT IT WAS FUNNY WHEN I OVERHEARD THE COLONEL TELL IT TO--
EXCUSE ME, ARE YOU RICHARD JONES?
I AM. AND YOU ARE...?
SAMUEL KINGSTON, I'M THE SYNDICATED COLUMNS EDITOR AT THE DAILY BUGLE.
I HATE TO COME BY SO LATE, BUT IT TOOK A WHILE TO GET PERMISSION TO SEE YOU AND I DIDN'T WANT TO WASTE ANY MORE TIME. I'M HERE--

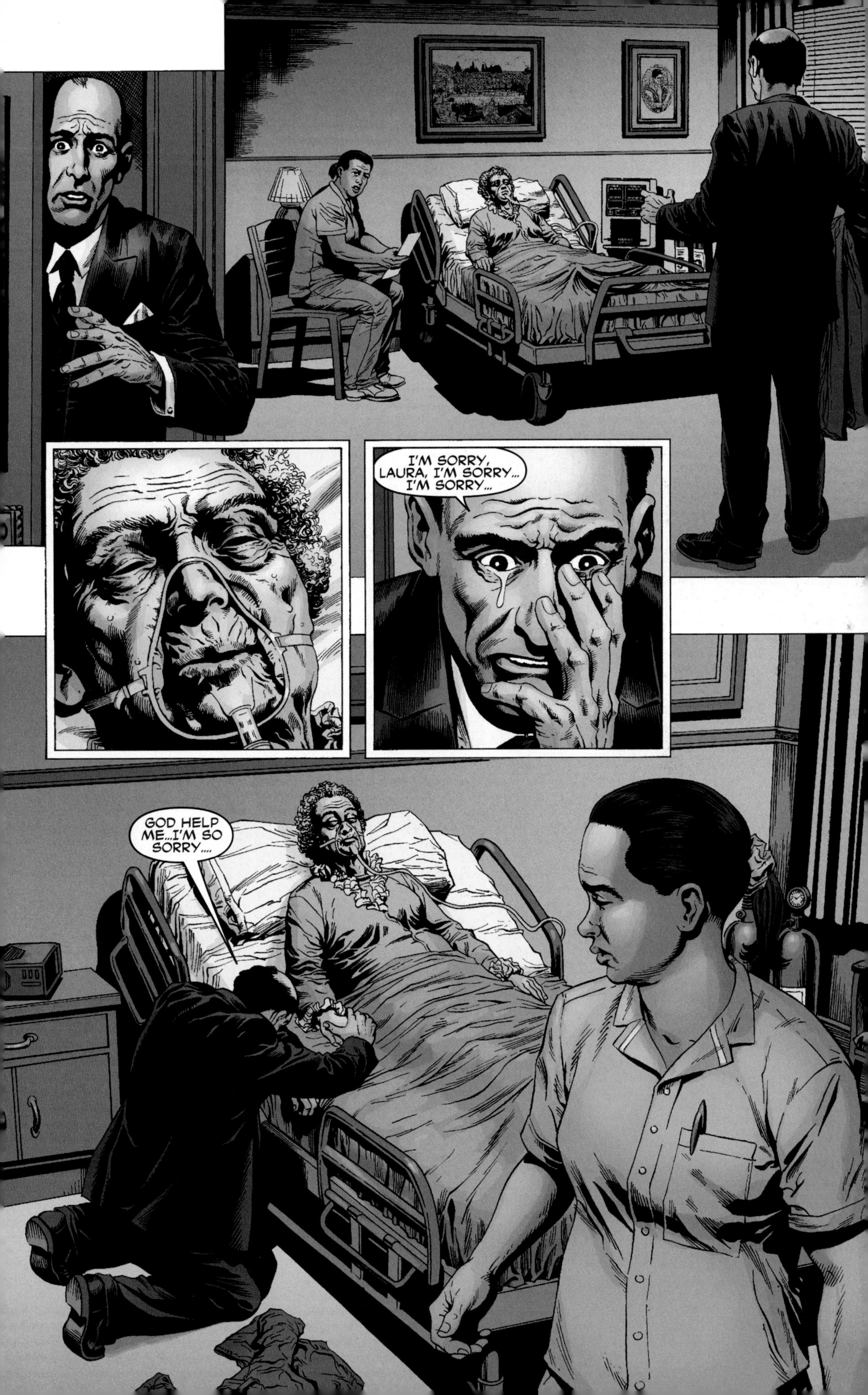
I'M SORRY, LAURA, I'M SORRY... I'M SORRY...
GOD HELP ME...I'M SO SORRY....

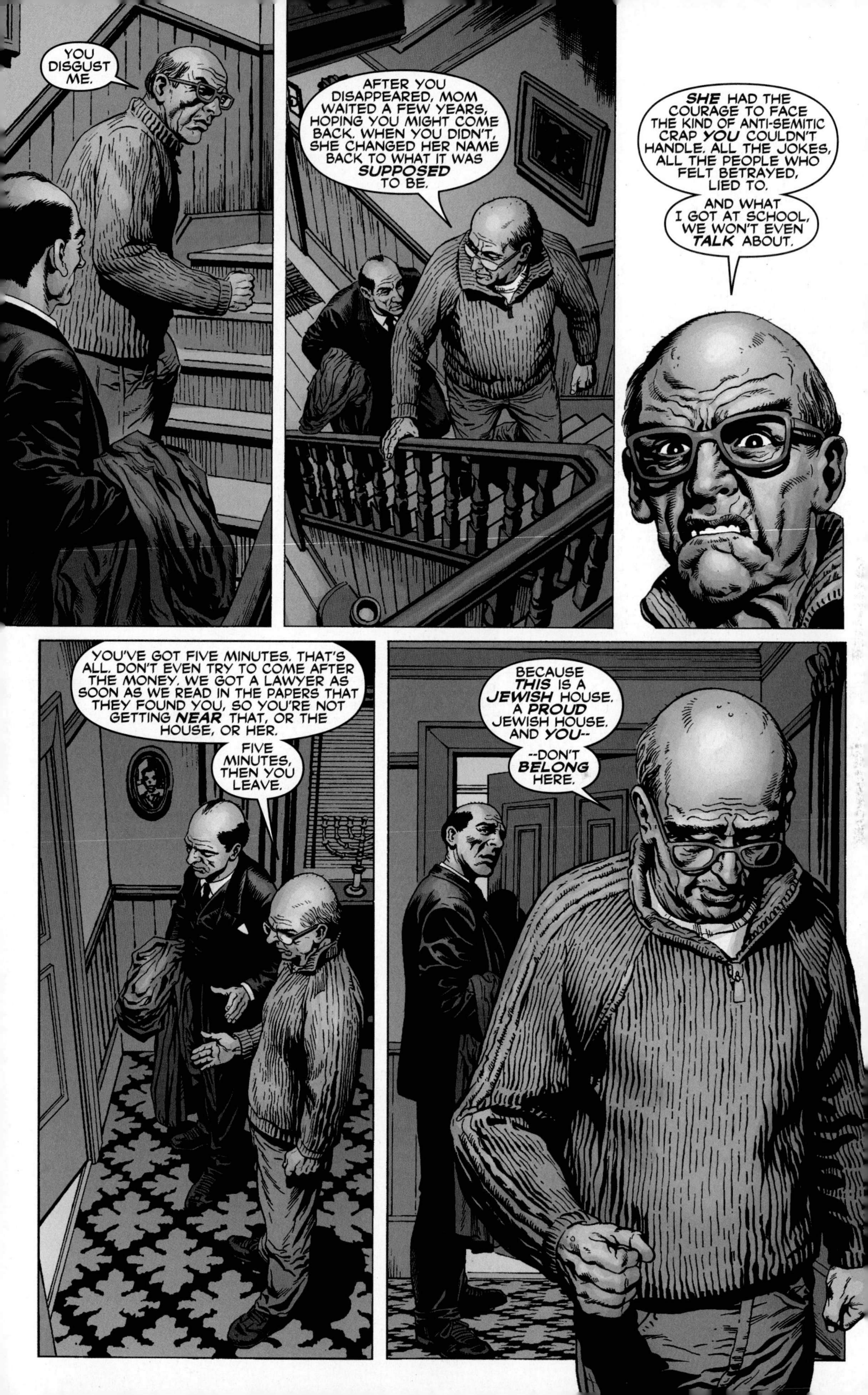
YOU DISGUST ME.
AFTER YOU DISAPPEARED, MOM WAITED A FEW YEARS, HOPING YOU MIGHT COME BACK. WHEN YOU DIDN'T, SHE CHANGED HER NAME BACK TO WHAT IT WAS *SUPPOSED* TO BE.
SHE HAD THE COURAGE TO FACE THE KIND OF ANTI-SEMITIC CRAP *YOU* COULDN'T HANDLE. ALL THE JOKES, ALL THE PEOPLE WHO FELT BETRAYED, LIED TO.
AND WHAT I GOT AT SCHOOL, WE WON'T EVEN *TALK* ABOUT.
YOU'VE GOT FIVE MINUTES. THAT'S ALL. DON'T EVEN TRY TO COME AFTER THE MONEY. WE GOT A LAWYER AS SOON AS WE READ IN THE PAPERS THAT THEY FOUND YOU, SO YOU'RE NOT GETTING *NEAR* THAT, OR THE HOUSE, OR HER.
FIVE MINUTES, THEN YOU LEAVE.
BECAUSE *THIS* IS A *JEWISH* HOUSE. A *PROUD* JEWISH HOUSE. AND *YOU*--
--DON'T *BELONG* HERE.

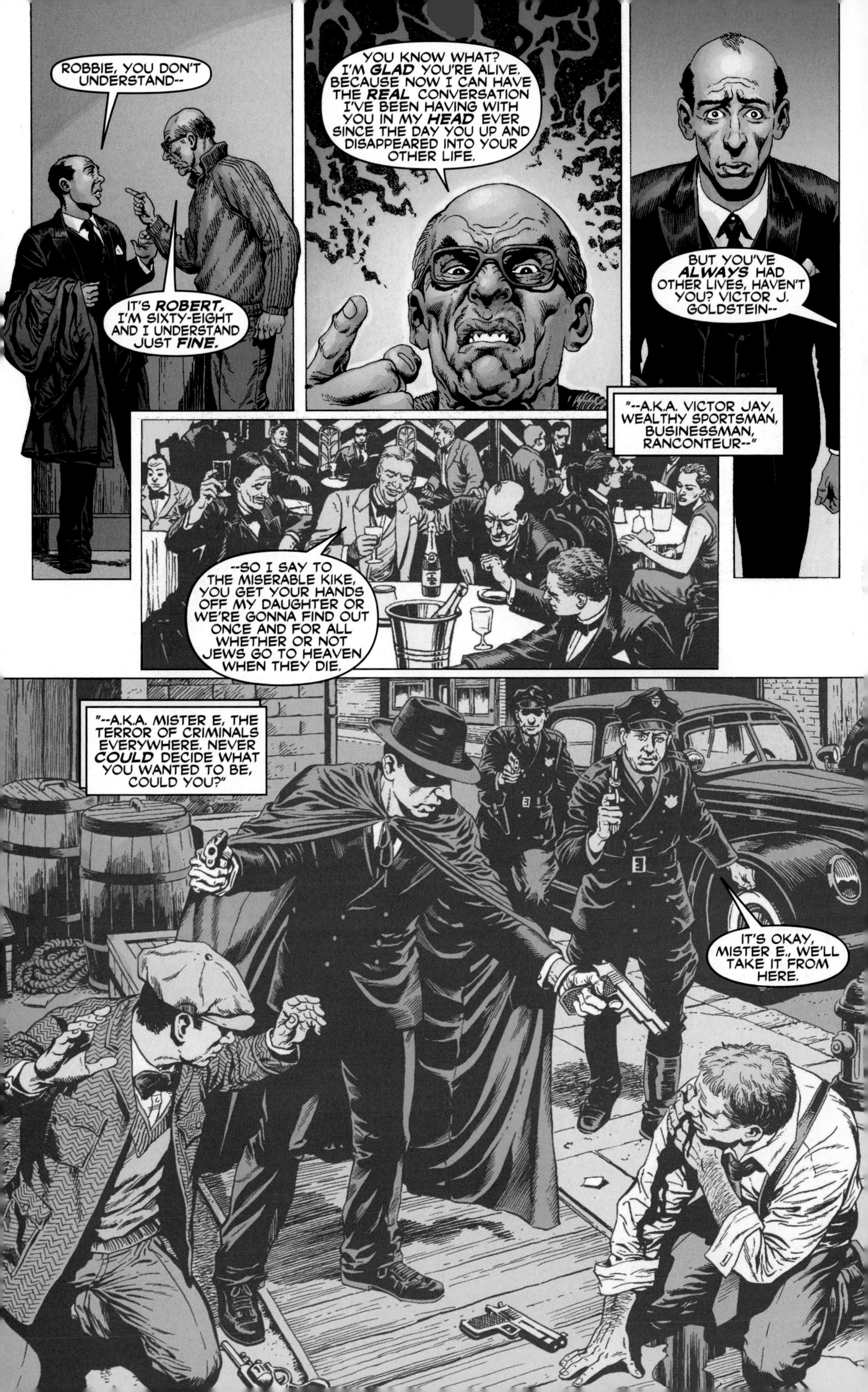
ROBBIE, YOU DON'T UNDERSTAND--
IT'S ROBERT, I'M SIXTY-EIGHT AND I UNDERSTAND JUST FINE.
YOU KNOW WHAT? I'M GLAD YOU'RE ALIVE. BECAUSE NOW I CAN HAVE THE REAL CONVERSATION I'VE BEEN HAVING WITH YOU IN MY HEAD EVER SINCE THE DAY YOU UP AND DISAPPEARED INTO YOUR OTHER LIFE.
BUT YOU'VE ALWAYS HAD OTHER LIVES, HAVEN'T YOU? VICTOR J. GOLDSTEIN--
"--A.K.A. VICTOR JAY, WEALTHY SPORTSMAN, BUSINESSMAN, RANCONTEUR--"
--SO I SAY TO THE MISERABLE KIKE, YOU GET YOUR HANDS OFF MY DAUGHTER OR WE'RE GONNA FIND OUT ONCE AND FOR ALL WHETHER OR NOT JEWS GO TO HEAVEN WHEN THEY DIE.
"--A.K.A. MISTER E, THE TERROR OF CRIMINALS EVERYWHERE. NEVER COULD DECIDE WHAT YOU WANTED TO BE, COULD YOU?"
IT'S OKAY, MISTER E., WE'LL TAKE IT FROM HERE.

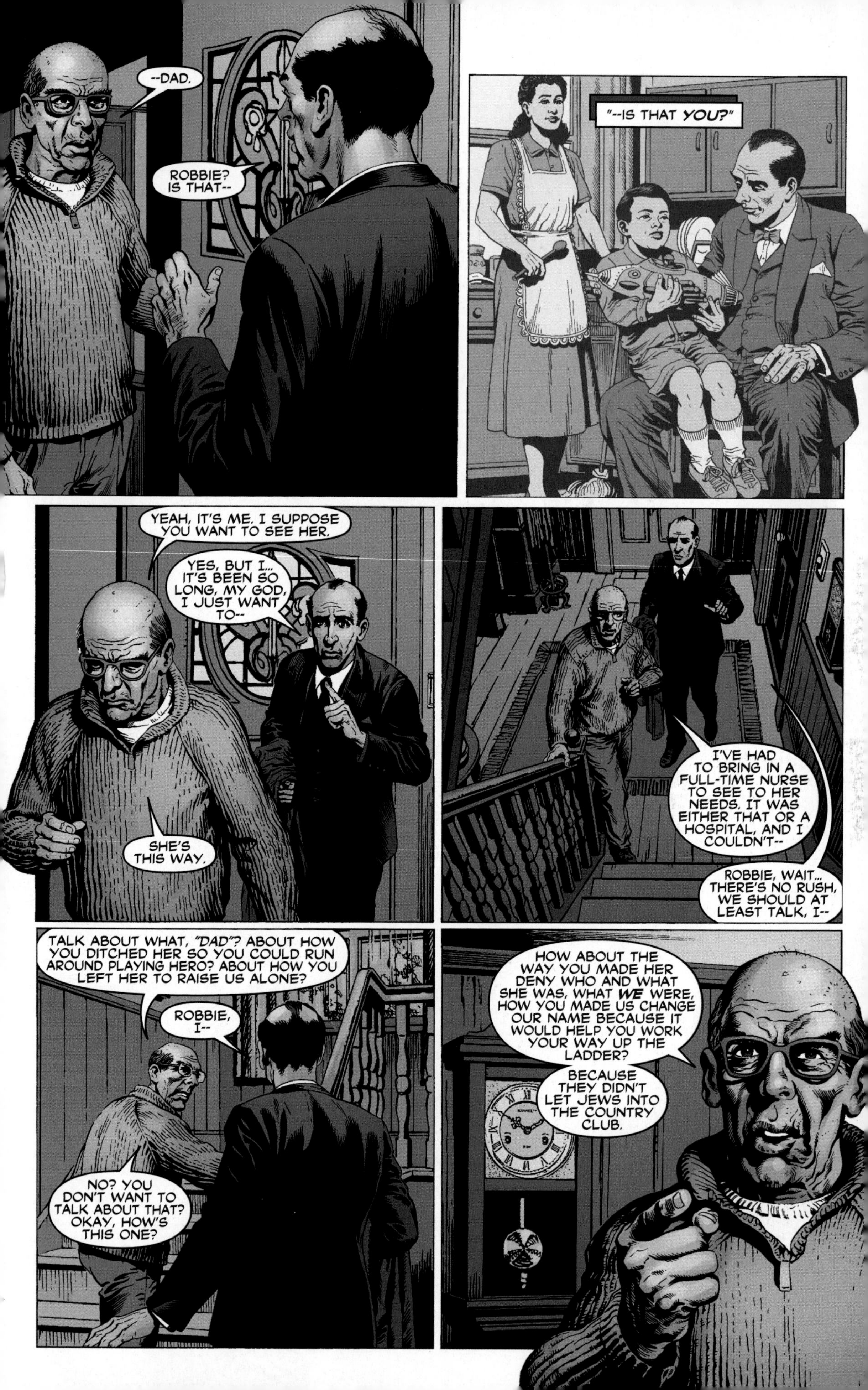
--DAD.
ROBBIE? IS THAT--
"--IS THAT *YOU?*"
YEAH, IT'S ME. I SUPPOSE YOU WANT TO SEE HER.
YES, BUT I... IT'S BEEN SO LONG, MY GOD, I JUST WANT TO--
SHE'S THIS WAY.
I'VE HAD TO BRING IN A FULL-TIME NURSE TO SEE TO HER NEEDS. IT WAS EITHER THAT OR A HOSPITAL, AND I COULDN'T--
ROBBIE, WAIT... THERE'S NO RUSH, WE SHOULD AT LEAST TALK, I--
TALK ABOUT WHAT, *"DAD"*? ABOUT HOW YOU DITCHED HER SO YOU COULD RUN AROUND PLAYING HERO? ABOUT HOW YOU LEFT HER TO RAISE US ALONE?
ROBBIE, I--
NO? YOU DON'T WANT TO TALK ABOUT THAT? OKAY, HOW'S THIS ONE?
HOW ABOUT THE WAY YOU MADE HER DENY WHO AND WHAT SHE WAS, WHAT *WE* WERE, HOW YOU MADE US CHANGE OUR NAME BECAUSE IT WOULD HELP YOU WORK YOUR WAY UP THE LADDER?
BECAUSE THEY DIDN'T LET JEWS INTO THE COUNTRY CLUB.

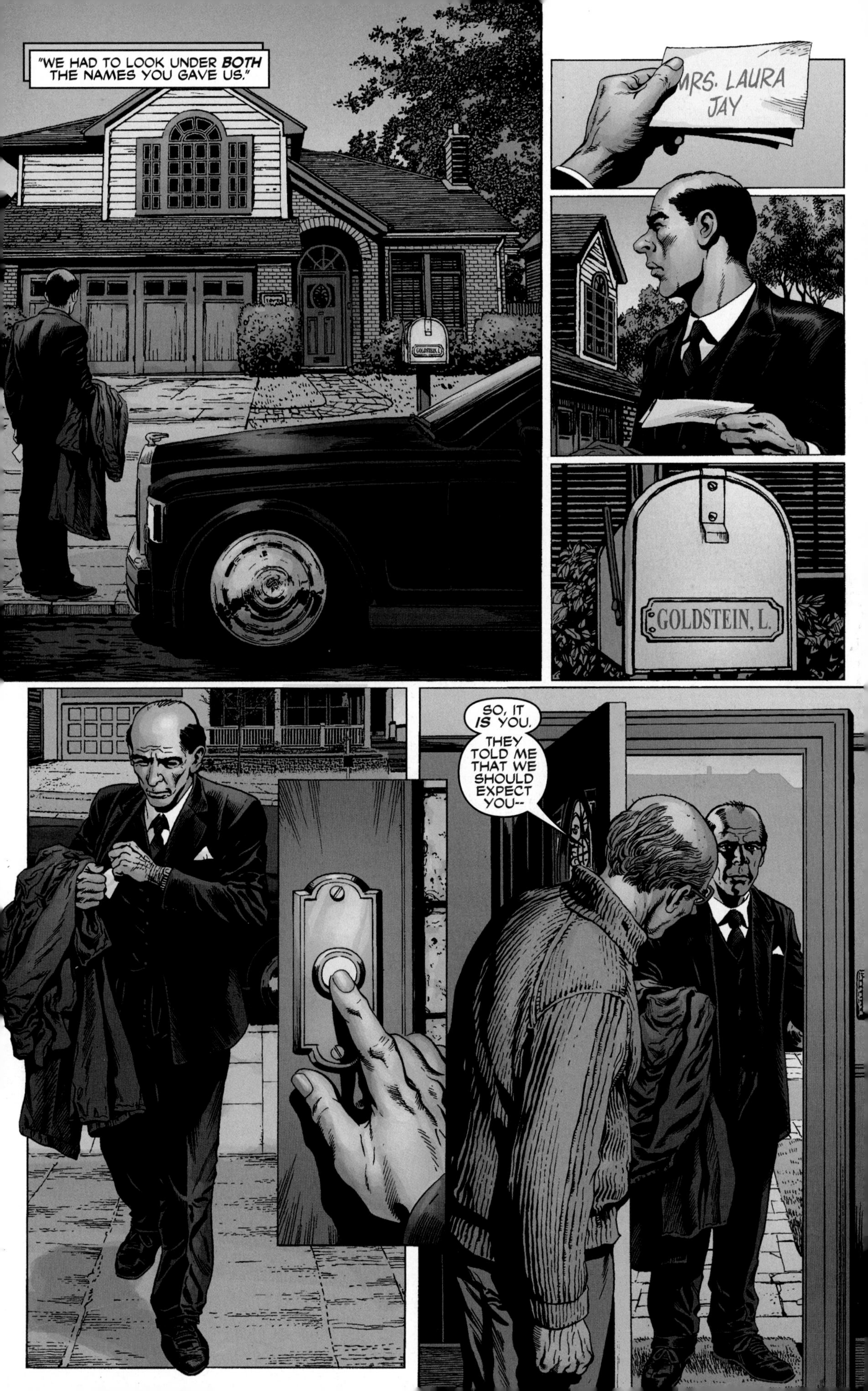
"WE HAD TO LOOK UNDER BOTH THE NAMES YOU GAVE US."
MRS. LAURA JAY
GOLDSTEIN, L.
SO, IT IS YOU.
THEY TOLD ME THAT WE SHOULD EXPECT YOU--

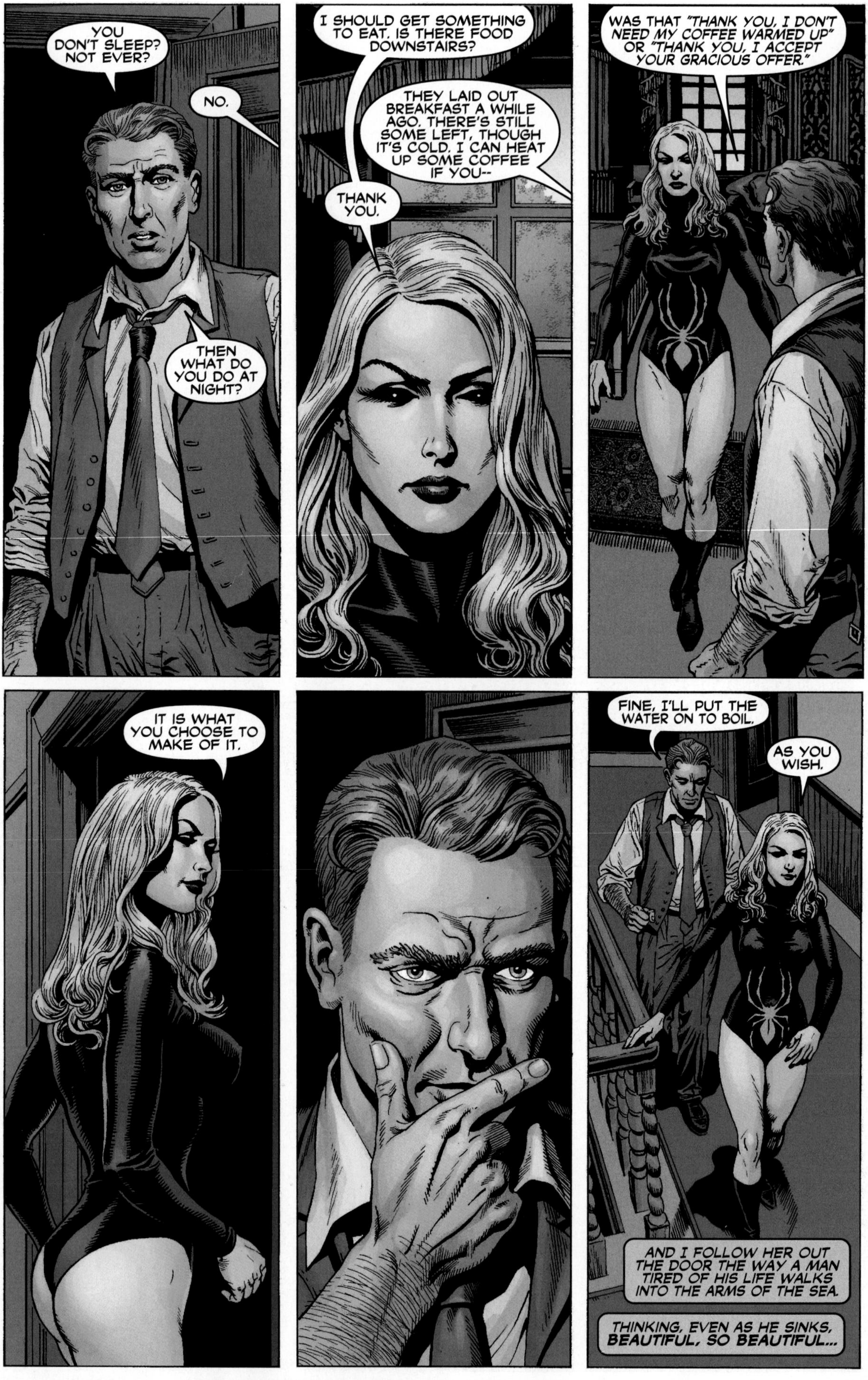
YOU DON'T SLEEP? NOT EVER?
NO.
THEN WHAT DO YOU DO AT NIGHT?
I SHOULD GET SOMETHING TO EAT. IS THERE FOOD DOWNSTAIRS?
THEY LAID OUT BREAKFAST A WHILE AGO. THERE'S STILL SOME LEFT, THOUGH IT'S COLD. I CAN HEAT UP SOME COFFEE IF YOU--
THANK YOU.
WAS THAT "THANK YOU, I DON'T NEED MY COFFEE WARMED UP" OR "THANK YOU, I ACCEPT YOUR GRACIOUS OFFER."
IT IS WHAT YOU CHOOSE TO MAKE OF IT.
FINE, I'LL PUT THE WATER ON TO BOIL.
AS YOU WISH.
AND I FOLLOW HER OUT THE DOOR THE WAY A MAN TIRED OF HIS LIFE WALKS INTO THE ARMS OF THE SEA.
THINKING, EVEN AS HE SINKS, BEAUTIFUL, SO BEAUTIFUL...

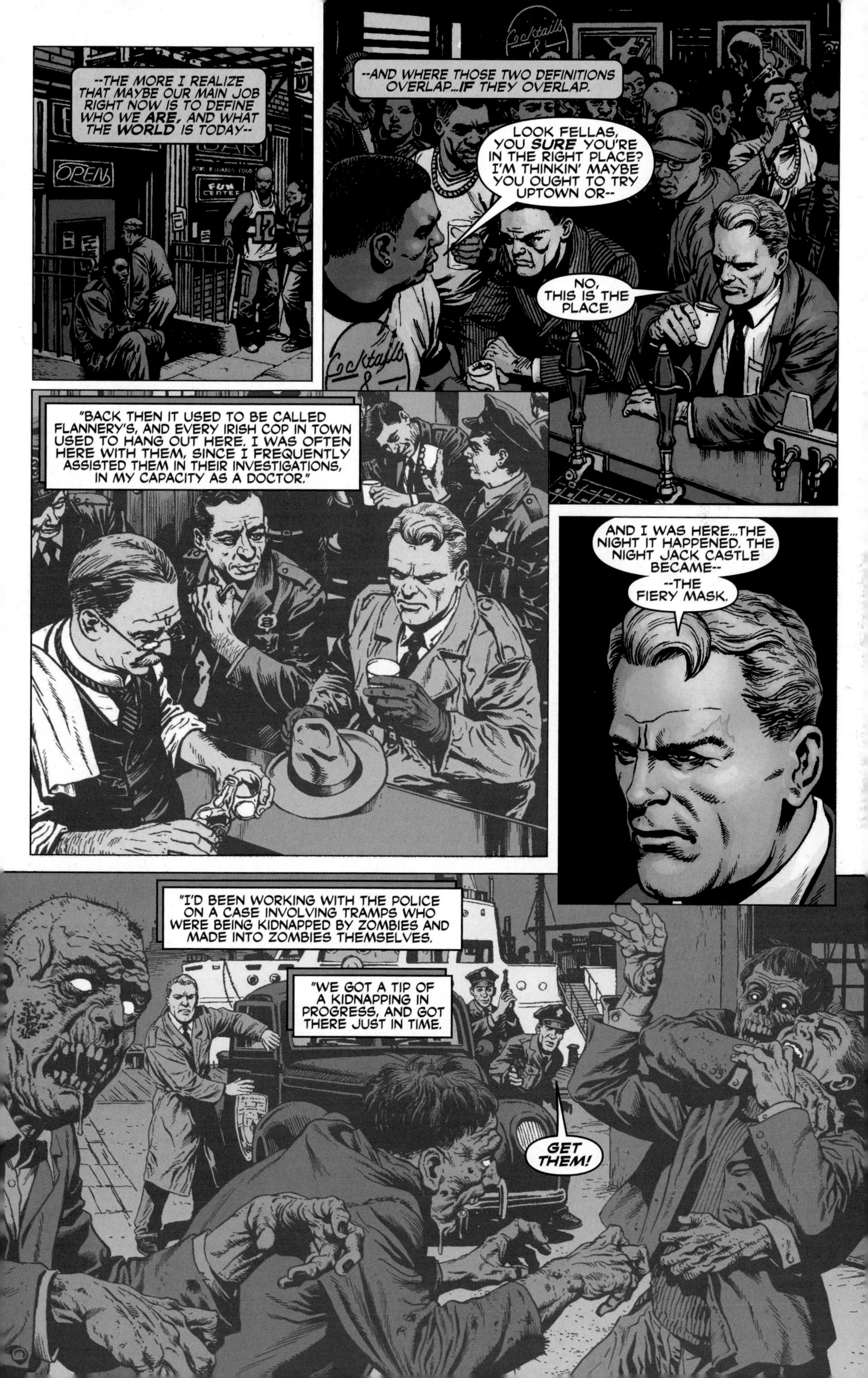
--THE MORE I REALIZE THAT MAYBE OUR MAIN JOB RIGHT NOW IS TO DEFINE WHO WE ARE, AND WHAT THE WORLD IS TODAY--
OPEN
FUN CENTER
--AND WHERE THOSE TWO DEFINITIONS OVERLAP...IF THEY OVERLAP.
LOOK FELLAS, YOU SURE YOU'RE IN THE RIGHT PLACE? I'M THINKIN' MAYBE YOU OUGHT TO TRY UPTOWN OR--
NO, THIS IS THE PLACE.
"BACK THEN IT USED TO BE CALLED FLANNERY'S, AND EVERY IRISH COP IN TOWN USED TO HANG OUT HERE. I WAS OFTEN HERE WITH THEM, SINCE I FREQUENTLY ASSISTED THEM IN THEIR INVESTIGATIONS, IN MY CAPACITY AS A DOCTOR."
AND I WAS HERE...THE NIGHT IT HAPPENED. THE NIGHT JACK CASTLE BECAME--
--THE FIERY MASK.
"I'D BEEN WORKING WITH THE POLICE ON A CASE INVOLVING TRAMPS WHO WERE BEING KIDNAPPED BY ZOMBIES AND MADE INTO ZOMBIES THEMSELVES.
"WE GOT A TIP OF A KIDNAPPING IN PROGRESS, AND GOT THERE JUST IN TIME.
GET THEM!

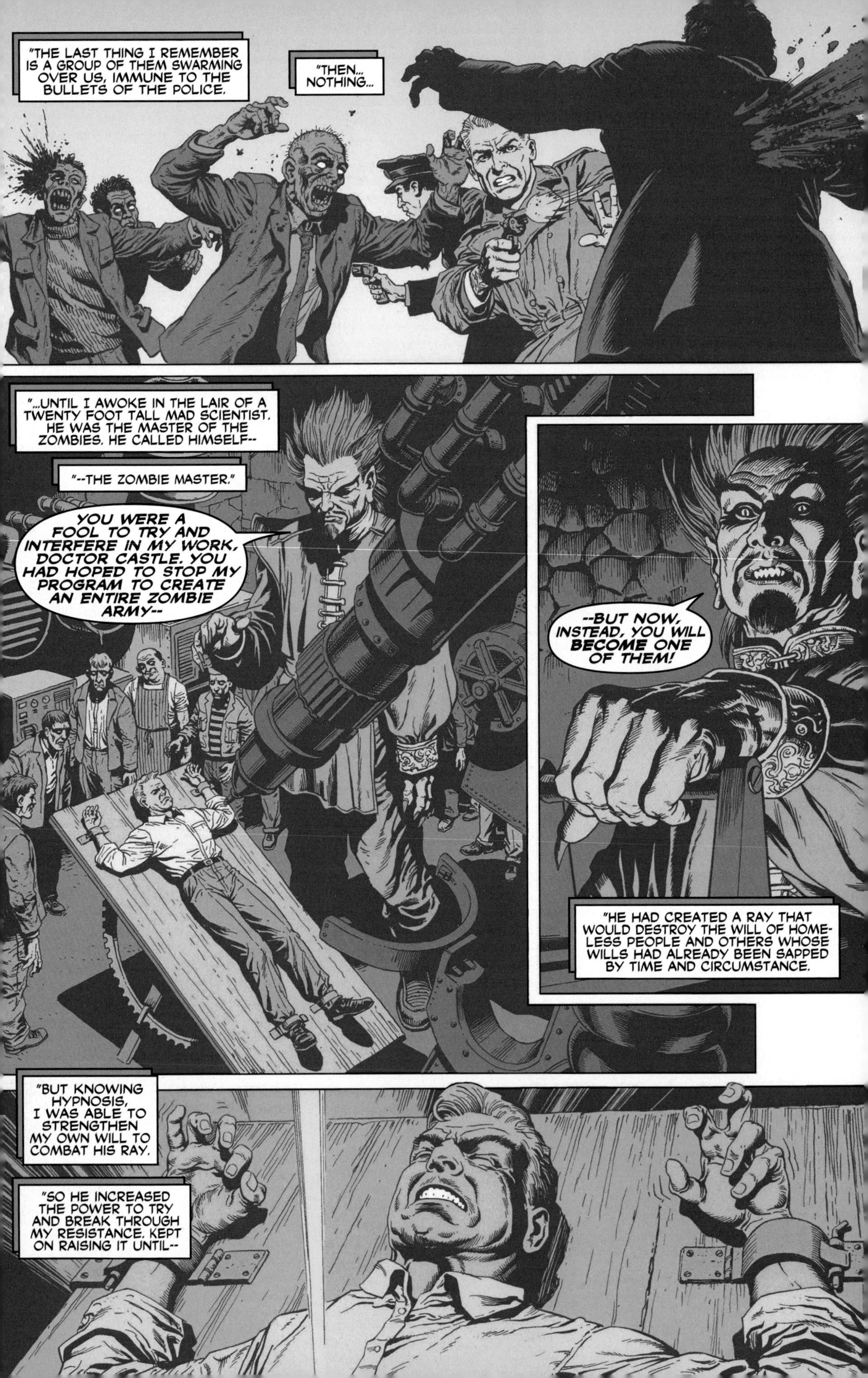
"THE LAST THING I REMEMBER IS A GROUP OF THEM SWARMING OVER US, IMMUNE TO THE BULLETS OF THE POLICE.
"THEN... NOTHING...
"...UNTIL I AWOKE IN THE LAIR OF A TWENTY FOOT TALL MAD SCIENTIST. HE WAS THE MASTER OF THE ZOMBIES. HE CALLED HIMSELF--
"--THE ZOMBIE MASTER."
YOU WERE A FOOL TO TRY AND INTERFERE IN MY WORK, DOCTOR CASTLE. YOU HAD HOPED TO STOP MY PROGRAM TO CREATE AN ENTIRE ZOMBIE ARMY--
--BUT NOW, INSTEAD, YOU WILL BECOME ONE OF THEM!
"HE HAD CREATED A RAY THAT WOULD DESTROY THE WILL OF HOMELESS PEOPLE AND OTHERS WHOSE WILLS HAD ALREADY BEEN SAPPED BY TIME AND CIRCUMSTANCE.
"BUT KNOWING HYPNOSIS, I WAS ABLE TO STRENGTHEN MY OWN WILL TO COMBAT HIS RAY.
"SO HE INCREASED THE POWER TO TRY AND BREAK THROUGH MY RESISTANCE. KEPT ON RAISING IT UNTIL--

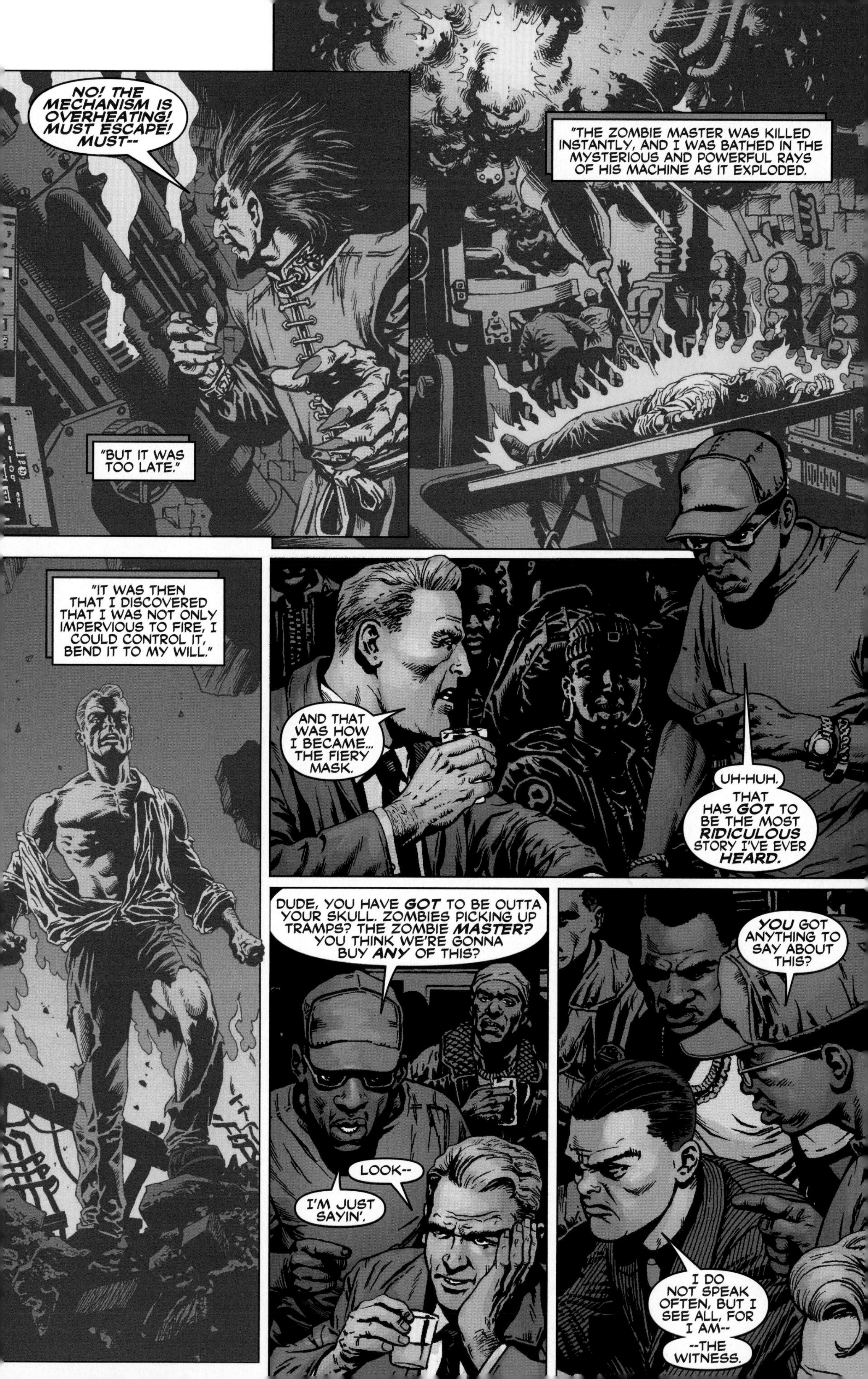
NO! THE MECHANISM IS OVERHEATING! MUST ESCAPE! MUST--
"BUT IT WAS TOO LATE."
"THE ZOMBIE MASTER WAS KILLED INSTANTLY, AND I WAS BATHED IN THE MYSTERIOUS AND POWERFUL RAYS OF HIS MACHINE AS IT EXPLODED.
"IT WAS THEN THAT I DISCOVERED THAT I WAS NOT ONLY IMPERVIOUS TO FIRE, I COULD CONTROL IT, BEND IT TO MY WILL."
AND THAT WAS HOW I BECAME... THE FIERY MASK.
UH-HUH. THAT HAS GOT TO BE THE MOST RIDICULOUS STORY I'VE EVER HEARD.
DUDE, YOU HAVE GOT TO BE OUTTA YOUR SKULL. ZOMBIES PICKING UP TRAMPS? THE ZOMBIE MASTER? YOU THINK WE'RE GONNA BUY ANY OF THIS?
LOOK--
I'M JUST SAYIN'.
YOU GOT ANYTHING TO SAY ABOUT THIS?
I DO NOT SPEAK OFTEN, BUT I SEE ALL, FOR I AM--
--THE WITNESS.

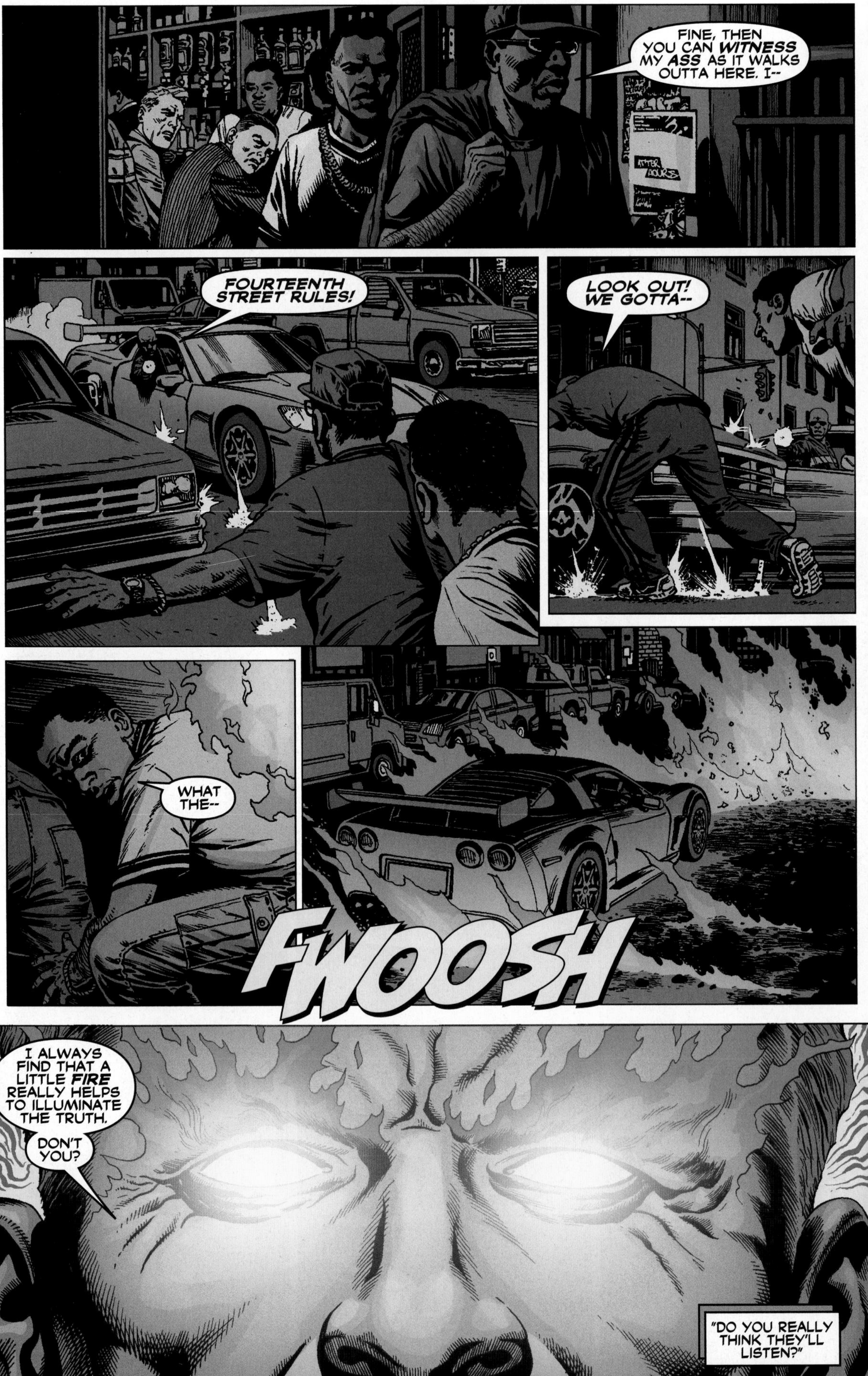
FINE, THEN YOU CAN WITNESS MY ASS AS IT WALKS OUTTA HERE. I--
FOURTEENTH STREET RULES!
LOOK OUT! WE GOTTA--
WHAT THE--
FWOOSH
I ALWAYS FIND THAT A LITTLE FIRE REALLY HELPS TO ILLUMINATE THE TRUTH.
DON'T YOU?
"DO YOU REALLY THINK THEY'LL LISTEN?"

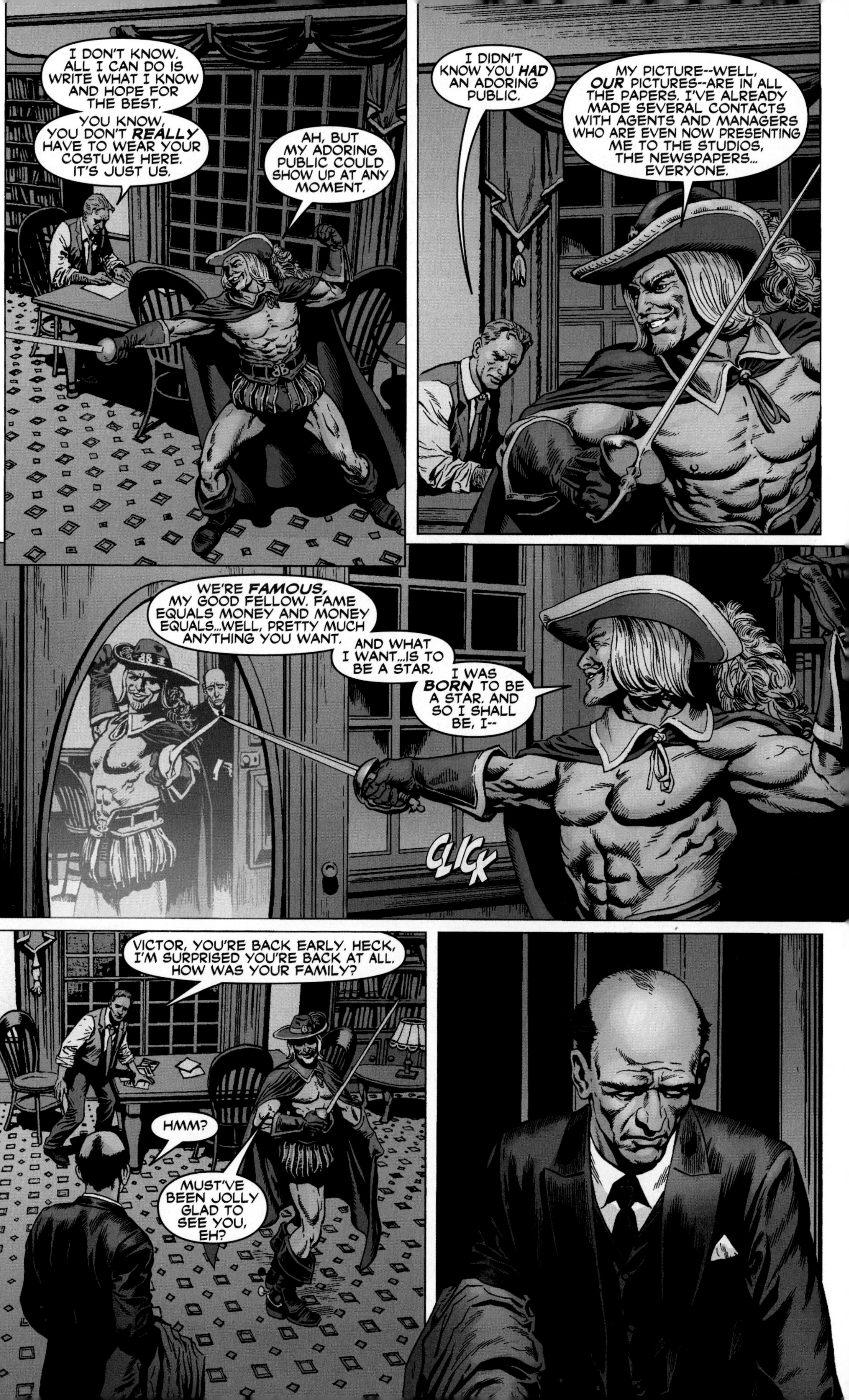
I DON'T KNOW. ALL I CAN DO IS WRITE WHAT I KNOW AND HOPE FOR THE BEST.
YOU KNOW, YOU DON'T REALLY HAVE TO WEAR YOUR COSTUME HERE. IT'S JUST US.
AH, BUT MY ADORING PUBLIC COULD SHOW UP AT ANY MOMENT.
I DIDN'T KNOW YOU HAD AN ADORING PUBLIC.
MY PICTURE--WELL, OUR PICTURES--ARE IN ALL THE PAPERS. I'VE ALREADY MADE SEVERAL CONTACTS WITH AGENTS AND MANAGERS WHO ARE EVEN NOW PRESENTING ME TO THE STUDIOS, THE NEWSPAPERS... EVERYONE.
WE'RE FAMOUS, MY GOOD FELLOW. FAME EQUALS MONEY AND MONEY EQUALS...WELL, PRETTY MUCH ANYTHING YOU WANT.
AND WHAT I WANT...IS TO BE A STAR.
I WAS BORN TO BE A STAR. AND SO I SHALL BE, I--
CLICK
VICTOR, YOU'RE BACK EARLY. HECK, I'M SURPRISED YOU'RE BACK AT ALL. HOW WAS YOUR FAMILY?
HMM?
MUST'VE BEEN JOLLY GLAD TO SEE YOU, EH?

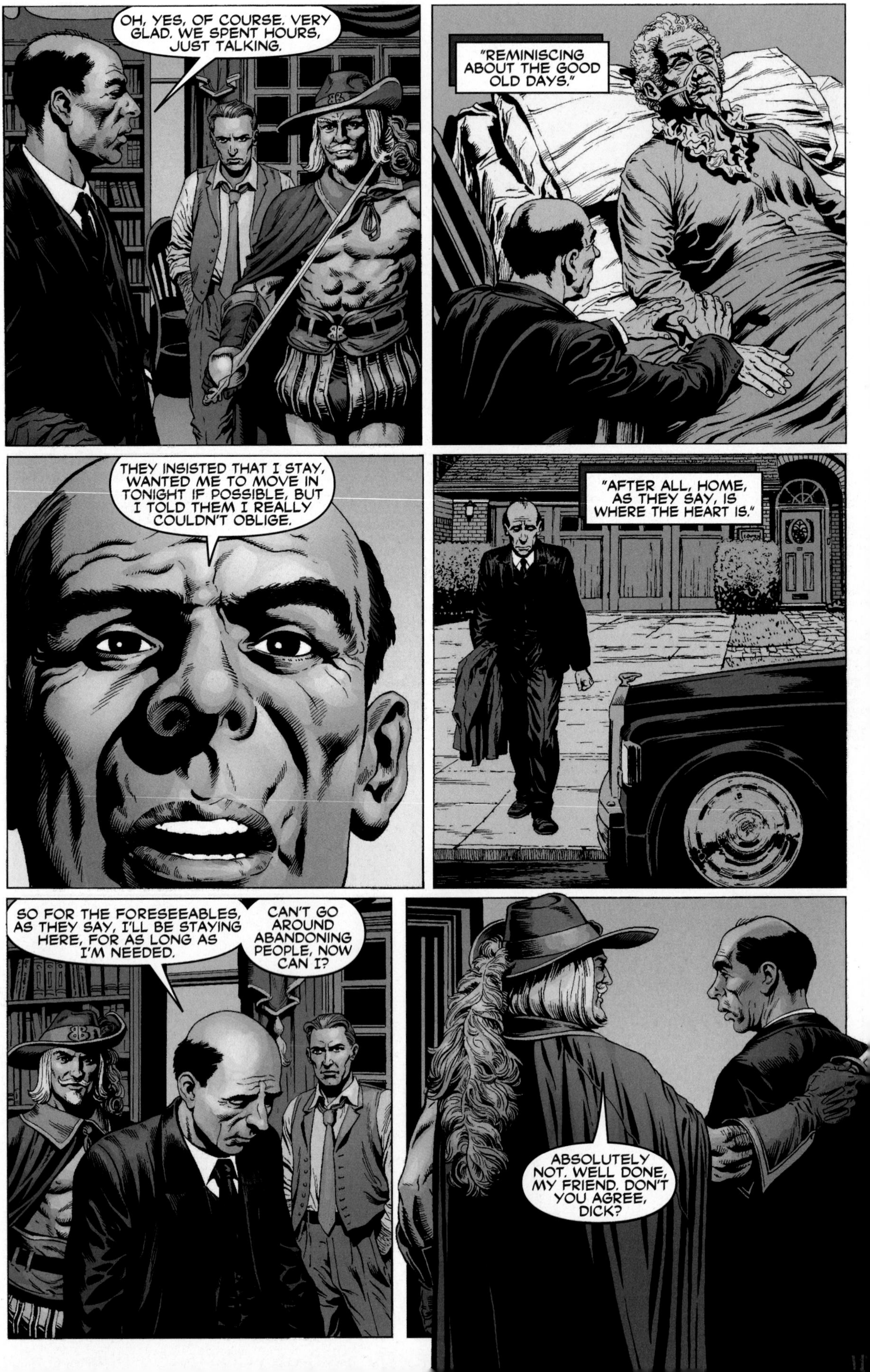
OH, YES, OF COURSE. VERY GLAD. WE SPENT HOURS, JUST TALKING.
"REMINISCING ABOUT THE GOOD OLD DAYS."
THEY INSISTED THAT I STAY, WANTED ME TO MOVE IN TONIGHT IF POSSIBLE, BUT I TOLD THEM I REALLY COULDN'T OBLIGE.
"AFTER ALL, HOME, AS THEY SAY, IS WHERE THE HEART IS."
SO FOR THE FORESEEABLES, AS THEY SAY, I'LL BE STAYING HERE, FOR AS LONG AS I'M NEEDED.
CAN'T GO AROUND ABANDONING PEOPLE, NOW CAN I?
ABSOLUTELY NOT. WELL DONE, MY FRIEND. DON'T YOU AGREE, DICK?

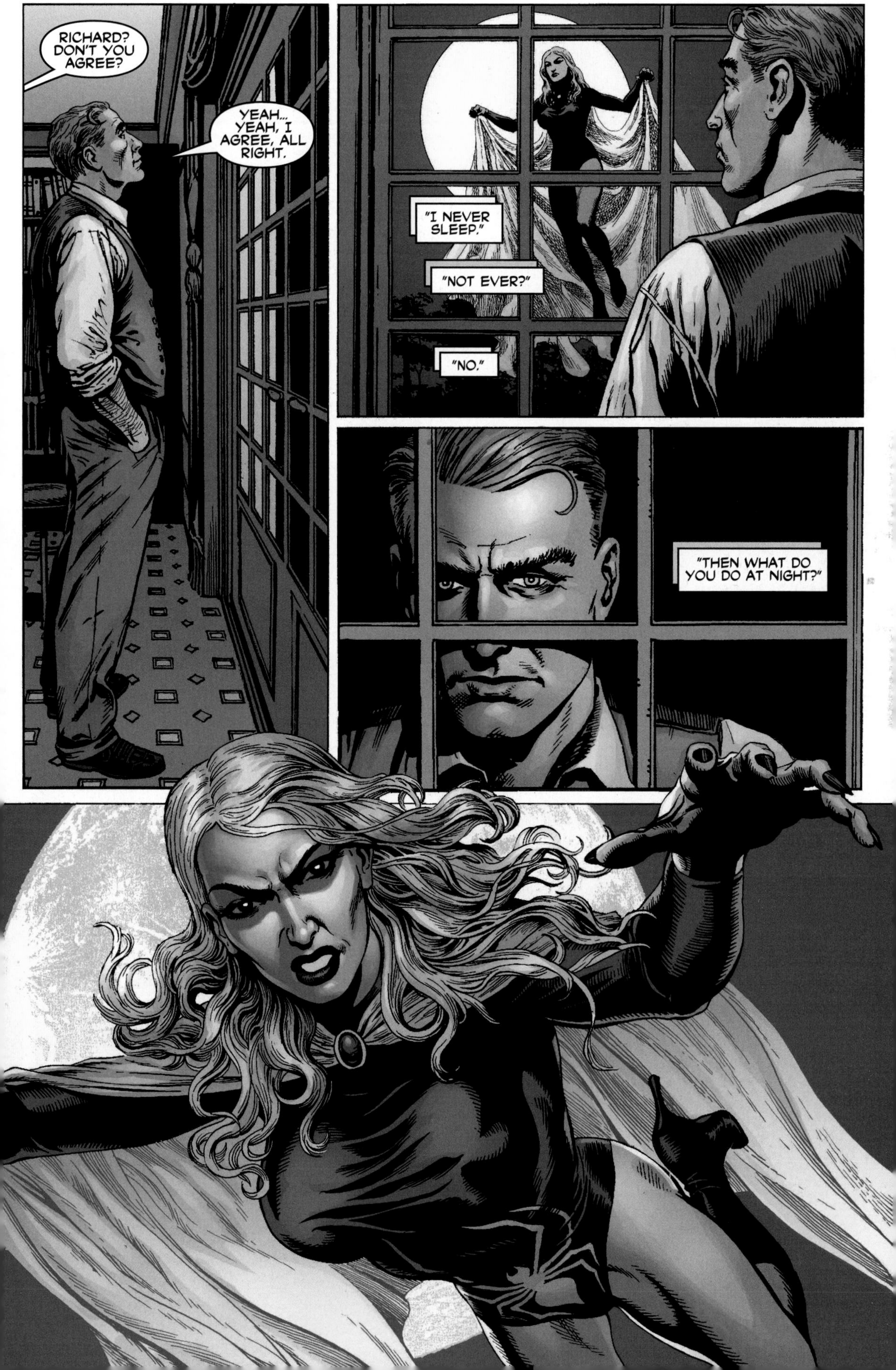
RICHARD? DON'T YOU AGREE?
YEAH... YEAH, I AGREE, ALL RIGHT.
"I NEVER SLEEP."
"NOT EVER?"
"NO."
"THEN WHAT DO YOU DO AT NIGHT?"

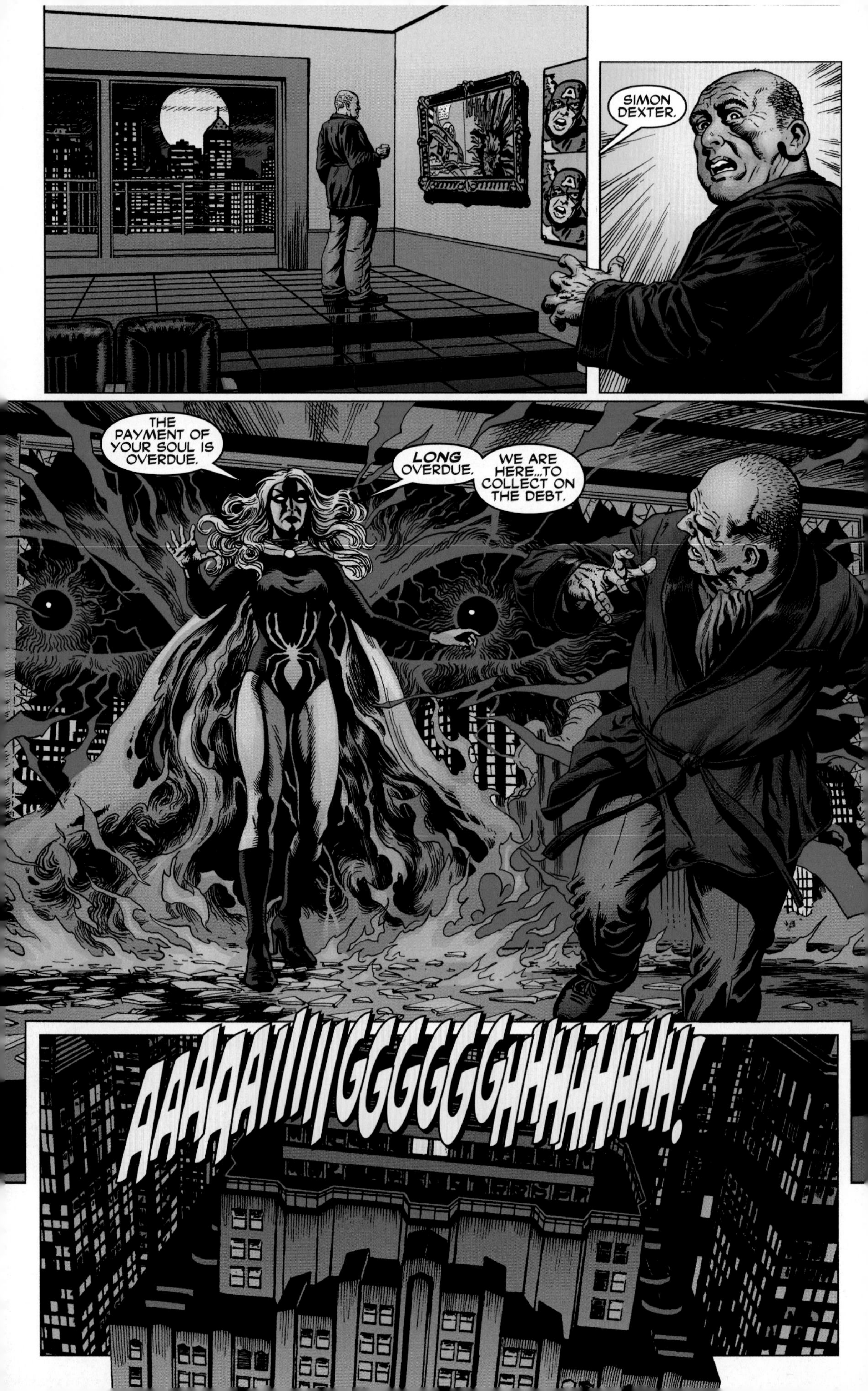
SIMON DEXTER.
THE PAYMENT OF YOUR SOUL IS OVERDUE.
LONG OVERDUE.
WE ARE HERE...TO COLLECT ON THE DEBT.
AAAAIIIIIGGGGGGHHHHHHH!

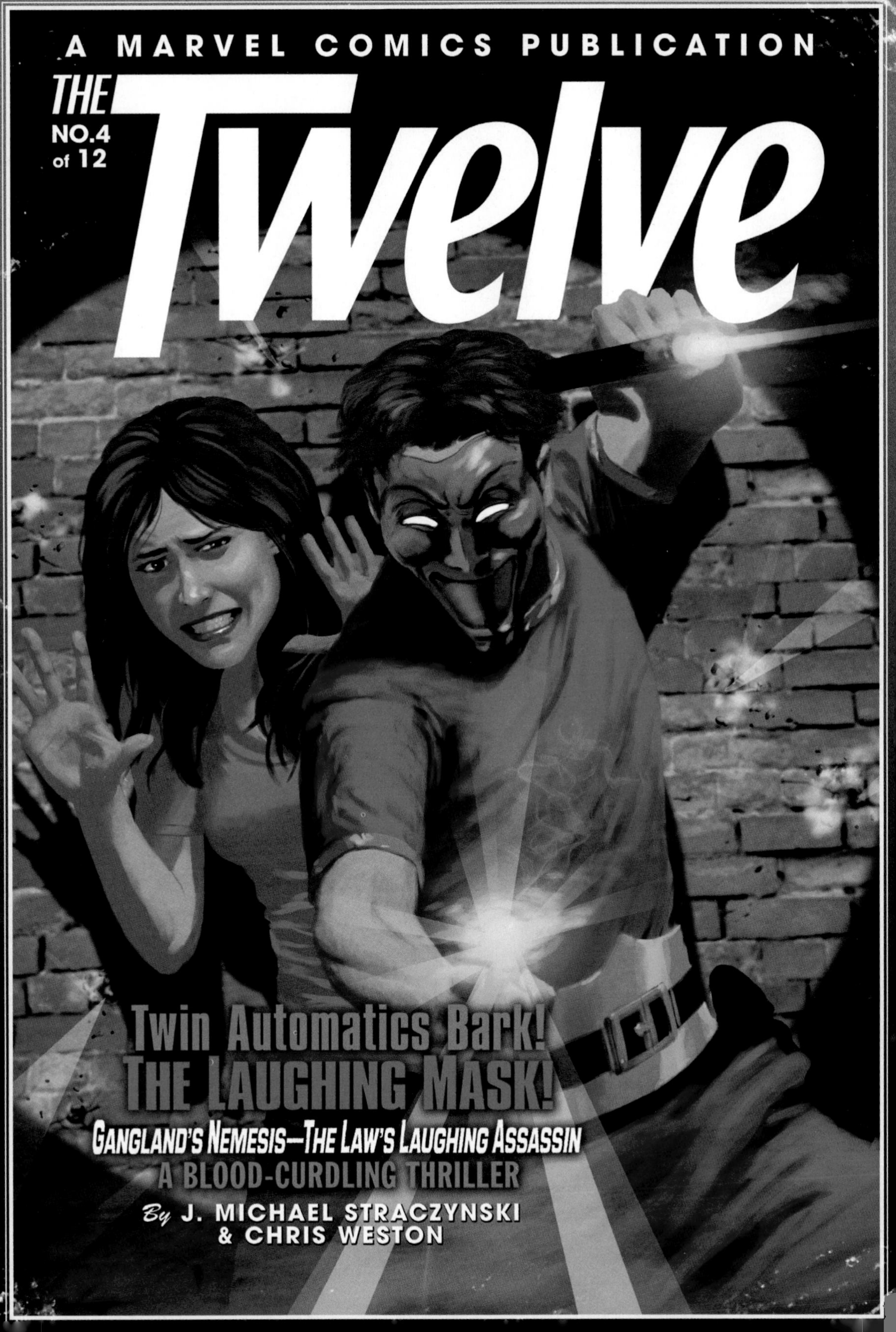
A MARVEL COMICS PUBLICATION
THE
NO.4
of 12
Twelve
Twin Automatics Bark!
THE LAUGHING MASK!
GANGLAND'S NEMESIS—THE LAW'S LAUGHING ASSASSIN
A BLOOD-CURDLING THRILLER
By J. MICHAEL STRACZYNSKI
& CHRIS WESTON

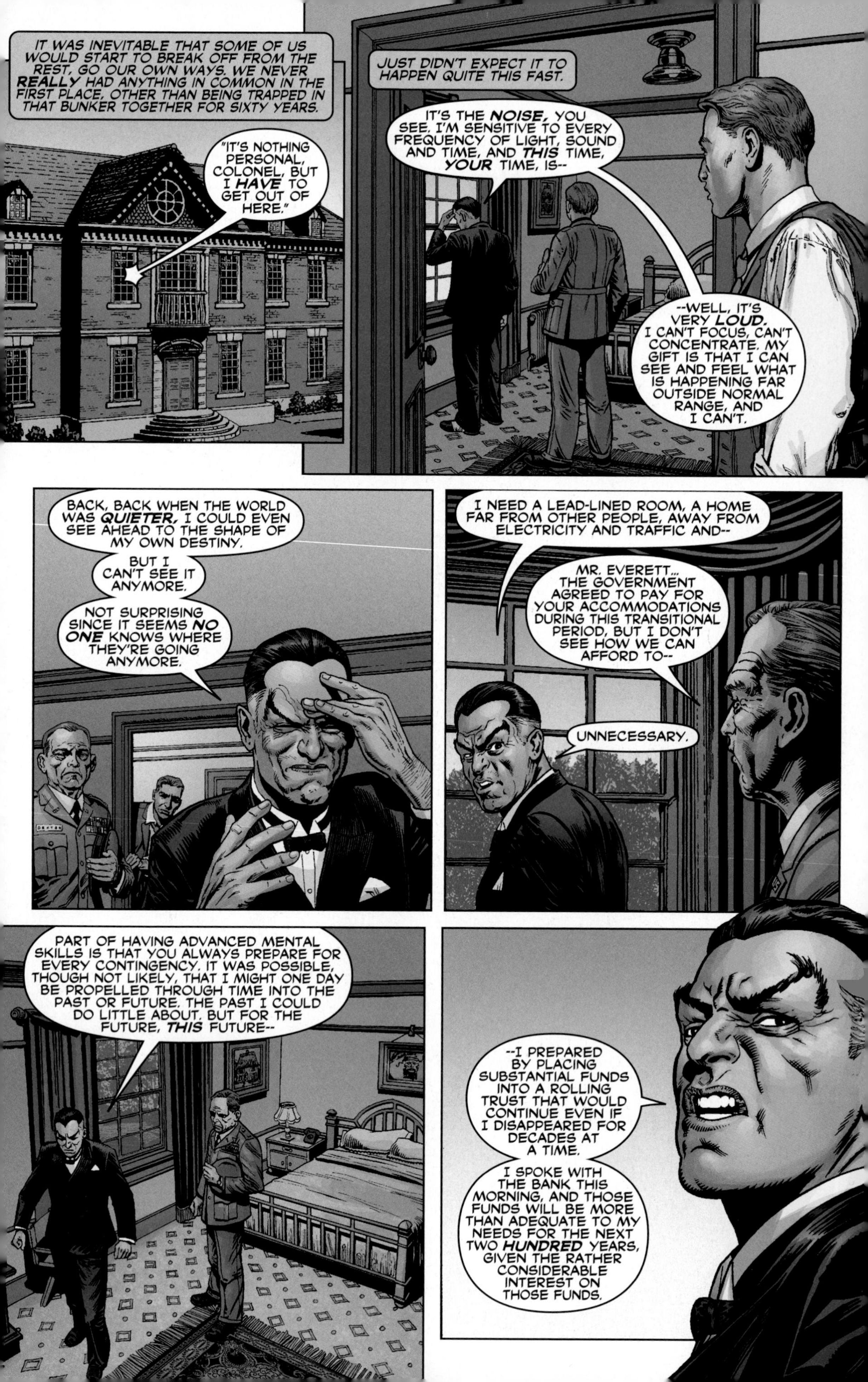
IT WAS INEVITABLE THAT SOME OF US WOULD START TO BREAK OFF FROM THE REST, GO OUR OWN WAYS. WE NEVER REALLY HAD ANYTHING IN COMMON IN THE FIRST PLACE, OTHER THAN BEING TRAPPED IN THAT BUNKER TOGETHER FOR SIXTY YEARS.
"IT'S NOTHING PERSONAL, COLONEL, BUT I HAVE TO GET OUT OF HERE."
JUST DIDN'T EXPECT IT TO HAPPEN QUITE THIS FAST.
IT'S THE NOISE, YOU SEE. I'M SENSITIVE TO EVERY FREQUENCY OF LIGHT, SOUND AND TIME, AND THIS TIME, YOUR TIME, IS--
--WELL, IT'S VERY LOUD. I CAN'T FOCUS, CAN'T CONCENTRATE. MY GIFT IS THAT I CAN SEE AND FEEL WHAT IS HAPPENING FAR OUTSIDE NORMAL RANGE, AND I CAN'T.
BACK, BACK WHEN THE WORLD WAS QUIETER, I COULD EVEN SEE AHEAD TO THE SHAPE OF MY OWN DESTINY.
BUT I CAN'T SEE IT ANYMORE.
NOT SURPRISING SINCE IT SEEMS NO ONE KNOWS WHERE THEY'RE GOING ANYMORE.
I NEED A LEAD-LINED ROOM, A HOME FAR FROM OTHER PEOPLE, AWAY FROM ELECTRICITY AND TRAFFIC AND--
MR. EVERETT... THE GOVERNMENT AGREED TO PAY FOR YOUR ACCOMMODATIONS DURING THIS TRANSITIONAL PERIOD, BUT I DON'T SEE HOW WE CAN AFFORD TO--
UNNECESSARY.
PART OF HAVING ADVANCED MENTAL SKILLS IS THAT YOU ALWAYS PREPARE FOR EVERY CONTINGENCY. IT WAS POSSIBLE, THOUGH NOT LIKELY, THAT I MIGHT ONE DAY BE PROPELLED THROUGH TIME INTO THE PAST OR FUTURE. THE PAST I COULD DO LITTLE ABOUT. BUT FOR THE FUTURE, THIS FUTURE--
--I PREPARED BY PLACING SUBSTANTIAL FUNDS INTO A ROLLING TRUST THAT WOULD CONTINUE EVEN IF I DISAPPEARED FOR DECADES AT A TIME.
I SPOKE WITH THE BANK THIS MORNING, AND THOSE FUNDS WILL BE MORE THAN ADEQUATE TO MY NEEDS FOR THE NEXT TWO HUNDRED YEARS, GIVEN THE RATHER CONSIDERABLE INTEREST ON THOSE FUNDS.

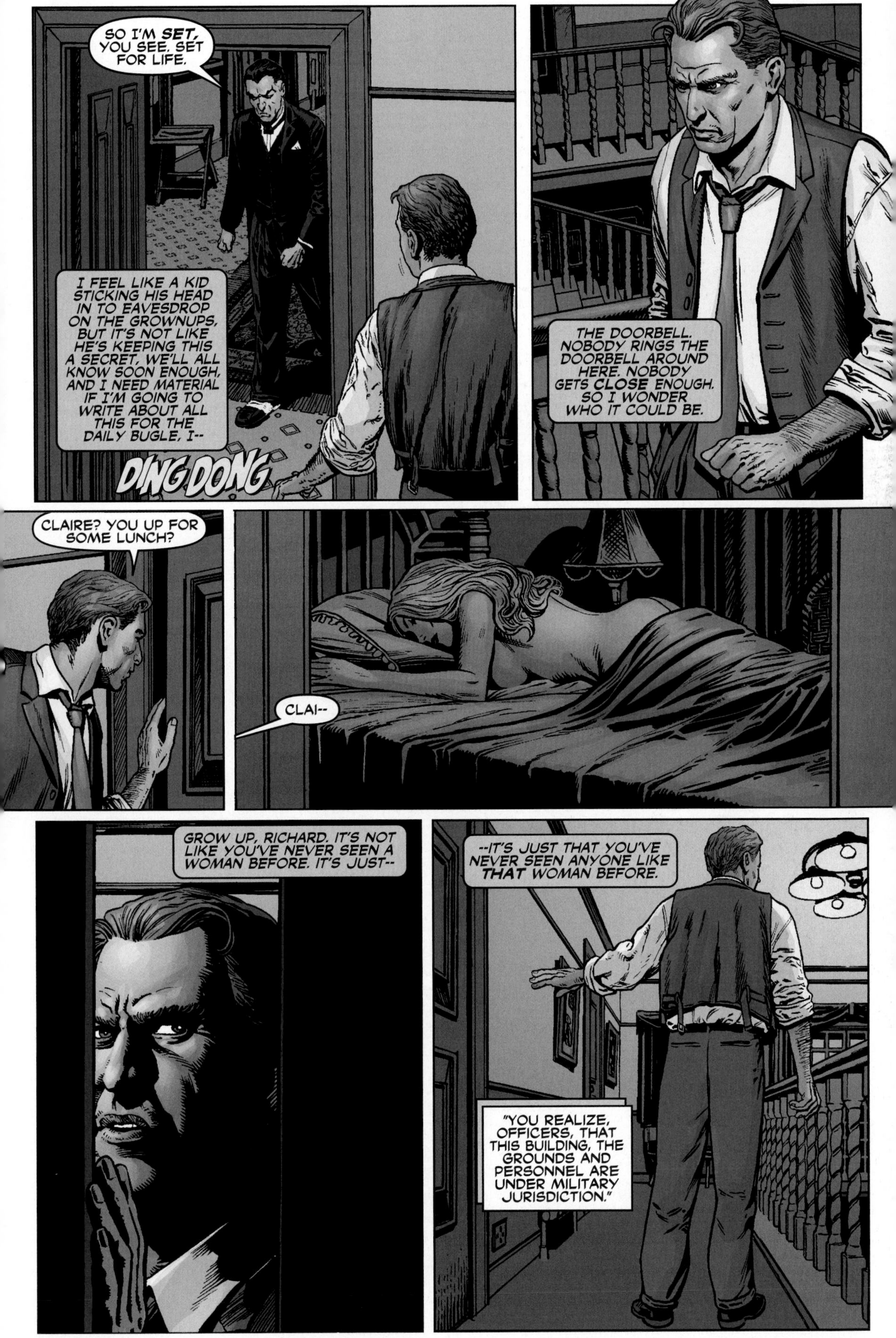
SO I'M SET, YOU SEE. SET FOR LIFE.
I FEEL LIKE A KID STICKING HIS HEAD IN TO EAVESDROP ON THE GROWNUPS, BUT IT'S NOT LIKE HE'S KEEPING THIS A SECRET, WE'LL ALL KNOW SOON ENOUGH, AND I NEED MATERIAL IF I'M GOING TO WRITE ABOUT ALL THIS FOR THE DAILY BUGLE, I--
DING DONG
THE DOORBELL. NOBODY RINGS THE DOORBELL AROUND HERE. NOBODY GETS CLOSE ENOUGH. SO I WONDER WHO IT COULD BE.
CLAIRE? YOU UP FOR SOME LUNCH?
CLAI--
GROW UP, RICHARD. IT'S NOT LIKE YOU'VE NEVER SEEN A WOMAN BEFORE. IT'S JUST--
--IT'S JUST THAT YOU'VE NEVER SEEN ANYONE LIKE THAT WOMAN BEFORE.
"YOU REALIZE, OFFICERS, THAT THIS BUILDING, THE GROUNDS AND PERSONNEL ARE UNDER MILITARY JURISDICTION."

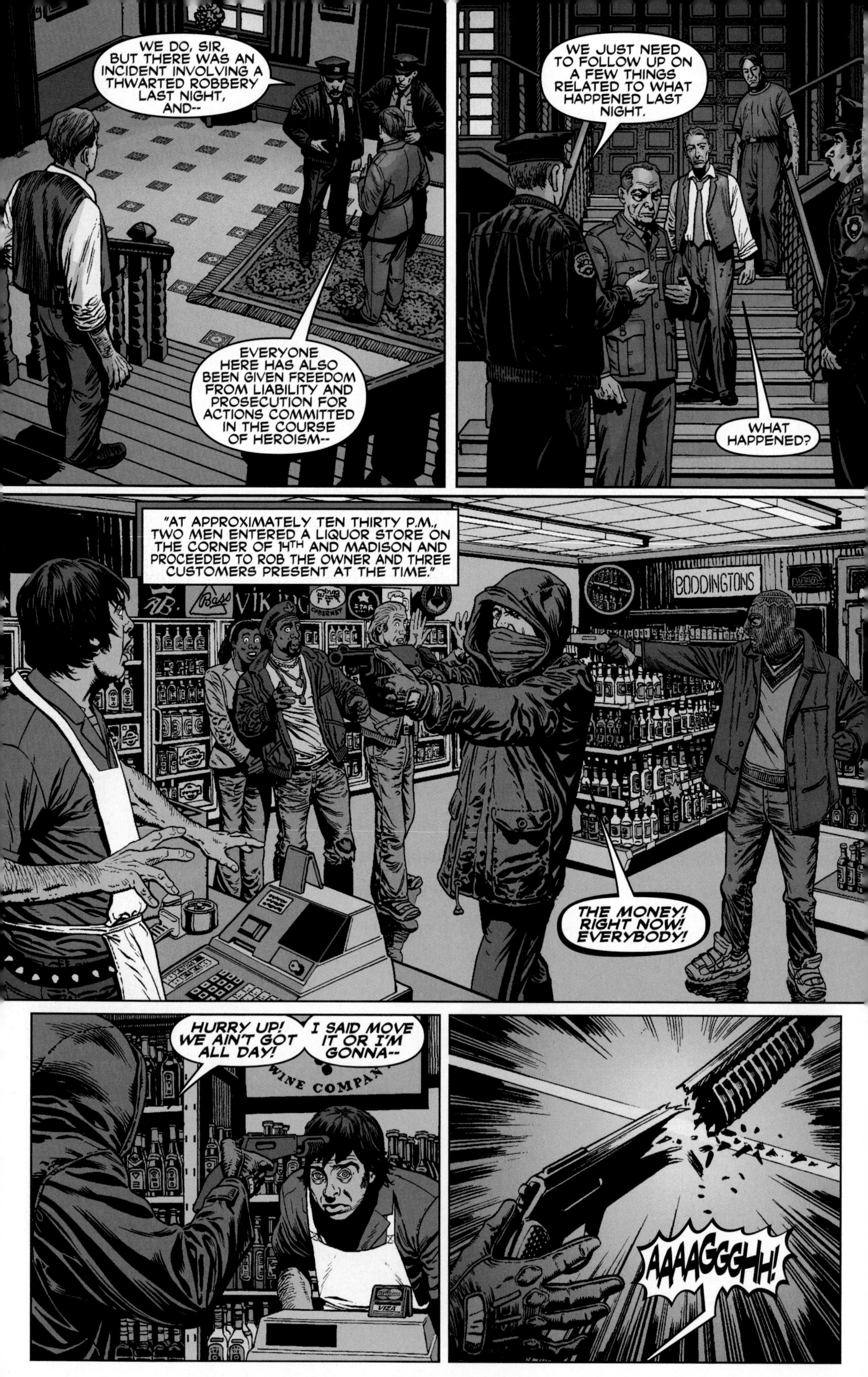
WE DO, SIR, BUT THERE WAS AN INCIDENT INVOLVING A THWARTED ROBBERY LAST NIGHT, AND--
EVERYONE HERE HAS ALSO BEEN GIVEN FREEDOM FROM LIABILITY AND PROSECUTION FOR ACTIONS COMMITTED IN THE COURSE OF HEROISM--
WE JUST NEED TO FOLLOW UP ON A FEW THINGS RELATED TO WHAT HAPPENED LAST NIGHT.
WHAT HAPPENED?
"AT APPROXIMATELY TEN THIRTY P.M., TWO MEN ENTERED A LIQUOR STORE ON THE CORNER OF 14TH AND MADISON AND PROCEEDED TO ROB THE OWNER AND THREE CUSTOMERS PRESENT AT THE TIME."
BODDINGTONS
THE MONEY! RIGHT NOW! EVERYBODY!
HURRY UP! WE AIN'T GOT ALL DAY!
I SAID MOVE IT OR I'M GONNA--
WINE COMPAN
VIZA
AAAAGGGHH!

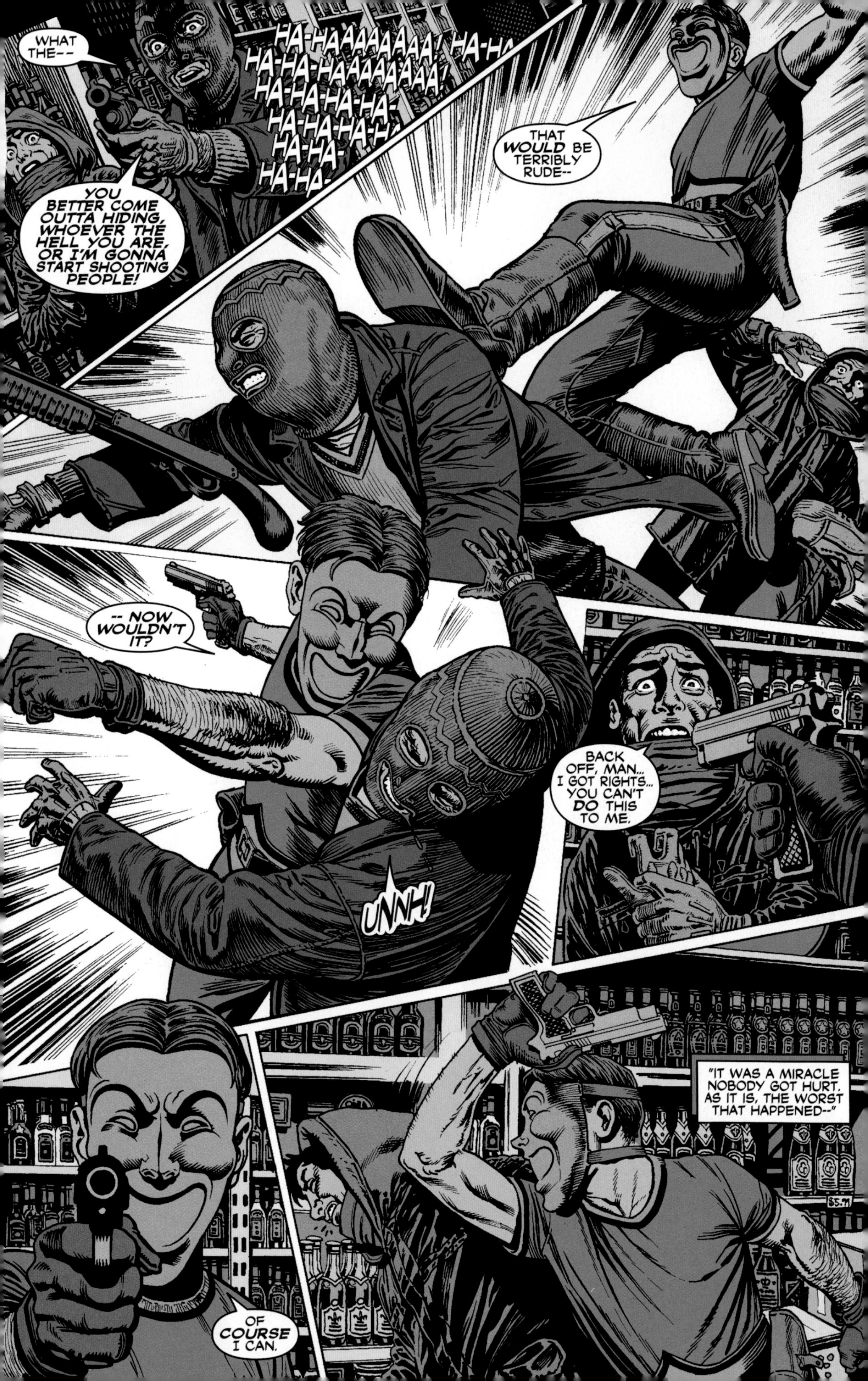
WHAT THE--
HA-HAAAAAAAA! HA-HA HA-HA-HAAAAAAAA! HA-HA-HA-HA- HA-HA-HA-HA- HA-HA- HA-HA-
YOU BETTER COME OUTTA HIDING, WHOEVER THE HELL YOU ARE, OR I'M GONNA START SHOOTING PEOPLE!
THAT WOULD BE TERRIBLY RUDE--
-- NOW WOULDN'T IT?
BACK OFF, MAN... I GOT RIGHTS... YOU CAN'T DO THIS TO ME.
UNNH!
OF COURSE I CAN.
"IT WAS A MIRACLE NOBODY GOT HURT. AS IT IS, THE WORST THAT HAPPENED--"

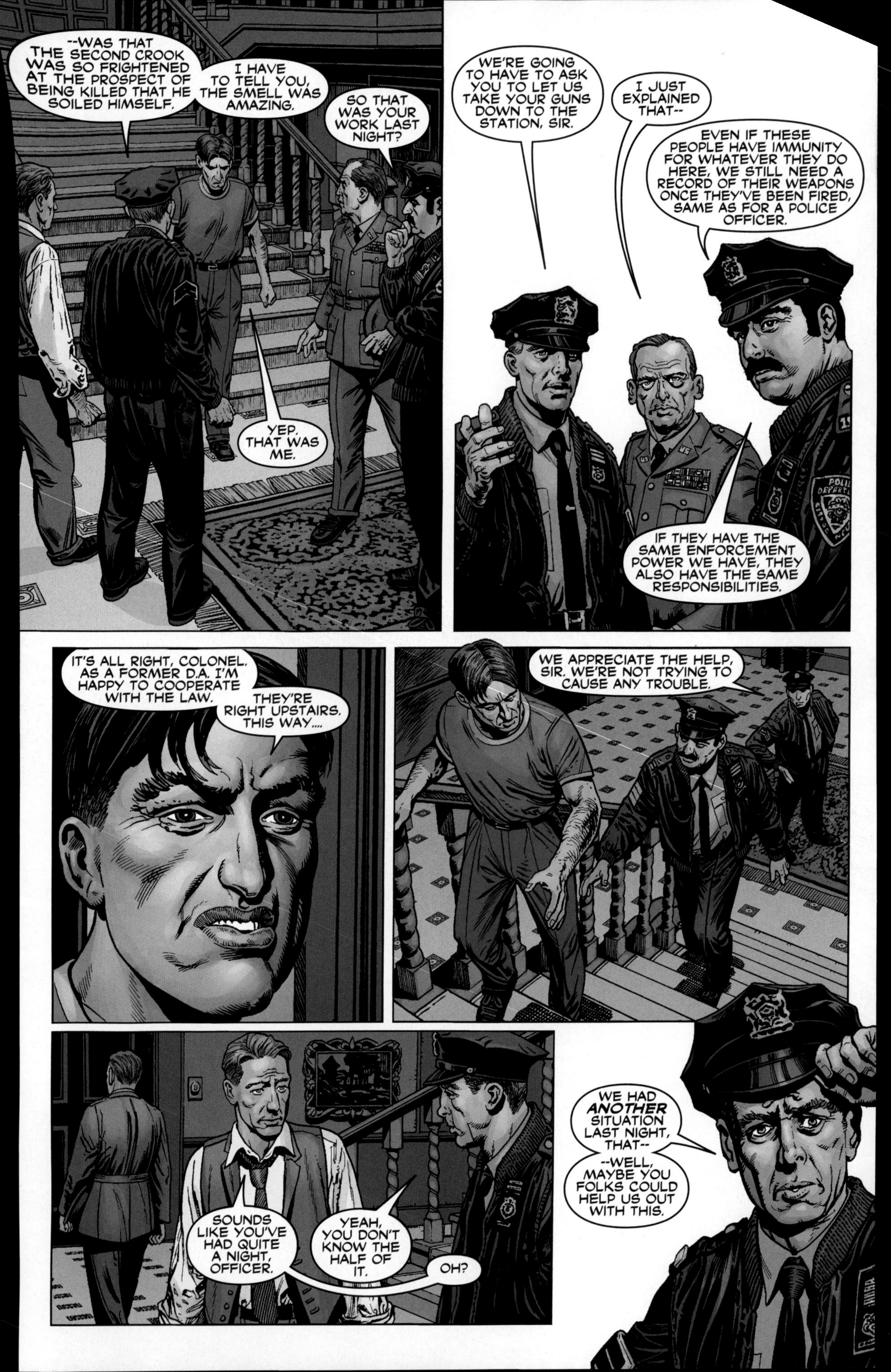
--WAS THAT THE SECOND CROOK WAS SO FRIGHTENED AT THE PROSPECT OF BEING KILLED THAT HE SOILED HIMSELF.
I HAVE TO TELL YOU, THE SMELL WAS AMAZING.
SO THAT WAS YOUR WORK LAST NIGHT?
YEP. THAT WAS ME.
WE'RE GOING TO HAVE TO ASK YOU TO LET US TAKE YOUR GUNS DOWN TO THE STATION, SIR.
I JUST EXPLAINED THAT--
EVEN IF THESE PEOPLE HAVE IMMUNITY FOR WHATEVER THEY DO HERE, WE STILL NEED A RECORD OF THEIR WEAPONS ONCE THEY'VE BEEN FIRED, SAME AS FOR A POLICE OFFICER.
IF THEY HAVE THE SAME ENFORCEMENT POWER WE HAVE, THEY ALSO HAVE THE SAME RESPONSIBILITIES.
IT'S ALL RIGHT, COLONEL. AS A FORMER D.A. I'M HAPPY TO COOPERATE WITH THE LAW.
THEY'RE RIGHT UPSTAIRS. THIS WAY....
WE APPRECIATE THE HELP, SIR. WE'RE NOT TRYING TO CAUSE ANY TROUBLE.
SOUNDS LIKE YOU'VE HAD QUITE A NIGHT, OFFICER.
YEAH, YOU DON'T KNOW THE HALF OF IT.
OH?
WE HAD ANOTHER SITUATION LAST NIGHT, THAT--
--WELL, MAYBE YOU FOLKS COULD HELP US OUT WITH THIS.

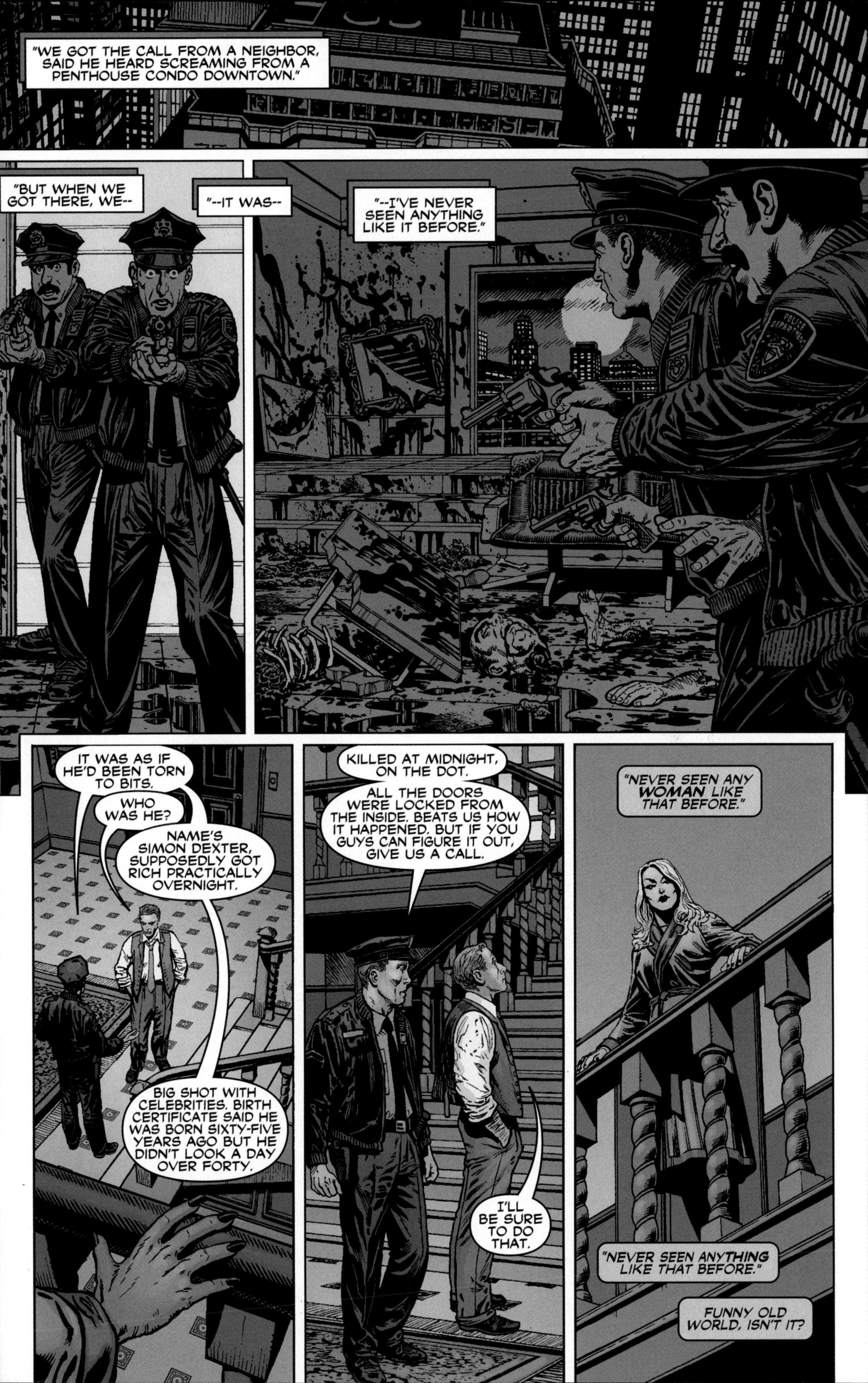
"WE GOT THE CALL FROM A NEIGHBOR, SAID HE HEARD SCREAMING FROM A PENTHOUSE CONDO DOWNTOWN."
"BUT WHEN WE GOT THERE, WE--
"--IT WAS--
"--I'VE NEVER SEEN ANYTHING LIKE IT BEFORE."
IT WAS AS IF HE'D BEEN TORN TO BITS.
WHO WAS HE?
NAME'S SIMON DEXTER, SUPPOSEDLY GOT RICH PRACTICALLY OVERNIGHT.
BIG SHOT WITH CELEBRITIES. BIRTH CERTIFICATE SAID HE WAS BORN SIXTY-FIVE YEARS AGO BUT HE DIDN'T LOOK A DAY OVER FORTY.
KILLED AT MIDNIGHT, ON THE DOT.
ALL THE DOORS WERE LOCKED FROM THE INSIDE. BEATS US HOW IT HAPPENED. BUT IF YOU GUYS CAN FIGURE IT OUT, GIVE US A CALL.
I'LL BE SURE TO DO THAT.
"NEVER SEEN ANY WOMAN LIKE THAT BEFORE."
"NEVER SEEN ANYTHING LIKE THAT BEFORE."
FUNNY OLD WORLD, ISN'T IT?

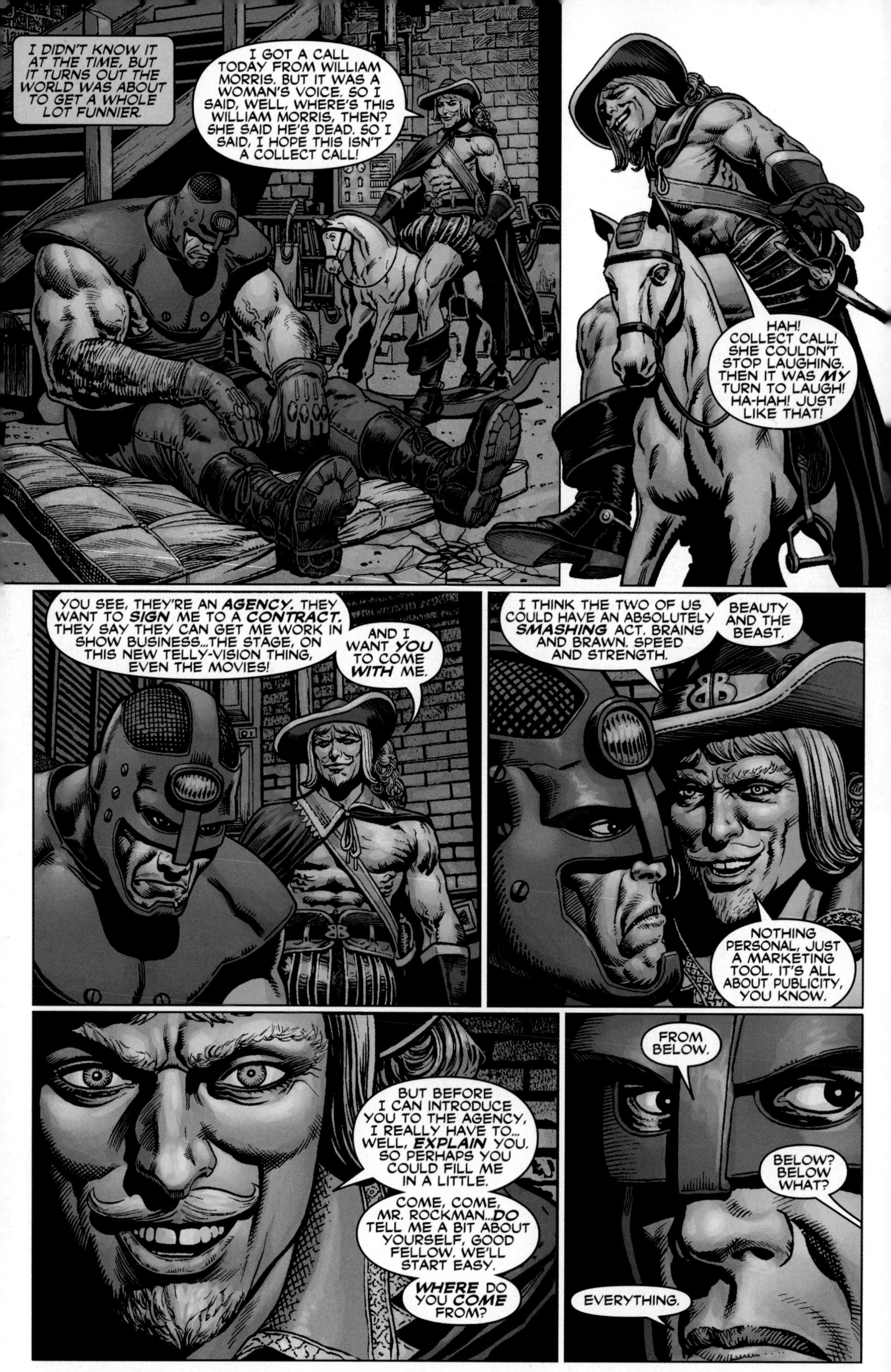
I DIDN'T KNOW IT AT THE TIME, BUT IT TURNS OUT THE WORLD WAS ABOUT TO GET A WHOLE LOT FUNNIER.
I GOT A CALL TODAY FROM WILLIAM MORRIS, BUT IT WAS A WOMAN'S VOICE. SO I SAID, WELL, WHERE'S THIS WILLIAM MORRIS, THEN? SHE SAID HE'S DEAD. SO I SAID, I HOPE THIS ISN'T A COLLECT CALL!
HAH! COLLECT CALL! SHE COULDN'T STOP LAUGHING. THEN IT WAS MY TURN TO LAUGH! HA-HAH! JUST LIKE THAT!
YOU SEE, THEY'RE AN AGENCY. THEY WANT TO SIGN ME TO A CONTRACT. THEY SAY THEY CAN GET ME WORK IN SHOW BUSINESS...THE STAGE, ON THIS NEW TELLY-VISION THING, EVEN THE MOVIES!
AND I WANT YOU TO COME WITH ME.
I THINK THE TWO OF US COULD HAVE AN ABSOLUTELY SMASHING ACT. BRAINS AND BRAWN. SPEED AND STRENGTH.
BEAUTY AND THE BEAST.
NOTHING PERSONAL, JUST A MARKETING TOOL. IT'S ALL ABOUT PUBLICITY, YOU KNOW.
BUT BEFORE I CAN INTRODUCE YOU TO THE AGENCY, I REALLY HAVE TO... WELL, EXPLAIN YOU. SO PERHAPS YOU COULD FILL ME IN A LITTLE.
COME, COME, MR. ROCKMAN...DO TELL ME A BIT ABOUT YOURSELF, GOOD FELLOW. WE'LL START EASY.
WHERE DO YOU COME FROM?
FROM BELOW.
BELOW? BELOW WHAT?
EVERYTHING.

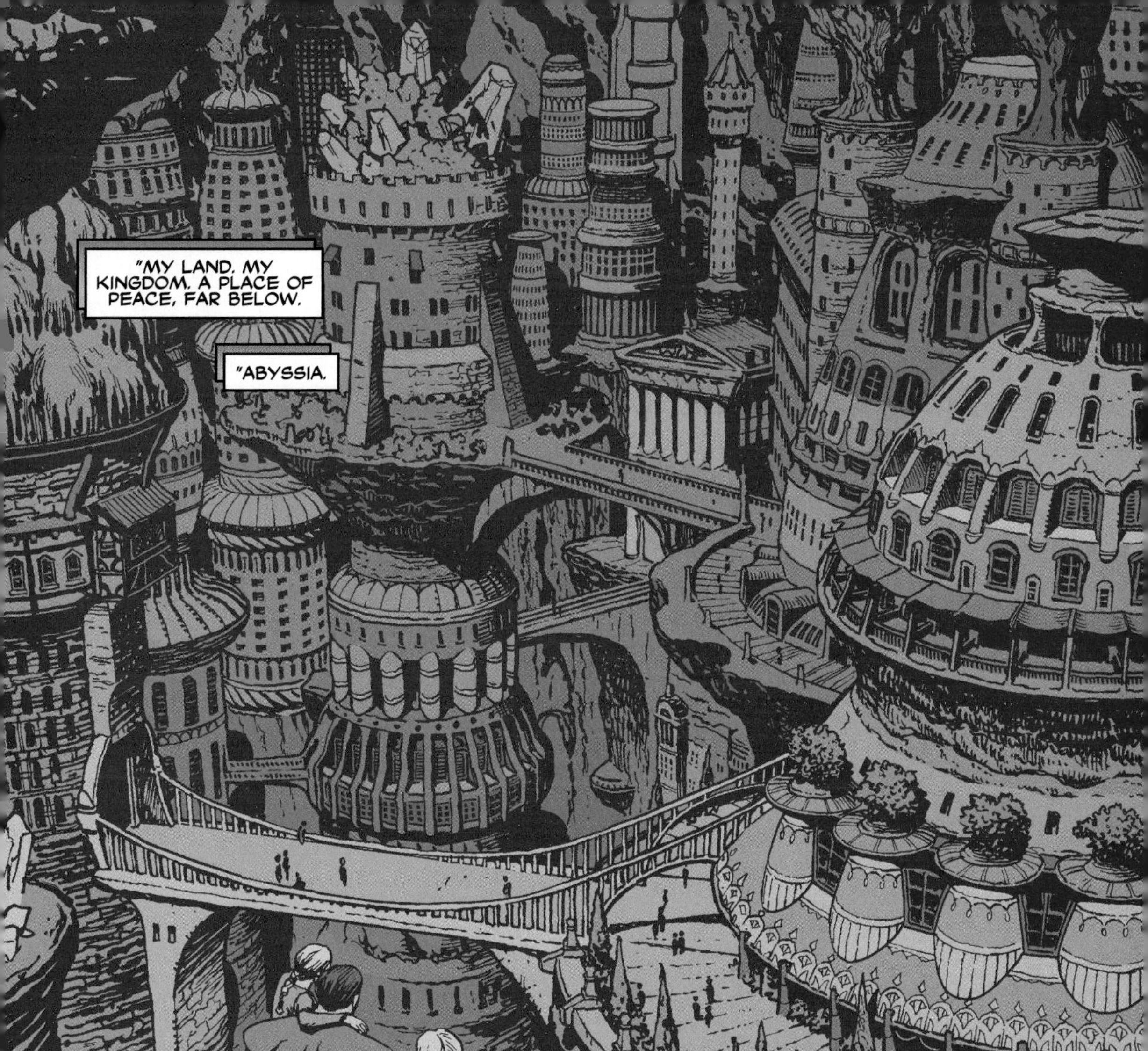
"MY LAND. MY KINGDOM. A PLACE OF PEACE, FAR BELOW.
"ABYSSIA.
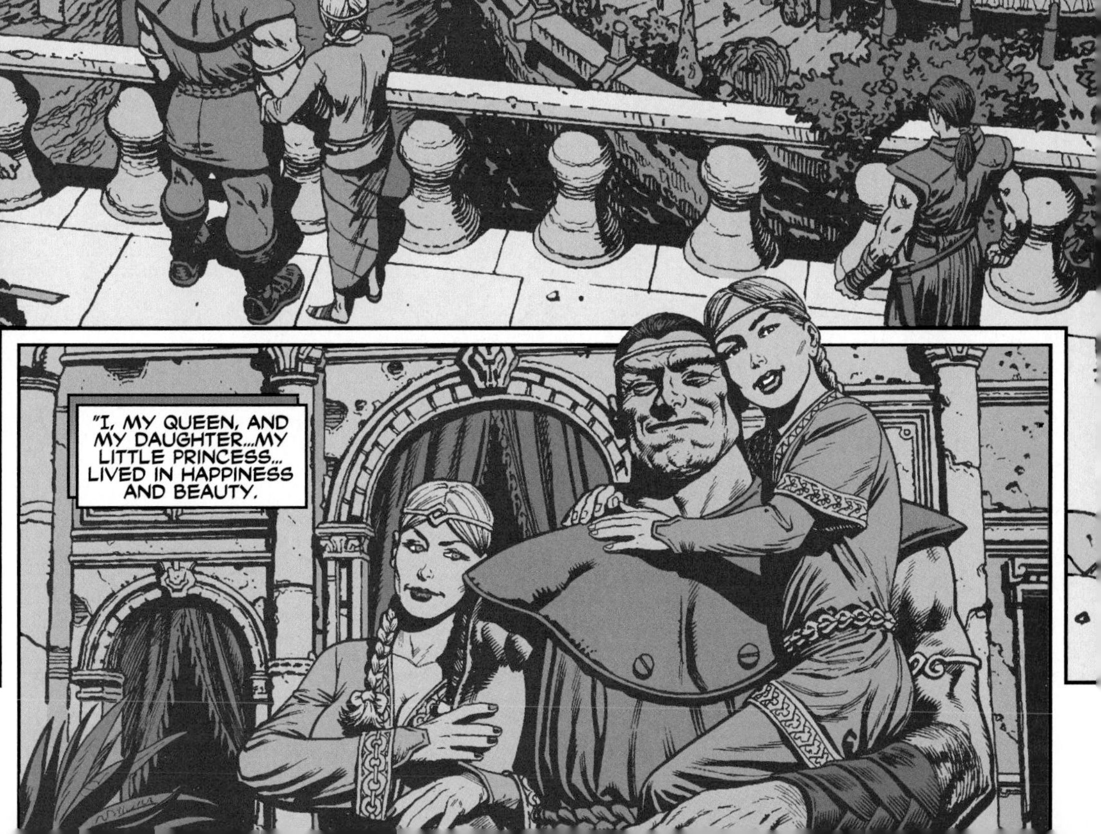
"I, MY QUEEN, AND MY DAUGHTER...MY LITTLE PRINCESS... LIVED IN HAPPINESS AND BEAUTY.

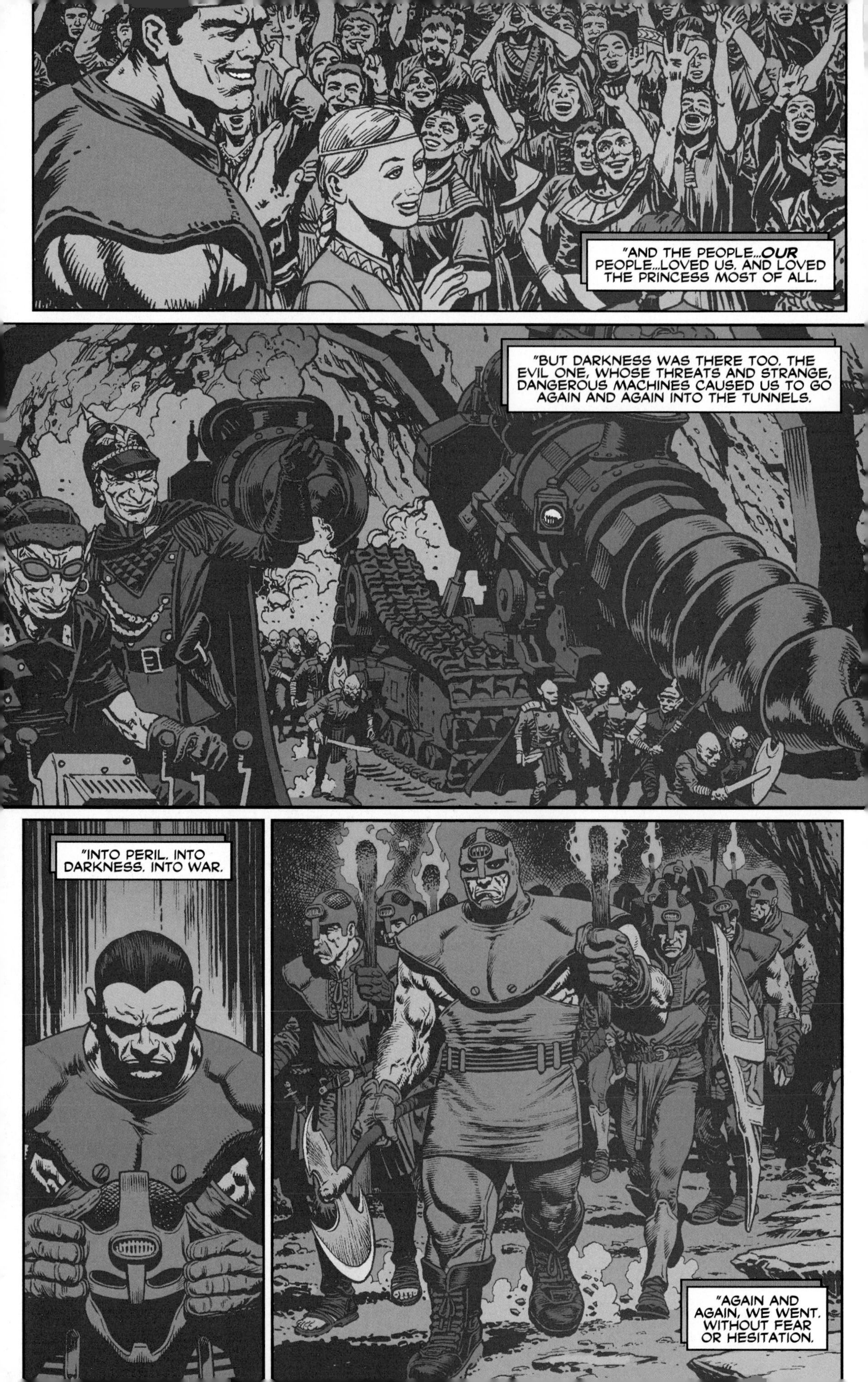
"AND THE PEOPLE...*OUR* PEOPLE...LOVED US. AND LOVED THE PRINCESS MOST OF ALL.
"BUT DARKNESS WAS THERE TOO. THE EVIL ONE, WHOSE THREATS AND STRANGE, DANGEROUS MACHINES CAUSED US TO GO AGAIN AND AGAIN INTO THE TUNNELS.
"INTO PERIL. INTO DARKNESS. INTO WAR.
"AGAIN AND AGAIN, WE WENT. WITHOUT FEAR OR HESITATION.

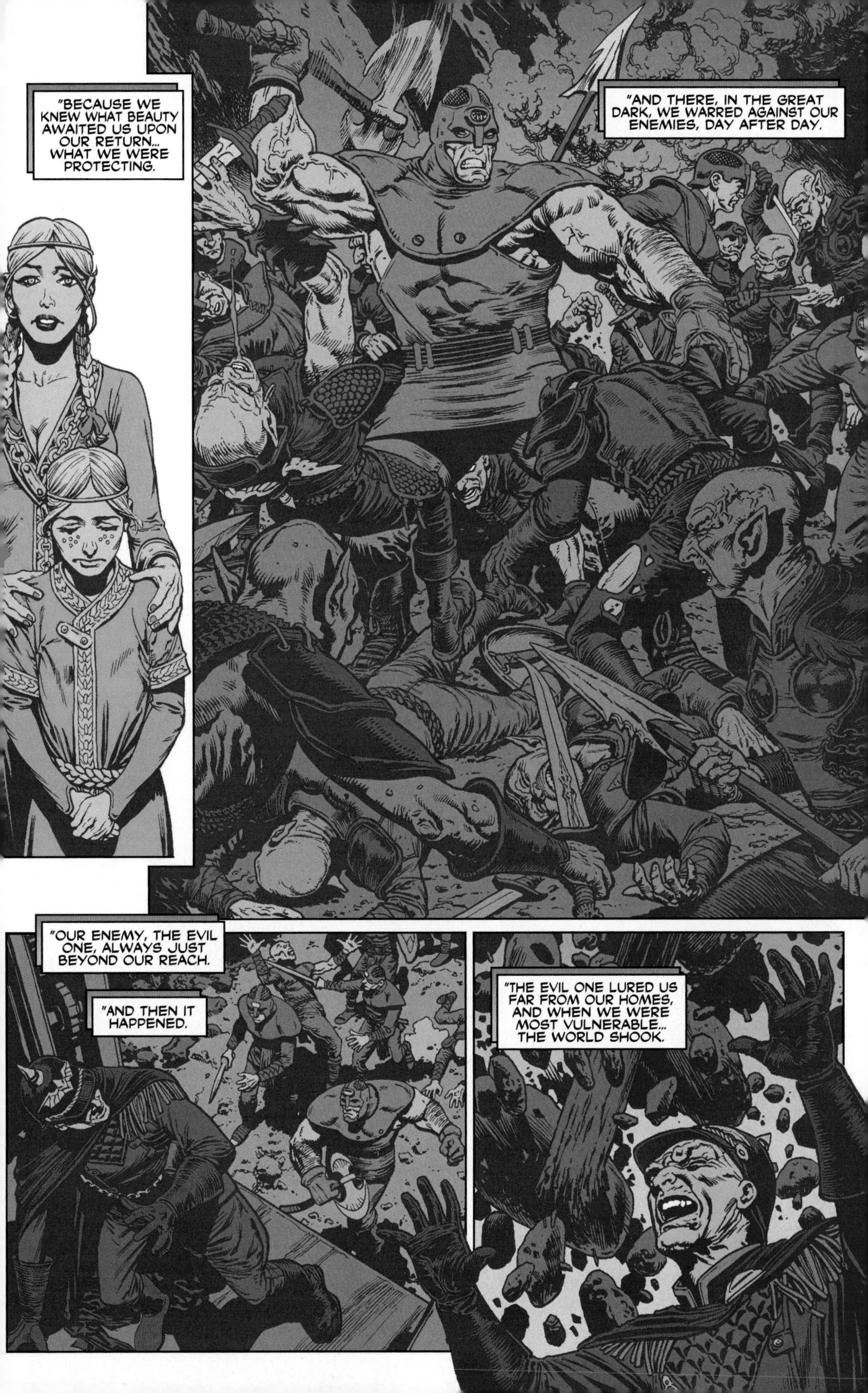
"BECAUSE WE KNEW WHAT BEAUTY AWAITED US UPON OUR RETURN... WHAT WE WERE PROTECTING.
"AND THERE, IN THE GREAT DARK, WE WARRED AGAINST OUR ENEMIES, DAY AFTER DAY.
"OUR ENEMY, THE EVIL ONE, ALWAYS JUST BEYOND OUR REACH.
"AND THEN IT HAPPENED.
"THE EVIL ONE LURED US FAR FROM OUR HOMES, AND WHEN WE WERE MOST VULNERABLE... THE WORLD SHOOK.

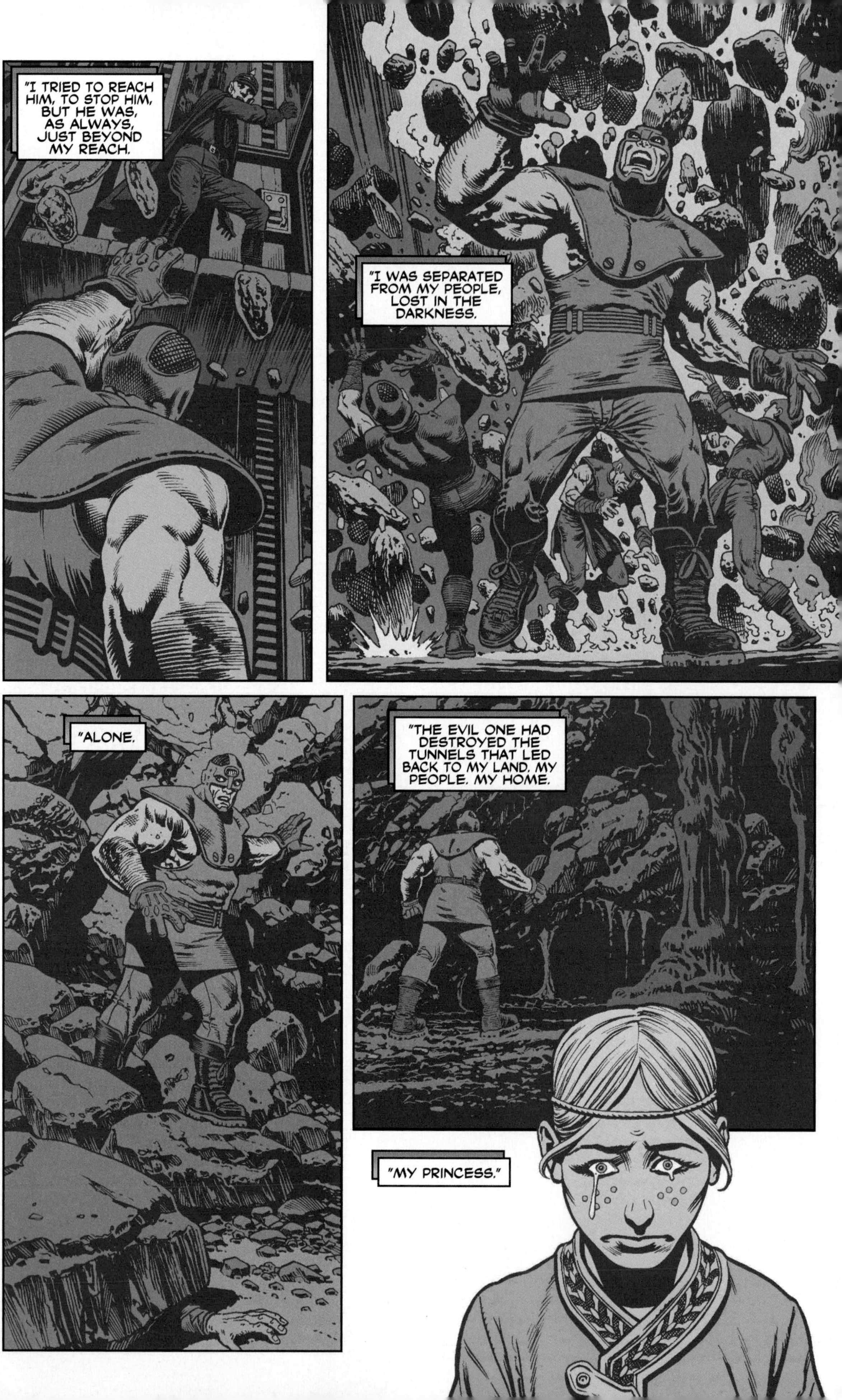
"I TRIED TO REACH HIM, TO STOP HIM, BUT HE WAS, AS ALWAYS, JUST BEYOND MY REACH.
"I WAS SEPARATED FROM MY PEOPLE, LOST IN THE DARKNESS.
"ALONE.
"THE EVIL ONE HAD DESTROYED THE TUNNELS THAT LED BACK TO MY LAND. MY PEOPLE. MY HOME.
"MY PRINCESS."

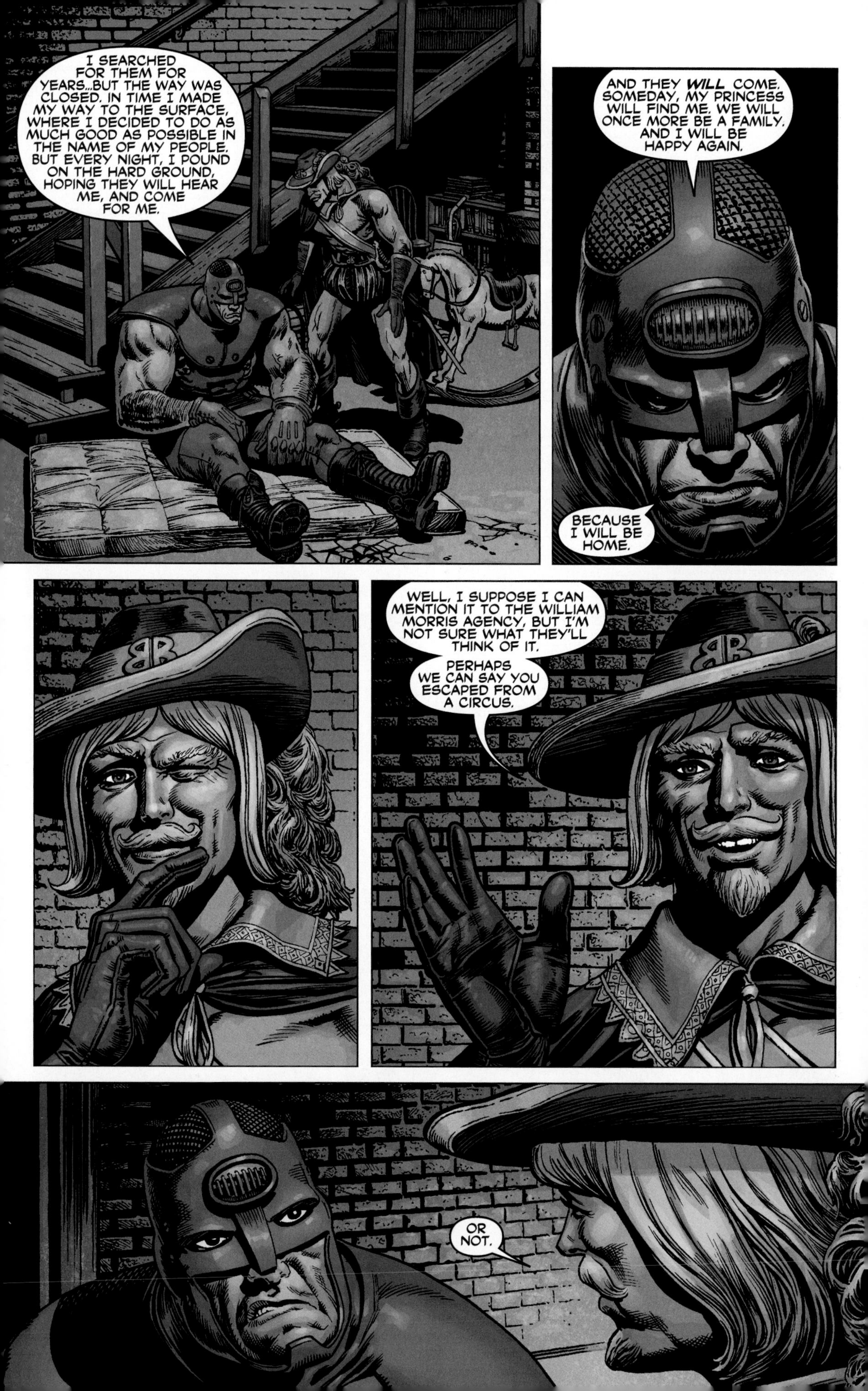
I SEARCHED FOR THEM FOR YEARS...BUT THE WAY WAS CLOSED. IN TIME I MADE MY WAY TO THE SURFACE, WHERE I DECIDED TO DO AS MUCH GOOD AS POSSIBLE IN THE NAME OF MY PEOPLE. BUT EVERY NIGHT, I POUND ON THE HARD GROUND, HOPING THEY WILL HEAR ME, AND COME FOR ME.
AND THEY WILL COME. SOMEDAY, MY PRINCESS WILL FIND ME. WE WILL ONCE MORE BE A FAMILY. AND I WILL BE HAPPY AGAIN.
BECAUSE I WILL BE HOME.
WELL, I SUPPOSE I CAN MENTION IT TO THE WILLIAM MORRIS AGENCY, BUT I'M NOT SURE WHAT THEY'LL THINK OF IT.
PERHAPS WE CAN SAY YOU ESCAPED FROM A CIRCUS.
OR NOT.

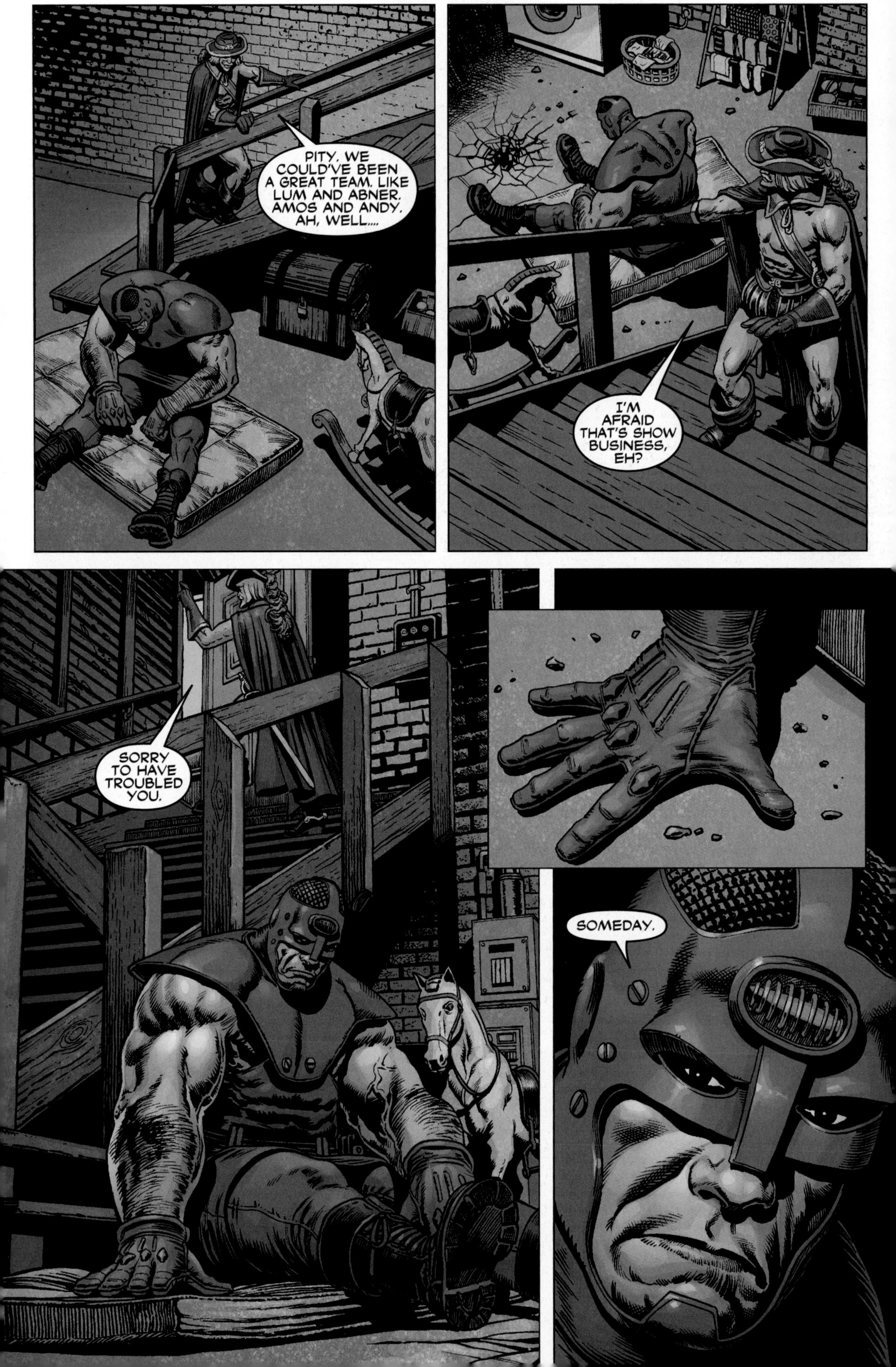
PITY. WE COULD'VE BEEN A GREAT TEAM. LIKE LUM AND ABNER. AMOS AND ANDY. AH, WELL....
I'M AFRAID THAT'S SHOW BUSINESS, EH?
SORRY TO HAVE TROUBLED YOU.
SOMEDAY.

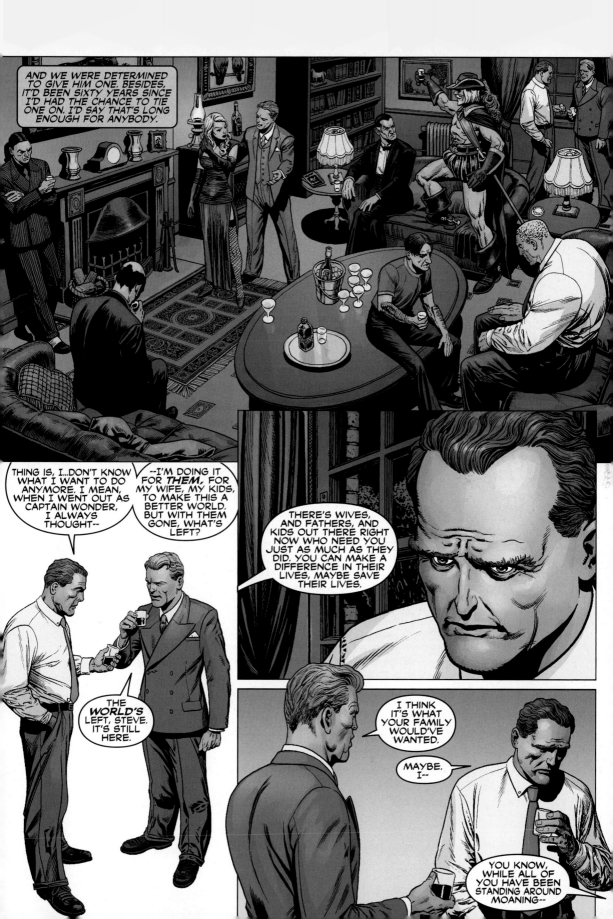

AND WE WERE DETERMINED TO GIVE HIM ONE. BESIDES, IT'D BEEN SIXTY YEARS SINCE I'D HAD THE CHANCE TO TIE ONE ON. I'D SAY THAT'S LONG ENOUGH FOR ANYBODY.

THING IS, I...DON'T KNOW WHAT I WANT TO DO ANYMORE. I MEAN, WHEN I WENT OUT AS CAPTAIN WONDER, I ALWAYS THOUGHT--

--I'M DOING IT FOR *THEM.* FOR MY WIFE, MY KIDS, TO MAKE THIS A BETTER WORLD. BUT WITH THEM GONE, WHAT'S LEFT?

THERE'S WIVES, AND FATHERS, AND KIDS OUT THERE RIGHT NOW WHO NEED YOU JUST AS MUCH AS THEY DID. YOU CAN MAKE A DIFFERENCE IN THEIR LIVES, MAYBE SAVE THEIR LIVES.

THE *WORLD'S* LEFT, STEVE. IT'S STILL HERE.

I THINK IT'S WHAT YOUR FAMILY WOULD'VE WANTED.

MAYBE. I--

YOU KNOW, WHILE ALL OF YOU HAVE BEEN STANDING AROUND MOANING--

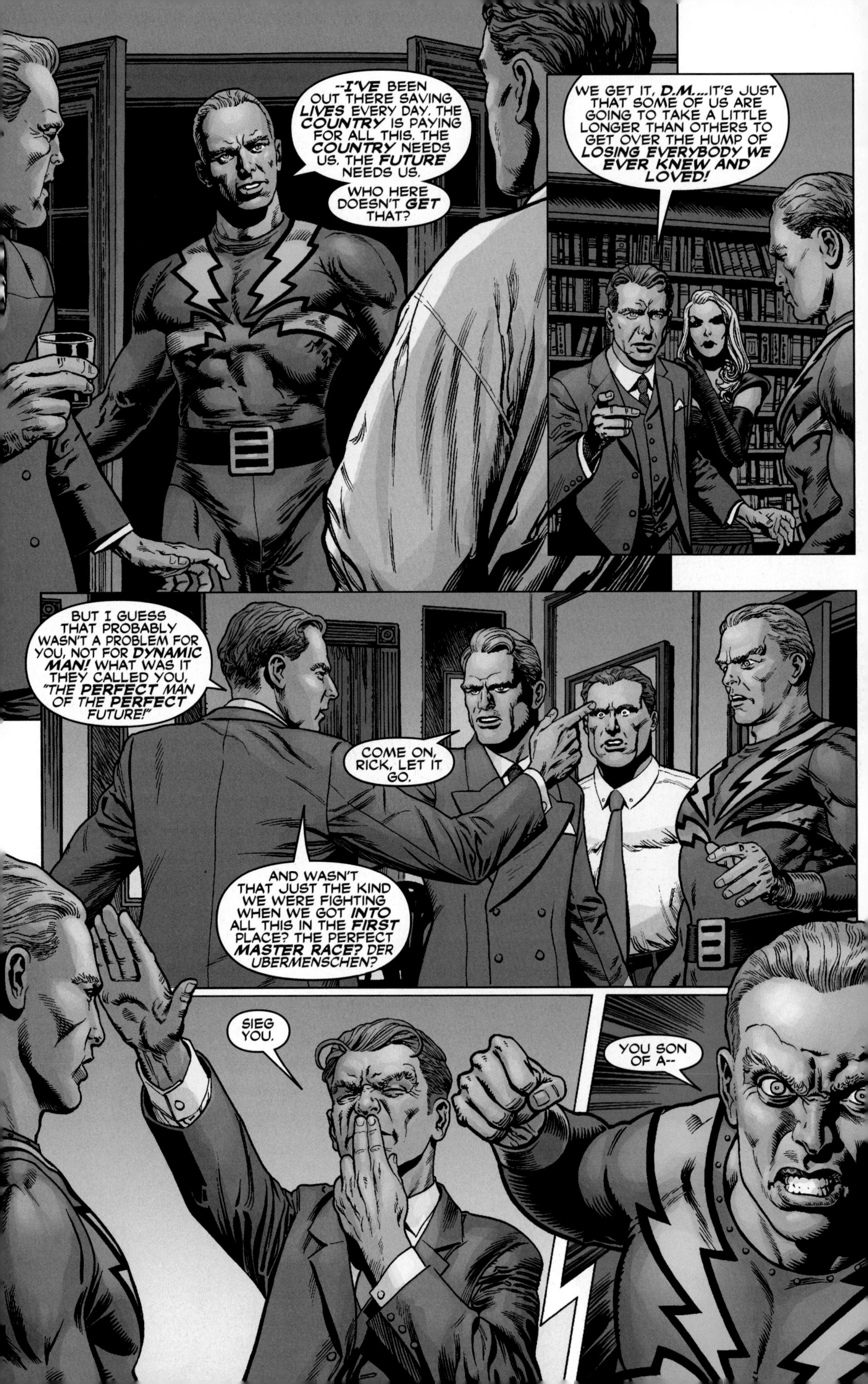
--I'VE BEEN OUT THERE SAVING LIVES EVERY DAY. THE COUNTRY IS PAYING FOR ALL THIS. THE COUNTRY NEEDS US. THE FUTURE NEEDS US.
WHO HERE DOESN'T GET THAT?
WE GET IT, D.M.... IT'S JUST THAT SOME OF US ARE GOING TO TAKE A LITTLE LONGER THAN OTHERS TO GET OVER THE HUMP OF LOSING EVERYBODY WE EVER KNEW AND LOVED!
BUT I GUESS THAT PROBABLY WASN'T A PROBLEM FOR YOU, NOT FOR DYNAMIC MAN! WHAT WAS IT THEY CALLED YOU, "THE PERFECT MAN OF THE PERFECT FUTURE!"
COME ON, RICK, LET IT GO.
AND WASN'T THAT JUST THE KIND WE WERE FIGHTING WHEN WE GOT INTO ALL THIS IN THE FIRST PLACE? THE PERFECT MASTER RACE? DER UBERMENSCHEN?
SIEG YOU.
YOU SON OF A--

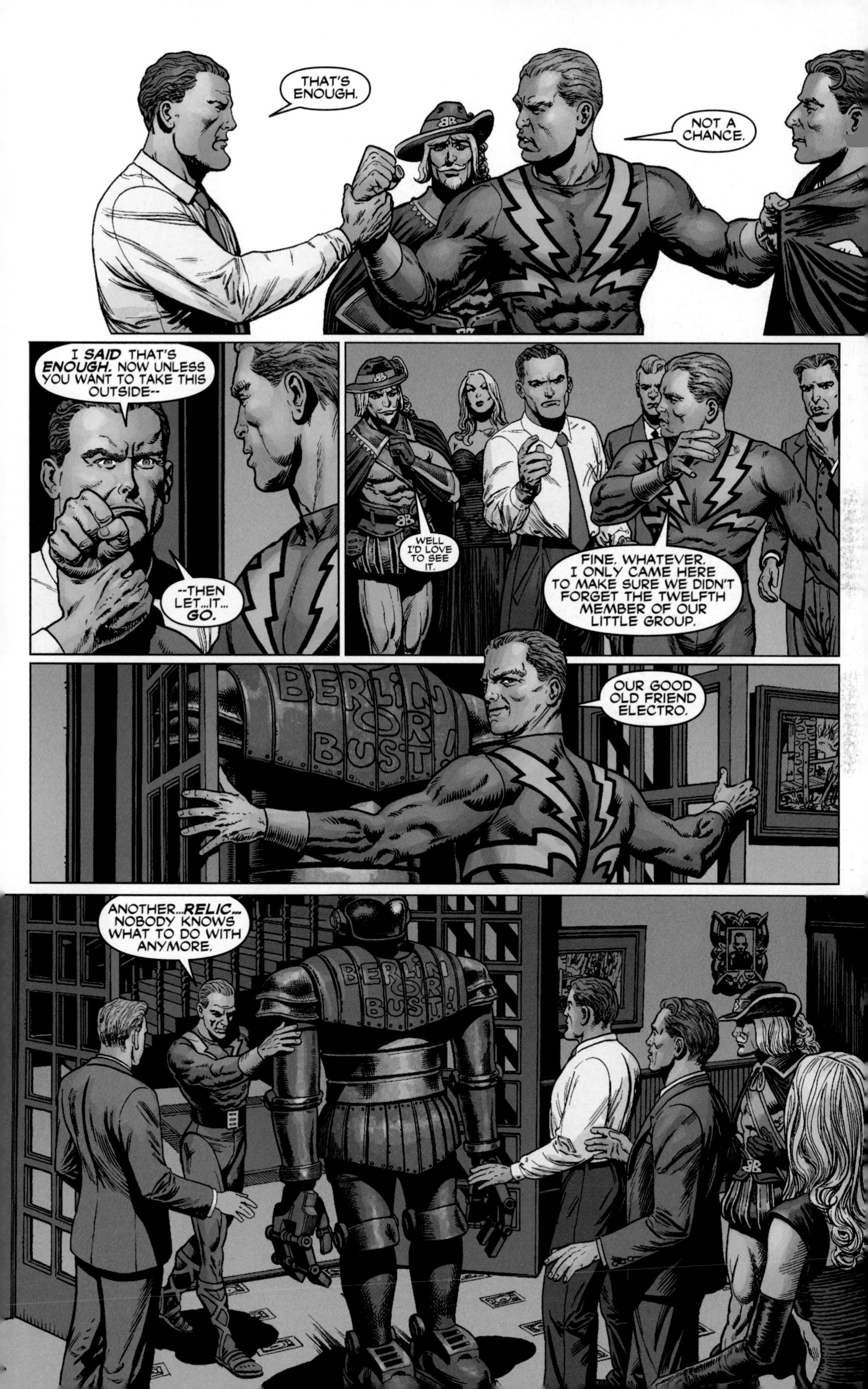
THAT'S ENOUGH.
NOT A CHANCE.
I SAID THAT'S ENOUGH. NOW UNLESS YOU WANT TO TAKE THIS OUTSIDE--
--THEN LET...IT... GO.
WELL I'D LOVE TO SEE IT.
FINE. WHATEVER. I ONLY CAME HERE TO MAKE SURE WE DIDN'T FORGET THE TWELFTH MEMBER OF OUR LITTLE GROUP.
BERLIN OR BUST!
OUR GOOD OLD FRIEND ELECTRO.
ANOTHER...RELIC... NOBODY KNOWS WHAT TO DO WITH ANYMORE.
BERLIN OR BUST!

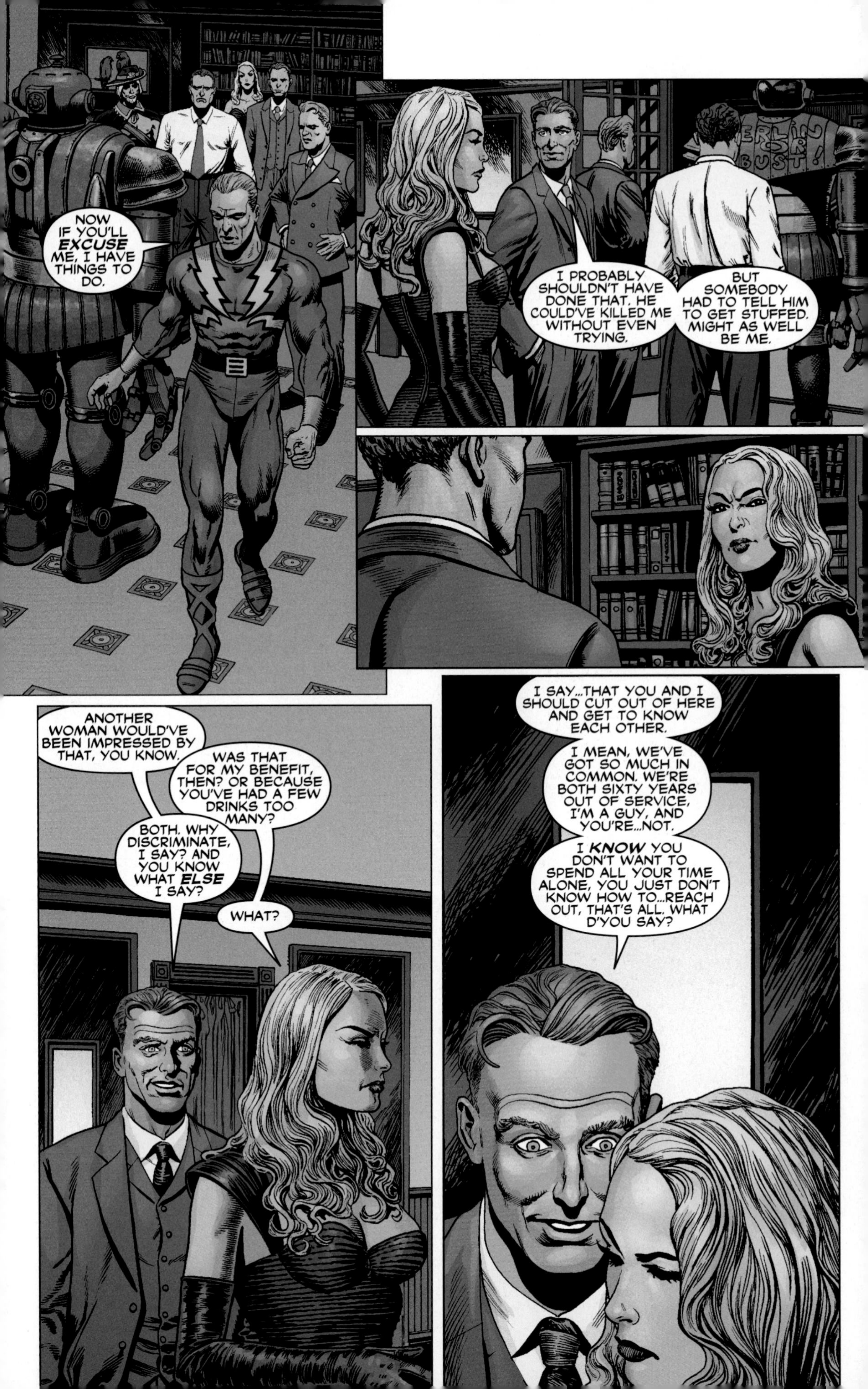
NOW IF YOU'LL EXCUSE ME, I HAVE THINGS TO DO.
I PROBABLY SHOULDN'T HAVE DONE THAT. HE COULD'VE KILLED ME WITHOUT EVEN TRYING.
BUT SOMEBODY HAD TO TELL HIM TO GET STUFFED. MIGHT AS WELL BE ME.
ANOTHER WOMAN WOULD'VE BEEN IMPRESSED BY THAT, YOU KNOW.
WAS THAT FOR MY BENEFIT, THEN? OR BECAUSE YOU'VE HAD A FEW DRINKS TOO MANY?
BOTH. WHY DISCRIMINATE, I SAY? AND YOU KNOW WHAT ELSE I SAY?
WHAT?
I SAY...THAT YOU AND I SHOULD CUT OUT OF HERE AND GET TO KNOW EACH OTHER.
I MEAN, WE'VE GOT SO MUCH IN COMMON. WE'RE BOTH SIXTY YEARS OUT OF SERVICE, I'M A GUY, AND YOU'RE...NOT.
I KNOW YOU DON'T WANT TO SPEND ALL YOUR TIME ALONE, YOU JUST DON'T KNOW HOW TO...REACH OUT, THAT'S ALL. WHAT D'YOU SAY?

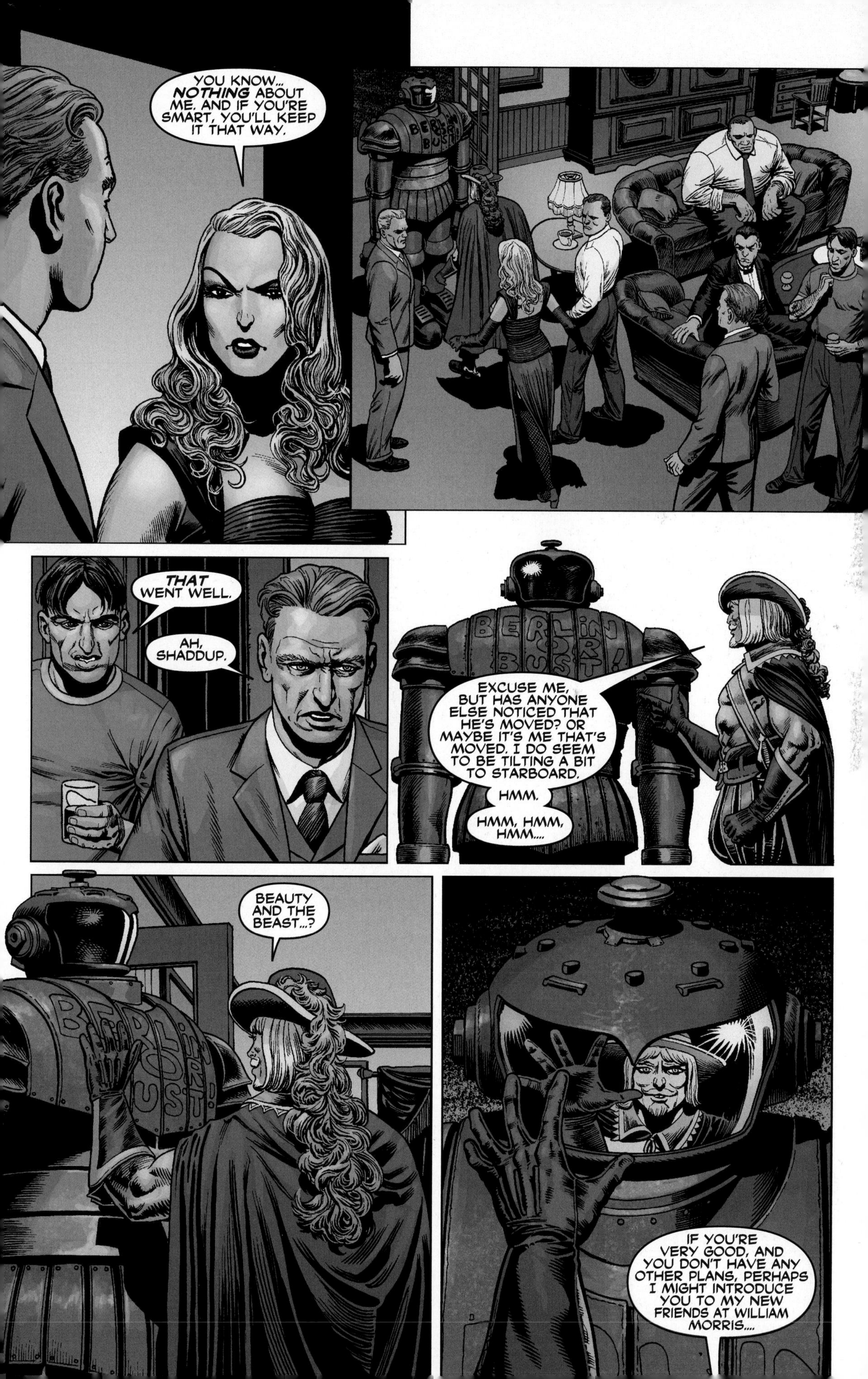
YOU KNOW... NOTHING ABOUT ME. AND IF YOU'RE SMART, YOU'LL KEEP IT THAT WAY.
BERLIN OR BUST
THAT WENT WELL.
AH, SHADDUP.
BERLIN OR BUST!
EXCUSE ME, BUT HAS ANYONE ELSE NOTICED THAT HE'S MOVED? OR MAYBE IT'S ME THAT'S MOVED. I DO SEEM TO BE TILTING A BIT TO STARBOARD.
HMM.
HMM, HMM, HMM....
BEAUTY AND THE BEAST...?
BERLIN OR BUST
IF YOU'RE VERY GOOD, AND YOU DON'T HAVE ANY OTHER PLANS, PERHAPS I MIGHT INTRODUCE YOU TO MY NEW FRIENDS AT WILLIAM MORRIS....

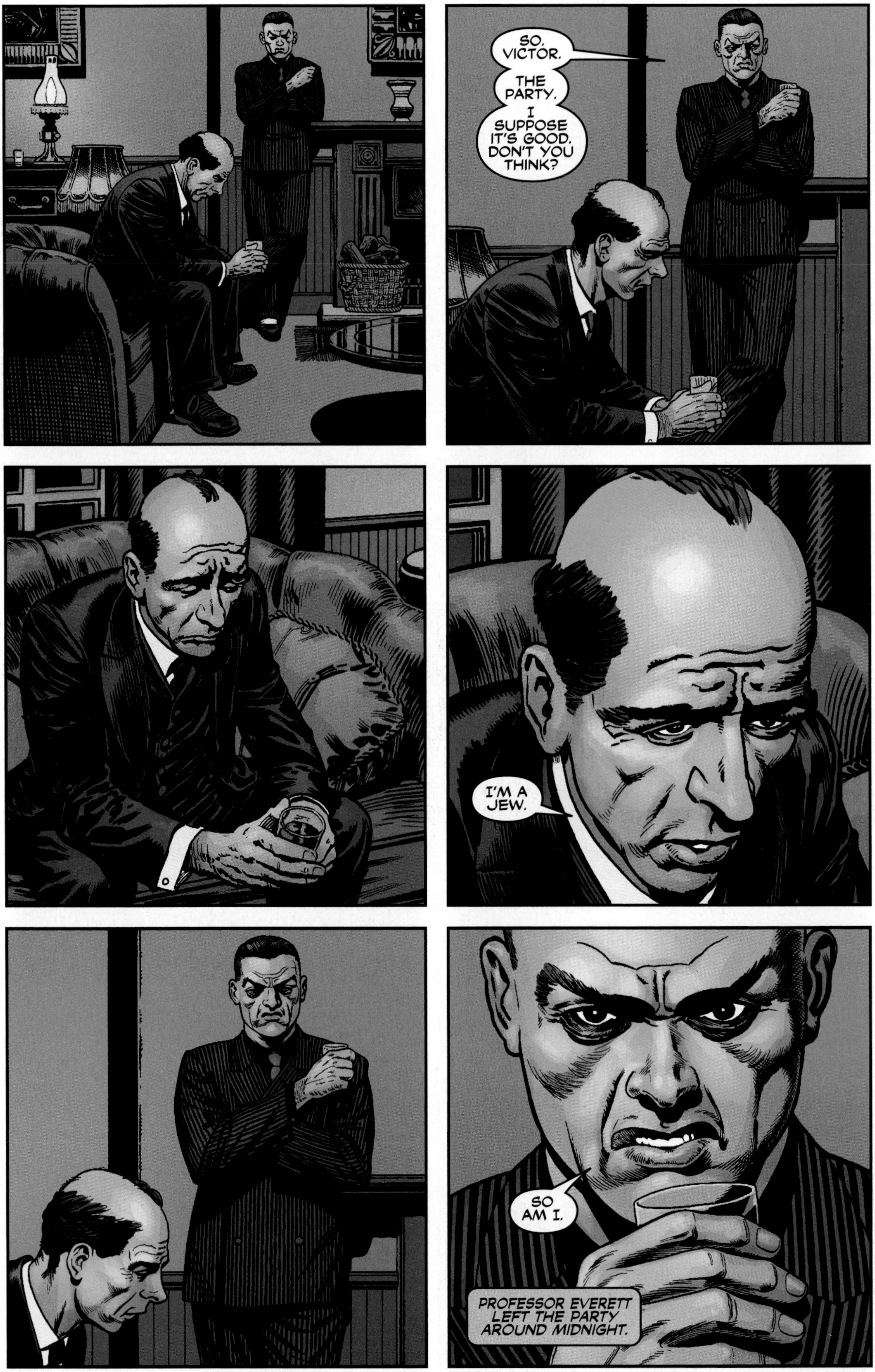

SO. VICTOR.
THE PARTY.
I SUPPOSE IT'S GOOD. DON'T YOU THINK?
I'M A JEW.
SO AM I.
PROFESSOR EVERETT LEFT THE PARTY AROUND MIDNIGHT.

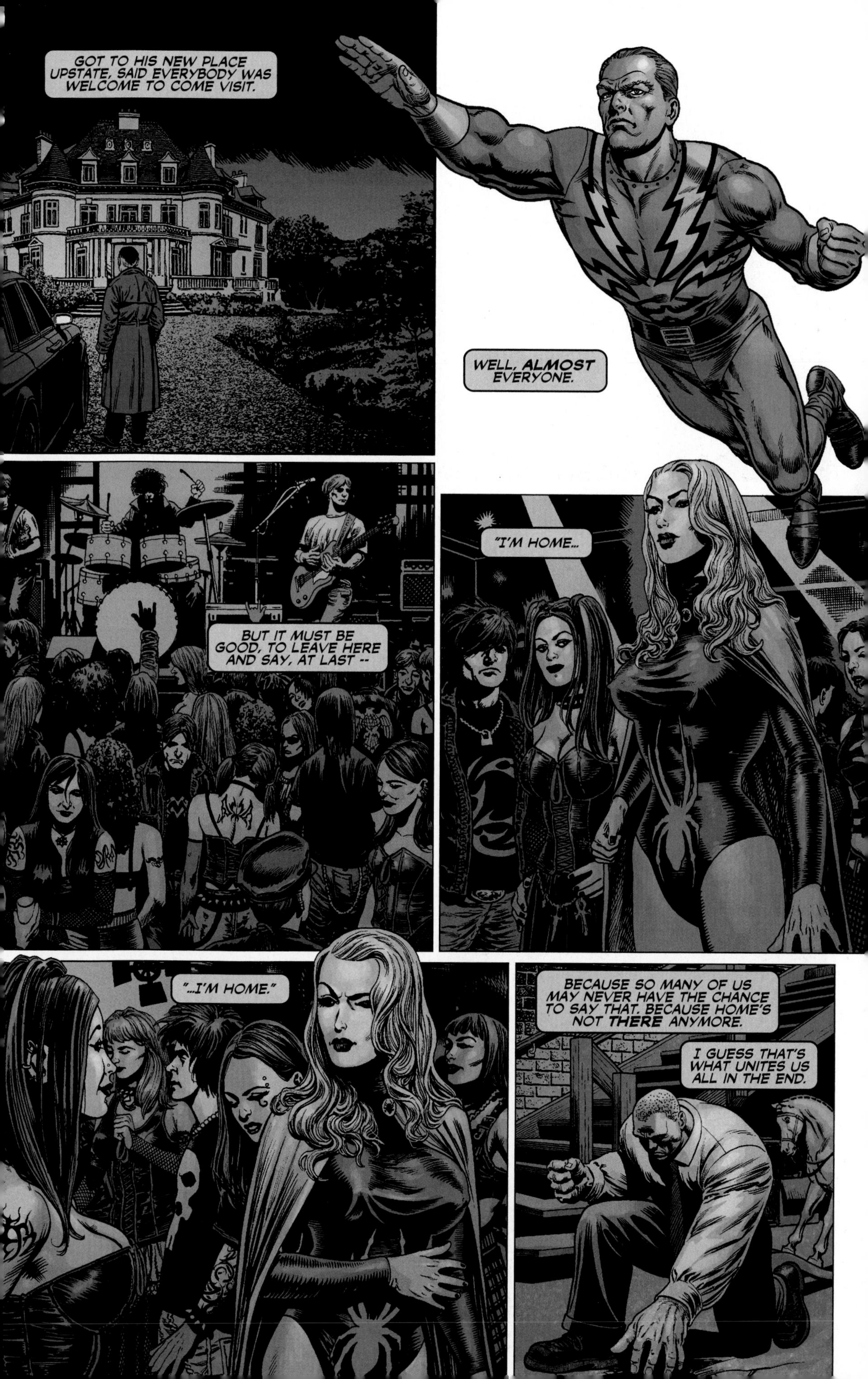
GOT TO HIS NEW PLACE UPSTATE, SAID EVERYBODY WAS WELCOME TO COME VISIT.
WELL, ALMOST EVERYONE.
BUT IT MUST BE GOOD, TO LEAVE HERE AND SAY, AT LAST --
"I'M HOME...
"...I'M HOME."
BECAUSE SO MANY OF US MAY NEVER HAVE THE CHANCE TO SAY THAT. BECAUSE HOME'S NOT THERE ANYMORE.
I GUESS THAT'S WHAT UNITES US ALL IN THE END.

ALL OF US, IN THE DARK...TRYING TO COME HOME.

OF COURSE, WHAT NOBODY KNEW WAS THAT SOMETIMES, IT'S THOSE LITTLE PIECES OF HOME THAT CAN COME BACK TO BITE YOU IN THE ASS IN A BIG WAY.

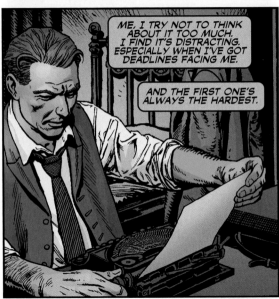

ME, I TRY NOT TO THINK ABOUT IT TOO MUCH. I FIND IT'S DISTRACTING. ESPECIALLY WHEN I'VE GOT DEADLINES FACING ME.

AND THE FIRST ONE'S ALWAYS THE HARDEST.

TAp·TAp·TAp·TAp·TAp·TAp·TAp

OKAY...HERE WE GO. HAVE TO GET THIS STARTED--

BOOM BOOM BOOM

--BECAUSE WHEN I'M HERE, BEHIND THE TYPEWRITER, I'M FINALLY WHERE I BELONG.

HOME.

DAILY BUGLE metro

Richard Jones, fighting crime in the forties as **The Phantom Reporter.**

LOOKING BOTH WAYS

By Richard Jones
Special Correspondent
Exclusive to the Daily Bugle

When I was approached by the Daily Bugle to write this column, I asked what they wanted me to write about. Having been sixty years and more in deep freeze, it's not exactly like I was going to be able to comment on the latest fashions. Heck, I'm still amazed to see women wearing stockings without seams up the back.

Their reply: Write about what it is to be a hero, then and now. Compare and contrast.

Thing of it is, I don't know what it is to be a hero. I know that I've put on a mask to fight what I believed in my heart was wrong, a system of corruption and greed and violence. But everyone who puts on a uniform, in a street or a foreign land, is doing the same thing, so I'm nothing special in that regard. I fought the Nazis, but then the whole world was fighting the Nazis. We did what we had to do. We did what we thought was right.

It would be easy to say that's the difference between now and then, that this is a world of grays, and back then it was all black and white. But the color gray has always been with us. There have always been those who put their own comfort and security above the safety and well-being of others, and those who are too politic, or too polite to point this out.

So, what is a hero? Who is a hero? I don't know, because honestly, I'm not one of them. I wish I was. But I'm not. So I can only tell you what I think a hero is, to me.

A hero is somebody who's scared out of his mind. He knows if he walks out onto the battlefield, he's going to get killed. He's shaking and his voice trembles as he hears the shells land, hears the guns fire, hears the cries of the wounded. Terrified. He wishes he had powers, wishes he could fly off and escape what's coming. But he doesn't, and he can't, and somehow, despite all of this, he straightens, and steps out onto the battlefield, to try to save some of the guys who came here with him. Knowing he'll probably die trying.

That was how my father died, in World War One, back before we realised we'd have to start numbering them. He was a hero. He was my hero.

And maybe, in the end, that's what it really comes down to. A hero isn't the loudest guy, or the bravest guy, or the guy who kills the most enemy soldiers. It's the guy who lays down his life, who gives everything he has, everything he is, and everything he will ever be... for us. For his children.

No, I'm not a hero.

But someday, maybe, with luck... I will be.

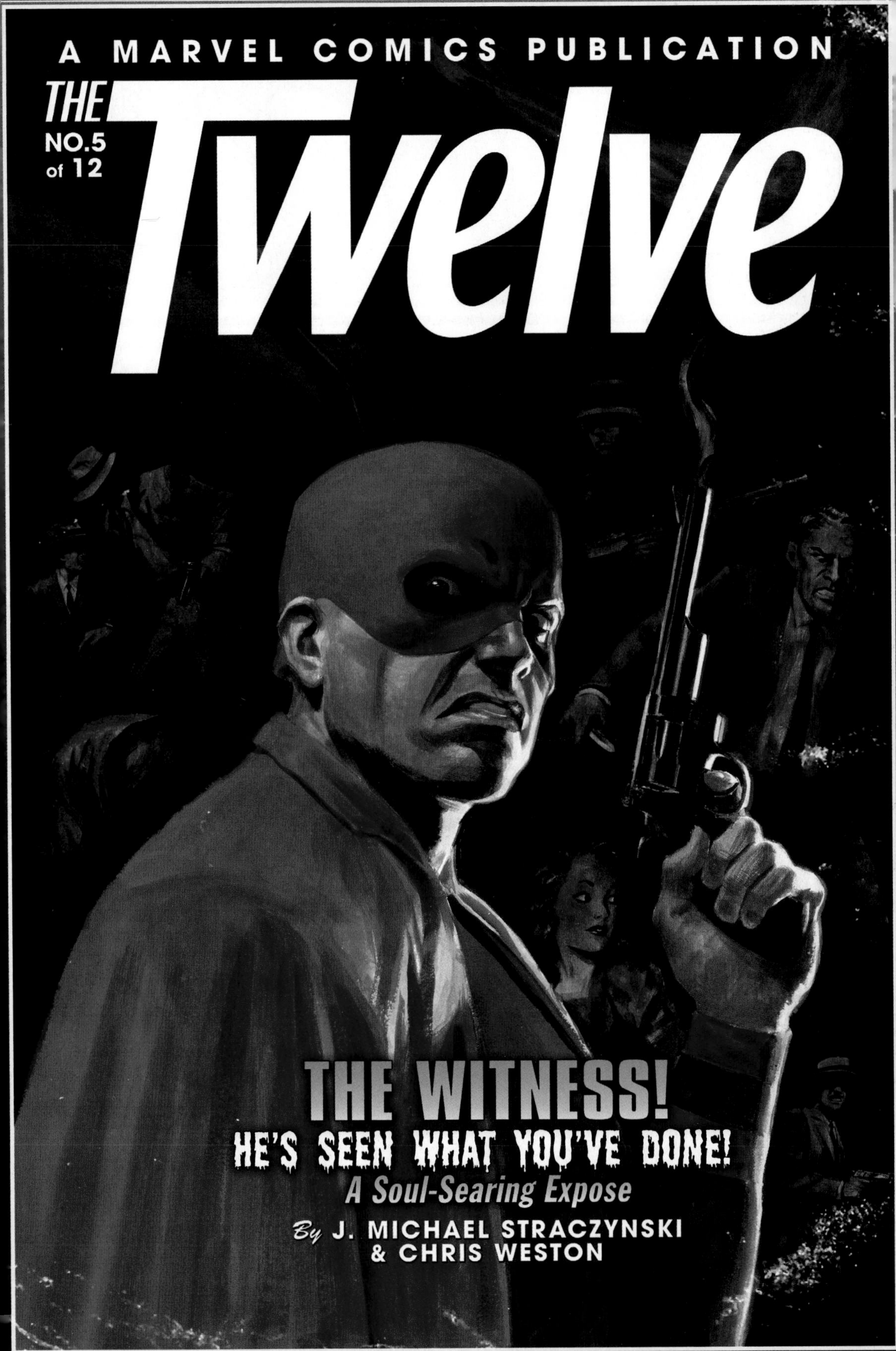
A MARVEL COMICS PUBLICATION
THE
NO.5
of 12
Twelve
THE WITNESS!
HE'S SEEN WHAT YOU'VE DONE!
A Soul-Searing Expose
By J. MICHAEL STRACZYNSKI
& CHRIS WESTON

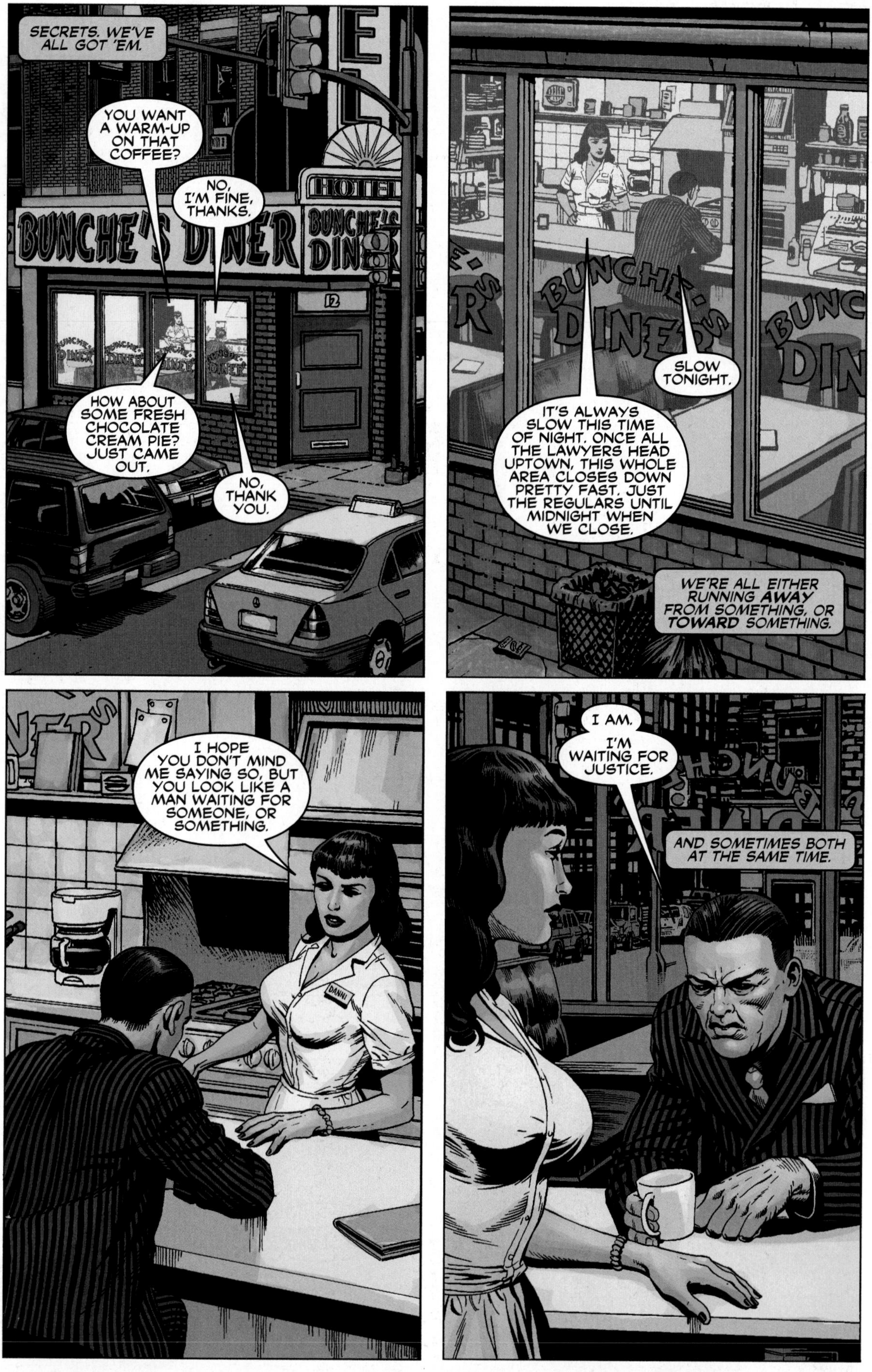
SECRETS. WE'VE ALL GOT 'EM.
YOU WANT A WARM-UP ON THAT COFFEE?
NO, I'M FINE, THANKS.
HOW ABOUT SOME FRESH CHOCOLATE CREAM PIE? JUST CAME OUT.
NO, THANK YOU.
BUNCHE'S DINER
HOTEL
SLOW TONIGHT.
IT'S ALWAYS SLOW THIS TIME OF NIGHT. ONCE ALL THE LAWYERS HEAD UPTOWN, THIS WHOLE AREA CLOSES DOWN PRETTY FAST. JUST THE REGULARS UNTIL MIDNIGHT WHEN WE CLOSE.
WE'RE ALL EITHER RUNNING AWAY FROM SOMETHING, OR TOWARD SOMETHING.
I HOPE YOU DON'T MIND ME SAYING SO, BUT YOU LOOK LIKE A MAN WAITING FOR SOMEONE, OR SOMETHING.
I AM.
I'M WAITING FOR JUSTICE.
AND SOMETIMES BOTH AT THE SAME TIME.

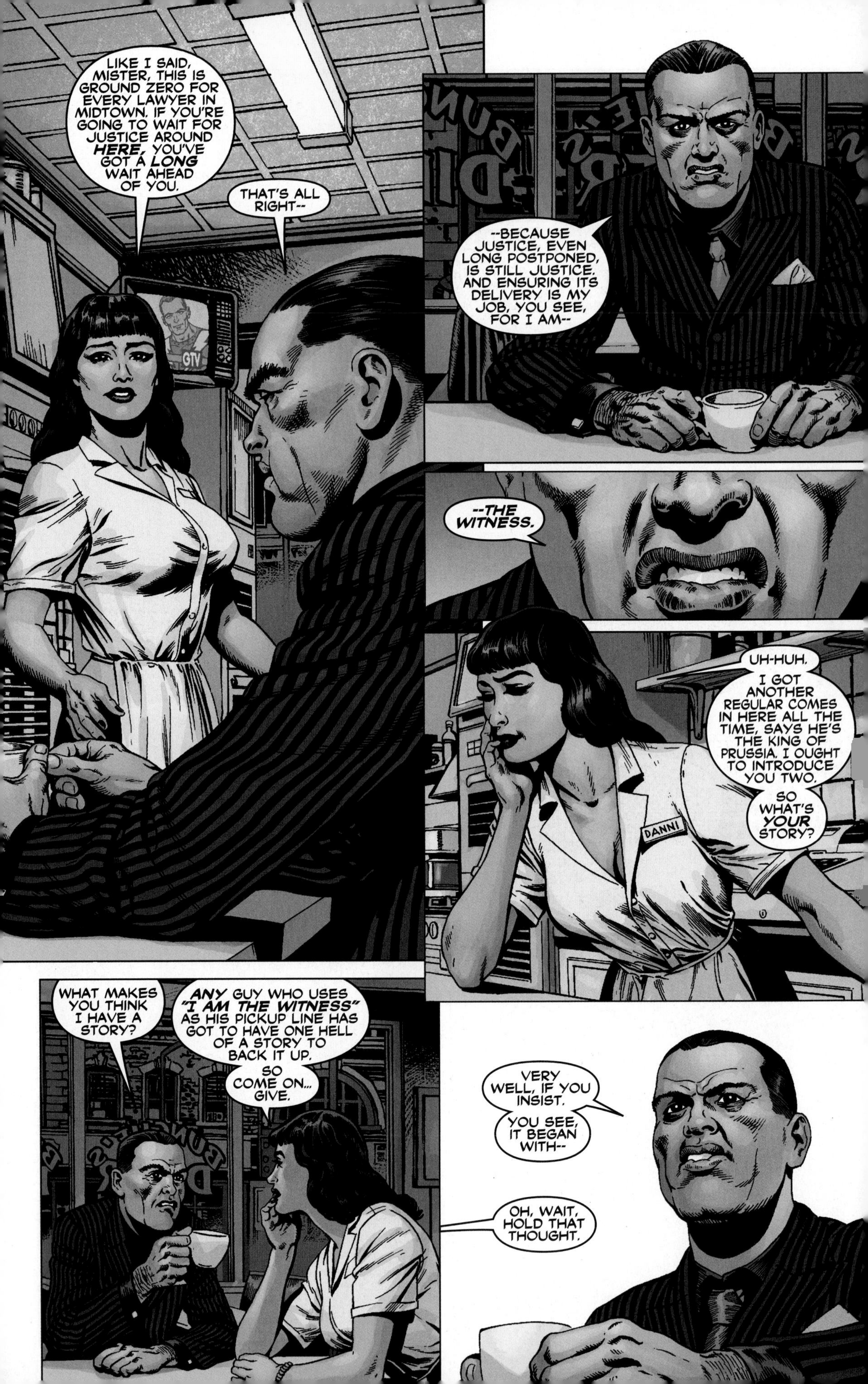
LIKE I SAID, MISTER, THIS IS GROUND ZERO FOR EVERY LAWYER IN MIDTOWN. IF YOU'RE GOING TO WAIT FOR JUSTICE AROUND HERE, YOU'VE GOT A LONG WAIT AHEAD OF YOU.
THAT'S ALL RIGHT--
GTV
--BECAUSE JUSTICE, EVEN LONG POSTPONED, IS STILL JUSTICE. AND ENSURING ITS DELIVERY IS MY JOB, YOU SEE, FOR I AM--
--THE WITNESS.
UH-HUH.
I GOT ANOTHER REGULAR COMES IN HERE ALL THE TIME, SAYS HE'S THE KING OF PRUSSIA. I OUGHT TO INTRODUCE YOU TWO.
SO WHAT'S YOUR STORY?
DANNI
WHAT MAKES YOU THINK I HAVE A STORY?
ANY GUY WHO USES "I AM THE WITNESS" AS HIS PICKUP LINE HAS GOT TO HAVE ONE HELL OF A STORY TO BACK IT UP.
SO COME ON... GIVE.
VERY WELL, IF YOU INSIST.
YOU SEE, IT BEGAN WITH--
OH, WAIT, HOLD THAT THOUGHT.

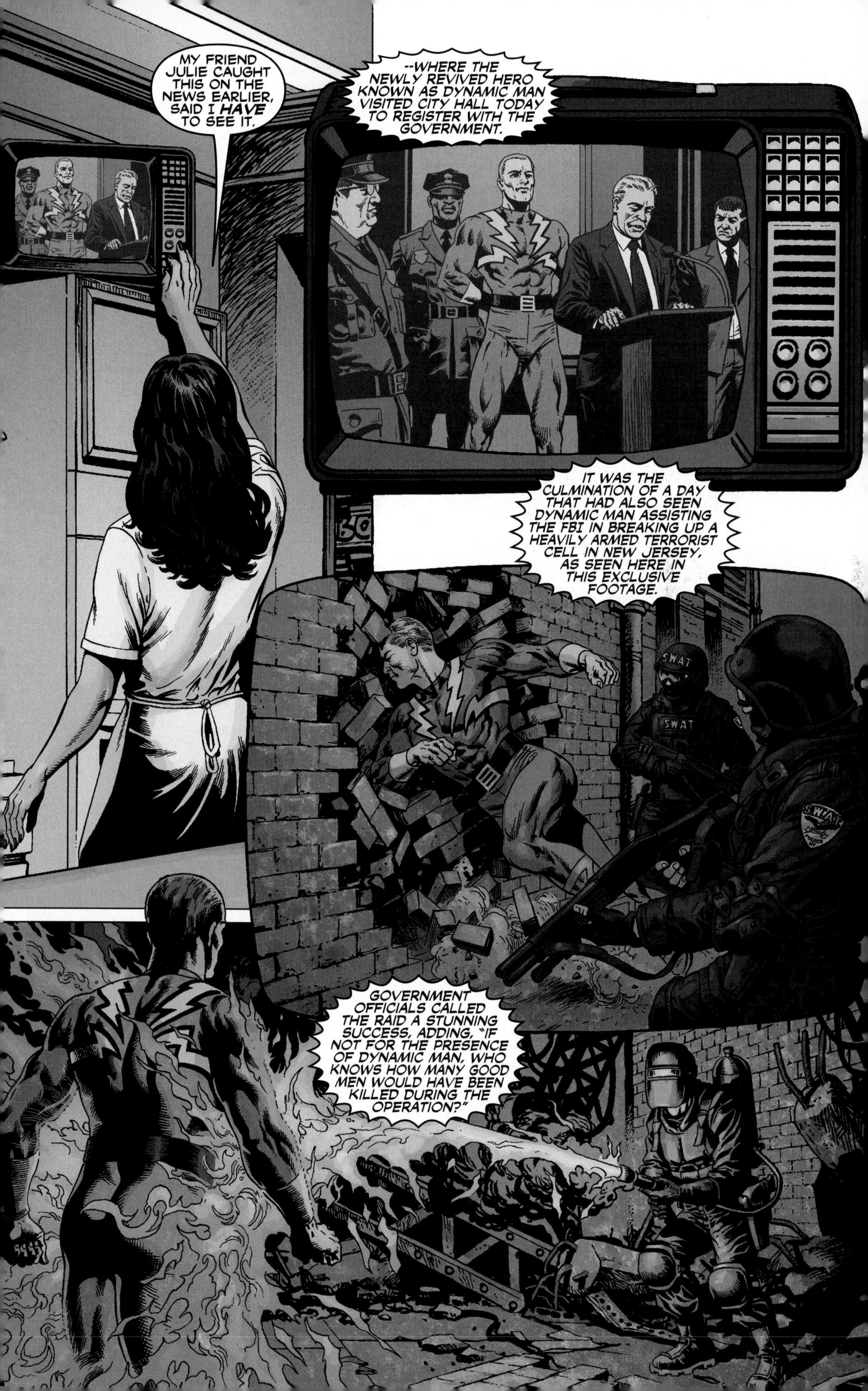
MY FRIEND JULIE CAUGHT THIS ON THE NEWS EARLIER, SAID I HAVE TO SEE IT.
--WHERE THE NEWLY REVIVED HERO KNOWN AS DYNAMIC MAN VISITED CITY HALL TODAY TO REGISTER WITH THE GOVERNMENT.
IT WAS THE CULMINATION OF A DAY THAT HAD ALSO SEEN DYNAMIC MAN ASSISTING THE FBI IN BREAKING UP A HEAVILY ARMED TERRORIST CELL IN NEW JERSEY, AS SEEN HERE IN THIS EXCLUSIVE FOOTAGE.
SWAT
SWAT
GOVERNMENT OFFICIALS CALLED THE RAID A STUNNING SUCCESS, ADDING, "IF NOT FOR THE PRESENCE OF DYNAMIC MAN, WHO KNOWS HOW MANY GOOD MEN WOULD HAVE BEEN KILLED DURING THE OPERATION?"

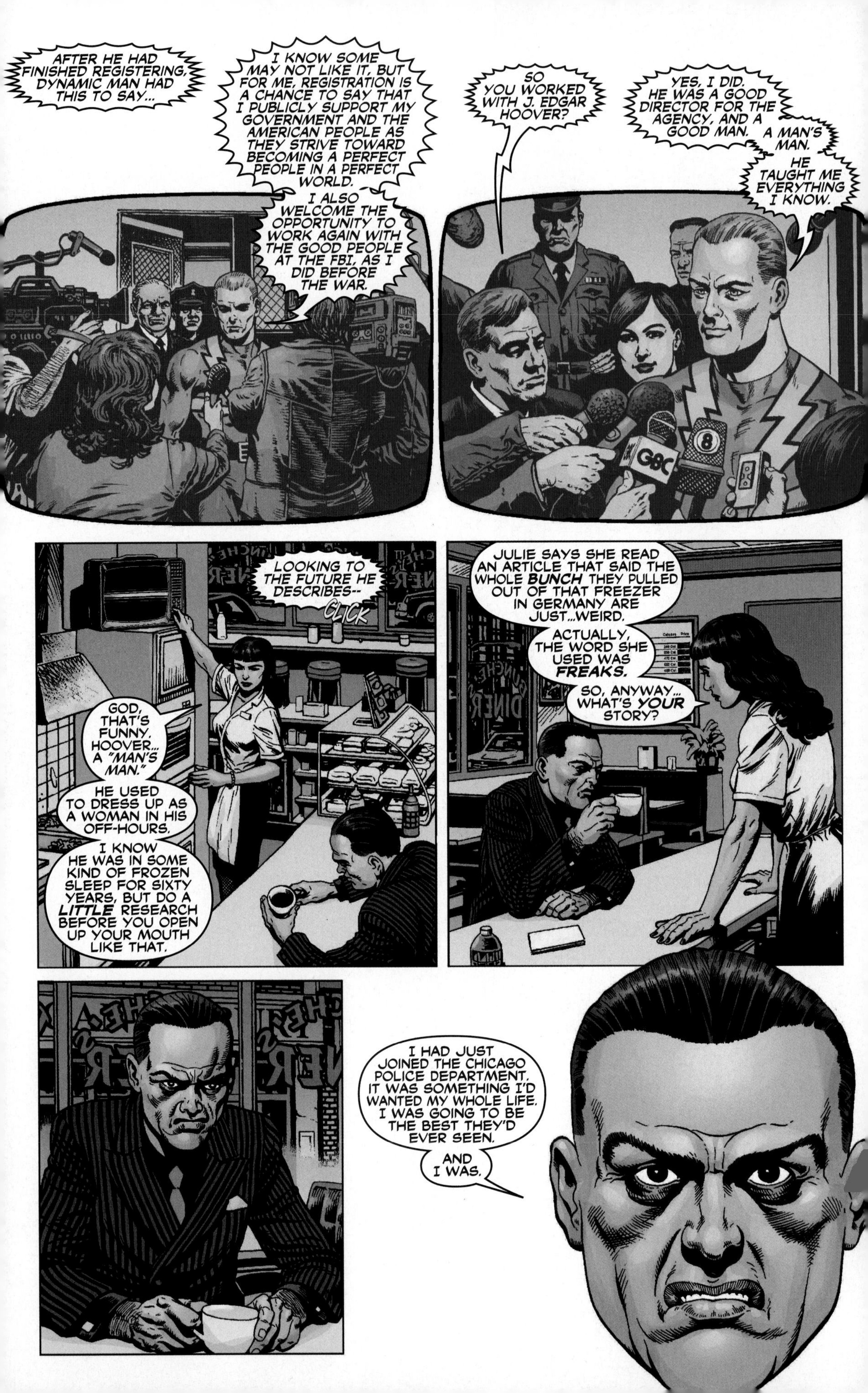
AFTER HE HAD FINISHED REGISTERING, DYNAMIC MAN HAD THIS TO SAY...
I KNOW SOME MAY NOT LIKE IT, BUT FOR ME, REGISTRATION IS A CHANCE TO SAY THAT I PUBLICLY SUPPORT MY GOVERNMENT AND THE AMERICAN PEOPLE AS THEY STRIVE TOWARD BECOMING A PERFECT PEOPLE IN A PERFECT WORLD.
I ALSO WELCOME THE OPPORTUNITY TO WORK AGAIN WITH THE GOOD PEOPLE AT THE FBI, AS I DID BEFORE THE WAR.
SO YOU WORKED WITH J. EDGAR HOOVER?
YES, I DID. HE WAS A GOOD DIRECTOR FOR THE AGENCY, AND A GOOD MAN.
A MAN'S MAN.
HE TAUGHT ME EVERYTHING I KNOW.
GBC
8
LOOKING TO THE FUTURE HE DESCRIBES--
CLICK
GOD, THAT'S FUNNY. HOOVER... A "MAN'S MAN."
HE USED TO DRESS UP AS A WOMAN IN HIS OFF-HOURS.
I KNOW HE WAS IN SOME KIND OF FROZEN SLEEP FOR SIXTY YEARS, BUT DO A LITTLE RESEARCH BEFORE YOU OPEN UP YOUR MOUTH LIKE THAT.
JULIE SAYS SHE READ AN ARTICLE THAT SAID THE WHOLE BUNCH THEY PULLED OUT OF THAT FREEZER IN GERMANY ARE JUST... WEIRD.
ACTUALLY, THE WORD SHE USED WAS FREAKS.
SO, ANYWAY... WHAT'S YOUR STORY?
I HAD JUST JOINED THE CHICAGO POLICE DEPARTMENT. IT WAS SOMETHING I'D WANTED MY WHOLE LIFE. I WAS GOING TO BE THE BEST THEY'D EVER SEEN.
AND I WAS.

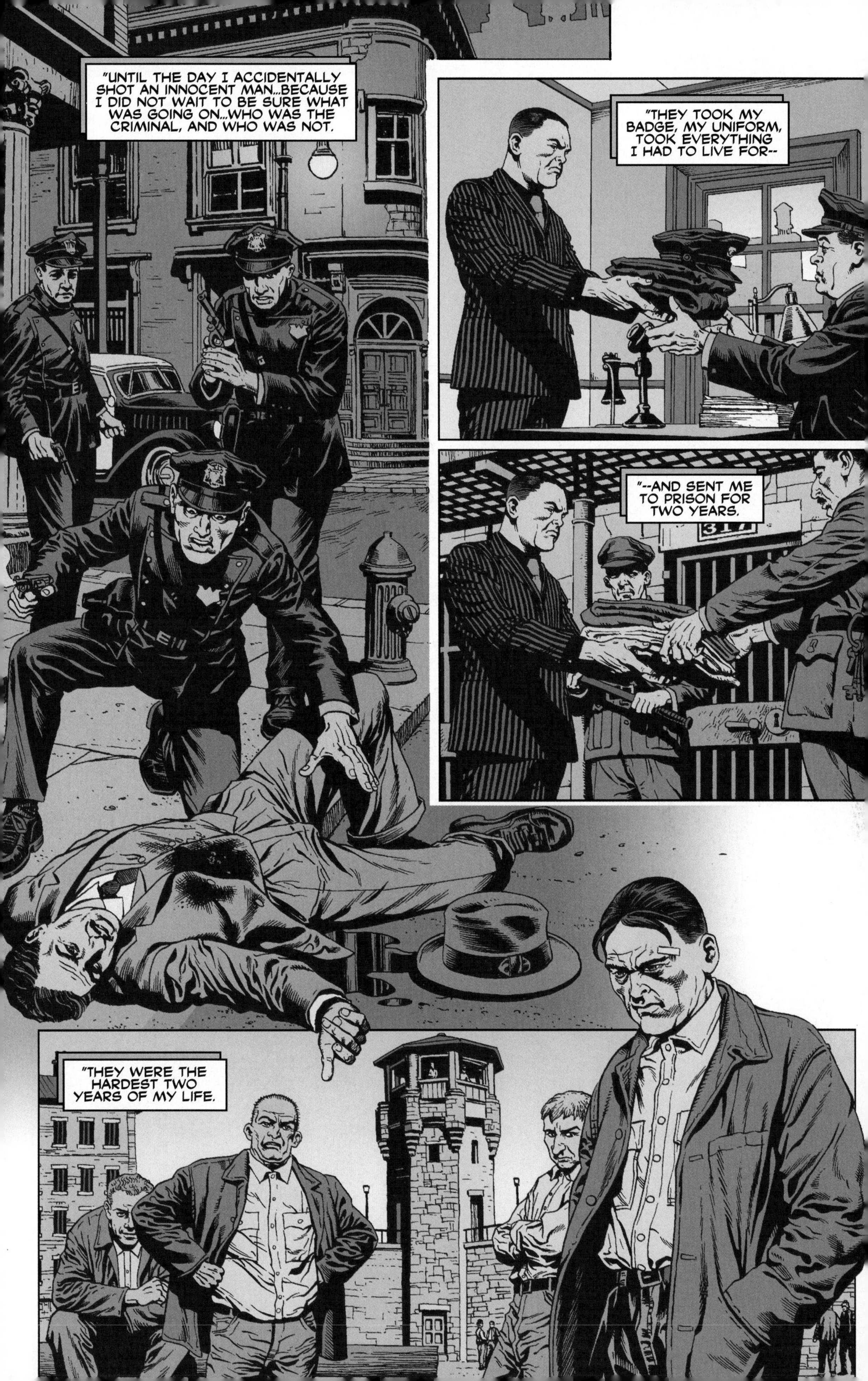
"UNTIL THE DAY I ACCIDENTALLY SHOT AN INNOCENT MAN...BECAUSE I DID NOT WAIT TO BE SURE WHAT WAS GOING ON...WHO WAS THE CRIMINAL, AND WHO WAS NOT.
"THEY TOOK MY BADGE, MY UNIFORM, TOOK EVERYTHING I HAD TO LIVE FOR--
"--AND SENT ME TO PRISON FOR TWO YEARS.
317
"THEY WERE THE HARDEST TWO YEARS OF MY LIFE.

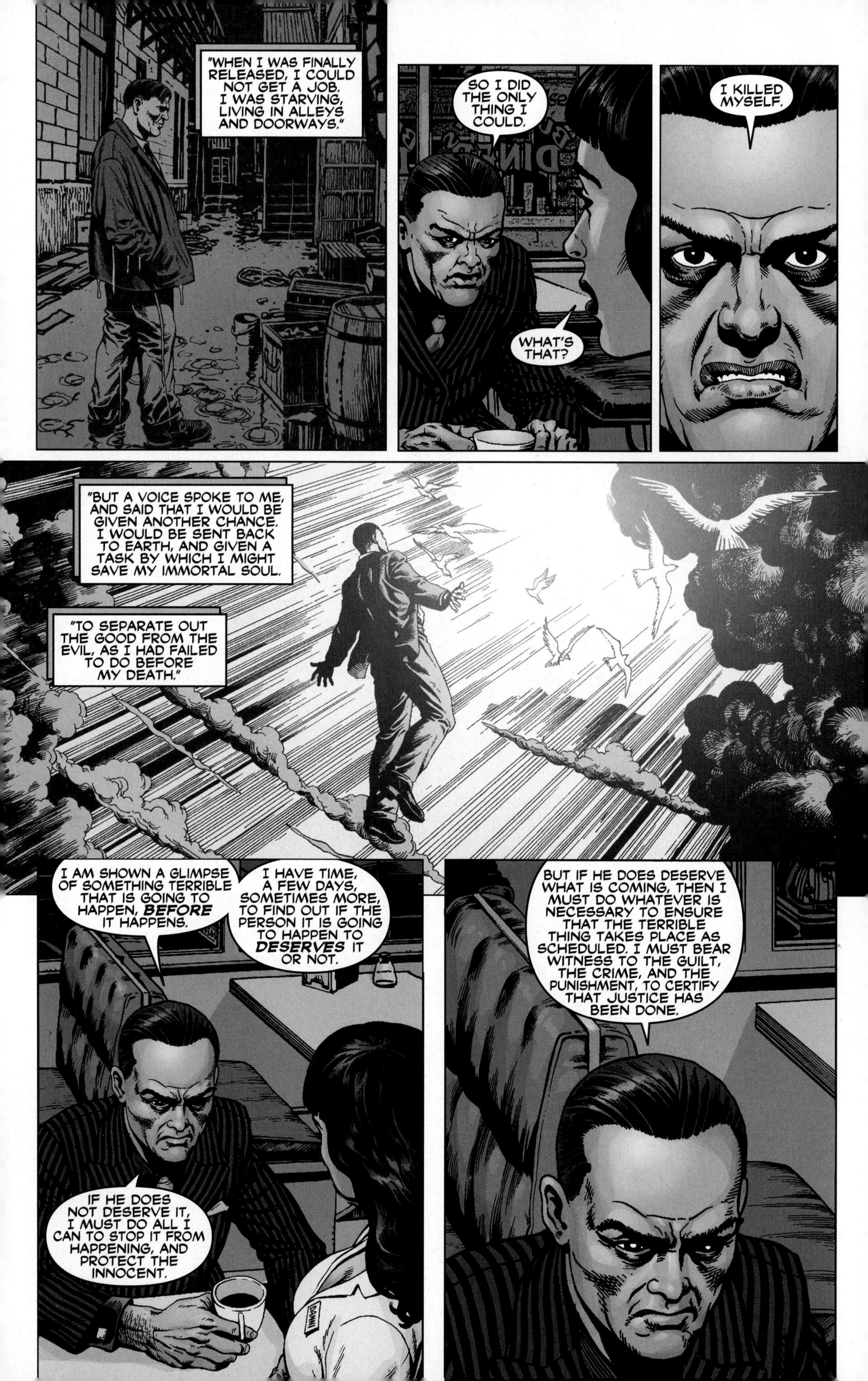
"WHEN I WAS FINALLY RELEASED, I COULD NOT GET A JOB. I WAS STARVING, LIVING IN ALLEYS AND DOORWAYS."
SO I DID THE ONLY THING I COULD.
WHAT'S THAT?
I KILLED MYSELF.
"BUT A VOICE SPOKE TO ME, AND SAID THAT I WOULD BE GIVEN ANOTHER CHANCE. I WOULD BE SENT BACK TO EARTH, AND GIVEN A TASK BY WHICH I MIGHT SAVE MY IMMORTAL SOUL.
"TO SEPARATE OUT THE GOOD FROM THE EVIL, AS I HAD FAILED TO DO BEFORE MY DEATH."
I AM SHOWN A GLIMPSE OF SOMETHING TERRIBLE THAT IS GOING TO HAPPEN, ***BEFORE*** IT HAPPENS.
I HAVE TIME, A FEW DAYS, SOMETIMES MORE, TO FIND OUT IF THE PERSON IT IS GOING TO HAPPEN TO ***DESERVES*** IT OR NOT.
IF HE DOES NOT DESERVE IT, I MUST DO ALL I CAN TO STOP IT FROM HAPPENING, AND PROTECT THE INNOCENT.
BUT IF HE DOES DESERVE WHAT IS COMING, THEN I MUST DO WHATEVER IS NECESSARY TO ENSURE THAT THE TERRIBLE THING TAKES PLACE AS SCHEDULED. I MUST BEAR WITNESS TO THE GUILT, THE CRIME, AND THE PUNISHMENT, TO CERTIFY THAT JUSTICE HAS BEEN DONE.

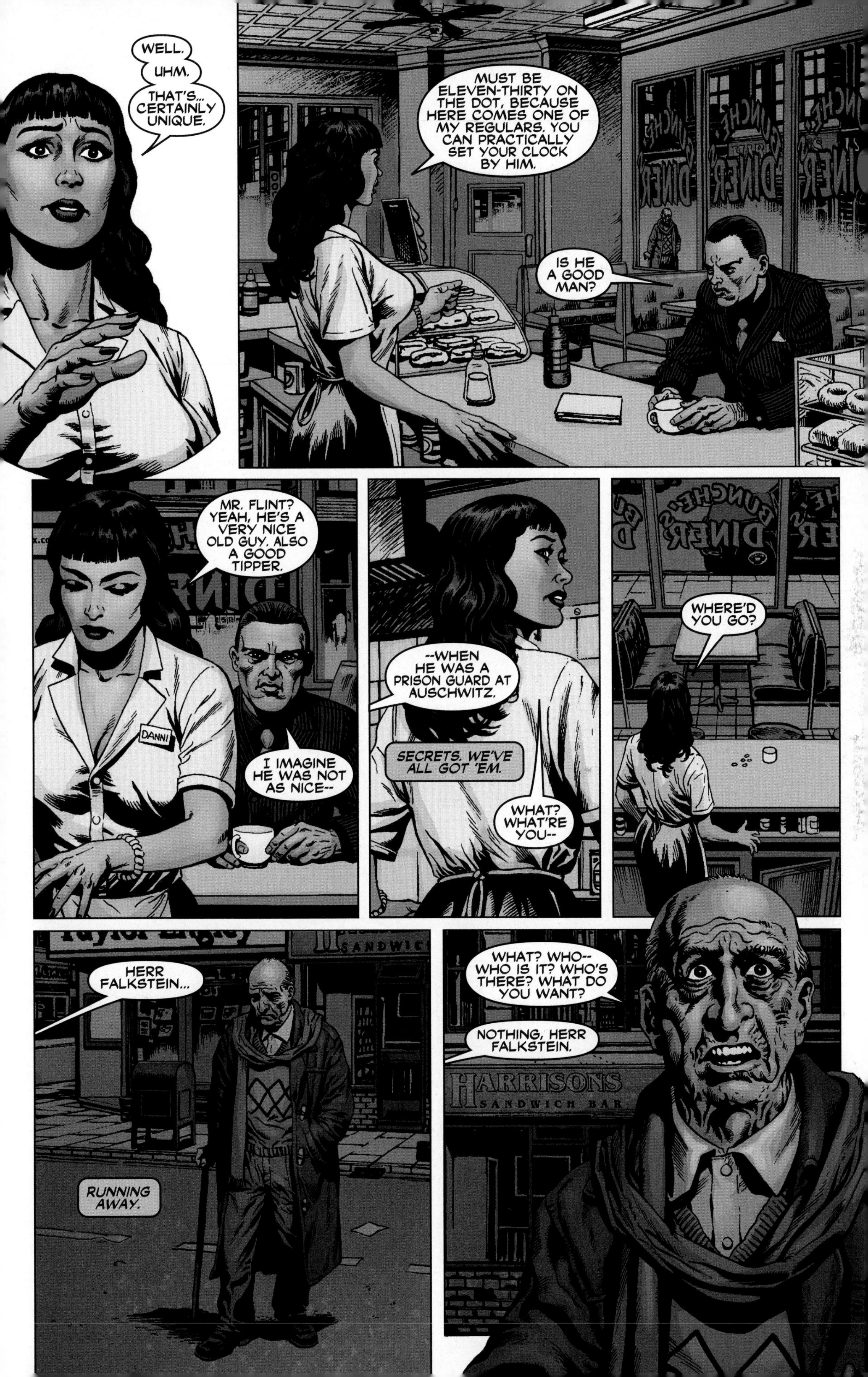
WELL.
UHM.
THAT'S... CERTAINLY UNIQUE.
MUST BE ELEVEN-THIRTY ON THE DOT, BECAUSE HERE COMES ONE OF MY REGULARS. YOU CAN PRACTICALLY SET YOUR CLOCK BY HIM.
IS HE A GOOD MAN?
MR. FLINT? YEAH, HE'S A VERY NICE OLD GUY. ALSO A GOOD TIPPER.
DANNI
I IMAGINE HE WAS NOT AS NICE--
--WHEN HE WAS A PRISON GUARD AT AUSCHWITZ.
SECRETS. WE'VE ALL GOT 'EM.
WHAT? WHAT'RE YOU--
WHERE'D YOU GO?
HERR FALKSTEIN...
RUNNING AWAY.
WHAT? WHO-- WHO IS IT? WHO'S THERE? WHAT DO YOU WANT?
NOTHING, HERR FALKSTEIN.
HARRISONS
SANDWICH BAR

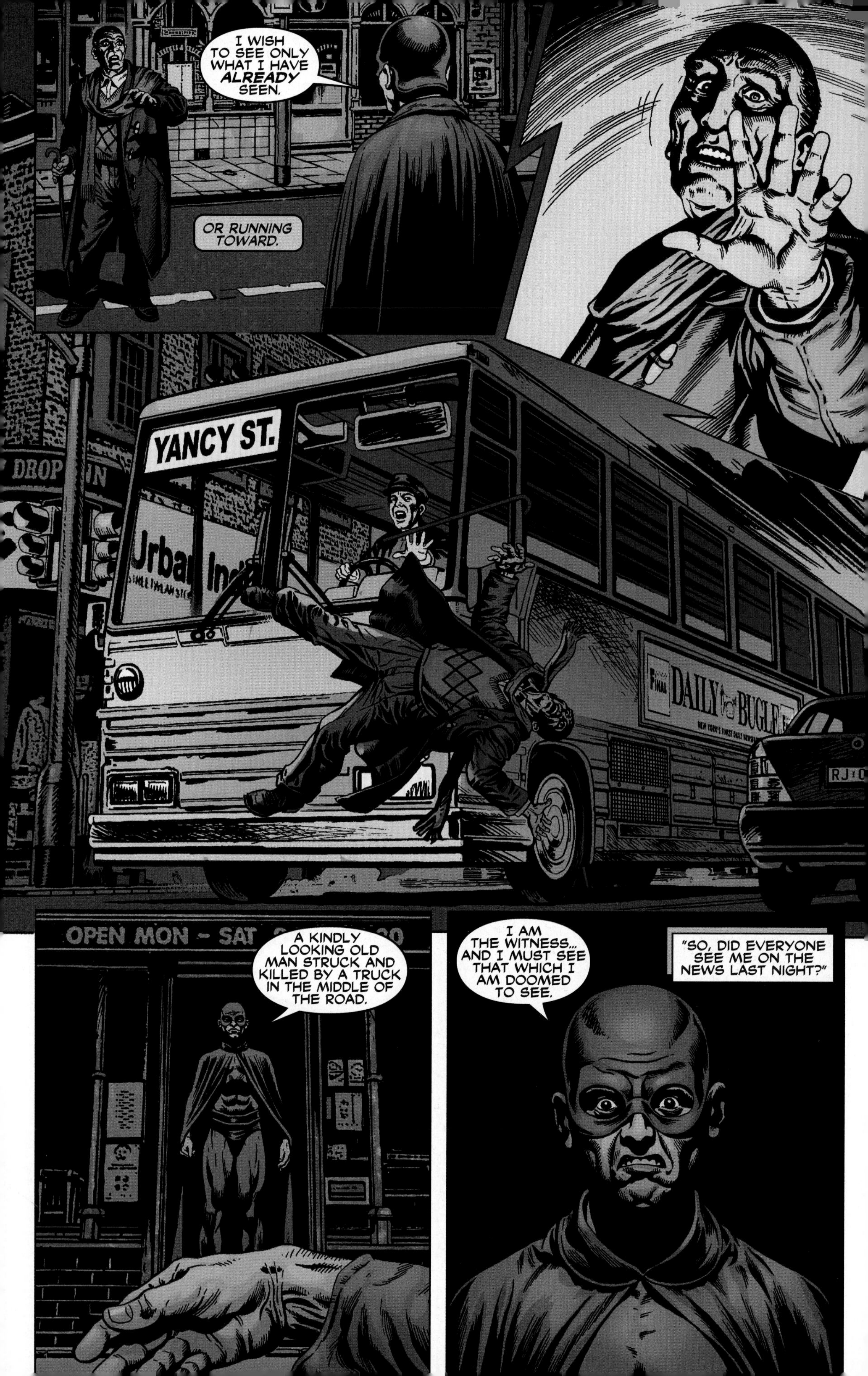
I WISH TO SEE ONLY WHAT I HAVE *ALREADY* SEEN.
OR RUNNING TOWARD.
YANCY ST.
DROP IN
DAILY BUGLE
OPEN MON - SAT
A KINDLY LOOKING OLD MAN STRUCK AND KILLED BY A TRUCK IN THE MIDDLE OF THE ROAD.
I AM THE WITNESS... AND I MUST SEE THAT WHICH I AM DOOMED TO SEE.
"SO, DID EVERYONE SEE ME ON THE NEWS LAST NIGHT?"

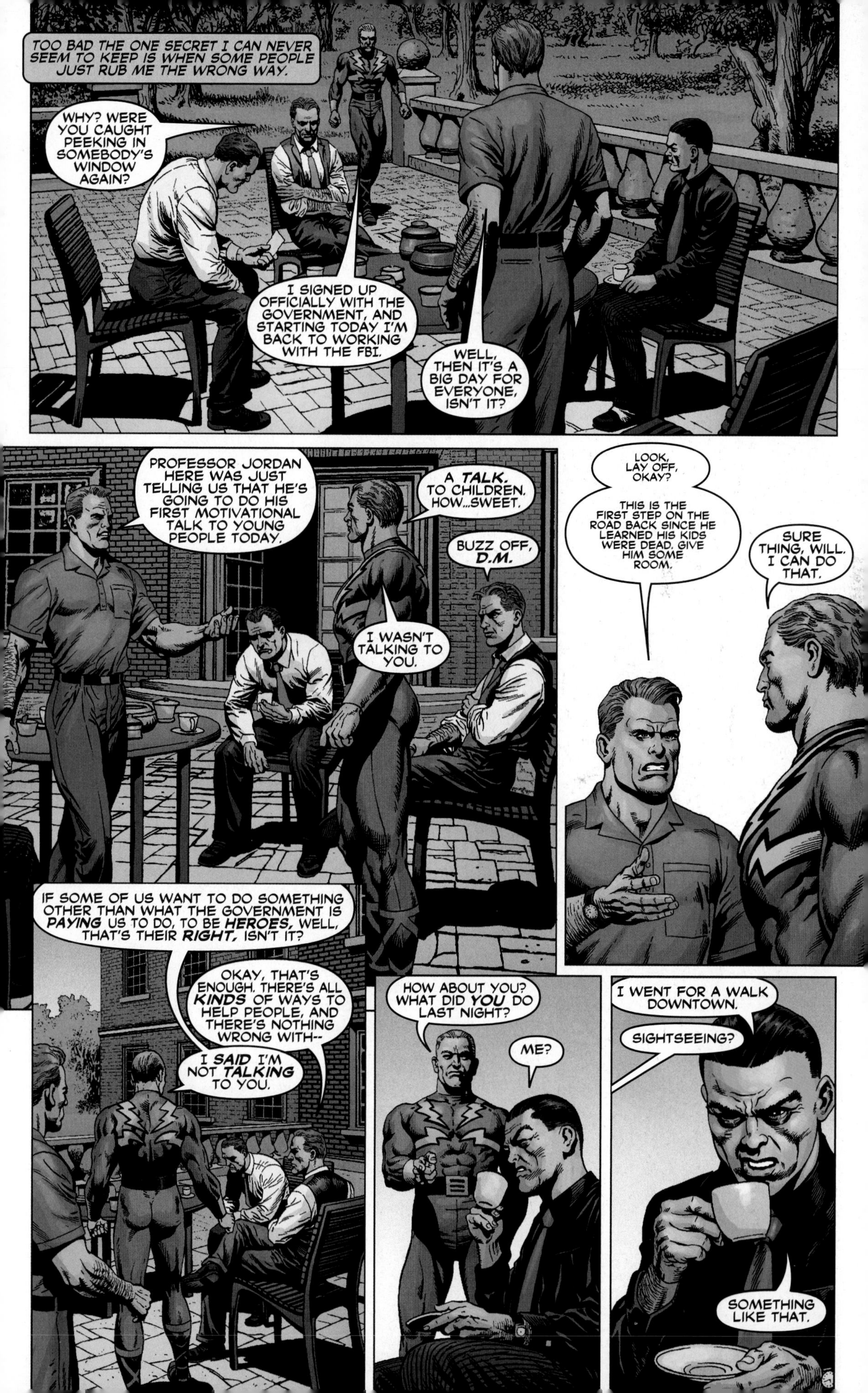

TOO BAD THE ONE SECRET I CAN NEVER SEEM TO KEEP IS WHEN SOME PEOPLE JUST RUB ME THE WRONG WAY.
WHY? WERE YOU CAUGHT PEEKING IN SOMEBODY'S WINDOW AGAIN?
I SIGNED UP OFFICIALLY WITH THE GOVERNMENT, AND STARTING TODAY I'M BACK TO WORKING WITH THE FBI.
WELL, THEN IT'S A BIG DAY FOR EVERYONE, ISN'T IT?
PROFESSOR JORDAN HERE WAS JUST TELLING US THAT HE'S GOING TO DO HIS FIRST MOTIVATIONAL TALK TO YOUNG PEOPLE TODAY.
A TALK. TO CHILDREN. HOW...SWEET.
BUZZ OFF, D.M.
I WASN'T TALKING TO YOU.
LOOK, LAY OFF, OKAY?
THIS IS THE FIRST STEP ON THE ROAD BACK SINCE HE LEARNED HIS KIDS WERE DEAD. GIVE HIM SOME ROOM.
SURE THING, WILL. I CAN DO THAT.
IF SOME OF US WANT TO DO SOMETHING OTHER THAN WHAT THE GOVERNMENT IS PAYING US TO DO, TO BE HEROES, WELL, THAT'S THEIR RIGHT, ISN'T IT?
OKAY, THAT'S ENOUGH. THERE'S ALL KINDS OF WAYS TO HELP PEOPLE, AND THERE'S NOTHING WRONG WITH--
I SAID I'M NOT TALKING TO YOU.
HOW ABOUT YOU? WHAT DID YOU DO LAST NIGHT?
ME?
I WENT FOR A WALK DOWNTOWN.
SIGHTSEEING?
SOMETHING LIKE THAT.

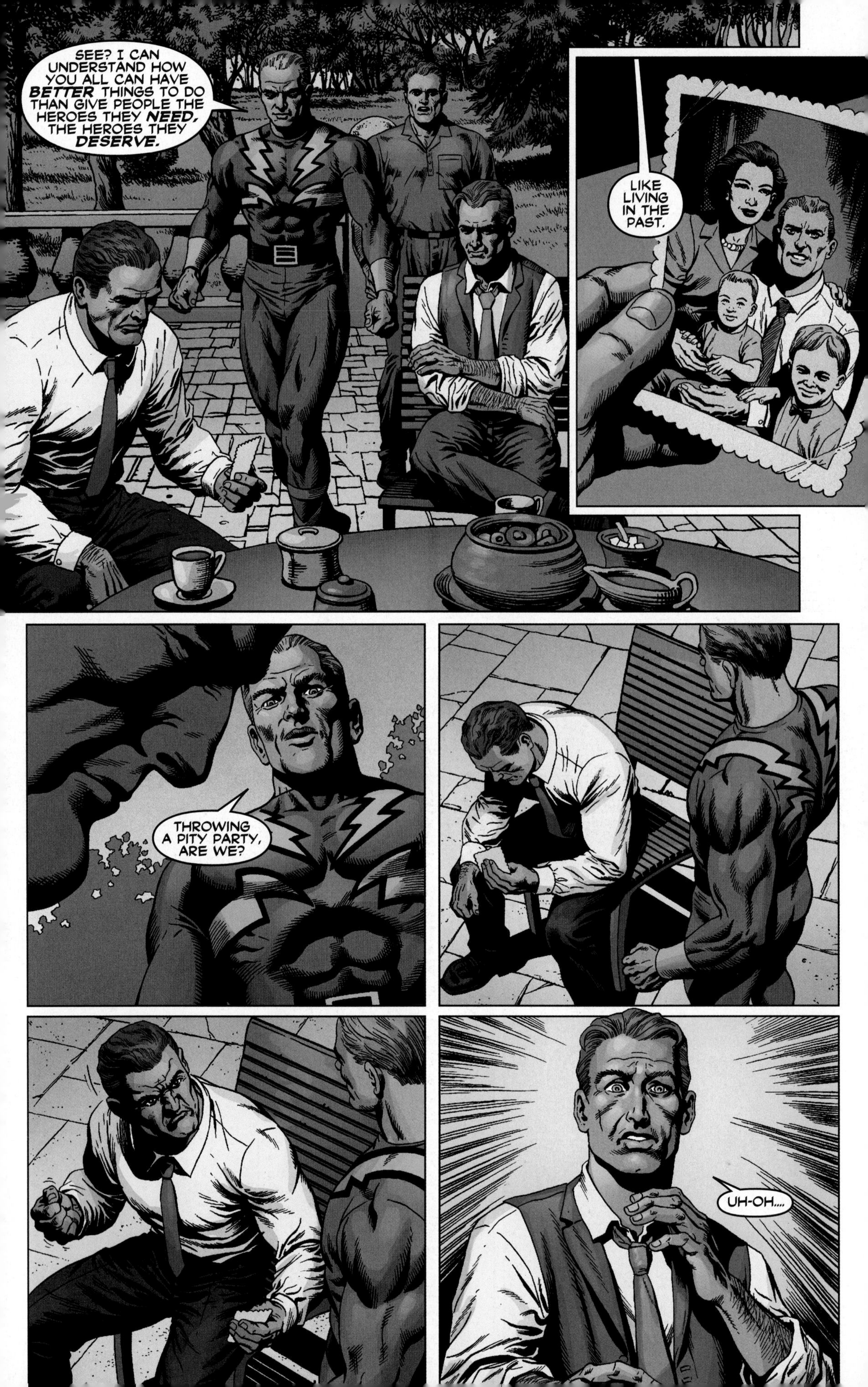
SEE? I CAN UNDERSTAND HOW YOU ALL CAN HAVE BETTER THINGS TO DO THAN GIVE PEOPLE THE HEROES THEY NEED, THE HEROES THEY DESERVE.
LIKE LIVING IN THE PAST.
THROWING A PITY PARTY, ARE WE?
UH-OH....

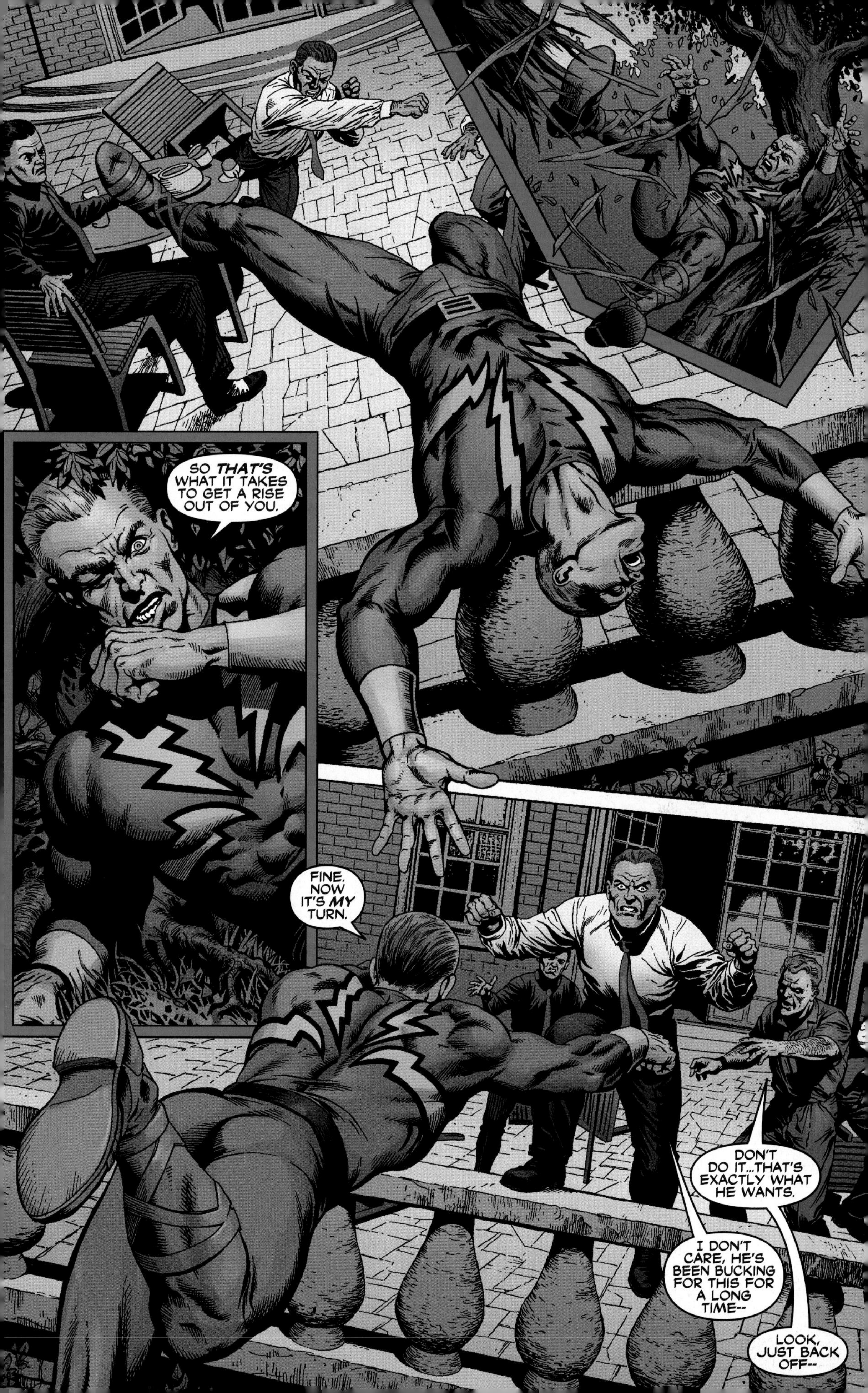
SO THAT'S WHAT IT TAKES TO GET A RISE OUT OF YOU.
FINE. NOW IT'S MY TURN.
DON'T DO IT...THAT'S EXACTLY WHAT HE WANTS.
I DON'T CARE, HE'S BEEN BUCKING FOR THIS FOR A LONG TIME--
LOOK, JUST BACK OFF--

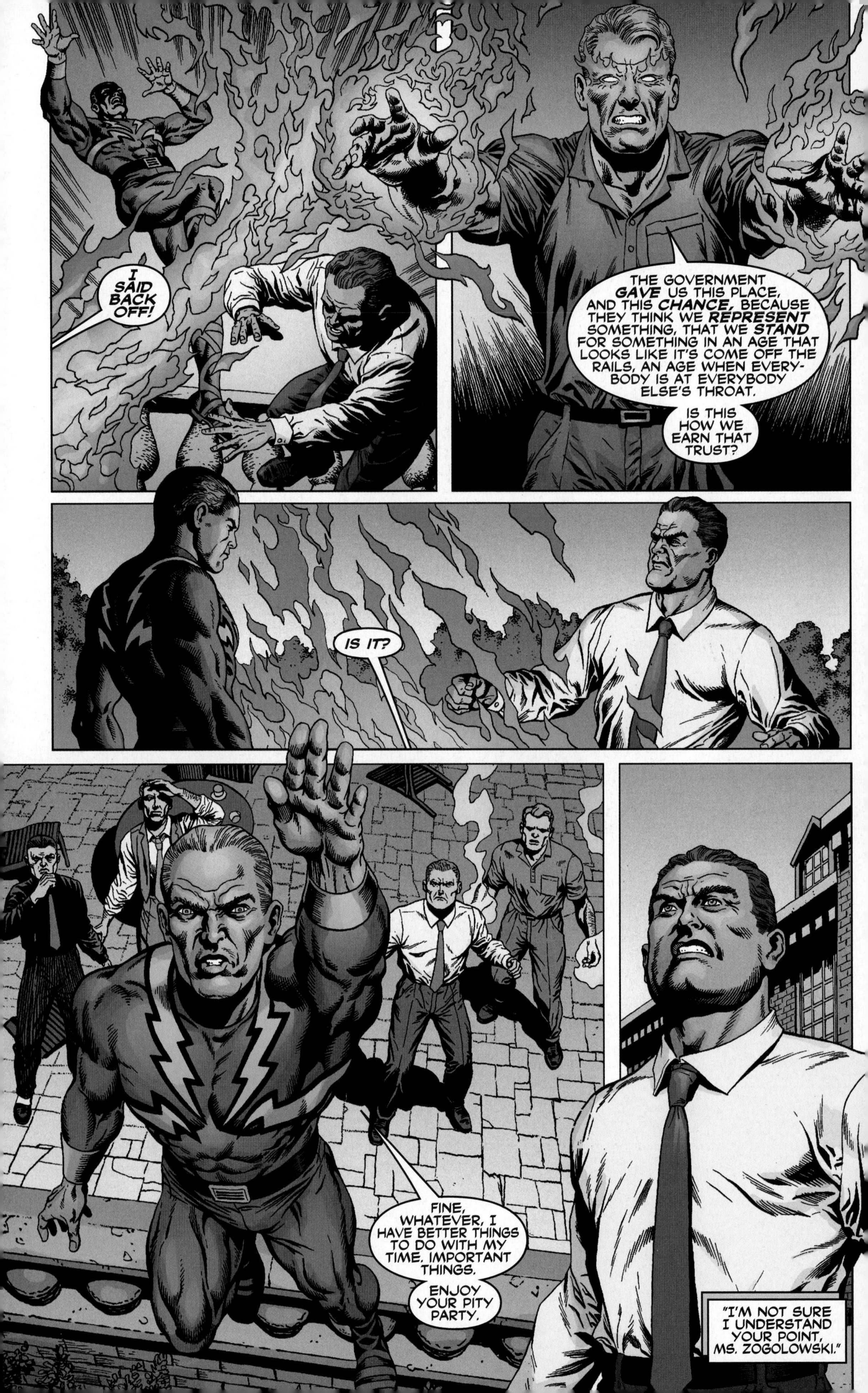
I SAID BACK OFF!
THE GOVERNMENT GAVE US THIS PLACE, AND THIS CHANCE, BECAUSE THEY THINK WE REPRESENT SOMETHING, THAT WE STAND FOR SOMETHING IN AN AGE THAT LOOKS LIKE IT'S COME OFF THE RAILS, AN AGE WHEN EVERY-BODY IS AT EVERYBODY ELSE'S THROAT.
IS THIS HOW WE EARN THAT TRUST?
IS IT?
FINE, WHATEVER, I HAVE BETTER THINGS TO DO WITH MY TIME. IMPORTANT THINGS.
ENJOY YOUR PITY PARTY.
"I'M NOT SURE I UNDERSTAND YOUR POINT, MS. ZOGOLOWSKI."

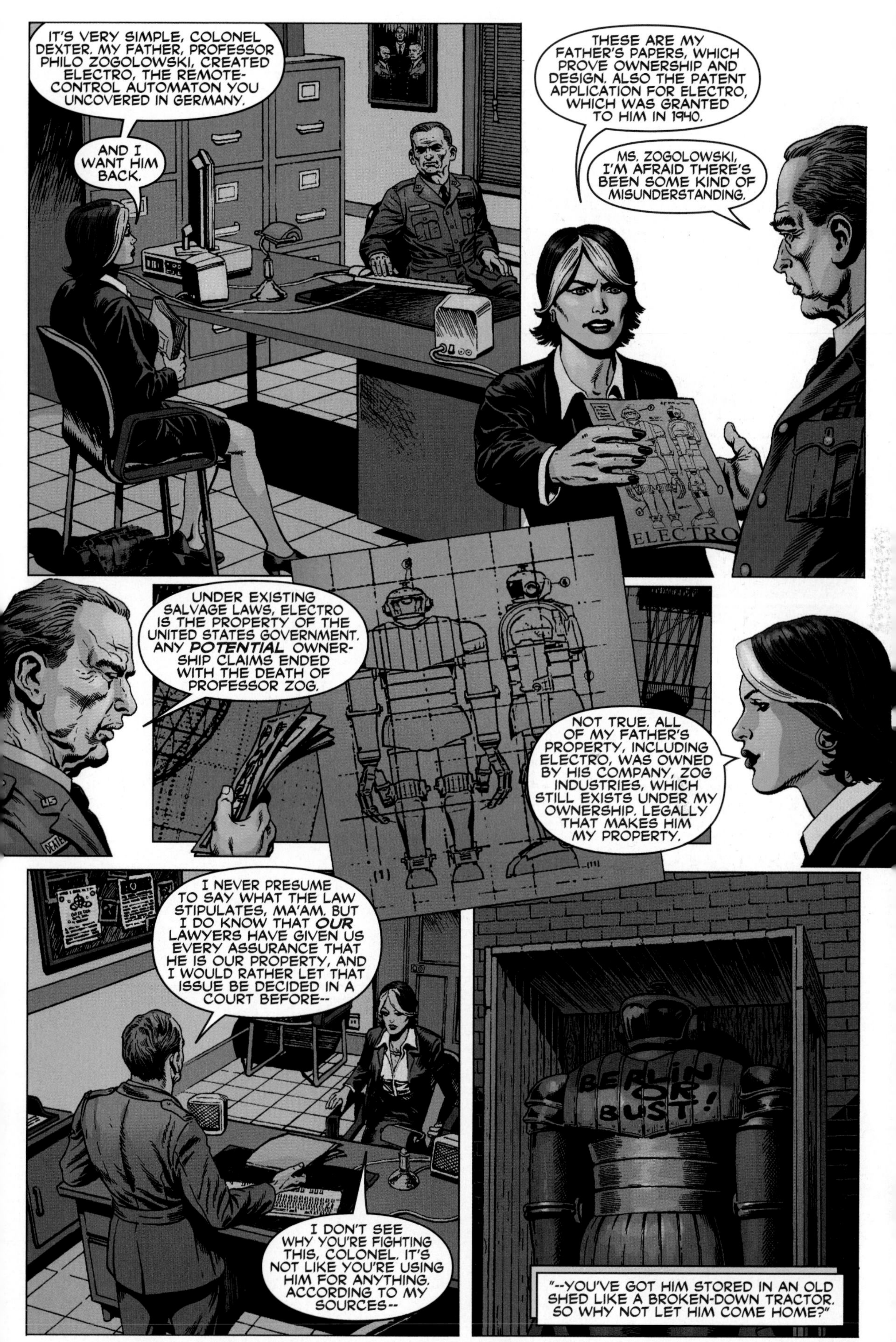
IT'S VERY SIMPLE, COLONEL DEXTER. MY FATHER, PROFESSOR PHILO ZOGOLOWSKI, CREATED ELECTRO, THE REMOTE-CONTROL AUTOMATON YOU UNCOVERED IN GERMANY.
AND I WANT HIM BACK.
THESE ARE MY FATHER'S PAPERS, WHICH PROVE OWNERSHIP AND DESIGN. ALSO THE PATENT APPLICATION FOR ELECTRO, WHICH WAS GRANTED TO HIM IN 1940.
MS. ZOGOLOWSKI, I'M AFRAID THERE'S BEEN SOME KIND OF MISUNDERSTANDING.
ELECTRO
UNDER EXISTING SALVAGE LAWS, ELECTRO IS THE PROPERTY OF THE UNITED STATES GOVERNMENT. ANY *POTENTIAL* OWNERSHIP CLAIMS ENDED WITH THE DEATH OF PROFESSOR ZOG.
NOT TRUE. ALL OF MY FATHER'S PROPERTY, INCLUDING ELECTRO, WAS OWNED BY HIS COMPANY, ZOG INDUSTRIES, WHICH STILL EXISTS UNDER MY OWNERSHIP. LEGALLY THAT MAKES HIM MY PROPERTY.
I NEVER PRESUME TO SAY WHAT THE LAW STIPULATES, MA'AM. BUT I DO KNOW THAT *OUR* LAWYERS HAVE GIVEN US EVERY ASSURANCE THAT HE IS OUR PROPERTY, AND I WOULD RATHER LET THAT ISSUE BE DECIDED IN A COURT BEFORE--
I DON'T SEE WHY YOU'RE FIGHTING THIS, COLONEL. IT'S NOT LIKE YOU'RE USING HIM FOR ANYTHING. ACCORDING TO MY SOURCES--
BERLIN OR BUST!
"--YOU'VE GOT HIM STORED IN AN OLD SHED LIKE A BROKEN-DOWN TRACTOR. SO WHY NOT LET HIM COME HOME?"

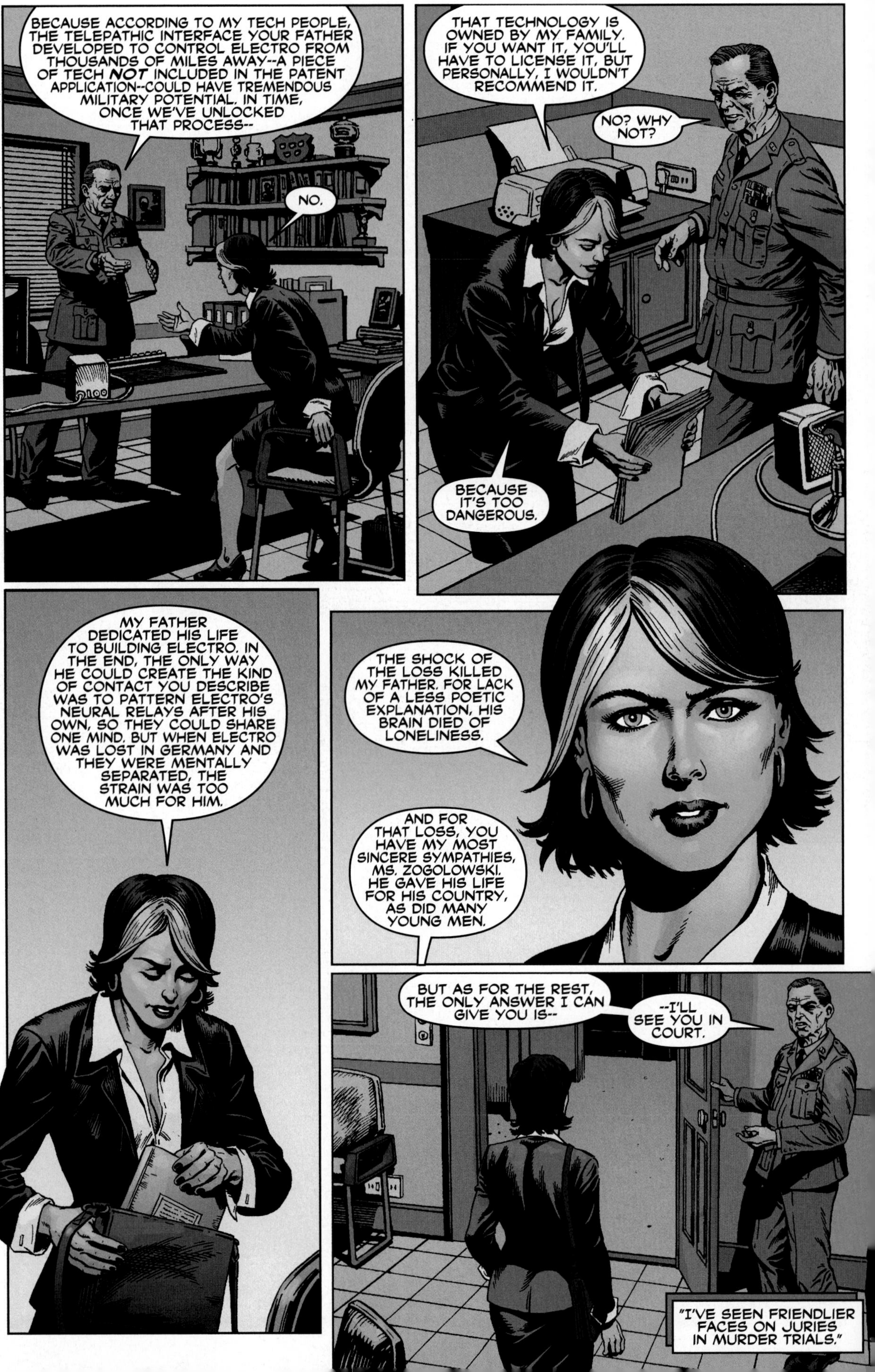
BECAUSE ACCORDING TO MY TECH PEOPLE, THE TELEPATHIC INTERFACE YOUR FATHER DEVELOPED TO CONTROL ELECTRO FROM THOUSANDS OF MILES AWAY--A PIECE OF TECH **NOT** INCLUDED IN THE PATENT APPLICATION--COULD HAVE TREMENDOUS MILITARY POTENTIAL. IN TIME, ONCE WE'VE UNLOCKED THAT PROCESS--
NO.
THAT TECHNOLOGY IS OWNED BY MY FAMILY. IF YOU WANT IT, YOU'LL HAVE TO LICENSE IT, BUT PERSONALLY, I WOULDN'T RECOMMEND IT.
NO? WHY NOT?
BECAUSE IT'S TOO DANGEROUS.
MY FATHER DEDICATED HIS LIFE TO BUILDING ELECTRO. IN THE END, THE ONLY WAY HE COULD CREATE THE KIND OF CONTACT YOU DESCRIBE WAS TO PATTERN ELECTRO'S NEURAL RELAYS AFTER HIS OWN, SO THEY COULD SHARE ONE MIND. BUT WHEN ELECTRO WAS LOST IN GERMANY AND THEY WERE MENTALLY SEPARATED, THE STRAIN WAS TOO MUCH FOR HIM.
THE SHOCK OF THE LOSS KILLED MY FATHER. FOR LACK OF A LESS POETIC EXPLANATION, HIS BRAIN DIED OF LONELINESS.
AND FOR THAT LOSS, YOU HAVE MY MOST SINCERE SYMPATHIES, MS. ZOGOLOWSKI. HE GAVE HIS LIFE FOR HIS COUNTRY, AS DID MANY YOUNG MEN.
BUT AS FOR THE REST, THE ONLY ANSWER I CAN GIVE YOU IS--
--I'LL SEE YOU IN COURT.
"I'VE SEEN FRIENDLIER FACES ON JURIES IN MURDER TRIALS."

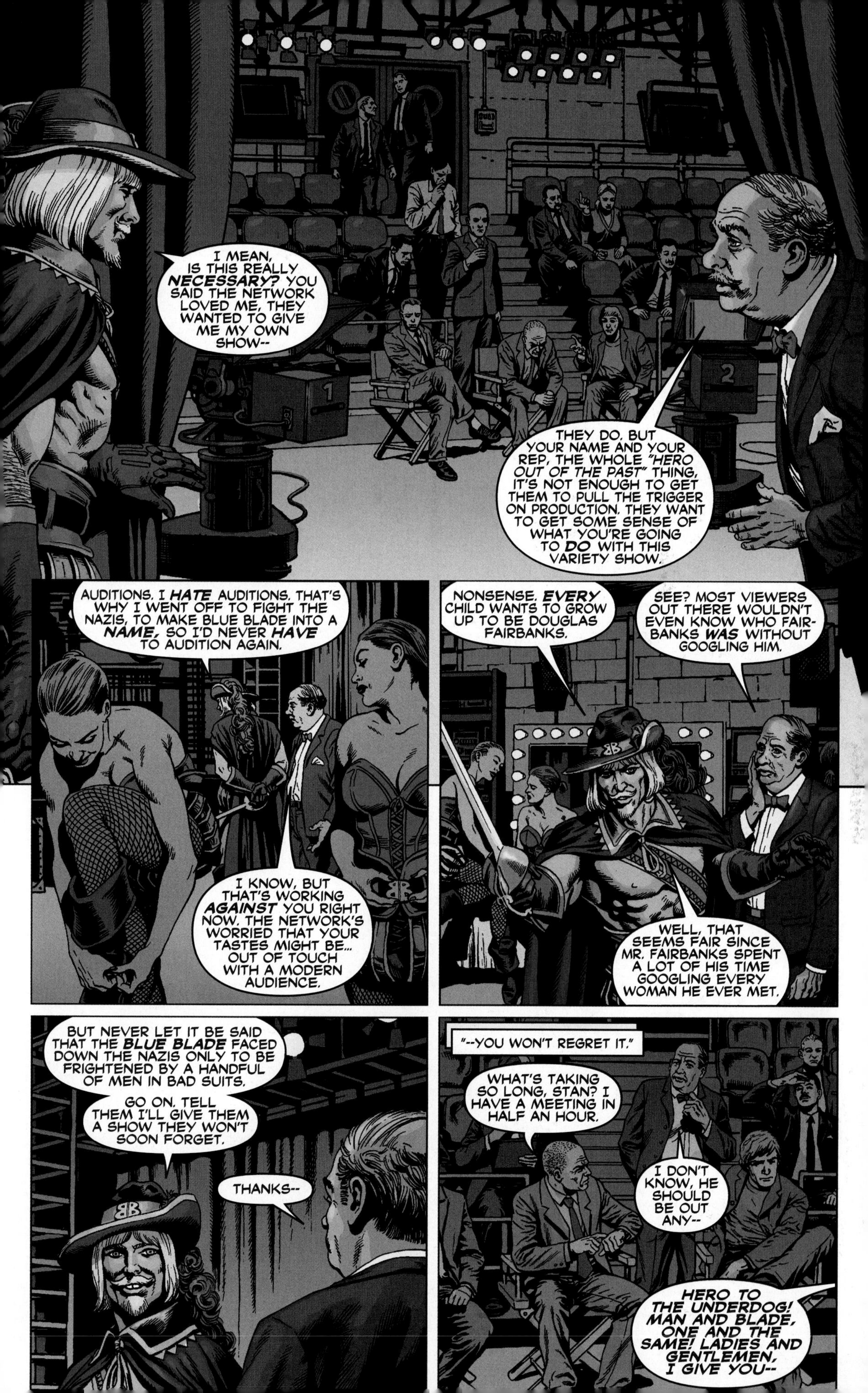

I MEAN, IS THIS REALLY NECESSARY? YOU SAID THE NETWORK LOVED ME, THEY WANTED TO GIVE ME MY OWN SHOW--
THEY DO. BUT YOUR NAME AND YOUR REP, THE WHOLE "HERO OUT OF THE PAST" THING, IT'S NOT ENOUGH TO GET THEM TO PULL THE TRIGGER ON PRODUCTION. THEY WANT TO GET SOME SENSE OF WHAT YOU'RE GOING TO DO WITH THIS VARIETY SHOW.
AUDITIONS. I HATE AUDITIONS. THAT'S WHY I WENT OFF TO FIGHT THE NAZIS, TO MAKE BLUE BLADE INTO A NAME, SO I'D NEVER HAVE TO AUDITION AGAIN.
I KNOW, BUT THAT'S WORKING AGAINST YOU RIGHT NOW. THE NETWORK'S WORRIED THAT YOUR TASTES MIGHT BE... OUT OF TOUCH WITH A MODERN AUDIENCE.
NONSENSE. EVERY CHILD WANTS TO GROW UP TO BE DOUGLAS FAIRBANKS.
SEE? MOST VIEWERS OUT THERE WOULDN'T EVEN KNOW WHO FAIRBANKS WAS WITHOUT GOOGLING HIM.
WELL, THAT SEEMS FAIR SINCE MR. FAIRBANKS SPENT A LOT OF HIS TIME GOOGLING EVERY WOMAN HE EVER MET.
BUT NEVER LET IT BE SAID THAT THE BLUE BLADE FACED DOWN THE NAZIS ONLY TO BE FRIGHTENED BY A HANDFUL OF MEN IN BAD SUITS.
GO ON. TELL THEM I'LL GIVE THEM A SHOW THEY WON'T SOON FORGET.
THANKS--
"--YOU WON'T REGRET IT."
WHAT'S TAKING SO LONG, STAN? I HAVE A MEETING IN HALF AN HOUR.
I DON'T KNOW, HE SHOULD BE OUT ANY--
HERO TO THE UNDERDOG! MAN AND BLADE, ONE AND THE SAME! LADIES AND GENTLEMEN, I GIVE YOU--

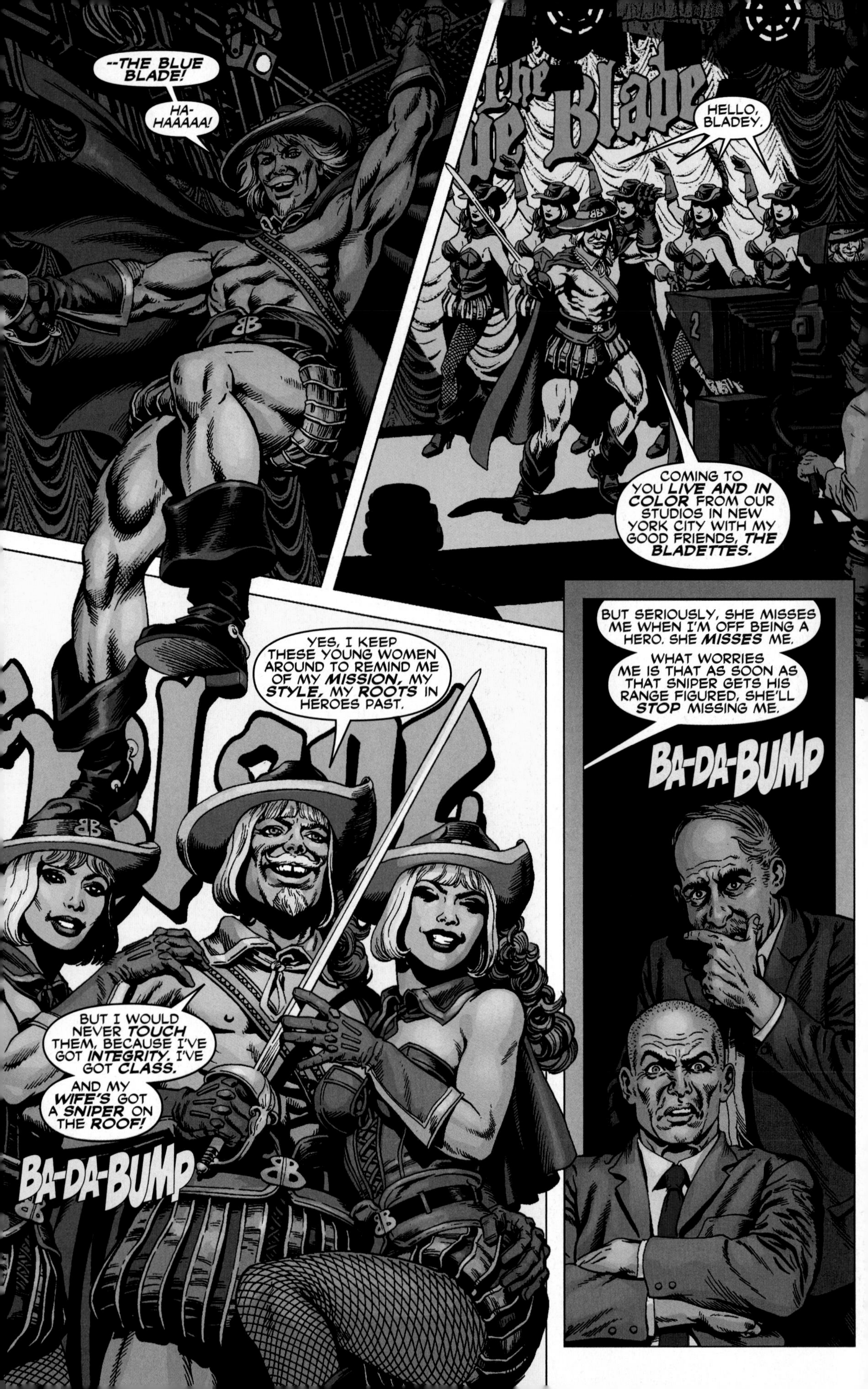

--THE BLUE BLADE!
HA-HAAAAA!
The Blue Blade
HELLO, BLADEY.
COMING TO YOU LIVE AND IN COLOR FROM OUR STUDIOS IN NEW YORK CITY WITH MY GOOD FRIENDS, THE BLADETTES.
YES, I KEEP THESE YOUNG WOMEN AROUND TO REMIND ME OF MY MISSION, MY STYLE, MY ROOTS IN HEROES PAST.
BUT I WOULD NEVER TOUCH THEM, BECAUSE I'VE GOT INTEGRITY. I'VE GOT CLASS.
AND MY WIFE'S GOT A SNIPER ON THE ROOF!
BA-DA-BUMP
BUT SERIOUSLY, SHE MISSES ME WHEN I'M OFF BEING A HERO. SHE MISSES ME.
WHAT WORRIES ME IS THAT AS SOON AS THAT SNIPER GETS HIS RANGE FIGURED, SHE'LL STOP MISSING ME.
BA-DA-BUMP

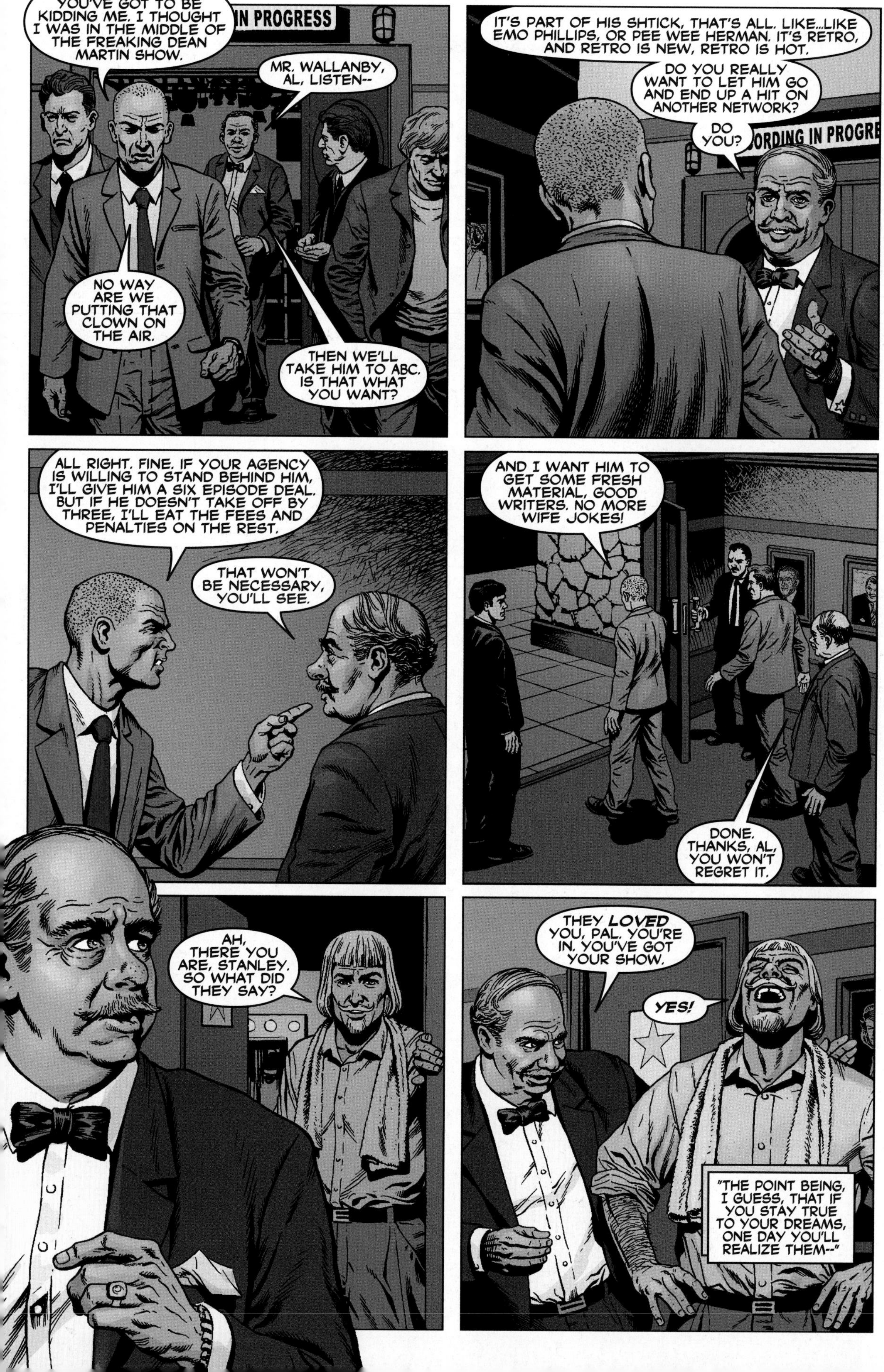

IN PROGRESS
WIFE JOKES? YOU'VE GOT TO BE KIDDING ME. I THOUGHT I WAS IN THE MIDDLE OF THE FREAKING DEAN MARTIN SHOW.
MR. WALLANBY, AL, LISTEN--
NO WAY ARE WE PUTTING THAT CLOWN ON THE AIR.
THEN WE'LL TAKE HIM TO ABC. IS THAT WHAT YOU WANT?
IT'S PART OF HIS SHTICK, THAT'S ALL. LIKE...LIKE EMO PHILLIPS, OR PEE WEE HERMAN. IT'S RETRO, AND RETRO IS NEW, RETRO IS HOT.
DO YOU REALLY WANT TO LET HIM GO AND END UP A HIT ON ANOTHER NETWORK?
DO YOU?
ORDING IN PROGRE
ALL RIGHT. FINE. IF YOUR AGENCY IS WILLING TO STAND BEHIND HIM, I'LL GIVE HIM A SIX EPISODE DEAL. BUT IF HE DOESN'T TAKE OFF BY THREE, I'LL EAT THE FEES AND PENALTIES ON THE REST.
THAT WON'T BE NECESSARY, YOU'LL SEE.
AND I WANT HIM TO GET SOME FRESH MATERIAL, GOOD WRITERS. NO MORE WIFE JOKES!
DONE. THANKS, AL, YOU WON'T REGRET IT.
AH, THERE YOU ARE, STANLEY. SO WHAT DID THEY SAY?
THEY *LOVED* YOU, PAL. YOU'RE IN. YOU'VE GOT YOUR SHOW.
YES!
"THE POINT BEING, I GUESS, THAT IF YOU STAY TRUE TO YOUR DREAMS, ONE DAY YOU'LL REALIZE THEM--"

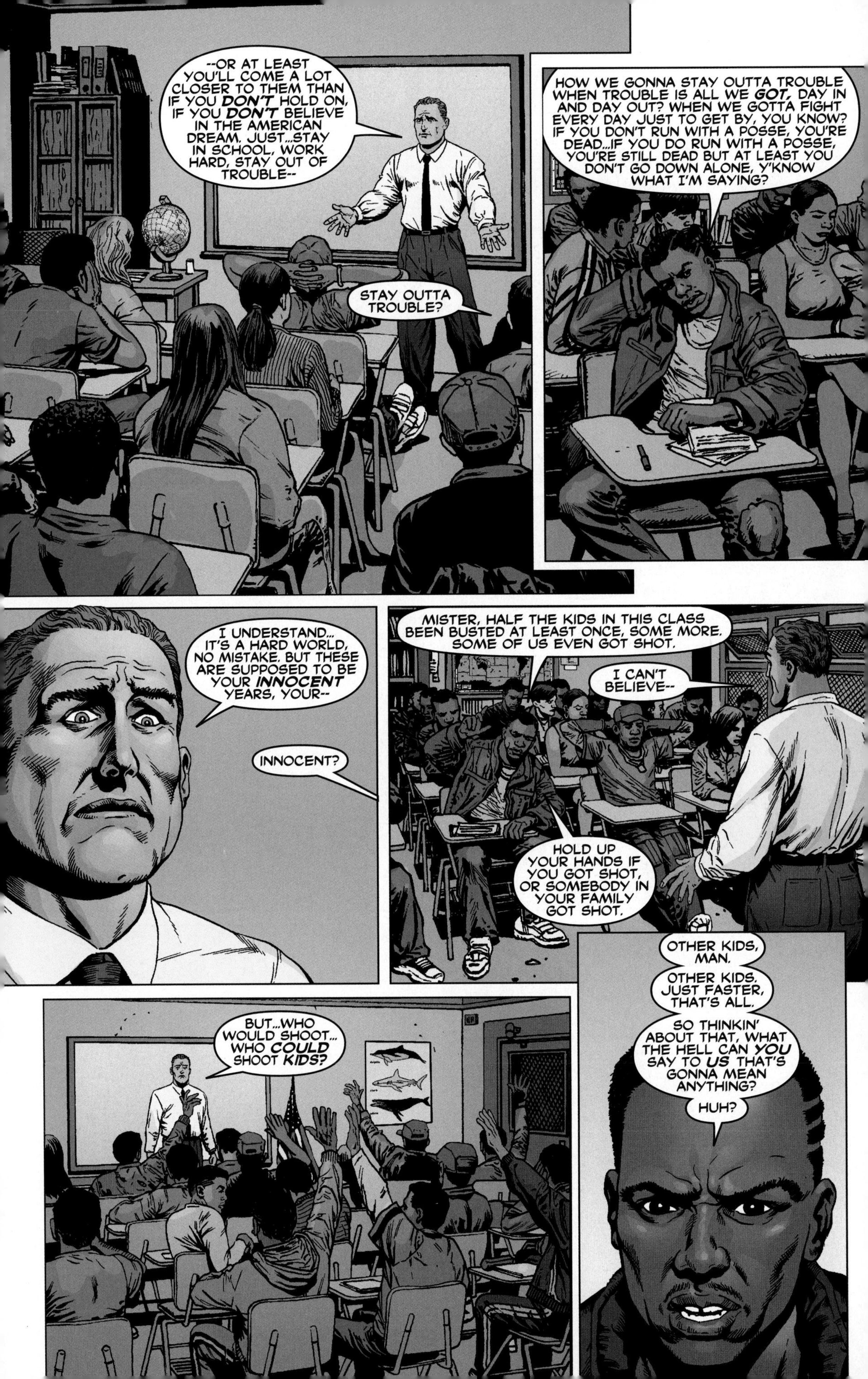
--OR AT LEAST YOU'LL COME A LOT CLOSER TO THEM THAN IF YOU DON'T HOLD ON, IF YOU DON'T BELIEVE IN THE AMERICAN DREAM. JUST...STAY IN SCHOOL, WORK HARD, STAY OUT OF TROUBLE--
STAY OUTTA TROUBLE?
HOW WE GONNA STAY OUTTA TROUBLE WHEN TROUBLE IS ALL WE GOT, DAY IN AND DAY OUT? WHEN WE GOTTA FIGHT EVERY DAY JUST TO GET BY, YOU KNOW? IF YOU DON'T RUN WITH A POSSE, YOU'RE DEAD...IF YOU DO RUN WITH A POSSE, YOU'RE STILL DEAD BUT AT LEAST YOU DON'T GO DOWN ALONE, Y'KNOW WHAT I'M SAYING?
I UNDERSTAND... IT'S A HARD WORLD, NO MISTAKE. BUT THESE ARE SUPPOSED TO BE YOUR INNOCENT YEARS, YOUR--
INNOCENT?
MISTER, HALF THE KIDS IN THIS CLASS BEEN BUSTED AT LEAST ONCE, SOME MORE. SOME OF US EVEN GOT SHOT.
I CAN'T BELIEVE--
HOLD UP YOUR HANDS IF YOU GOT SHOT, OR SOMEBODY IN YOUR FAMILY GOT SHOT.
BUT...WHO WOULD SHOOT... WHO COULD SHOOT KIDS?
OTHER KIDS, MAN.
OTHER KIDS. JUST FASTER, THAT'S ALL.
SO THINKIN' ABOUT THAT, WHAT THE HELL CAN YOU SAY TO US THAT'S GONNA MEAN ANYTHING?
HUH?

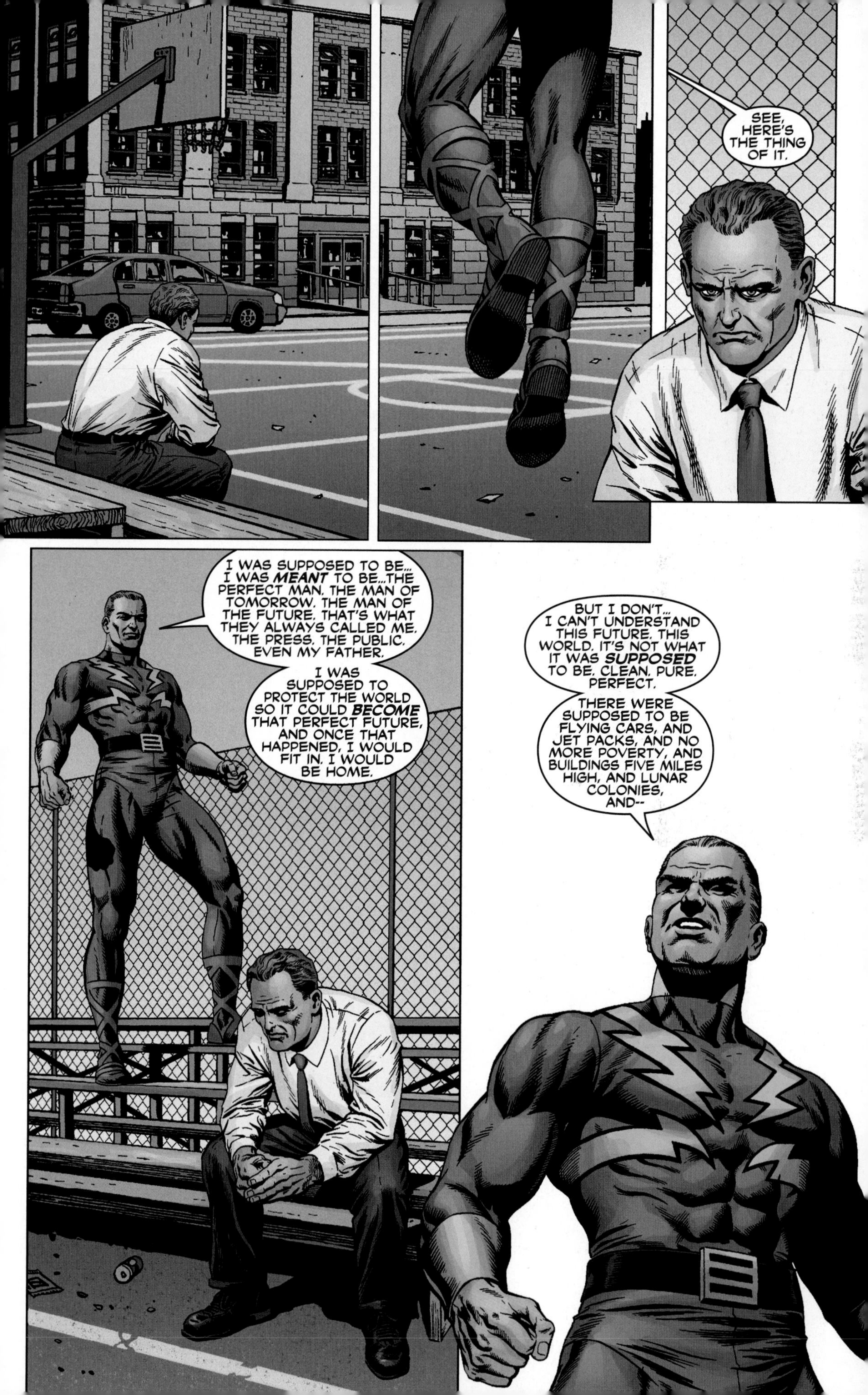
SEE, HERE'S THE THING OF IT.
I WAS SUPPOSED TO BE... I WAS *MEANT* TO BE...THE PERFECT MAN. THE MAN OF TOMORROW. THE MAN OF THE FUTURE. THAT'S WHAT THEY ALWAYS CALLED ME. THE PRESS. THE PUBLIC. EVEN MY FATHER.
I WAS SUPPOSED TO PROTECT THE WORLD SO IT COULD *BECOME* THAT PERFECT FUTURE, AND ONCE THAT HAPPENED, I WOULD FIT IN. I WOULD BE HOME.
BUT I DON'T... I CAN'T UNDERSTAND THIS FUTURE. THIS WORLD. IT'S NOT WHAT IT WAS *SUPPOSED* TO BE. CLEAN. PURE. PERFECT.
THERE WERE SUPPOSED TO BE FLYING CARS, AND JET PACKS, AND NO MORE POVERTY, AND BUILDINGS FIVE MILES HIGH, AND LUNAR COLONIES, AND--

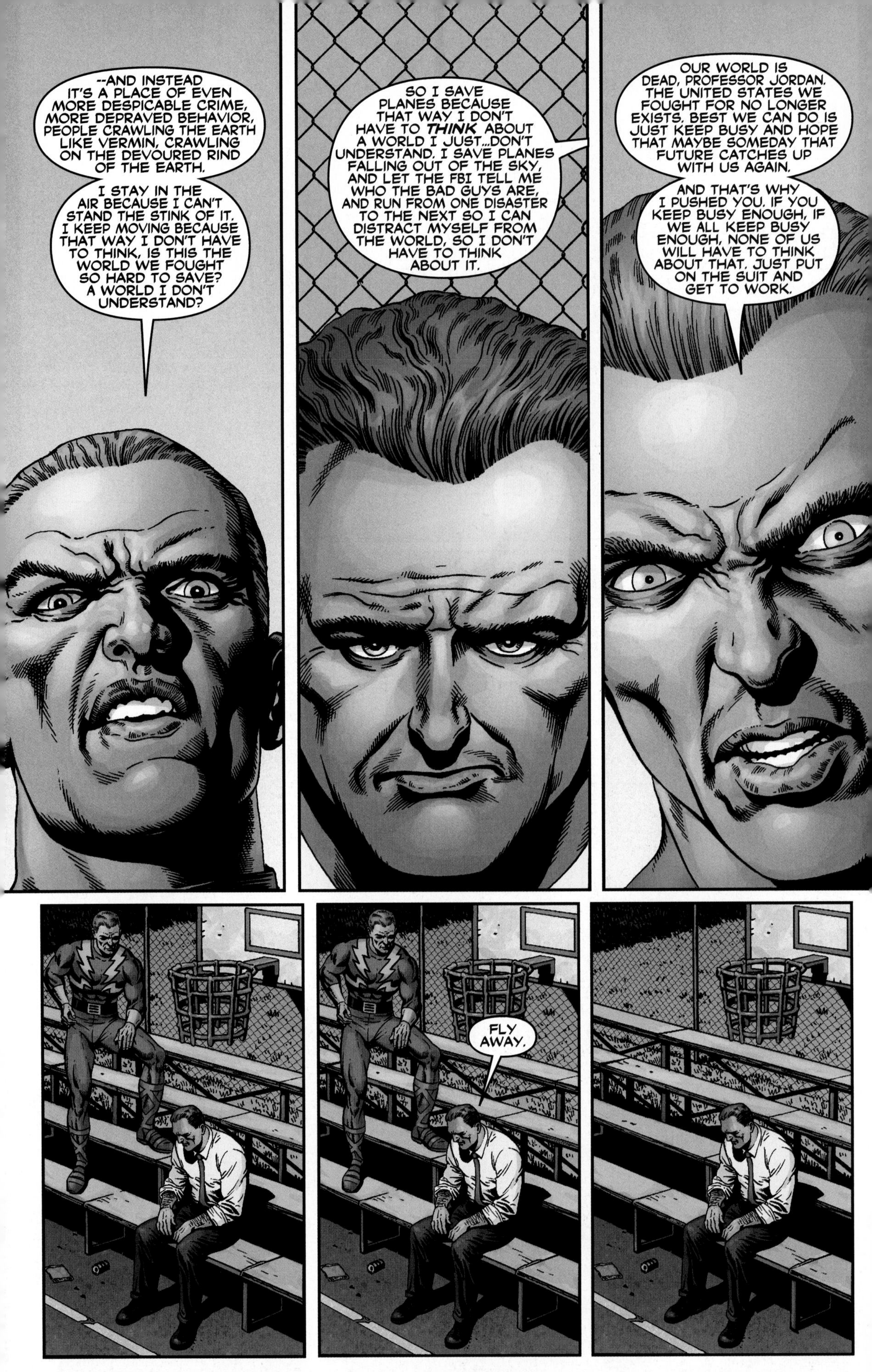
--AND INSTEAD IT'S A PLACE OF EVEN MORE DESPICABLE CRIME, MORE DEPRAVED BEHAVIOR, PEOPLE CRAWLING THE EARTH LIKE VERMIN, CRAWLING ON THE DEVOURED RIND OF THE EARTH.
I STAY IN THE AIR BECAUSE I CAN'T STAND THE STINK OF IT. I KEEP MOVING BECAUSE THAT WAY I DON'T HAVE TO THINK, IS THIS THE WORLD WE FOUGHT SO HARD TO SAVE? A WORLD I DON'T UNDERSTAND?
SO I SAVE PLANES BECAUSE THAT WAY I DON'T HAVE TO *THINK* ABOUT A WORLD I JUST...DON'T UNDERSTAND. I SAVE PLANES FALLING OUT OF THE SKY, AND LET THE FBI TELL ME WHO THE BAD GUYS ARE, AND RUN FROM ONE DISASTER TO THE NEXT SO I CAN DISTRACT MYSELF FROM THE WORLD, SO I DON'T HAVE TO THINK ABOUT IT.
OUR WORLD IS DEAD, PROFESSOR JORDAN. THE UNITED STATES WE FOUGHT FOR NO LONGER EXISTS. BEST WE CAN DO IS JUST KEEP BUSY AND HOPE THAT MAYBE SOMEDAY THAT FUTURE CATCHES UP WITH US AGAIN.
AND THAT'S WHY I PUSHED YOU. IF YOU KEEP BUSY ENOUGH, IF WE ALL KEEP BUSY ENOUGH, NONE OF US WILL HAVE TO THINK ABOUT THAT. JUST PUT ON THE SUIT AND GET TO WORK.
FLY AWAY.

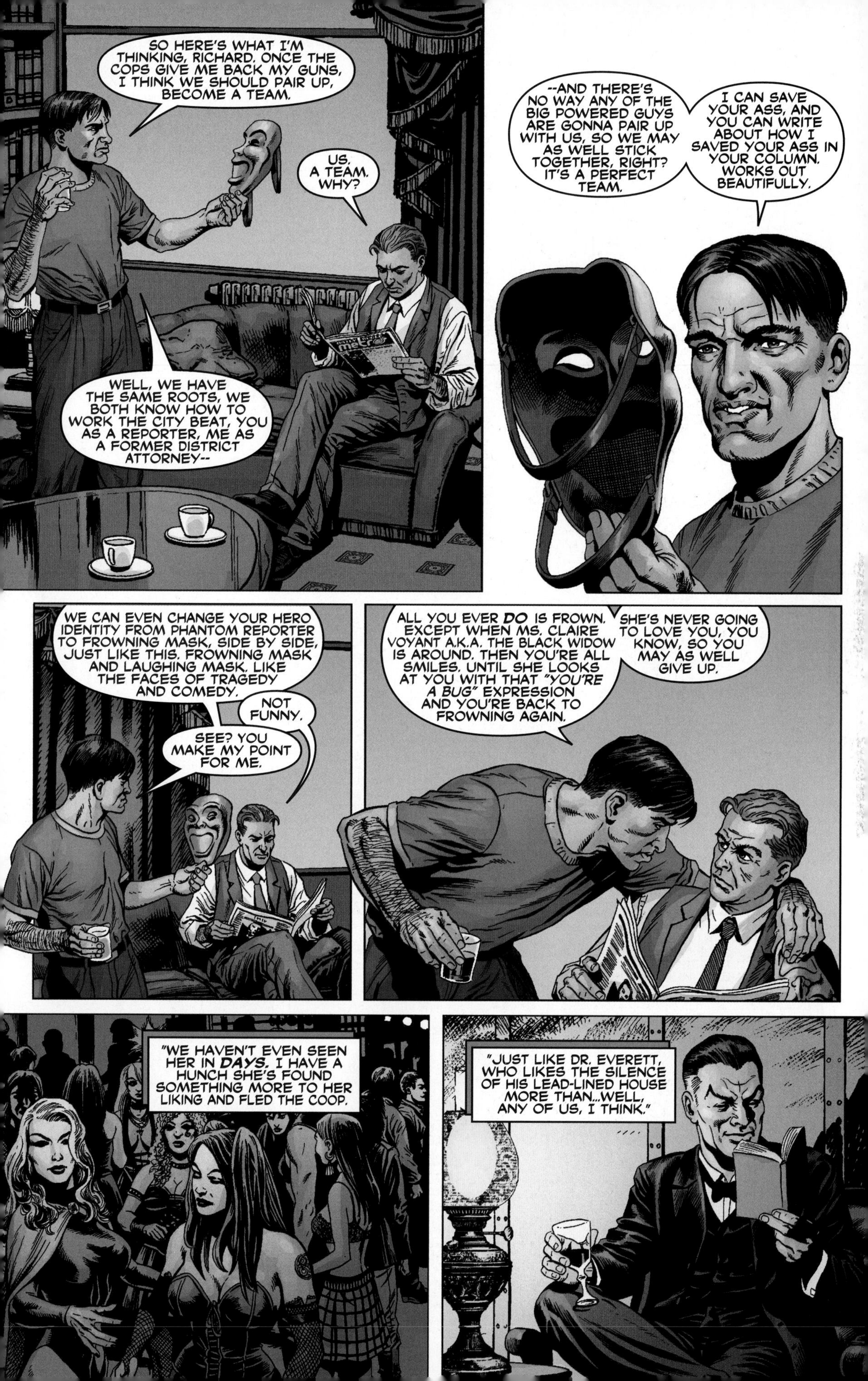

SO HERE'S WHAT I'M THINKING, RICHARD. ONCE THE COPS GIVE ME BACK MY GUNS, I THINK WE SHOULD PAIR UP, BECOME A TEAM.
US. A TEAM. WHY?
WELL, WE HAVE THE SAME ROOTS, WE BOTH KNOW HOW TO WORK THE CITY BEAT, YOU AS A REPORTER, ME AS A FORMER DISTRICT ATTORNEY--
--AND THERE'S NO WAY ANY OF THE BIG POWERED GUYS ARE GONNA PAIR UP WITH US, SO WE MAY AS WELL STICK TOGETHER, RIGHT? IT'S A PERFECT TEAM.
I CAN SAVE YOUR ASS, AND YOU CAN WRITE ABOUT HOW I SAVED YOUR ASS IN YOUR COLUMN. WORKS OUT BEAUTIFULLY.
WE CAN EVEN CHANGE YOUR HERO IDENTITY FROM PHANTOM REPORTER TO FROWNING MASK, SIDE BY SIDE, JUST LIKE THIS. FROWNING MASK AND LAUGHING MASK. LIKE THE FACES OF TRAGEDY AND COMEDY.
NOT FUNNY.
SEE? YOU MAKE MY POINT FOR ME.
ALL YOU EVER *DO* IS FROWN. EXCEPT WHEN MS. CLAIRE VOYANT A.K.A. THE BLACK WIDOW IS AROUND. THEN YOU'RE ALL SMILES. UNTIL SHE LOOKS AT YOU WITH THAT *"YOU'RE A BUG"* EXPRESSION AND YOU'RE BACK TO FROWNING AGAIN.
SHE'S NEVER GOING TO LOVE YOU, YOU KNOW, SO YOU MAY AS WELL GIVE UP.
"WE HAVEN'T EVEN SEEN HER IN *DAYS*. I HAVE A HUNCH SHE'S FOUND SOMETHING MORE TO HER LIKING AND FLED THE COOP.
"JUST LIKE DR. EVERETT, WHO LIKES THE SILENCE OF HIS LEAD-LINED HOUSE MORE THAN...WELL, ANY OF US, I THINK."

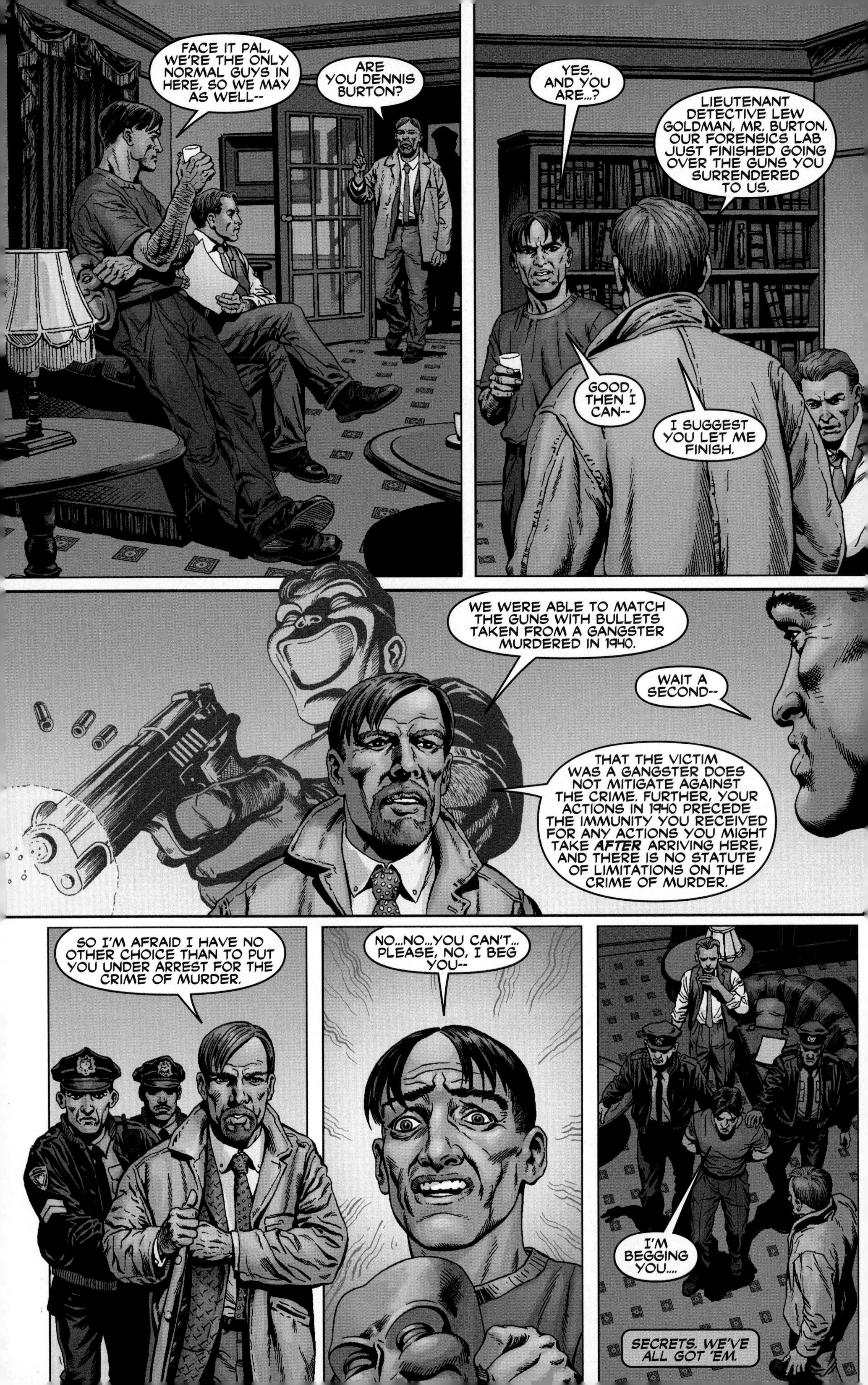
FACE IT PAL, WE'RE THE ONLY NORMAL GUYS IN HERE, SO WE MAY AS WELL--
ARE YOU DENNIS BURTON?
YES. AND YOU ARE...?
LIEUTENANT DETECTIVE LEW GOLDMAN, MR. BURTON. OUR FORENSICS LAB JUST FINISHED GOING OVER THE GUNS YOU SURRENDERED TO US.
GOOD, THEN I CAN--
I SUGGEST YOU LET ME FINISH.
WE WERE ABLE TO MATCH THE GUNS WITH BULLETS TAKEN FROM A GANGSTER MURDERED IN 1940.
WAIT A SECOND--
THAT THE VICTIM WAS A GANGSTER DOES NOT MITIGATE AGAINST THE CRIME. FURTHER, YOUR ACTIONS IN 1940 PRECEDE THE IMMUNITY YOU RECEIVED FOR ANY ACTIONS YOU MIGHT TAKE *AFTER* ARRIVING HERE, AND THERE IS NO STATUTE OF LIMITATIONS ON THE CRIME OF MURDER.
SO I'M AFRAID I HAVE NO OTHER CHOICE THAN TO PUT YOU UNDER ARREST FOR THE CRIME OF MURDER.
NO...NO...YOU CAN'T... PLEASE, NO, I BEG YOU--
I'M BEGGING YOU....
SECRETS. WE'VE ALL GOT 'EM.

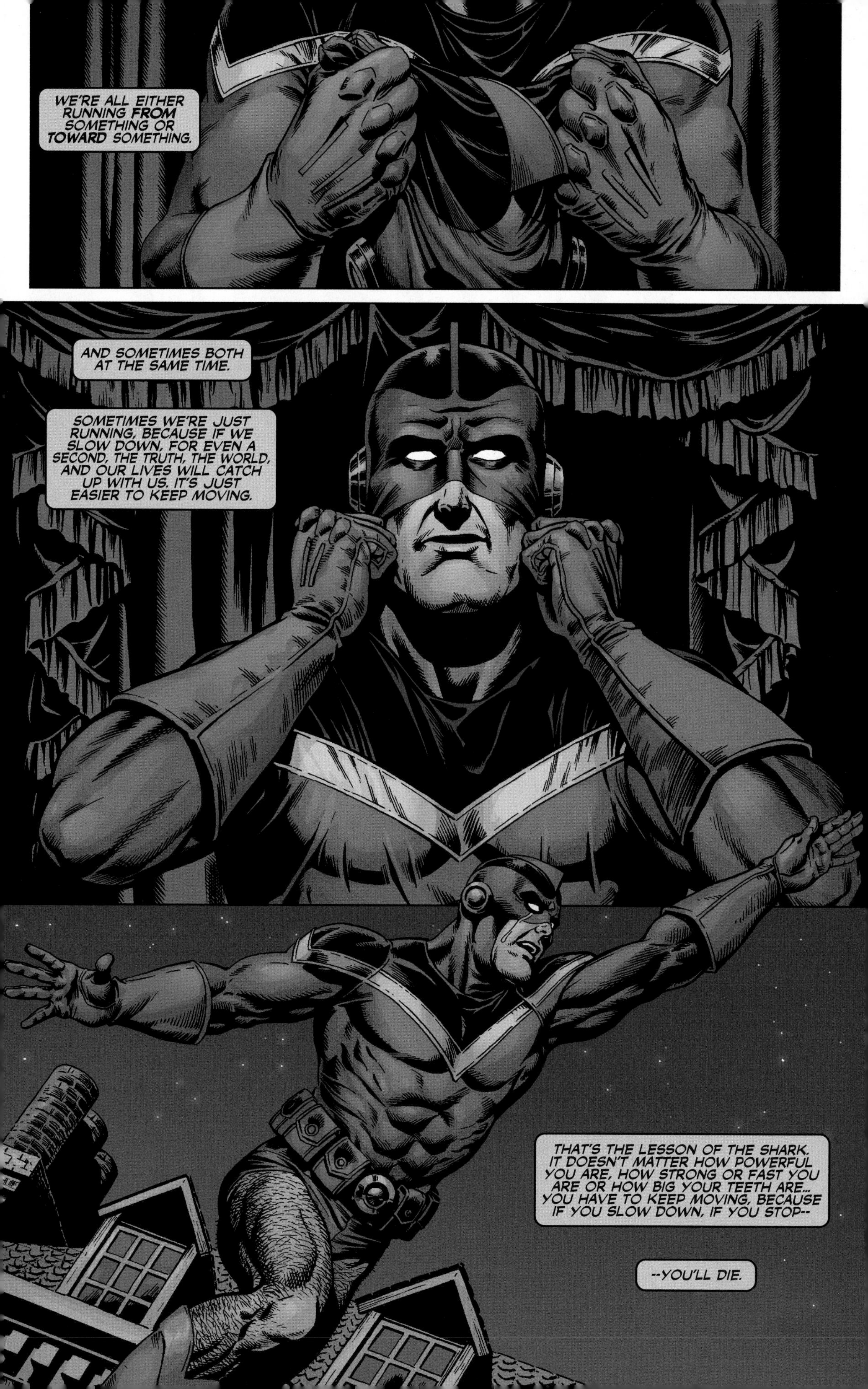
WE'RE ALL EITHER RUNNING FROM SOMETHING OR TOWARD SOMETHING.
AND SOMETIMES BOTH AT THE SAME TIME.
SOMETIMES WE'RE JUST RUNNING, BECAUSE IF WE SLOW DOWN, FOR EVEN A SECOND, THE TRUTH, THE WORLD, AND OUR LIVES WILL CATCH UP WITH US. IT'S JUST EASIER TO KEEP MOVING.
THAT'S THE LESSON OF THE SHARK. IT DOESN'T MATTER HOW POWERFUL YOU ARE, HOW STRONG OR FAST YOU ARE OR HOW BIG YOUR TEETH ARE... YOU HAVE TO KEEP MOVING, BECAUSE IF YOU SLOW DOWN, IF YOU STOP--
--YOU'LL DIE.

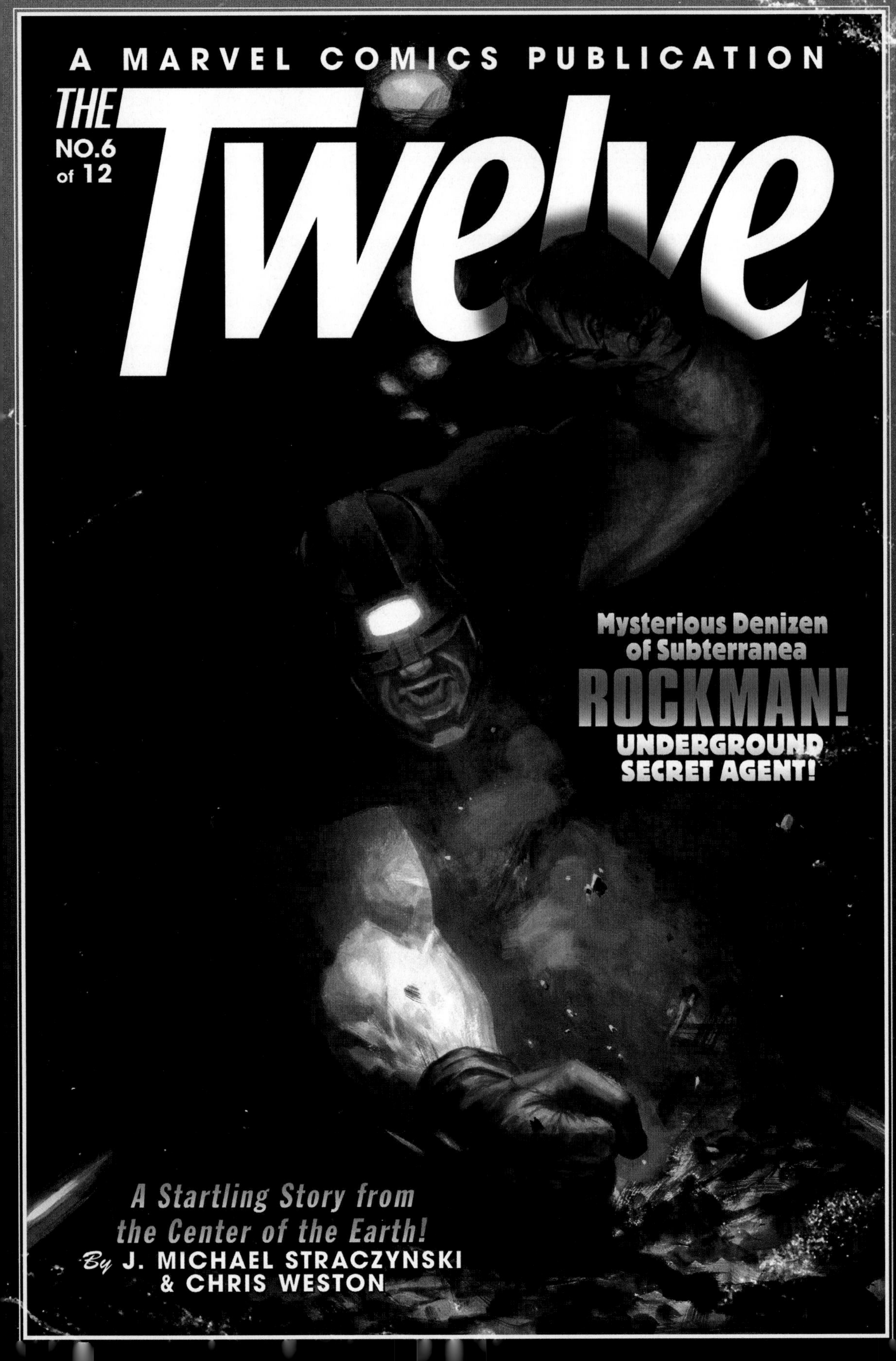
A MARVEL COMICS PUBLICATION
THE
NO.6
of 12
Twelve
Mysterious Denizen
of Subterranea
ROCKMAN!
UNDERGROUND
SECRET AGENT!
A Startling Story from
the Center of the Earth!
By J. MICHAEL STRACZYNSKI
& CHRIS WESTON

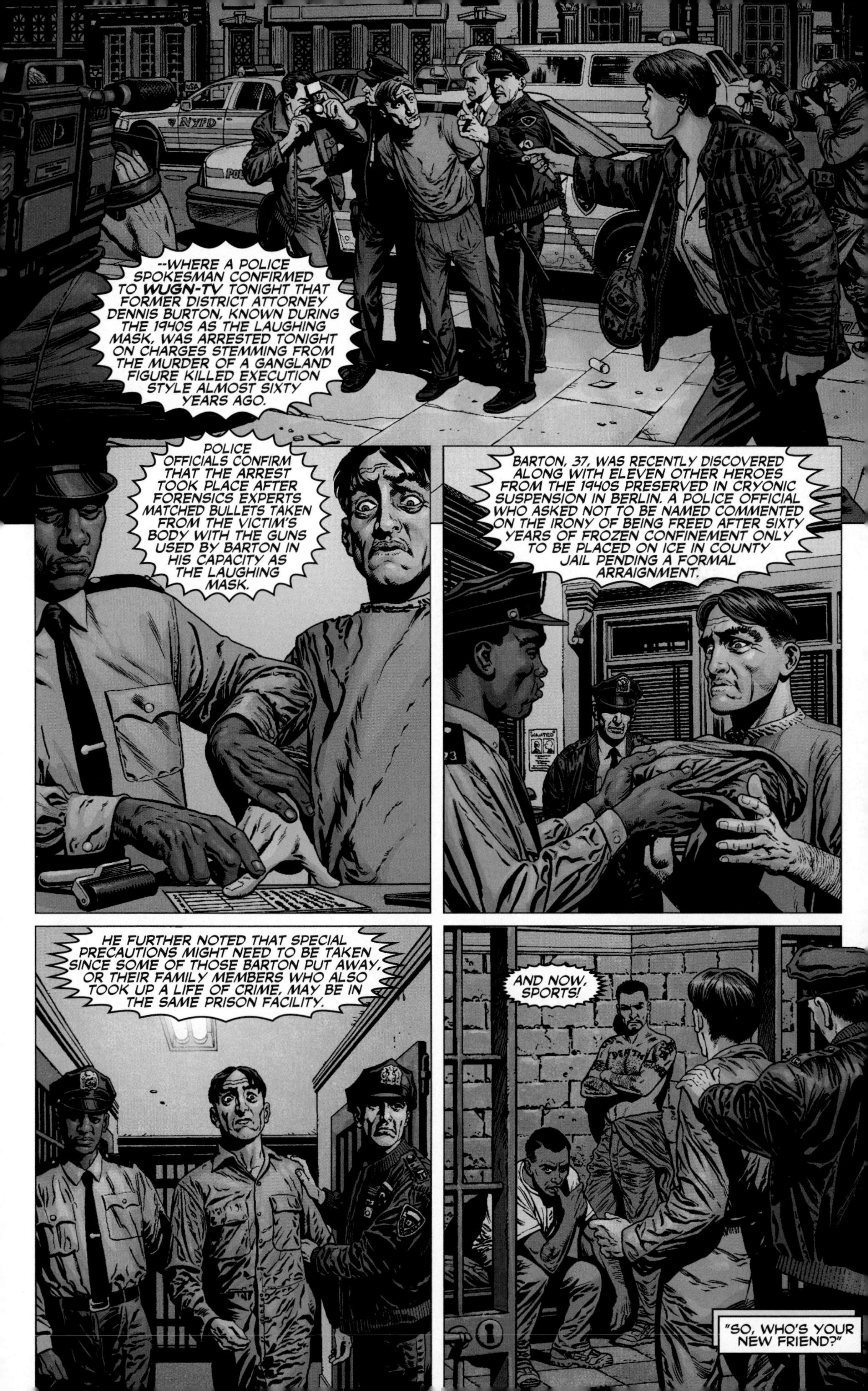
--WHERE A POLICE SPOKESMAN CONFIRMED TO WUGN-TV TONIGHT THAT FORMER DISTRICT ATTORNEY DENNIS BURTON, KNOWN DURING THE 1940S AS THE LAUGHING MASK, WAS ARRESTED TONIGHT ON CHARGES STEMMING FROM THE MURDER OF A GANGLAND FIGURE KILLED EXECUTION STYLE ALMOST SIXTY YEARS AGO.
POLICE OFFICIALS CONFIRM THAT THE ARREST TOOK PLACE AFTER FORENSICS EXPERTS MATCHED BULLETS TAKEN FROM THE VICTIM'S BODY WITH THE GUNS USED BY BARTON IN HIS CAPACITY AS THE LAUGHING MASK.
BARTON, 37, WAS RECENTLY DISCOVERED ALONG WITH ELEVEN OTHER HEROES FROM THE 1940S PRESERVED IN CRYONIC SUSPENSION IN BERLIN. A POLICE OFFICIAL WHO ASKED NOT TO BE NAMED COMMENTED ON THE IRONY OF BEING FREED AFTER SIXTY YEARS OF FROZEN CONFINEMENT ONLY TO BE PLACED ON ICE IN COUNTY JAIL PENDING A FORMAL ARRAIGNMENT.
HE FURTHER NOTED THAT SPECIAL PRECAUTIONS MIGHT NEED TO BE TAKEN SINCE SOME OF THOSE BARTON PUT AWAY, OR THEIR FAMILY MEMBERS WHO ALSO TOOK UP A LIFE OF CRIME, MAY BE IN THE SAME PRISON FACILITY.
AND NOW, SPORTS!
"SO, WHO'S YOUR NEW FRIEND?"

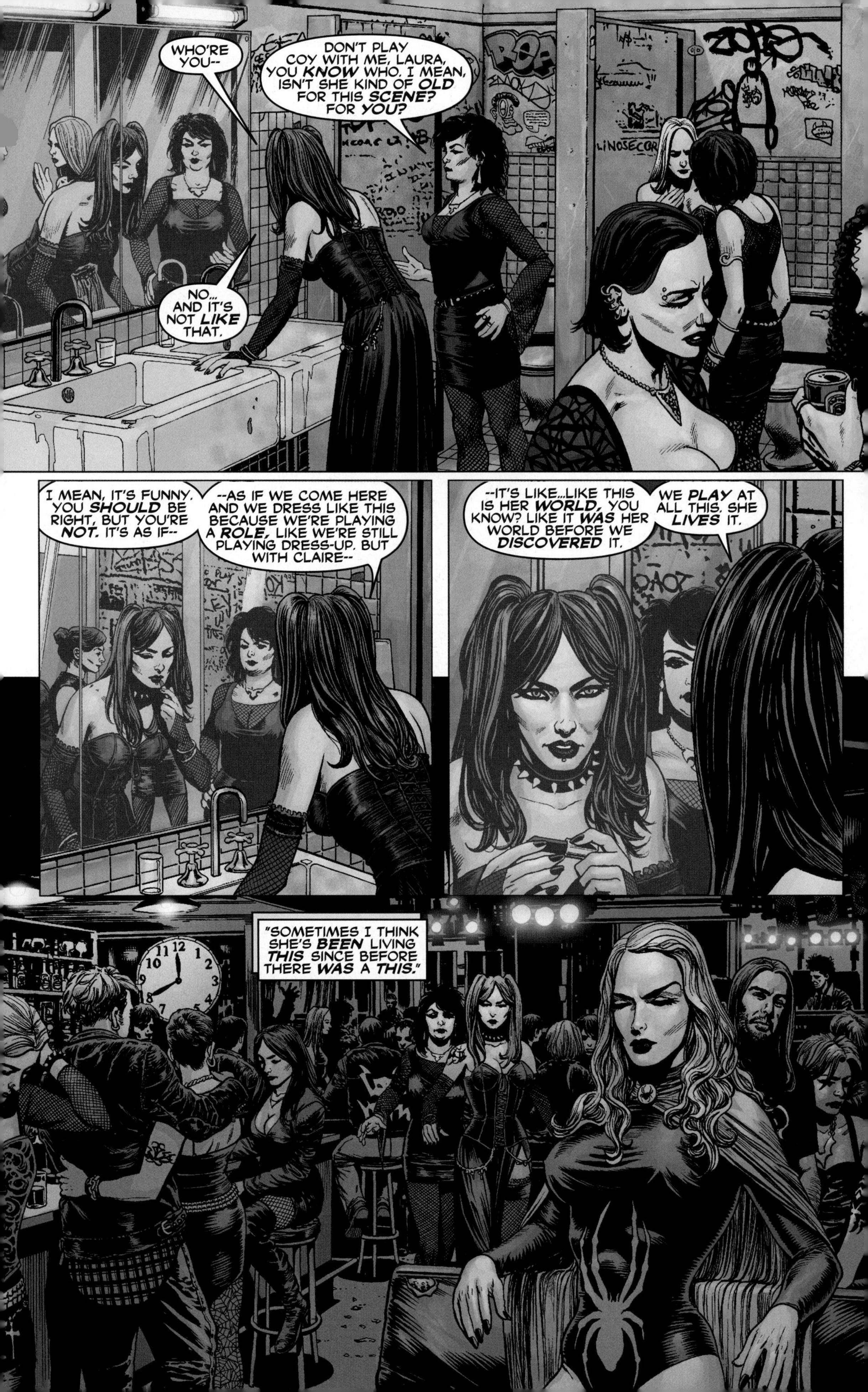
WHO'RE YOU--
DON'T PLAY COY WITH ME, LAURA, YOU KNOW WHO. I MEAN, ISN'T SHE KIND OF OLD FOR THIS SCENE? FOR YOU?
NO... AND IT'S NOT LIKE THAT.
I MEAN, IT'S FUNNY. YOU SHOULD BE RIGHT, BUT YOU'RE NOT. IT'S AS IF--
--AS IF WE COME HERE AND WE DRESS LIKE THIS BECAUSE WE'RE PLAYING A ROLE, LIKE WE'RE PLAYING STILL PLAYING DRESS-UP. BUT WITH CLAIRE--
--IT'S LIKE...LIKE THIS IS HER WORLD, YOU KNOW? LIKE IT WAS HER WORLD BEFORE WE DISCOVERED IT.
WE PLAY AT ALL THIS. SHE LIVES IT.
"SOMETIMES I THINK SHE'S BEEN LIVING THIS SINCE BEFORE THERE WAS A THIS."

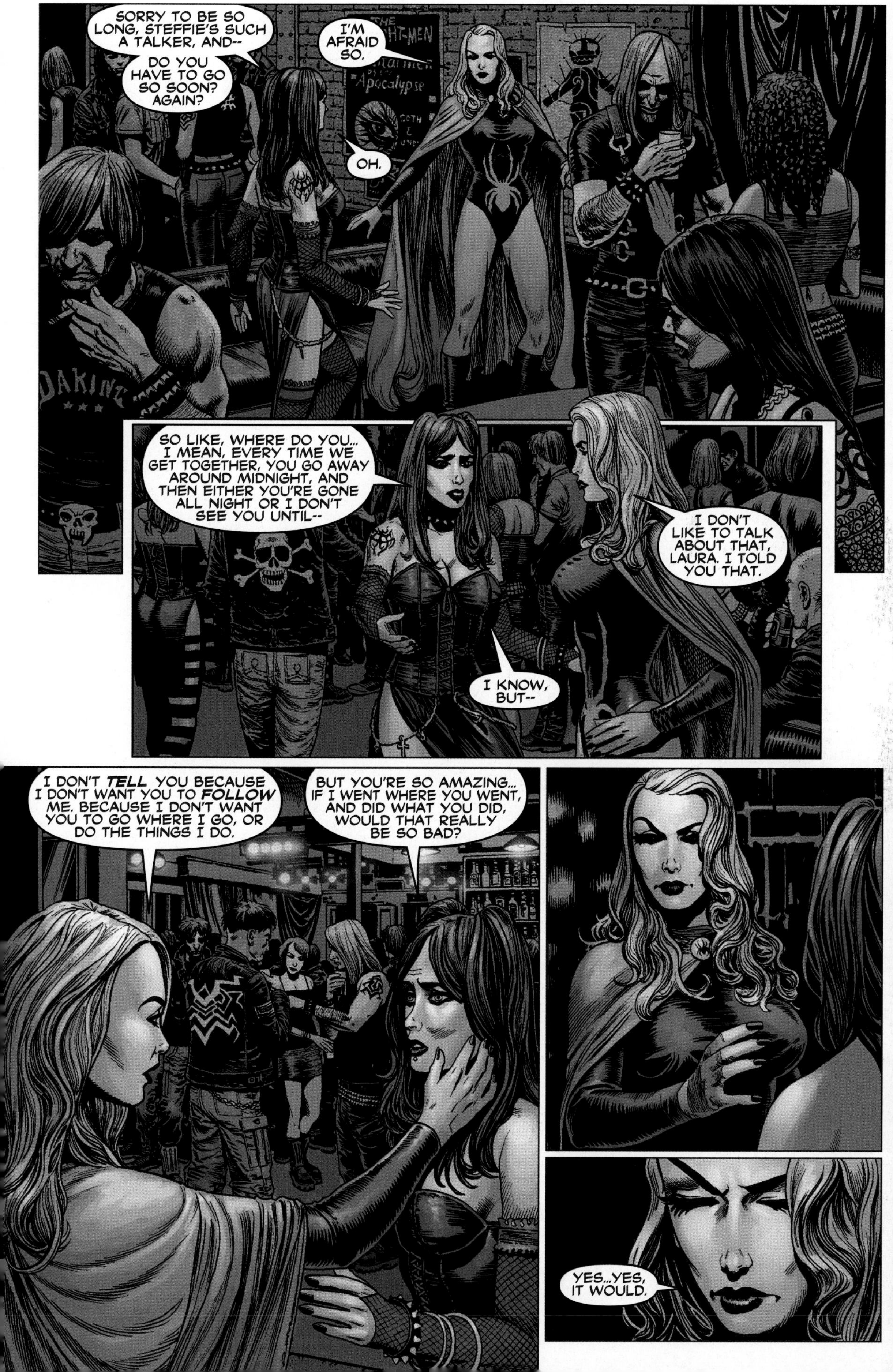
SORRY TO BE SO LONG, STEFFIE'S SUCH A TALKER, AND--
DO YOU HAVE TO GO SO SOON? AGAIN?
I'M AFRAID SO.
OH.
SO LIKE, WHERE DO YOU... I MEAN, EVERY TIME WE GET TOGETHER, YOU GO AWAY AROUND MIDNIGHT, AND THEN EITHER YOU'RE GONE ALL NIGHT OR I DON'T SEE YOU UNTIL--
I DON'T LIKE TO TALK ABOUT THAT, LAURA. I TOLD YOU THAT.
I KNOW, BUT--
I DON'T TELL YOU BECAUSE I DON'T WANT YOU TO FOLLOW ME. BECAUSE I DON'T WANT YOU TO GO WHERE I GO, OR DO THE THINGS I DO.
BUT YOU'RE SO AMAZING... IF I WENT WHERE YOU WENT, AND DID WHAT YOU DID, WOULD THAT REALLY BE SO BAD?
YES...YES, IT WOULD.

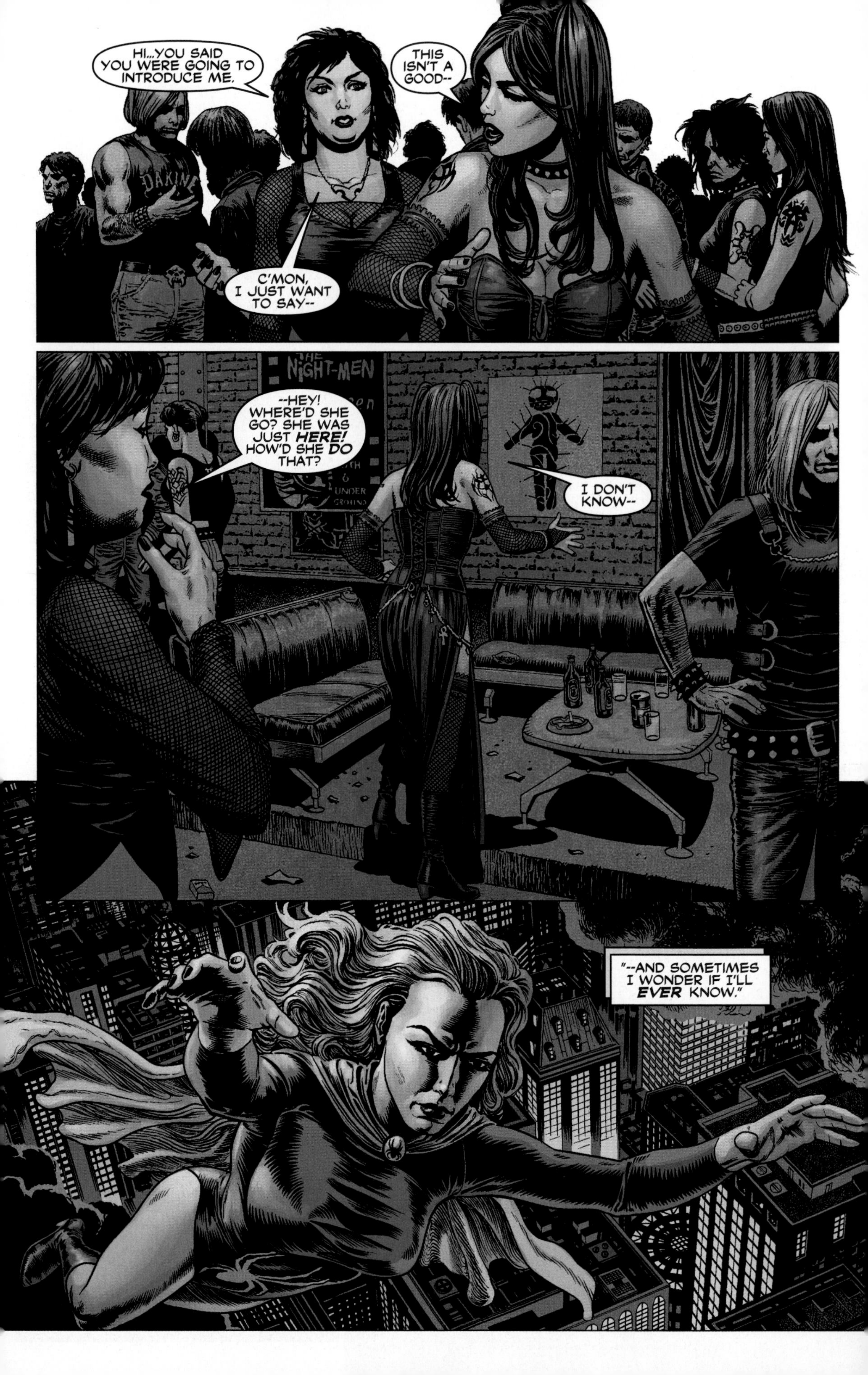
HI...YOU SAID YOU WERE GOING TO INTRODUCE ME.
THIS ISN'T A GOOD--
C'MON, I JUST WANT TO SAY--
THE NIGHT-MEN
--HEY! WHERE'D SHE GO? SHE WAS JUST **HERE!** HOW'D SHE **DO** THAT?
I DON'T KNOW--
"--AND SOMETIMES I WONDER IF I'LL **EVER** KNOW."

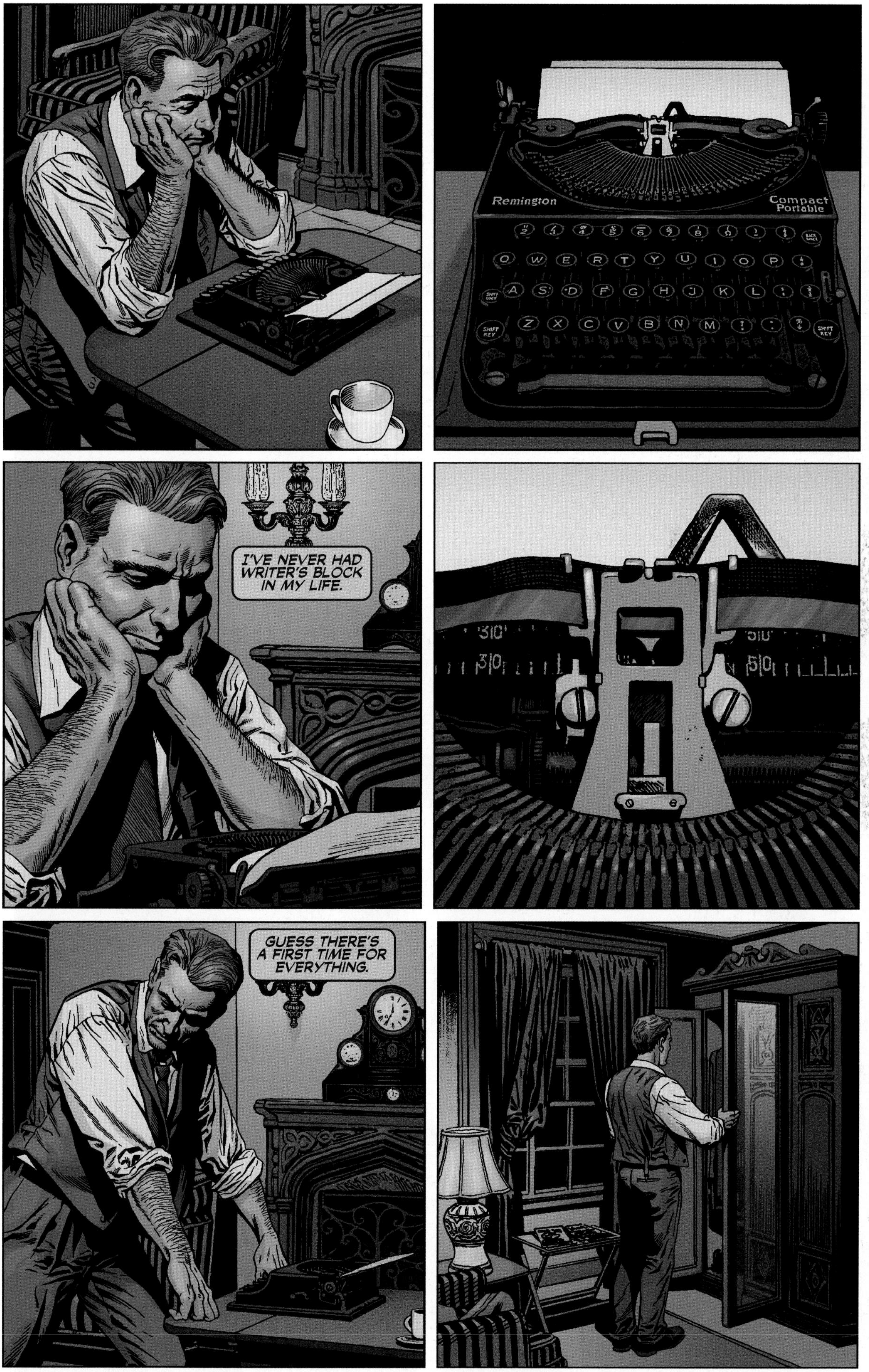
Remington
Compact Portable
I'VE NEVER HAD WRITER'S BLOCK IN MY LIFE.
GUESS THERE'S A FIRST TIME FOR EVERYTHING.

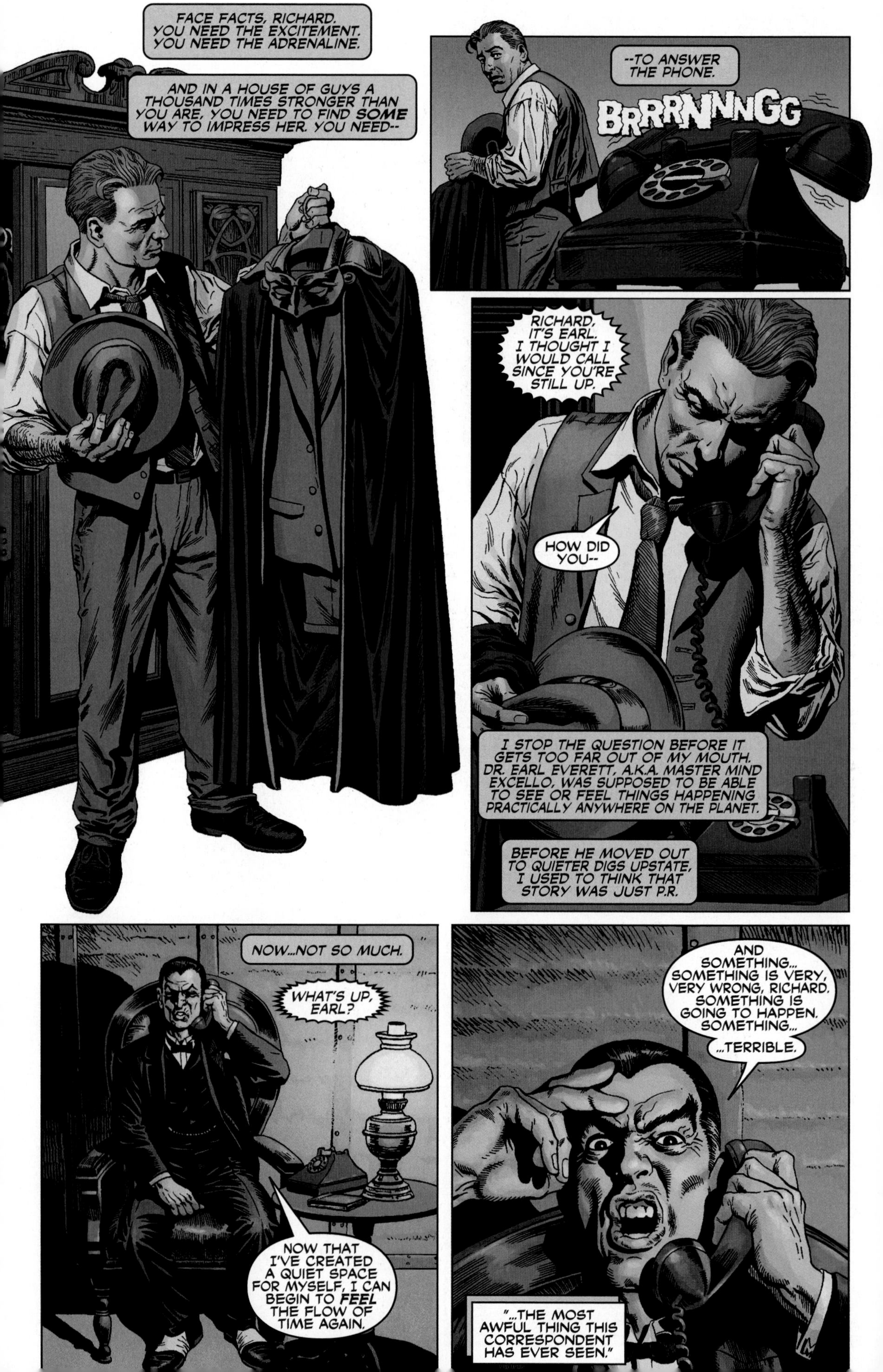

FACE FACTS, RICHARD. YOU NEED THE EXCITEMENT. YOU NEED THE ADRENALINE.
AND IN A HOUSE OF GUYS A THOUSAND TIMES STRONGER THAN YOU ARE, YOU NEED TO FIND SOME WAY TO IMPRESS HER. YOU NEED--
--TO ANSWER THE PHONE.
BRRRNNNGG
RICHARD, IT'S EARL. I THOUGHT I WOULD CALL SINCE YOU'RE STILL UP.
HOW DID YOU--
I STOP THE QUESTION BEFORE IT GETS TOO FAR OUT OF MY MOUTH. DR. EARL EVERETT, A.K.A. MASTER MIND EXCELLO, WAS SUPPOSED TO BE ABLE TO SEE OR FEEL THINGS HAPPENING PRACTICALLY ANYWHERE ON THE PLANET.
BEFORE HE MOVED OUT TO QUIETER DIGS UPSTATE, I USED TO THINK THAT STORY WAS JUST P.R.
NOW...NOT SO MUCH.
WHAT'S UP, EARL?
NOW THAT I'VE CREATED A QUIET SPACE FOR MYSELF, I CAN BEGIN TO FEEL THE FLOW OF TIME AGAIN.
AND SOMETHING... SOMETHING IS VERY, VERY WRONG, RICHARD. SOMETHING IS GOING TO HAPPEN. SOMETHING...
...TERRIBLE.
"...THE MOST AWFUL THING THIS CORRESPONDENT HAS EVER SEEN."

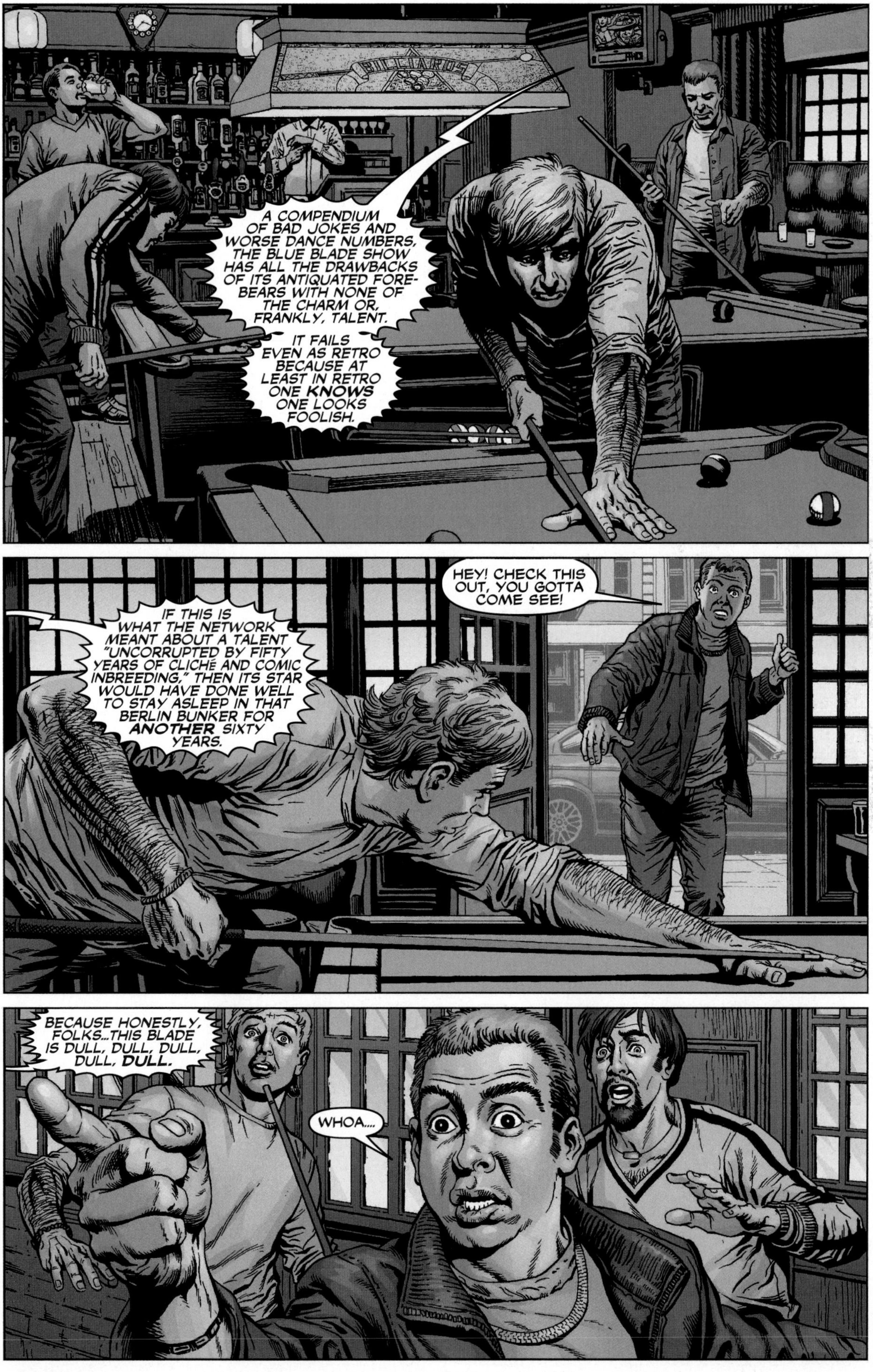
A COMPENDIUM OF BAD JOKES AND WORSE DANCE NUMBERS, THE BLUE BLADE SHOW HAS ALL THE DRAWBACKS OF ITS ANTIQUATED FORE-BEARS WITH NONE OF THE CHARM OR, FRANKLY, TALENT.
IT FAILS EVEN AS RETRO BECAUSE AT LEAST IN RETRO ONE **KNOWS** ONE LOOKS FOOLISH.
BILLIARDS
HEY! CHECK THIS OUT, YOU GOTTA COME SEE!
IF THIS IS WHAT THE NETWORK MEANT ABOUT A TALENT "UNCORRUPTED BY FIFTY YEARS OF CLICHÉ AND COMIC INBREEDING," THEN ITS STAR WOULD HAVE DONE WELL TO STAY ASLEEP IN THAT BERLIN BUNKER FOR **ANOTHER** SIXTY YEARS.
BECAUSE HONESTLY, FOLKS...THIS BLADE IS DULL, DULL, DULL, DULL, **DULL.**
WHOA....

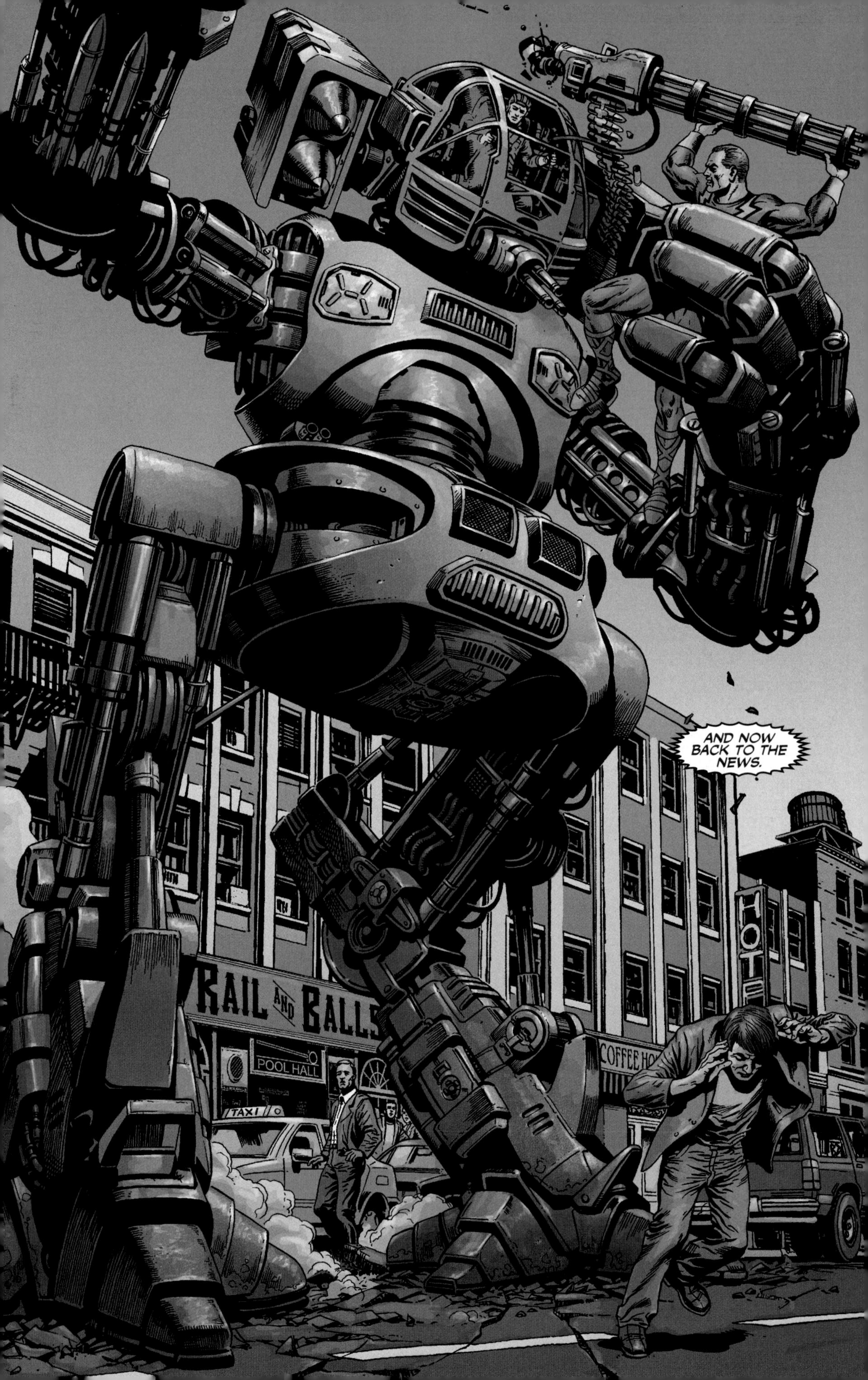
AND NOW BACK TO THE NEWS.
RAIL AND BALLS
POOL HALL
TAXI
COFFEE HO
HOT

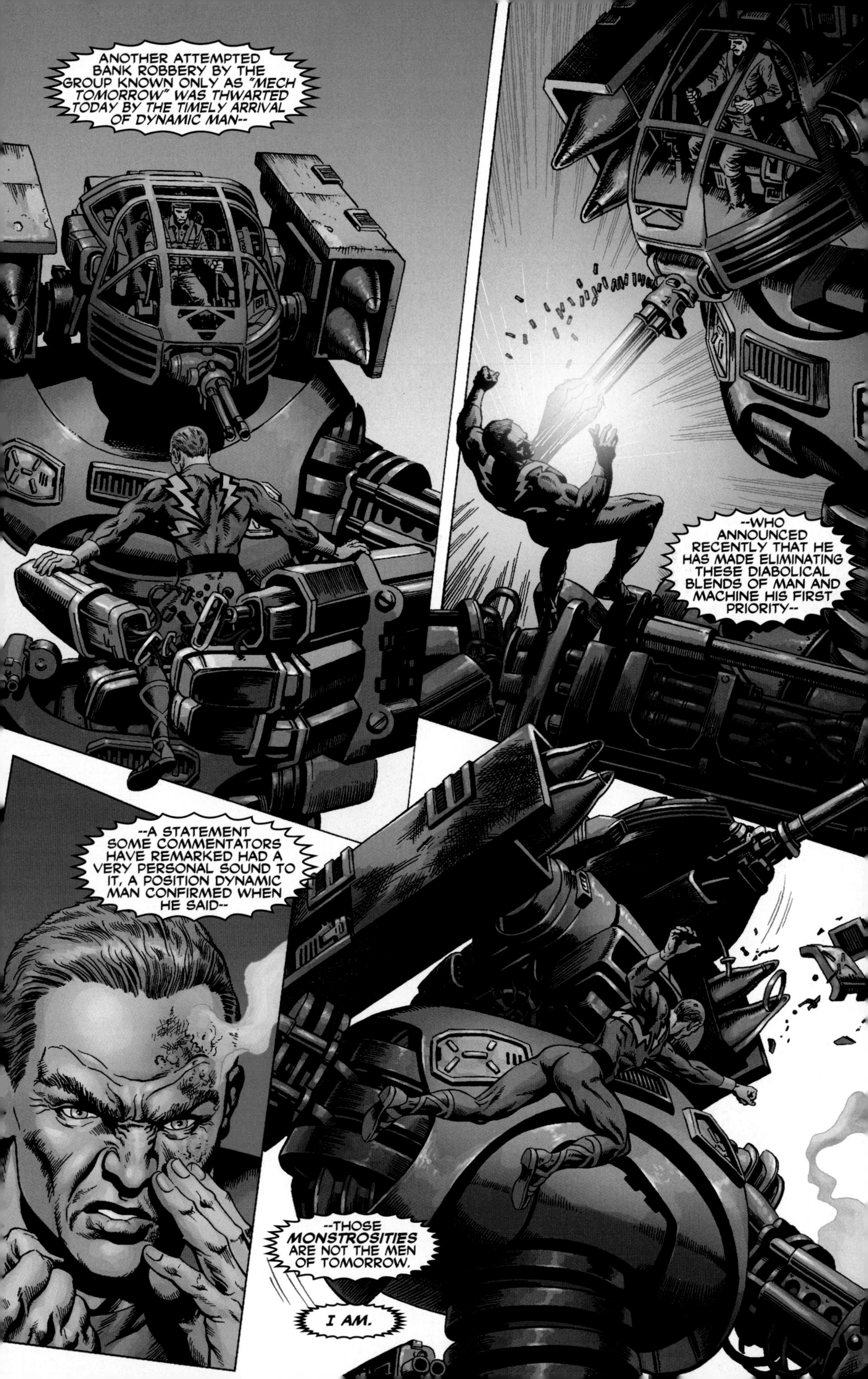
ANOTHER ATTEMPTED BANK ROBBERY BY THE GROUP KNOWN ONLY AS "MECH TOMORROW" WAS THWARTED TODAY BY THE TIMELY ARRIVAL OF DYNAMIC MAN--
--WHO ANNOUNCED RECENTLY THAT HE HAS MADE ELIMINATING THESE DIABOLICAL BLENDS OF MAN AND MACHINE HIS FIRST PRIORITY--
--A STATEMENT SOME COMMENTATORS HAVE REMARKED HAD A VERY PERSONAL SOUND TO IT, A POSITION DYNAMIC MAN CONFIRMED WHEN HE SAID--
--THOSE MONSTROSITIES ARE NOT THE MEN OF TOMORROW.
I AM.

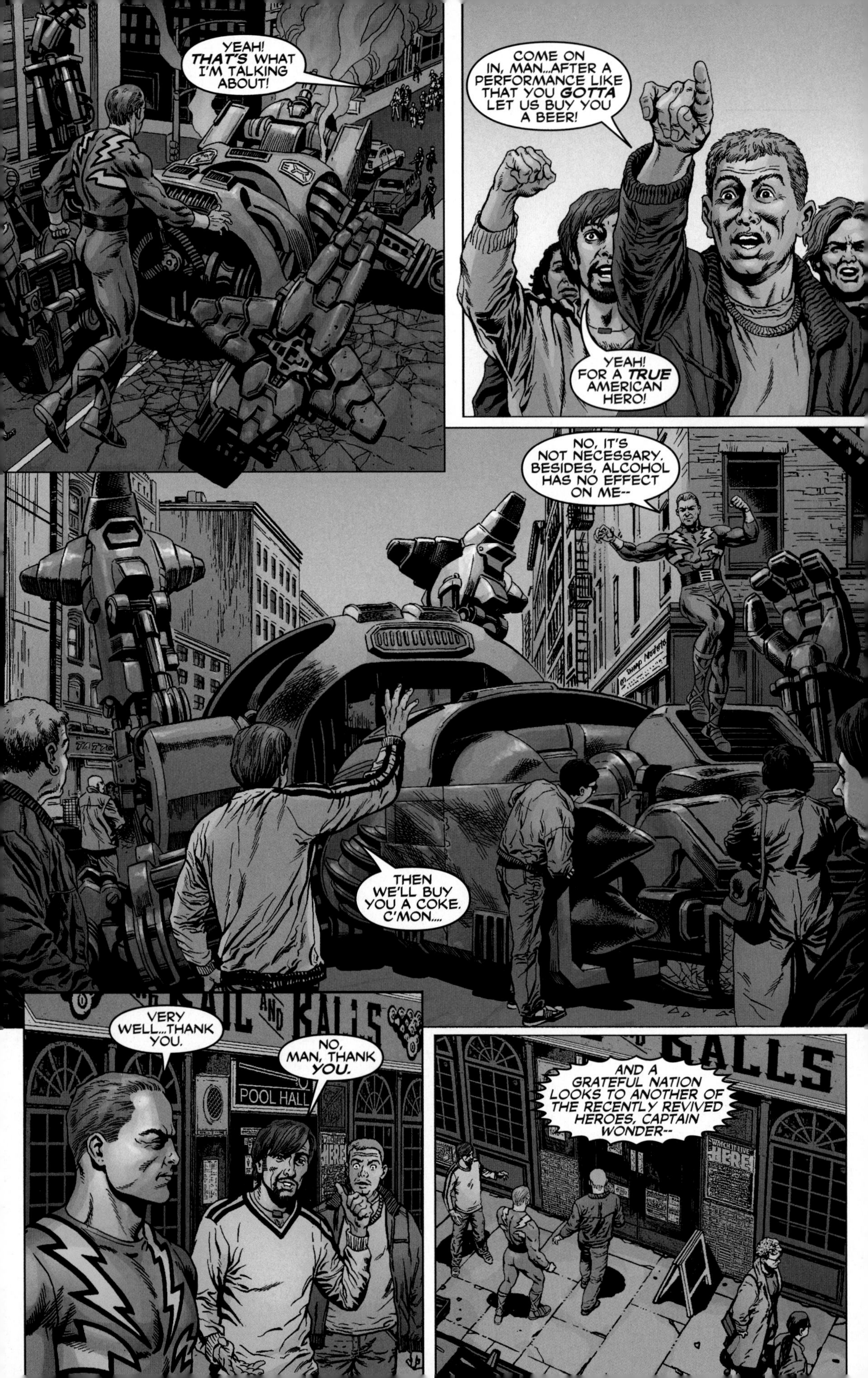
YEAH! THAT'S WHAT I'M TALKING ABOUT!
COME ON IN, MAN...AFTER A PERFORMANCE LIKE THAT YOU GOTTA LET US BUY YOU A BEER!
YEAH! FOR A TRUE AMERICAN HERO!
NO, IT'S NOT NECESSARY. BESIDES, ALCOHOL HAS NO EFFECT ON ME--
THEN WE'LL BUY YOU A COKE. C'MON....
VERY WELL...THANK YOU.
NO, MAN, THANK YOU.
POOL HALL
AND A GRATEFUL NATION LOOKS TO ANOTHER OF THE RECENTLY REVIVED HEROES, CAPTAIN WONDER--

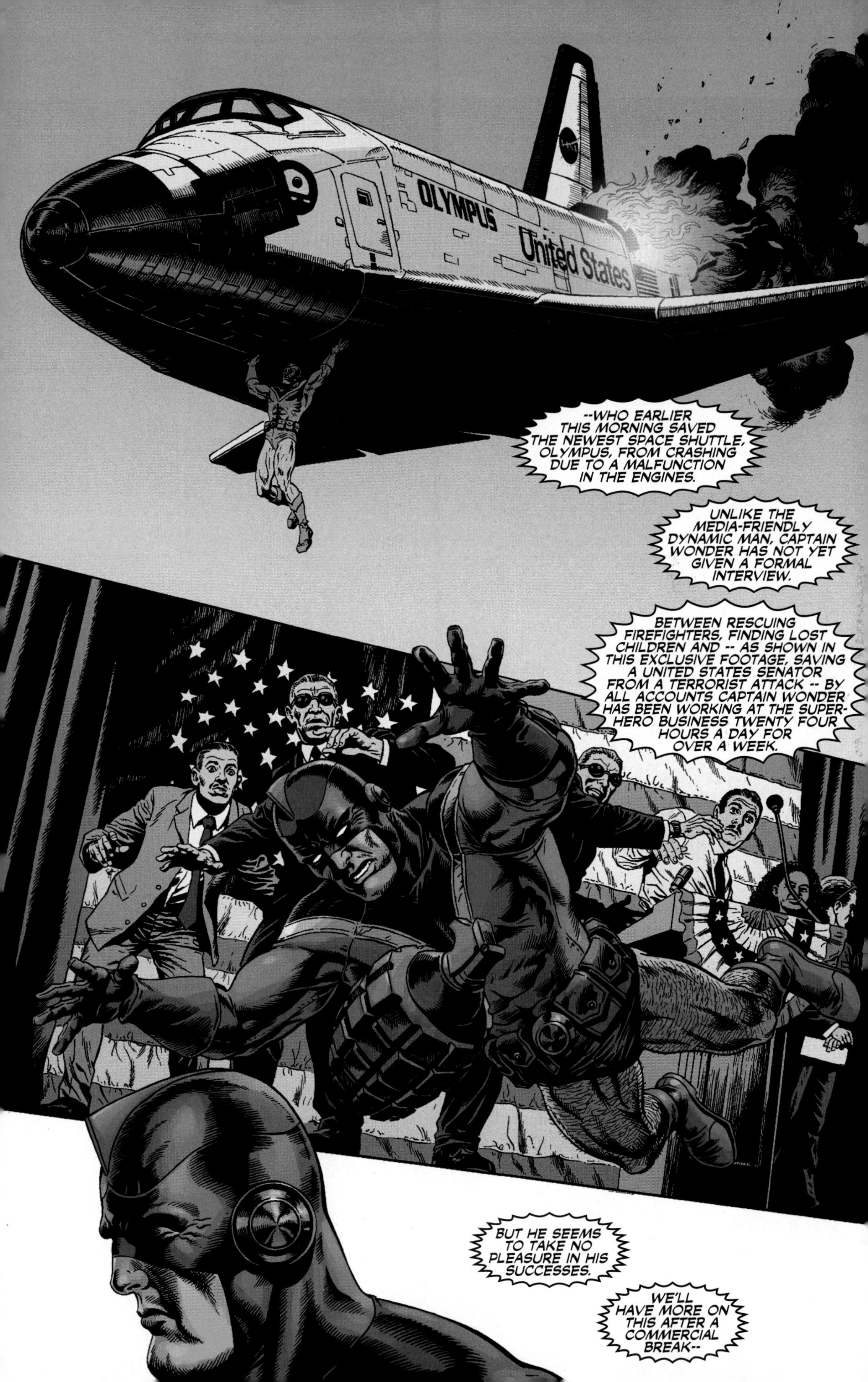
--WHO EARLIER THIS MORNING SAVED THE NEWEST SPACE SHUTTLE, OLYMPUS, FROM CRASHING DUE TO A MALFUNCTION IN THE ENGINES.
UNLIKE THE MEDIA-FRIENDLY DYNAMIC MAN, CAPTAIN WONDER HAS NOT YET GIVEN A FORMAL INTERVIEW.
BETWEEN RESCUING FIREFIGHTERS, FINDING LOST CHILDREN AND -- AS SHOWN IN THIS EXCLUSIVE FOOTAGE, SAVING A UNITED STATES SENATOR FROM A TERRORIST ATTACK -- BY ALL ACCOUNTS CAPTAIN WONDER HAS BEEN WORKING AT THE SUPER-HERO BUSINESS TWENTY FOUR HOURS A DAY FOR OVER A WEEK.
BUT HE SEEMS TO TAKE NO PLEASURE IN HIS SUCCESSES.
WE'LL HAVE MORE ON THIS AFTER A COMMERCIAL BREAK--

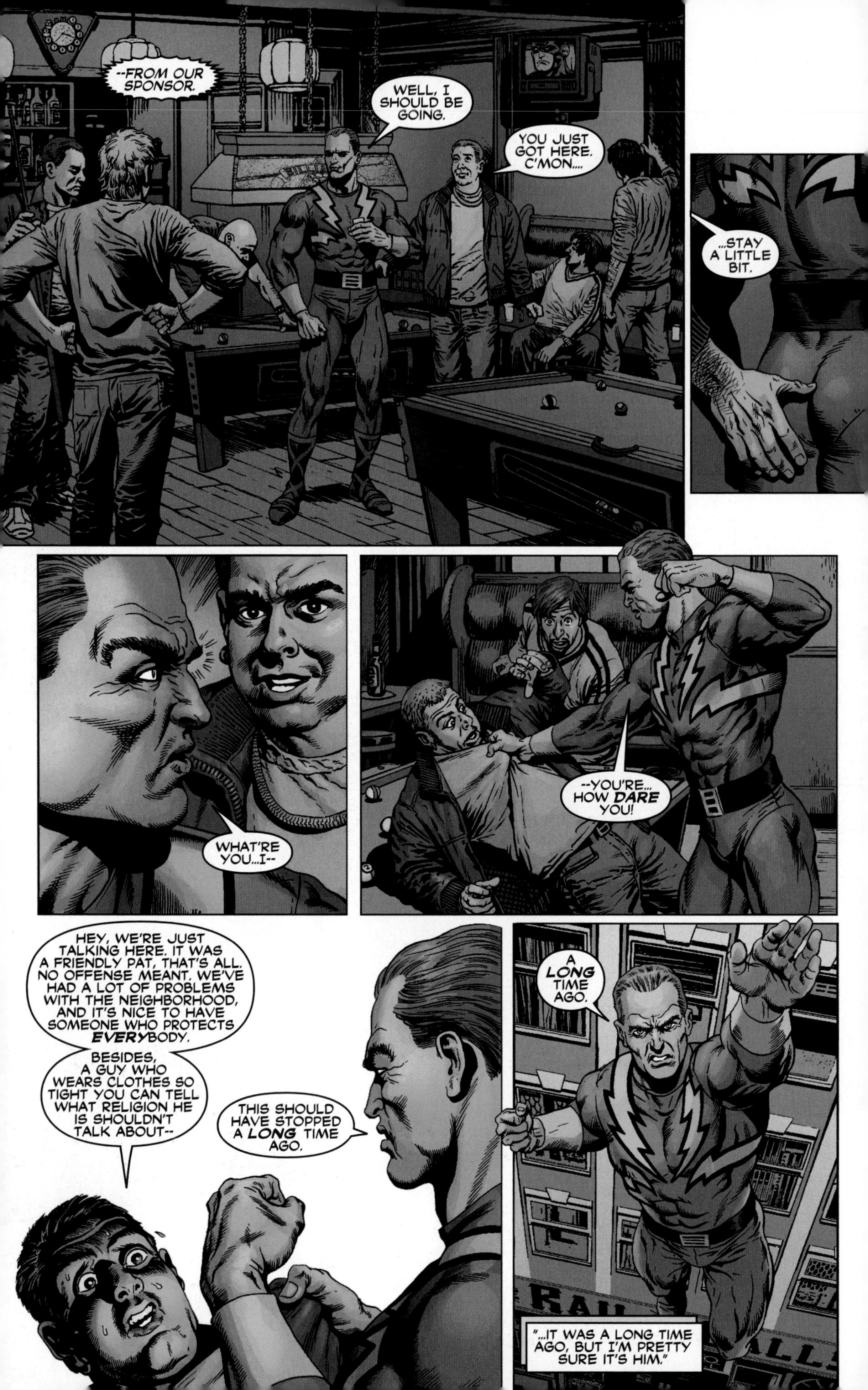
--FROM OUR SPONSOR.
WELL, I SHOULD BE GOING.
YOU JUST GOT HERE. C'MON....
...STAY A LITTLE BIT.
WHAT'RE YOU...I--
--YOU'RE... HOW DARE YOU!
HEY, WE'RE JUST TALKING HERE. IT WAS A FRIENDLY PAT, THAT'S ALL. NO OFFENSE MEANT. WE'VE HAD A LOT OF PROBLEMS WITH THE NEIGHBORHOOD, AND IT'S NICE TO HAVE SOMEONE WHO PROTECTS EVERYBODY.
BESIDES, A GUY WHO WEARS CLOTHES SO TIGHT YOU CAN TELL WHAT RELIGION HE IS SHOULDN'T TALK ABOUT--
THIS SHOULD HAVE STOPPED A LONG TIME AGO.
A LONG TIME AGO.
"...IT WAS A LONG TIME AGO, BUT I'M PRETTY SURE IT'S HIM."

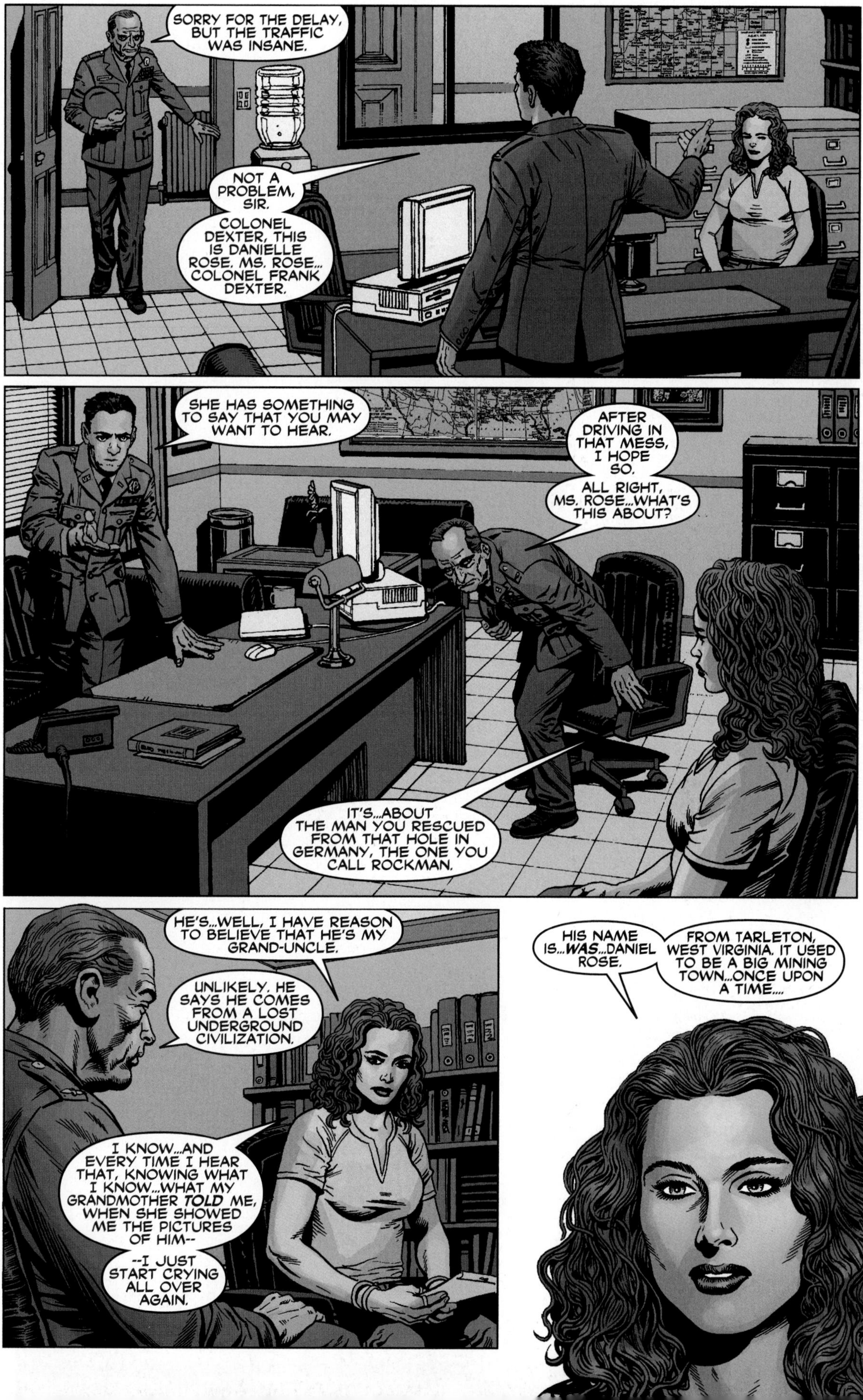
SORRY FOR THE DELAY, BUT THE TRAFFIC WAS INSANE.
NOT A PROBLEM, SIR.
COLONEL DEXTER, THIS IS DANIELLE ROSE. MS. ROSE... COLONEL FRANK DEXTER.
SHE HAS SOMETHING TO SAY THAT YOU MAY WANT TO HEAR.
AFTER DRIVING IN THAT MESS, I HOPE SO.
ALL RIGHT, MS. ROSE...WHAT'S THIS ABOUT?
IT'S...ABOUT THE MAN YOU RESCUED FROM THAT HOLE IN GERMANY, THE ONE YOU CALL ROCKMAN.
HE'S...WELL, I HAVE REASON TO BELIEVE THAT HE'S MY GRAND-UNCLE.
UNLIKELY. HE SAYS HE COMES FROM A LOST UNDERGROUND CIVILIZATION.
I KNOW...AND EVERY TIME I HEAR THAT, KNOWING WHAT I KNOW...WHAT MY GRANDMOTHER *TOLD* ME, WHEN SHE SHOWED ME THE PICTURES OF HIM--
--I JUST START CRYING ALL OVER AGAIN.
HIS NAME IS...*WAS*...DANIEL ROSE.
FROM TARLETON, WEST VIRGINIA. IT USED TO BE A BIG MINING TOWN...ONCE UPON A TIME....

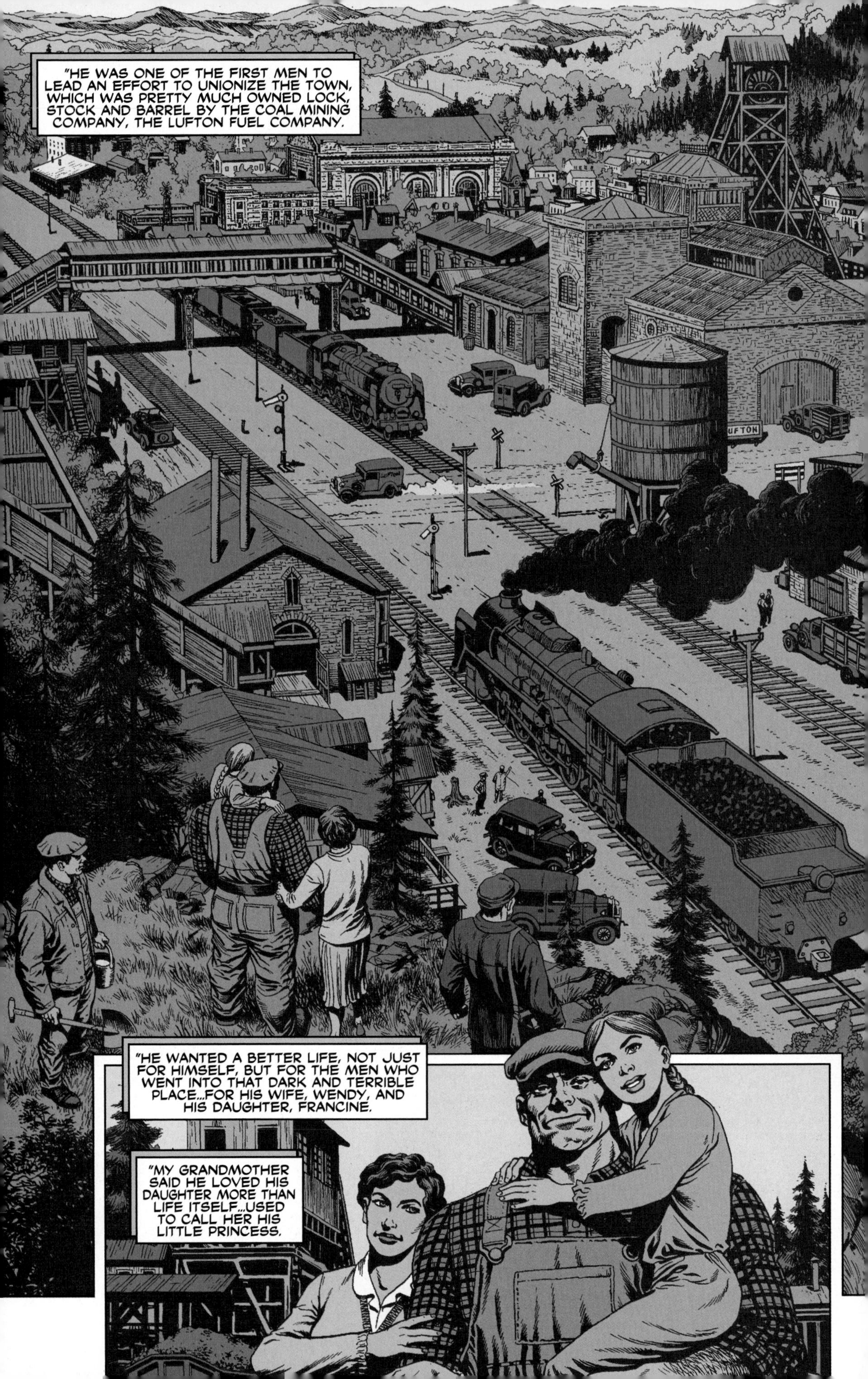
"HE WAS ONE OF THE FIRST MEN TO LEAD AN EFFORT TO UNIONIZE THE TOWN, WHICH WAS PRETTY MUCH OWNED LOCK, STOCK AND BARREL BY THE COAL MINING COMPANY, THE LUFTON FUEL COMPANY.
LUFTON
"HE WANTED A BETTER LIFE, NOT JUST FOR HIMSELF, BUT FOR THE MEN WHO WENT INTO THAT DARK AND TERRIBLE PLACE...FOR HIS WIFE, WENDY, AND HIS DAUGHTER, FRANCINE.
"MY GRANDMOTHER SAID HE LOVED HIS DAUGHTER MORE THAN LIFE ITSELF...USED TO CALL HER HIS LITTLE PRINCESS.

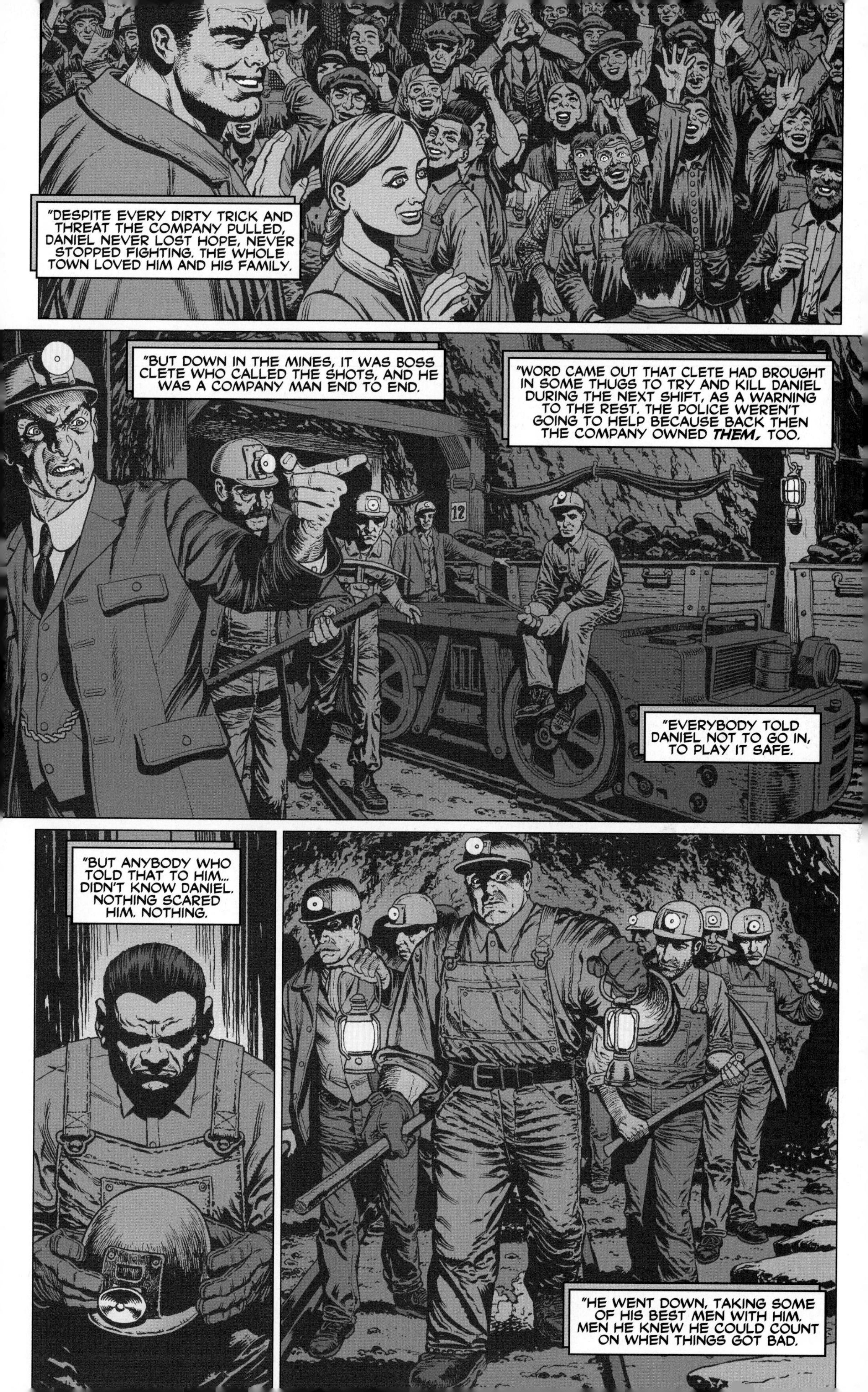
"DESPITE EVERY DIRTY TRICK AND THREAT THE COMPANY PULLED, DANIEL NEVER LOST HOPE, NEVER STOPPED FIGHTING. THE WHOLE TOWN LOVED HIM AND HIS FAMILY.
"BUT DOWN IN THE MINES, IT WAS BOSS CLETE WHO CALLED THE SHOTS, AND HE WAS A COMPANY MAN END TO END.
"WORD CAME OUT THAT CLETE HAD BROUGHT IN SOME THUGS TO TRY AND KILL DANIEL DURING THE NEXT SHIFT, AS A WARNING TO THE REST. THE POLICE WEREN'T GOING TO HELP BECAUSE BACK THEN THE COMPANY OWNED THEM, TOO.
12
"EVERYBODY TOLD DANIEL NOT TO GO IN, TO PLAY IT SAFE.
"BUT ANYBODY WHO TOLD THAT TO HIM... DIDN'T KNOW DANIEL. NOTHING SCARED HIM. NOTHING.
"HE WENT DOWN, TAKING SOME OF HIS BEST MEN WITH HIM, MEN HE KNEW HE COULD COUNT ON WHEN THINGS GOT BAD.

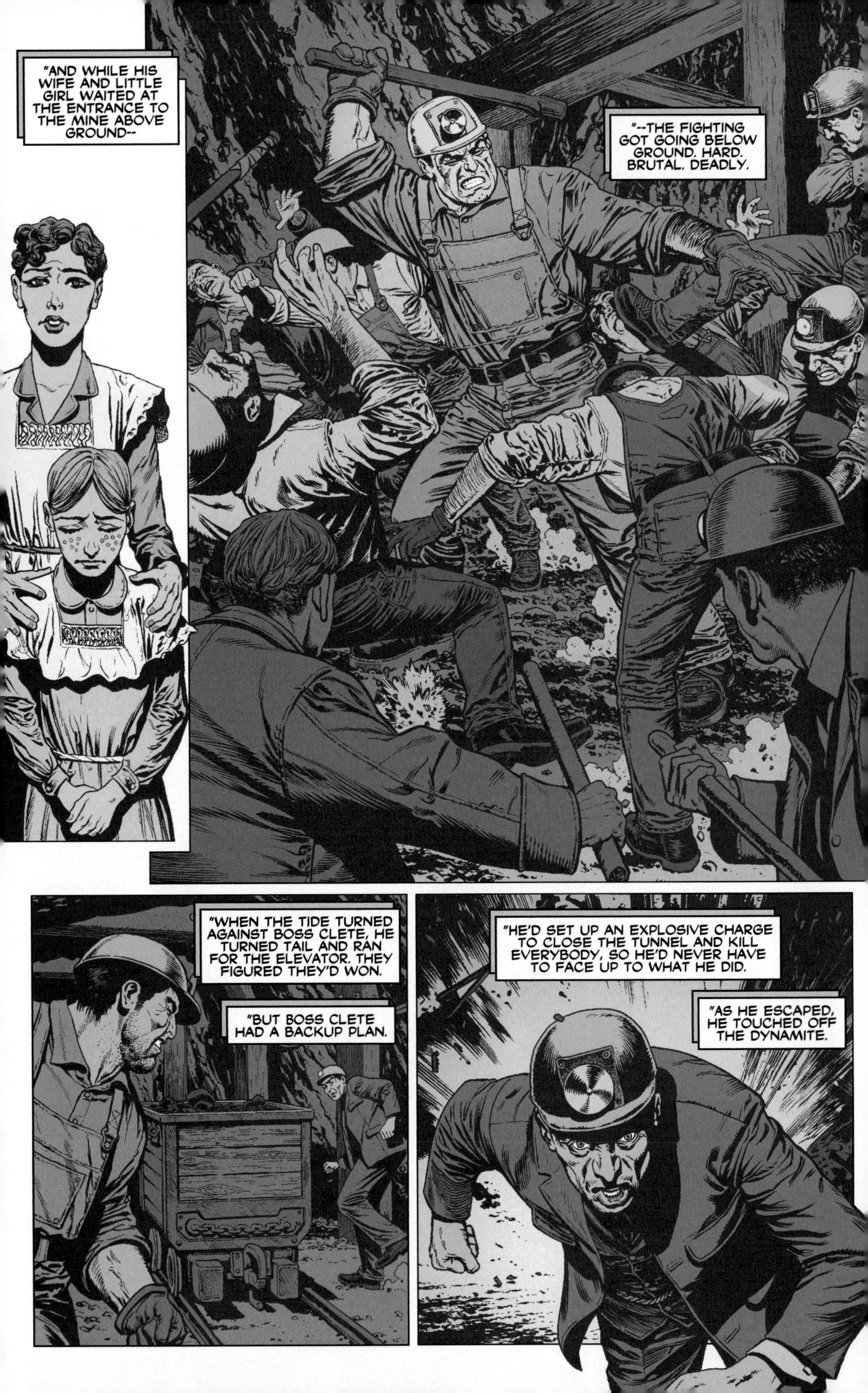
"AND WHILE HIS WIFE AND LITTLE GIRL WAITED AT THE ENTRANCE TO THE MINE ABOVE GROUND--
"--THE FIGHTING GOT GOING BELOW GROUND. HARD. BRUTAL. DEADLY.
"WHEN THE TIDE TURNED AGAINST BOSS CLETE, HE TURNED TAIL AND RAN FOR THE ELEVATOR. THEY FIGURED THEY'D WON.
"BUT BOSS CLETE HAD A BACKUP PLAN.
"HE'D SET UP AN EXPLOSIVE CHARGE TO CLOSE THE TUNNEL AND KILL EVERYBODY, SO HE'D NEVER HAVE TO FACE UP TO WHAT HE DID.
"AS HE ESCAPED, HE TOUCHED OFF THE DYNAMITE.

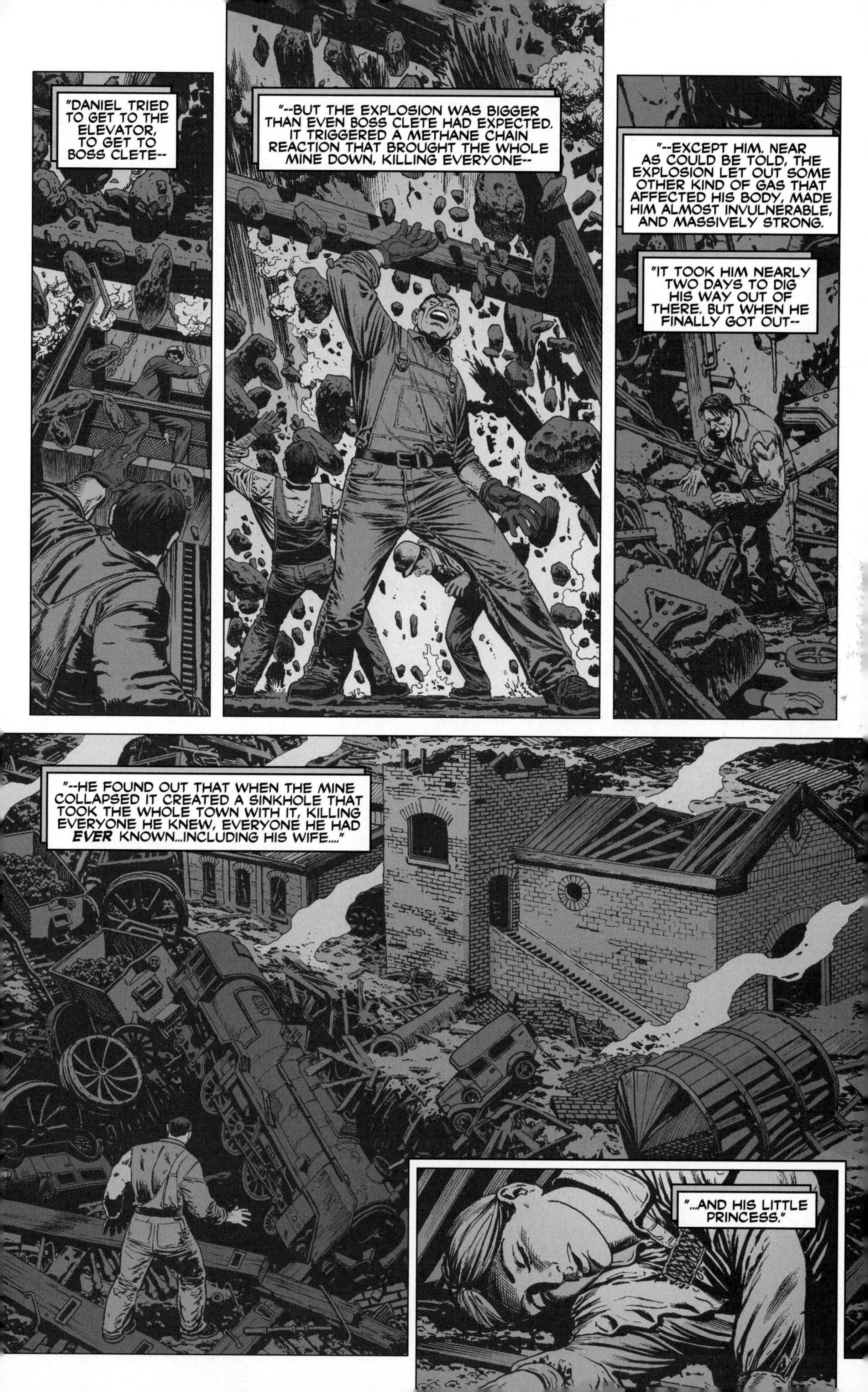
"DANIEL TRIED TO GET TO THE ELEVATOR, TO GET TO BOSS CLETE--
"--BUT THE EXPLOSION WAS BIGGER THAN EVEN BOSS CLETE HAD EXPECTED. IT TRIGGERED A METHANE CHAIN REACTION THAT BROUGHT THE WHOLE MINE DOWN, KILLING EVERYONE--
"--EXCEPT HIM. NEAR AS COULD BE TOLD, THE EXPLOSION LET OUT SOME OTHER KIND OF GAS THAT AFFECTED HIS BODY, MADE HIM ALMOST INVULNERABLE, AND MASSIVELY STRONG.
"IT TOOK HIM NEARLY TWO DAYS TO DIG HIS WAY OUT OF THERE. BUT WHEN HE FINALLY GOT OUT--
"--HE FOUND OUT THAT WHEN THE MINE COLLAPSED IT CREATED A SINKHOLE THAT TOOK THE WHOLE TOWN WITH IT, KILLING EVERYONE HE KNEW, EVERYONE HE HAD ***EVER*** KNOWN...INCLUDING HIS WIFE...."
"...AND HIS LITTLE PRINCESS."

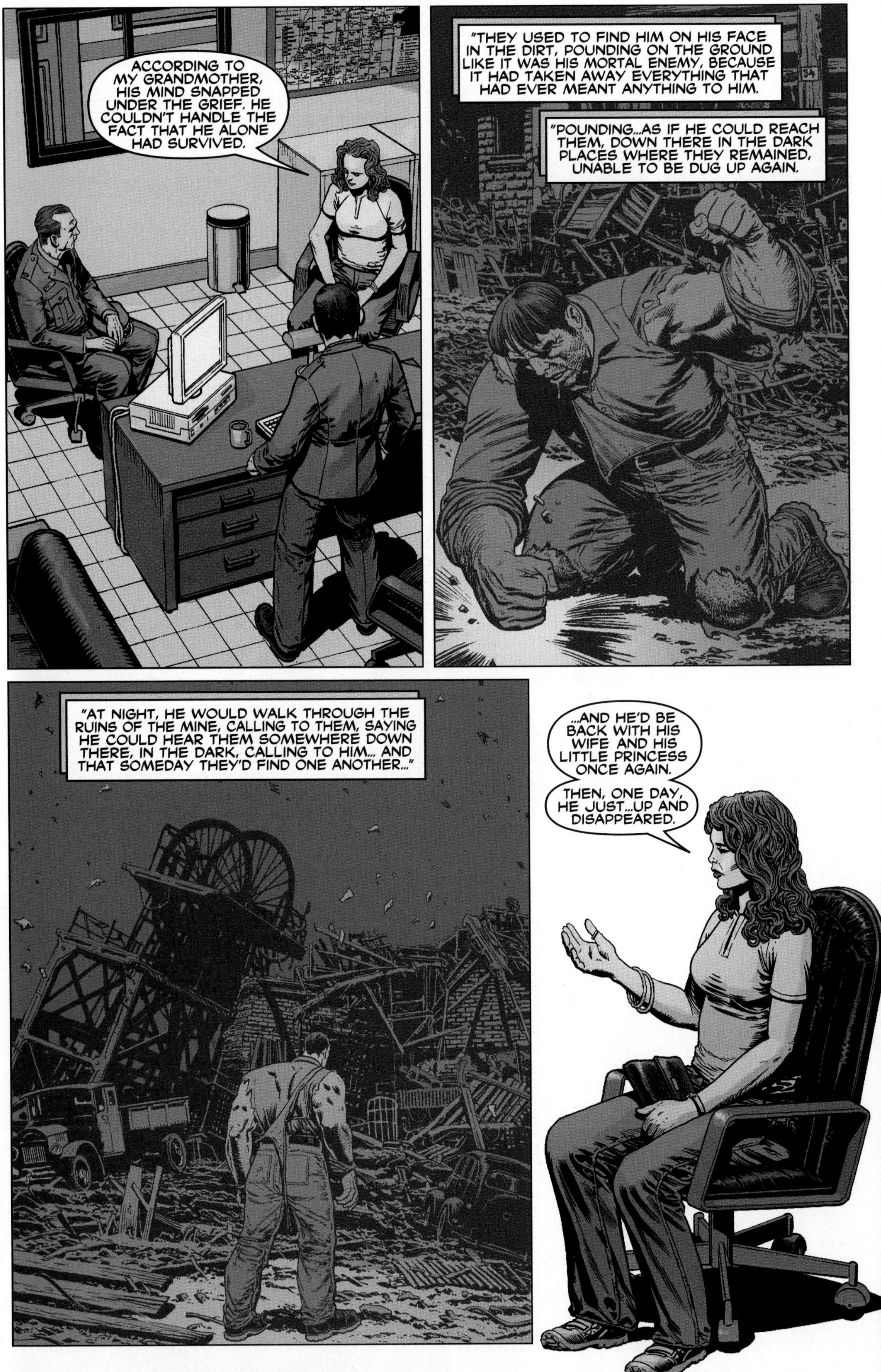
ACCORDING TO MY GRANDMOTHER, HIS MIND SNAPPED UNDER THE GRIEF. HE COULDN'T HANDLE THE FACT THAT HE ALONE HAD SURVIVED.
"THEY USED TO FIND HIM ON HIS FACE IN THE DIRT, POUNDING ON THE GROUND LIKE IT WAS HIS MORTAL ENEMY, BECAUSE IT HAD TAKEN AWAY EVERYTHING THAT HAD EVER MEANT ANYTHING TO HIM.
"POUNDING...AS IF HE COULD REACH THEM, DOWN THERE IN THE DARK PLACES WHERE THEY REMAINED, UNABLE TO BE DUG UP AGAIN.
"AT NIGHT, HE WOULD WALK THROUGH THE RUINS OF THE MINE, CALLING TO THEM, SAYING HE COULD HEAR THEM SOMEWHERE DOWN THERE, IN THE DARK, CALLING TO HIM... AND THAT SOMEDAY THEY'D FIND ONE ANOTHER..."
...AND HE'D BE BACK WITH HIS WIFE AND HIS LITTLE PRINCESS ONCE AGAIN.
THEN, ONE DAY, HE JUST...UP AND DISAPPEARED.

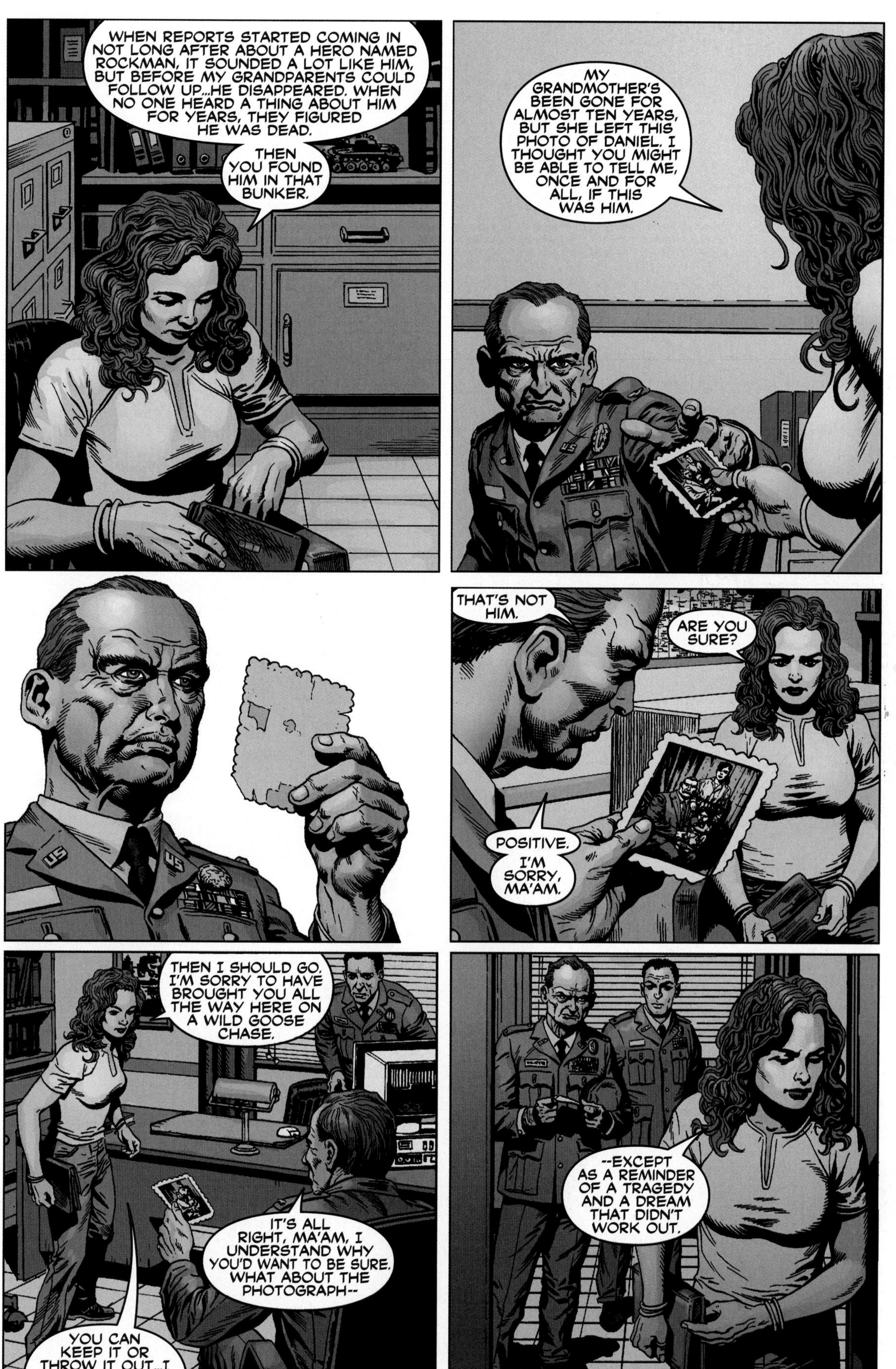
WHEN REPORTS STARTED COMING IN NOT LONG AFTER ABOUT A HERO NAMED ROCKMAN, IT SOUNDED A LOT LIKE HIM, BUT BEFORE MY GRANDPARENTS COULD FOLLOW UP...HE DISAPPEARED. WHEN NO ONE HEARD A THING ABOUT HIM FOR YEARS, THEY FIGURED HE WAS DEAD.
THEN YOU FOUND HIM IN THAT BUNKER.
MY GRANDMOTHER'S BEEN GONE FOR ALMOST TEN YEARS, BUT SHE LEFT THIS PHOTO OF DANIEL. I THOUGHT YOU MIGHT BE ABLE TO TELL ME, ONCE AND FOR ALL, IF THIS WAS HIM.
THAT'S NOT HIM.
ARE YOU SURE?
POSITIVE. I'M SORRY, MA'AM.
THEN I SHOULD GO. I'M SORRY TO HAVE BROUGHT YOU ALL THE WAY HERE ON A WILD GOOSE CHASE.
IT'S ALL RIGHT, MA'AM, I UNDERSTAND WHY YOU'D WANT TO BE SURE. WHAT ABOUT THE PHOTOGRAPH--
YOU CAN KEEP IT OR THROW IT OUT...I DON'T HAVE ANY MORE USE FOR IT--
--EXCEPT AS A REMINDER OF A TRAGEDY AND A DREAM THAT DIDN'T WORK OUT.

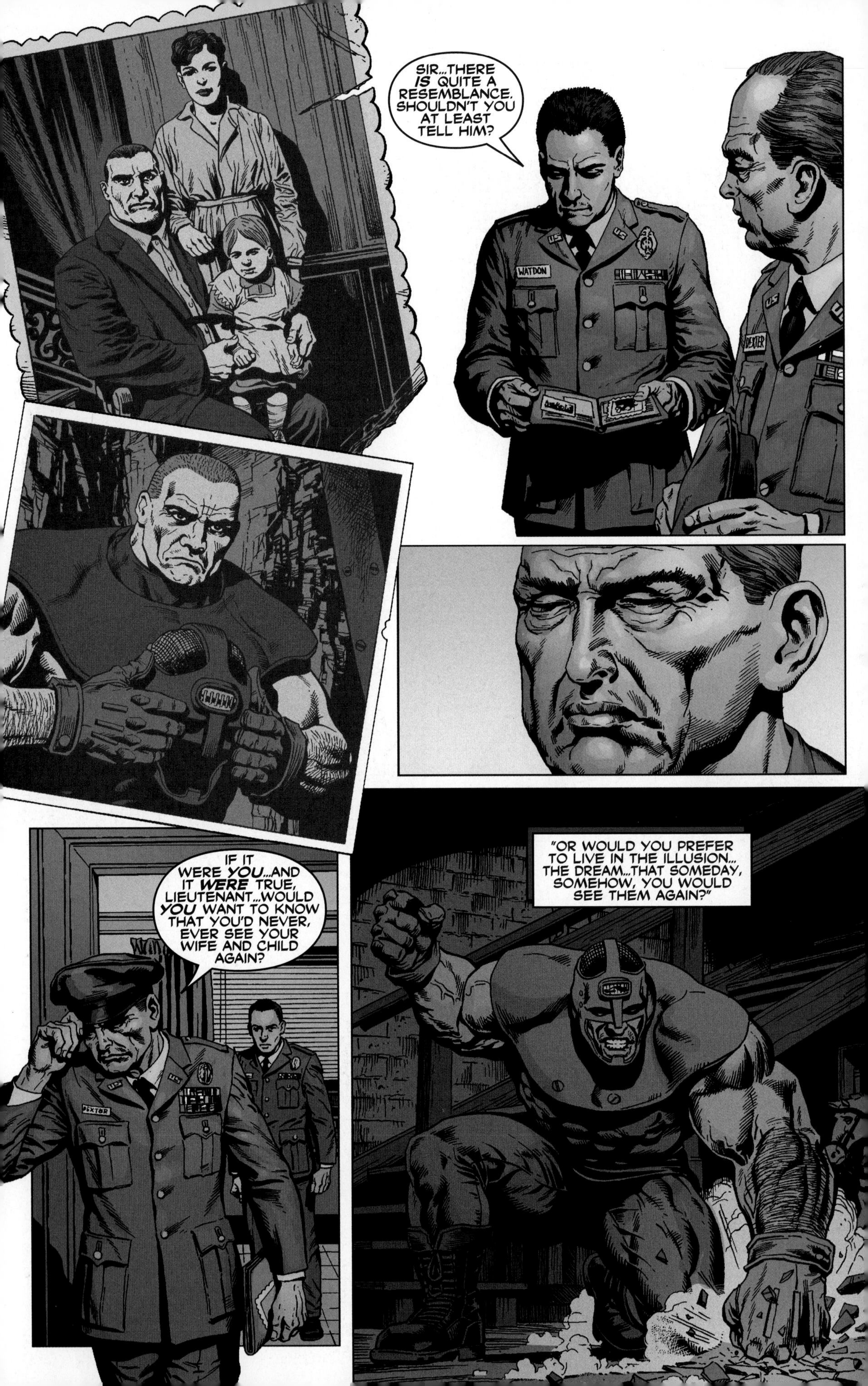
SIR...THERE IS QUITE A RESEMBLANCE. SHOULDN'T YOU AT LEAST TELL HIM?
WATDON
DEXTER
IF IT WERE YOU...AND IT WERE TRUE, LIEUTENANT...WOULD YOU WANT TO KNOW THAT YOU'D NEVER, EVER SEE YOUR WIFE AND CHILD AGAIN?
"OR WOULD YOU PREFER TO LIVE IN THE ILLUSION... THE DREAM...THAT SOMEDAY, SOMEHOW, YOU WOULD SEE THEM AGAIN?"

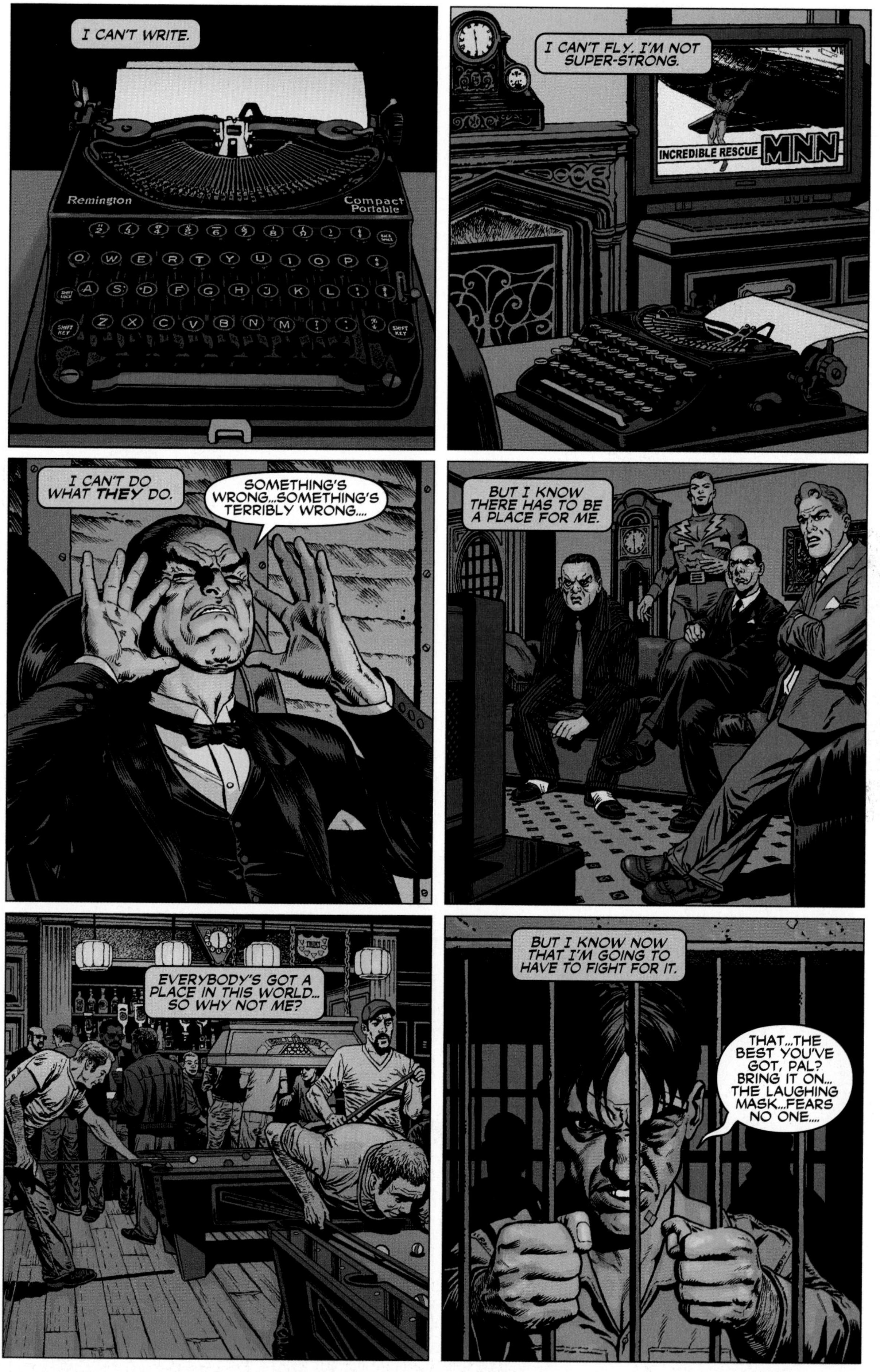
I CAN'T WRITE.
Remington
Compact Portable
I CAN'T FLY. I'M NOT SUPER-STRONG.
INCREDIBLE RESCUE
MNN
I CAN'T DO WHAT *THEY* DO.
SOMETHING'S WRONG...SOMETHING'S TERRIBLY WRONG....
BUT I KNOW THERE HAS TO BE A PLACE FOR ME.
EVERYBODY'S GOT A PLACE IN THIS WORLD... SO WHY NOT ME?
BUT I KNOW NOW THAT I'M GOING TO HAVE TO FIGHT FOR IT.
THAT...THE BEST YOU'VE GOT, PAL? BRING IT ON... THE LAUGHING MASK...FEARS NO ONE....

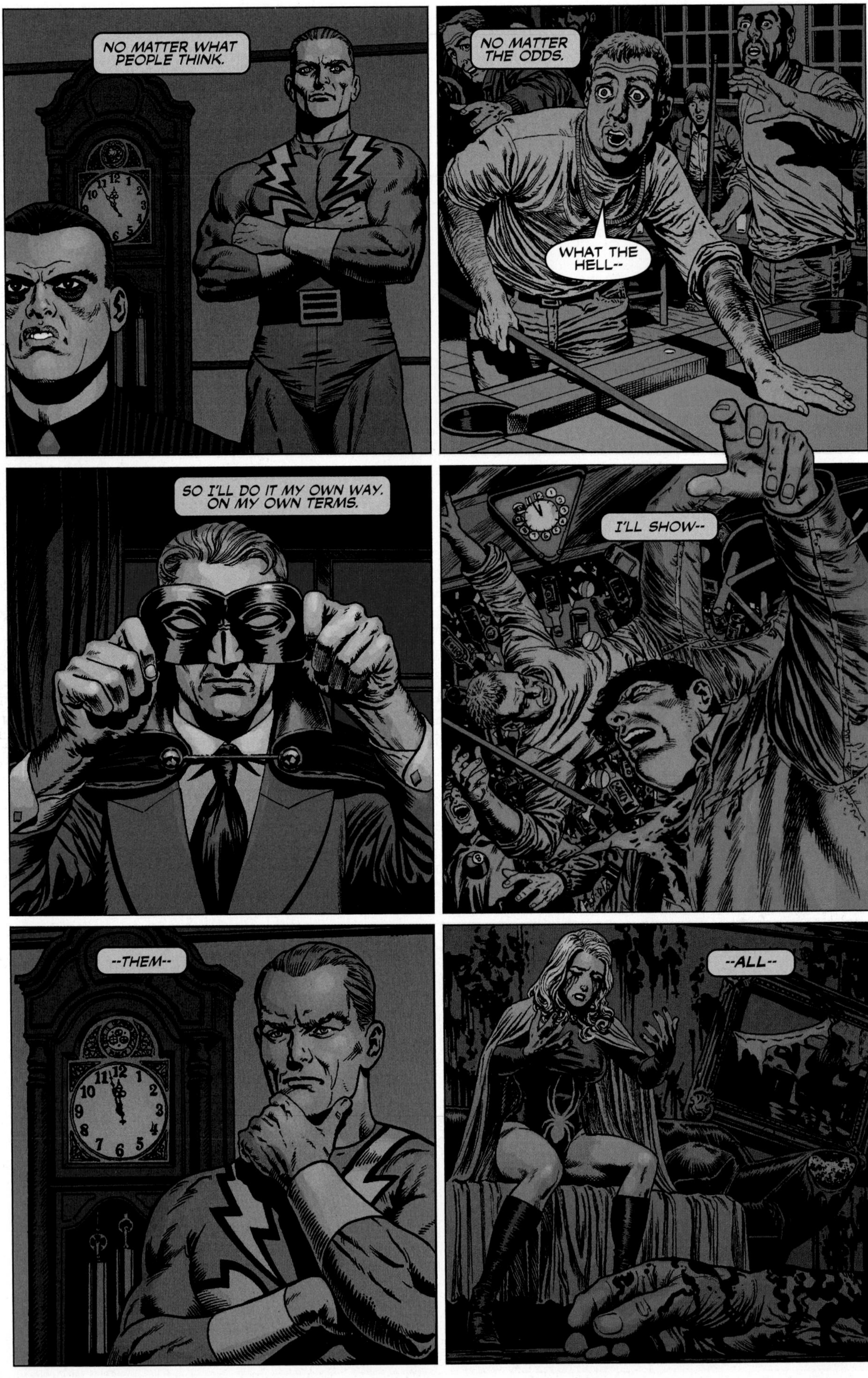
NO MATTER WHAT PEOPLE THINK.
NO MATTER THE ODDS.
WHAT THE HELL--
SO I'LL DO IT MY OWN WAY. ON MY OWN TERMS.
I'LL SHOW--
--THEM--
--ALL--